Taste of Home

quick COOKING

ANNUAL RECIPES

Taste of Home

RDA ENTHUSIAST BRANDS, LLC • MILWAUKEE, WI

Taste of Home quick COOKING
ANNUAL RECIPES

■ EDITORIAL
Editor-in-Chief **Catherine Cassidy**
Creative Director **Howard Greenberg**
Editorial Operations Director **Kerri Balliet**

Managing Editor/Print & Digital Books **Mark Hagen**
Associate Creative Director **Edwin Robles Jr.**

Editor **Christine Rukavena**
Associate Editor **Molly Jasinski**
Art Director **Maggie Conners**
Layout Designer **Courtney Lovetere**
Contributing Layout Designer **Siya Motamedi**
Editorial Production Manager **Dena Ahlers**
Copy Chief **Deb Warlaumont Mulvey**
Copy Editors **Kaitlin Stainbrook,**
Joanne Weintraub
Contributing Copy Editor **Valerie Phillips**

Chief Food Editor **Karen Berner**
Food Editors **James Schend; Peggy Woodward, RD**
Recipe Editors **Mary King; Annie Rundle;**
Jenni Sharp, RD; Irene Yeh
Content Operations Manager **Colleen King**
Content Operations Assistant **Shannon Stroud**
Executive Assistant **Marie Brannon**

Test Kitchen & Food Styling Manager
Sarah Thompson
Test Cooks **Nicholas Iverson (lead),**
Matthew Hass, Lauren Knoelke
Food Stylists **Kathryn Conrad (senior),**
Shannon Roum, Leah Rekau
Prep Cooks **Megumi Garcia, Melissa Hansen,**
Bethany Van Jacobson, Sara Wirtz

Photography Director **Stephanie Marchese**
Photographers **Dan Roberts, Jim Wieland**
Photographer/Set Stylist **Grace Natoli Sheldon**
Set Stylists **Stacey Genaw, Melissa Haberman,**
Dee Dee Jacq

Editorial Business Manager **Kristy Martin**
Editorial Business Associate **Samantha Lea Stoeger**

Editor, *Simple & Delicious* **Jeanne Ambrose**
Associate Creative Director, *Simple & Delicious*
Erin Burns
Art Director, *Simple & Delicious* **Kristen Johnson**

■ BUSINESS
Vice President, Chief Sales Officer
Mark S. Josephson
General Manager, Taste of Home Cooking School
Erin Puariea
Vice President, Digital Experience & E-Commerce
Jennifer Smith

■ THE READER'S DIGEST ASSOCIATION, INC.
President and Chief Executive Officer
Bonnie Kintzer
Chief Financial Officer **Colette Chestnut**
Vice President, Chief Operating Officer,
North America **Howard Halligan**
Vice President, EnthusiastBrands, Books & Retail
Harold Clarke
Vice President, North American Operations
Philippe Cloutier
Chief Marketing Officer **Leslie Dukker Doty**
Vice President, North American Human Resources
Phyllis E. Gebhardt, SPHR
Vice President, Brand Marketing **Beth Gorry**
Vice President, Global Communications
Susan Russ
Vice President, North American Technology
Aneel Tejwaney
Vice President, Consumer Marketing Planning
Jim Woods

Cover Photography
Taste of Home Photo Studio

© 2015 RDA Enthusiast Brands, LLC
1610 N. 2nd St., Suite 102, Milwaukee WI 53212-3906

International Standard Book Number:
978-1-61765-347-6

International Standard Serial Number: 1522-6603

Component Number: 117800050H00

Easy MEALS *for* BUSY FAMILIES

PICTURED ON FRONT COVER Sweet & Spicy Chicken Drummies (p. 91), Rhubarb Berry Cheesecake Pie (p. 314), Slow-Cooked Loaded Potato Soup (p. 181), Garden-Fresh Chef Salad (p. 243) and Garlic Toast Pizzas (p. 81).
PICTURED ON PAGE 1 Grilled Sausage-Basil Pizzas (p. 204).
PICTURED AT LEFT Snowman Christmas Cookies (p. 289), Mushroom Tortellini Soup (p. 133) and On-the-Go Breakfast Muffins (p. 105).
PICTURED ON PAGE 4 Crispy Shrimp Caesar Salad (p. 224), Greek Stuffed Mini Potatoes (p. 119), Peach Melba Trifle (p. 308).
PICTURED ON BACK COVER Reuben Bread Pudding (p. 160), Swiss Ham Kabobs (p. 82), Buffalo Turkey Burgers (p. 140), Peanut Butter Cup Trifle (p. 60) and Stovetop Macaroni and Cheese (p. 84).

contents

HANDY ICONS IN THIS BOOK

FAST FIX Recipes
are table-ready in
30 minutes or less.
Over 285 in all!

⑤INGREDIENTS 141 dishes use
5 or fewer ingredients. Recipes
may also call for water, salt,
pepper, and canola or olive oil.

EAT SMART Dietitian-
approved recipes that are
lower in calories, fat and
sodium. Find 174 in all!

FREEZE IT Save time with
93 freezer-friendly recipes
that make for quick meals
when the clock is ticking.

LIKE US
facebook.com/tasteofhome

TWEET US
@tasteofhome

FOLLOW US
pinterest.com/taste_of_home

SHARE A RECIPE
tasteofhome.com/submit

SHOP WITH US
shoptasteofhome.com

E-MAIL US
bookeditors@tasteofhome.com

VISIT
tasteofhome.com
for
MORE!

Make it fast and fabulous with
600+ RECIPES & TIPS!

DELICIOUS HOME COOKING doesn't require you to spend hours in the kitchen—and the 600+ tasty recipes and clever tips you'll find here are the proof! Just take a look at the all-new collection of readers' best dishes in this brand-new edition of *Quick Cooking Annual Recipes*.

Inside, we've included every recipe that appeared in *Simple & Delicious* magazine over the past year, as well as 100+ bonus dishes! Every recipe comes together in a wink, and because each one uses affordable, easy-to-find ingredients, you're guaranteed no-hassle success! This value-packed volume is bursting with quick dinners, impressive desserts, party-perfect munchies and other in-a-dash favorites.

You'll also find showstopping brunch entrees, sizzling grilled foods, fresh-baked breads, steaming soups and much more. Best of all, you can prepare more than half of these no-fuss favorites in 30 minutes or less!

FRESH IN THIS EDITION

Tasteful Holidays
Celebrate special occassions from Mardi Gras to Christmas with the fun menus, lip-smacking treats and irresistible food gifts you'll find right here. Best of all, these fun-to-share dishes are a cinch to make!

Kid-Friendly Foods
Have a picky eater? Turn here for 60+ kid-approved breakfasts, lunches, dinners, classroom treats, after-school snacks and everything in between. Not only are they sure to inspire and delight, but each item comes together easily.

Slow-Simmered Favorites
To feed your family right on even your busiest nights, just reach for the satisfying slow-cooked recipes in this popular chapter. Serve up soups, sandwiches, roasts, appetizers, and even beverages and desserts with more than three dozen hot new favorites.

Simple Breads to Savor
Enjoy the hot yummy goodness of buttery bread, anytime! Easily whip up some fresh-baked biscuits, rolls, muffins and more. Because nearly all recipes start with a handy mix or ready-made dough, you'll be amazed at what you can bake up in no time flat.

Helpful Icons
At-a-glance icons help you quickly locate the recipes you need. New this year, the useful Freeze It icon and accompanying freezer directions maximize your time in the kitchen. See page 3 to learn how the icons can work for you.

Plus...
Discover dozens of delicious contest winners, readers' favorite kitchen shortcuts, simple snacks, cookout favorites and more. Now dig in, and enjoy this best-loved collection from the recipe boxes of home cooks across the country!

The Past Year's
RECIPE CONTESTS & THEIR WINNERS

ONE-PAN WONDERS

GRAND PRIZE

CREAMY BUFFALO CHICKEN ENCHILADAS

I make my enchilada filling with shredded chicken and cheese and wrap it in warm corn tortillas, just like I would if I were making the traditional dish. But tangy blue cheese and Buffalo wing sauce make this version more American. Serve these enchiladas with a simple green salad and a side of chips and salsa, plus a cold beer or some limeade to wash it down.

—**CRYSTAL SCHLUETER** NORTHGLENN, CO

POTATO, POTAHHTO

GRAND PRIZE

LEMON ROASTED FINGERLINGS AND BRUSSELS SPROUTS

Roasting veggies makes them so toasty and flavorful. In fact, I've never met a veggie I wouldn't roast (except maybe cucumbers). For this dish, I combined two of my husband's favorites—potatoes and Brussels sprouts—for one of our weekly date nights, when the two of us eat dinner after our three kids are asleep. The lemony dressing is one I use on almost everything. When I tossed it with these particular veggies—well, you see what happened. Yum.

—**COURTNEY GAYLORD** COLUMBUS, IN

SLIMMING PICKIN'S

SOUTHWEST HASH WITH ADOBO-LIME CREMA

This dish came about because I love eggs Benedict but not all the fat and carbs in the original's English muffins and hollandaise. The adobo cream sauce layers on so much flavor, you don't even miss the extra butter and yolks. The recipe is terrific for brunch guests because it's kind of fancy, but everyone can eat as much as they want. When I'm in the mood to splurge, I throw some leftover pulled pork into the mix. It's an awesome addition.

—**BROOKE KELLER** LEXINGTON, KY

HOMEMADE IN A HURRY

SIMPLE CHICKEN STIR-FRY

Our kids have always loved ethnic foods, so everything I need for this stir-fry is usually on hand. Start the chicken and rice, then work on the sauce. It's so quick because you can basically dump in everything at once. I like to cook this in large batches so we have leftovers for lunches. Recently, I made it for my dad—when he asked for the recipe, I had to pare it down. A few days later, I saw this contest and decided to enter. Glad I did!

—**CHERYL MURPHY** DELTA, BC

FROM FREEZER TO FABULOUS

GRAND PRIZE

MOROCCAN APPLE BEEF STEW

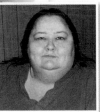

My inspiration for this dish was my Middle Eastern heritage. Cooks in that region often use meat and fruit in slow-cooked tajines with big flavors, like cinnamon, cardamom and even chiles. In Morocco, this would be a special meal for company. In Idaho, I serve it to family because it's easy and they love it—especially over couscous. If I don't have dried plums, other dried fruits (try apricots) work nicely. This is not a persnickety dish!

—TRISHA KRUSE EAGLE, ID

5-INGREDIENT FIX

GRAND PRIZE

HADDOCK WITH LIME-CILANTRO BUTTER

My family loves any dish that has fruit in it, especially citrus. When a friend gave me a type of fish fillet I wasn't familiar with, I took a cod recipe and adjusted the seasoning until I got this blend. What a success. Instead of lime, I've also used lemon or orange, and sometimes I add parsley in place of cilantro. If you want more heat, try Cajun seasoning and skip the salt and pepper. The recipe works with ocean perch, too—and cod, of course.

—DARLENE MORRIS FRANKLINTON, LA

Linguine with Broccoli Rabe & Peppers
PAGE 25

30-Minute Main Dishes

Every delicious entree on the following pages is table-ready in just 30 minutes or less. Short on ingredients and quick to prep, yet big on flavor, these recipes will be your new go-to for busy nights.

Shrimp Lettuce Wraps
PAGE 16

Spicy Tilapia Rice Bowl
PAGE 20

Blackberry-Sauced Pork Chops
PAGE 27

Smoky Sausage & Pepper Skillet

My family loves this combination of sausage, green peppers and onions. Everyone asks for it on their birthday!

—**CELINDA KULP** HUMMELSTOWN, PA

START TO FINISH: 30 MIN.
MAKES: 4 SERVINGS

- 1 **pound smoked sausage, sliced**
- 2 **large green peppers, thinly sliced**
- 1 **medium onion, thinly sliced**
- 1 **garlic clove, minced**
- 4 **teaspoons cornstarch**
- 2 **cups whole milk**
- ¼ **cup minced fresh parsley**
- ¾ **teaspoon dried marjoram**
- ½ **teaspoon pepper**
- ½ **cup shredded Parmesan cheese**
  Hot cooked rice or pasta

1. In a large skillet, brown sausage over medium heat. Remove with a slotted spoon; drain on paper towels.
2. Add green peppers and onion to same skillet; cook and stir until vegetables are crisp-tender. Add garlic; cook 1 minute longer. In a small bowl, mix cornstarch, milk, parsley, marjoram and pepper until blended; stir into pan. Bring to a boil; cook and stir 2 minutes or until sauce is thickened.
3. Return sausage to pan and heat through. Stir in cheese until blended. Serve with rice.

SMOKY SAUSAGE & PEPPER SKILLET

CHICKEN CACCIATORE WITH POLENTA

FREEZE IT

Chicken Cacciatore with Polenta

The microwave makes quick work of homemade polenta, and the rest is done in one skillet. Save a little Parmesan for sprinkling on top before serving.

—**YVONNE STARLIN** HERMITAGE, TN

START TO FINISH: 30 MIN.
MAKES: 4 SERVINGS

- 3 **cups water**
- ¾ **cup cornmeal**
- ½ **cup grated Parmesan cheese**
- ¾ **teaspoon salt**

CACCIATORE

- 1 **pound boneless skinless chicken thighs, cut into 1-inch pieces**
- ⅛ **teaspoon salt**
- ⅛ **teaspoon pepper**
- 1 **tablespoon olive oil**
- 1 **large onion, sliced**
- 1 **garlic clove, minced**
- 1 **can (14½ ounces) fire-roasted crushed tomatoes**
- ½ **cup pitted Greek olives**

1. In a microwave-safe bowl, whisk water and cornmeal; microwave, covered, on high for 6 minutes. Stir; cook, covered, 5-7 minutes longer or until polenta is thickened, stirring every 2 minutes. Stir in cheese and salt.
2. Meanwhile, sprinkle chicken with salt and pepper. In a large skillet, heat oil over medium-high heat. Add chicken; cook and stir until browned. Remove with a slotted spoon.
3. Add onion to the same pan; cook and stir 2-4 minutes or until tender. Add garlic; cook 1 minute longer. Return chicken to pan; stir in tomatoes and olives. Bring to a boil. Reduce heat; simmer, uncovered, 6-8 minutes or until chicken is no longer pink. Serve with polenta.
FREEZE OPTION *Freeze cooled chicken mixture in freezer containers. To use, partially thaw in refrigerator overnight. Heat through in saucepan, stirring occasionally and adding a little water if necessary.*

Fettuccine Carbonara

START TO FINISH: 30 MIN.
MAKES: 6 SERVINGS

- ½ pound bacon strips, chopped
- 1 package (16 ounces) fettuccine
- 1 small onion, finely chopped
- 2 garlic cloves, minced
- 1 cup half-and-half cream
- 4 eggs, lightly beaten
- ½ cup grated Romano cheese
- ½ teaspoon salt
- ¼ teaspoon pepper
- 1 tablespoon minced fresh parsley
  Additional grated Romano cheese, optional

1. In a large skillet, cook bacon over medium heat until crisp, stirring occasionally. Remove with a slotted spoon; drain on paper towels. Discard drippings, reserving 1 tablespoon in pan.
2. Meanwhile, in a Dutch oven, cook fettuccine according to package directions. Drain; return to pan.
3. Add onion to drippings in skillet; cook and stir over medium heat 2-3 minutes or until tender. Add garlic; cook 1 minute longer. Reduce heat to medium-low. Stir in cream. In a small bowl, whisk a small amount of warm cream into eggs; return all to pan, whisking constantly. Cook 8-10 minutes or until a thermometer reads 160°, stirring constantly.
4. Stir the cheese, salt, pepper and bacon into sauce. Add to fettuccine and toss to combine. Sprinkle with parsley and, if desired, additional cheese. Serve immediately.

When a man at church found out how much my family likes fettuccine carbonara, he shared his Italian grandmother's recipe with us. It is quick to prepare and absolutely delicious! Grated Parmesan cheese works just as well as Romano. —**KRISTINE CHAYES** SMITHTOWN, NY

FETTUCCINE CARBONARA

TILAPIA WITH FIESTA RICE

Tilapia with Fiesta Rice

I often use my husband's fresh-caught bass or catfish for this recipe, but tilapia, salmon and even chicken will do.
—**TARIN HAUCK** MINNEAPOLIS, KS

START TO FINISH: 25 MIN.
MAKES: 4 SERVINGS

- 4 tilapia fillets (6 ounces each)
- ½ teaspoon chili powder
- ⅛ teaspoon salt
- ⅛ teaspoon ground cumin
- ⅛ teaspoon pepper
- 1 package (8.8 ounces) ready-to-serve brown rice
- 1 can (15 ounces) black beans, rinsed and drained
- 1½ cups frozen corn, thawed
- 1½ cups salsa

1. Place tilapia in a 15x10x1-in. baking pan. Mix chili powder, salt, cumin and pepper; sprinkle over fish. Broil 3-4 in. from heat 10-12 minutes or until fish just begins to flake easily with a fork.
2. Meanwhile, prepare rice according to package directions. Transfer to a microwave-safe bowl; stir in beans, corn and salsa. Microwave, covered, on high for 2-3 minutes or until heated through, stirring once. Serve with fish.
PER SERVING *424 cal., 3 g fat (1 g sat. fat), 83 mg chol., 874 mg sodium, 53 g carb., 7 g fiber, 41 g pro.*

CRAN-APPLE TURKEY SKILLET

You need only one skillet to pull off this delicious meal. Talk about simple!
—LISA RENSHAW KANSAS CITY, MO

Cran-Apple Turkey Skillet

START TO FINISH: 20 MIN.
MAKES: 6 SERVINGS

- 2 medium apples, peeled and thinly sliced
- ¾ cup apple cider or unsweetened apple juice
- ¾ cup reduced-sodium chicken broth
- ⅓ cup dried cranberries
- ⅛ teaspoon ground nutmeg
- 3 cups cubed cooked turkey breast
- 1 package (6 ounces) corn bread stuffing mix

1. In a large skillet, combine apples, cider, broth, cranberries and nutmeg; bring to a boil. Reduce heat; simmer, covered, 4-5 minutes or until apples are tender, stirring occasionally.
2. Stir in turkey and stuffing mix. Cook, covered, 2-3 minutes or until liquid is almost absorbed.

Rigatoni with Sausage & Peas

With a meaty tomato sauce and tangy goat cheese, this weeknight wonder is my own personal version of comfort food. You will want to have bowl after bowl.
—LIZZIE MUNRO BROOKLYN, NY

START TO FINISH: 30 MIN.
MAKES: 6 SERVINGS

- 12 ounces uncooked rigatoni or large tube pasta
- 1 pound bulk Italian sausage
- 4 garlic cloves, minced
- ¼ cup tomato paste
- 1 can (28 ounces) crushed tomatoes
- ½ teaspoon dried basil
- ¼ to ½ teaspoon crushed red pepper flakes
- 1½ cups frozen peas
- ½ cup heavy whipping cream
- ½ cup crumbled goat or feta cheese Thinly sliced fresh basil, optional

1. Cook rigatoni according to package directions.
2. Meanwhile, in a Dutch oven, cook sausage over medium heat 6-8 minutes or until no longer pink, breaking into crumbles. Add garlic; cook 1 minute longer. Drain. Add tomato paste; cook and stir 2-3 minutes or until meat is coated. Stir in tomatoes, dried basil and pepper flakes; bring to a boil. Reduce heat; simmer, uncovered, 10-15 minutes or until thickened, stirring occasionally.
3. Drain rigatoni; stir into sausage mixture. Add peas and cream; heat through. Top with cheese and, if desired, fresh basil.

RIGATONI WITH SAUSAGE & PEAS

CHIPOTLE CHICKEN
WITH SPANISH RICE

Chipotle Chicken with Spanish Rice

Here in Texas, we love Southwestern cooking. Chipotle pepper adds a nice smoky heat to this zesty chicken and rice dish. It's so quick and easy. Enjoy!
—**CAROLYN COLLINS** FREEPORT, TX

START TO FINISH: 25 MIN.
MAKES: 4 SERVINGS

- 4 **boneless skinless chicken thighs (about 1 pound)**
- ½ **teaspoon garlic salt**
- 2 **tablespoons canola oil**
- 1 **can (15 ounces) black beans, rinsed and drained**
- 1 **cup chunky salsa**
- 1 **chipotle pepper in adobo sauce, finely chopped**
- 2 **packages (8.8 ounces each) ready-to-serve Spanish rice**
- ½ **cup shredded Mexican cheese blend or Monterey Jack cheese**
- 2 **tablespoons minced fresh cilantro or parsley**

1. Sprinkle chicken with garlic salt. In a large skillet, heat oil over medium-high heat. Brown chicken on both sides. Stir in beans, salsa and chipotle pepper; bring to a boil. Reduce heat; simmer, covered, 6-8 minutes or until a thermometer inserted in chicken reads 170°.
2. Meanwhile, prepare rice according to package directions. Serve chicken with beans and rice; sprinkle with cheese and cilantro.

Pork Chops with Blue Cheese Sauce

Sometimes a sauce is just a sauce, but with these juicy chops, it really makes the dish. If you like a little spice, mix a small pinch of nutmeg with the black pepper before you sprinkle it on the meat.
—**KATHLEEN SPECHT** CLINTON, MT

START TO FINISH: 25 MIN.
MAKES: 4 SERVINGS

- 4 **bone-in pork loin chops (7 ounces each)**
- 1 **teaspoon coarsely ground pepper**
- 1 **teaspoon butter**
- 1 **green onion, finely chopped**
- 1 **garlic clove, minced**
- 1 **tablespoon all-purpose flour**
- ⅔ **cup fat-free milk**
- 3 **tablespoons crumbled blue cheese**
- 1 **tablespoon white wine or reduced-sodium chicken broth**

1. Preheat broiler. Sprinkle pork chops on both sides with pepper; place on a broiler pan coated with cooking spray. Broil 4-5 in. from heat 4-5 minutes on each side or until a thermometer reads 145°. Let stand 5 minutes before serving.
2. Meanwhile, in a small saucepan, heat butter over medium-high heat. Add green onion and garlic; cook and stir until tender.
3. Stir in flour until blended; gradually whisk in milk. Bring to a boil, stirring constantly; cook and stir 1-2 minutes or until thickened. Add cheese and wine; heat through. Serve pork chops with sauce.

PER SERVING *263 cal., 11 g fat (5 g sat. fat), 94 mg chol., 176 mg sodium, 5 g carb., trace fiber, 33 g pro.* **Diabetic Exchanges:** *5 lean meat, ½ fat.*

PORK CHOPS WITH
BLUE CHEESE SAUCE

SAUSAGE SKILLET WITH
PASTA & HERBS

Sausage Skillet with Pasta & Herbs

The fresh herbs really pop in this cinch of a weekday meal. If you want a break from pasta, serve the savory sausages on polenta instead. It would easily make a fantastic hoagie filling, too.

—VICTORIA DAVIS WILDER, VT

START TO FINISH: 30 MIN.
MAKES: 4 SERVINGS

- 2 tablespoons olive oil, divided
- 2 medium sweet red peppers, sliced
- 1 medium onion, halved and sliced
- 4 garlic cloves, minced
- 1 package (12 ounces) fully cooked Italian chicken sausage links, halved lengthwise and sliced
- 2 tablespoons balsamic vinegar
- ¼ teaspoon salt
- ¼ teaspoon pepper
- 2 tablespoons minced fresh parsley
- 2 teaspoons minced fresh rosemary
  Hot cooked cellentani or spiral pasta
  Shredded Parmesan cheese

1. In a large skillet, heat 1 tablespoon oil over medium-high heat. Add red peppers and onion; cook and stir 6-8 minutes or until crisp-tender. Add garlic; cook 1 minute longer. Remove from pan.

2. In same skillet, heat remaining oil over medium-high heat. Add sausage; cook and stir until browned. Stir in pepper mixture, vinegar, salt and pepper; heat through. Stir in herbs. Serve with pasta; sprinkle with cheese.

Tortellini with Asparagus & Lemon

This is a terrific warm-weather dish, loaded with fresh flavors. I make mine meatless, but some sliced grilled chicken on top would be delicious as well.

—CRYSTAL SCHLUETER NORTHGLENN, CO

START TO FINISH: 30 MIN.
MAKES: 4 SERVINGS

- 2 packages (9 ounces each) refrigerated cheese tortellini
- 3 tablespoons butter
- 1 tablespoon olive oil
- 2 cups cut fresh asparagus (2-inch pieces)
- 3 garlic cloves, minced
- ⅛ teaspoon pepper
- 2 teaspoons chopped chives
- 1 teaspoon minced fresh parsley
- ½ teaspoon chopped fresh dill
- ½ teaspoon grated lemon peel
- 2 tablespoons lemon juice
- ⅔ cup crumbled feta cheese
- ⅓ cup grated Parmesan cheese

1. Cook tortellini according to package directions. Meanwhile, in a large skillet, heat butter and oil over medium-high heat. Add asparagus; cook and stir 3-4 minutes or until crisp-tender. Add garlic and pepper; cook 1 minute longer.

2. Remove from heat; stir in herbs, lemon peel and lemon juice. Drain tortellini; transfer to a large bowl. Stir in cheeses and asparagus mixture.

Moo Shu Mushroom Wraps

With so many great veggies out there, I'm always playing around with the ingredients in these wraps. Sometimes I add extra protein—chicken, shrimp, pork, beef and tofu all work. Check for Sriracha and hoisin sauces in the Asian or international foods section of your grocery store.

—**ATHENA RUSSELL** FLORENCE, SC

START TO FINISH: 30 MIN.
MAKES: 5 SERVINGS

- 4 teaspoons sesame or canola oil, divided
- 4 eggs, lightly beaten
- ½ pound sliced fresh mushrooms
- 1 package (12 ounces) broccoli coleslaw mix
- 2 garlic cloves, minced
- 2 teaspoons minced fresh gingerroot
- 2 tablespoons rice vinegar
- 2 tablespoons reduced-sodium soy sauce
- 2 teaspoons Sriracha Asian hot chili sauce
- 1 cup fresh bean sprouts
- ½ cup hoisin sauce
- 10 flour tortillas (6 inches), warmed
- 6 green onions, sliced

1. In a large nonstick skillet, heat 1 teaspoon oil over medium heat. Pour in eggs; cook and stir until eggs are thickened and no liquid egg remains. Remove from pan.

2. In same skillet, heat remaining oil over medium-high heat. Add mushrooms; cook and stir until tender. Add coleslaw mix, garlic and ginger; cook 1-2 minutes longer or until slaw is crisp-tender. In a small bowl, mix vinegar, soy sauce and chili sauce; add to pan. Stir in sprouts and eggs; heat through.

3. Spread about 2 teaspoons hoisin sauce over each tortilla to within ¼ in. of edges. Layer with ½ cup vegetable mixture and about 1 tablespoon green onion. Roll up tightly.

EAT SMART
Cod Delight

START TO FINISH: 15 MIN.
MAKES: 4 SERVINGS

- 1 small tomato, chopped
- ⅓ cup finely chopped onion
- 2 tablespoons water
- 2 tablespoons canola oil
- 4 to 5 teaspoons lemon juice
- 1 teaspoon dried parsley flakes
- ½ teaspoon dried basil
- 1 small garlic clove, minced
- ⅛ teaspoon salt
- 4 cod fillets (4 ounces each)
- 1 teaspoon seafood seasoning

In a small bowl, combine the first nine ingredients. Place cod in an 11x7-in. baking dish; top with tomato mixture. Sprinkle with seafood seasoning. Microwave, covered, on high 5-6 minutes or until fish just begins to flake easily with a fork.

NOTE *This recipe was tested in a 1,100-watt microwave.*

PER SERVING *154 cal., 8 g fat (1 g sat. fat), 43 mg chol., 304 mg sodium, 3 g carb., 1 g fiber, 18 g pro.* **Diabetic Exchanges:** *3 lean meat, 1 fat.*

I used to make this in the oven, but then I discovered that the microwave lets me enjoy it even faster. It's a pretty dish to serve company. In fact, many of my friends and family now cook this at home.

—**NANCY DAUGHERTY** CORTLAND, OH

COD DELIGHT

Shrimp Lettuce Wraps

Lettuce forms a crispy shell that's full of possibilities, depending on what's in your fridge. Swap shrimp for cooked chicken, pork or tofu. Mix in any veggies you want: Carrots, broccoli, snow peas and chopped zucchini are all fantastic add-ins.

—**TASTE OF HOME** TEST KITCHEN

START TO FINISH: 30 MIN.
MAKES: 4 SERVINGS

- ¼ **cup reduced-sodium soy sauce**
- 3 **tablespoons lime juice**
- 2 **tablespoons plus 1 teaspoon apricot preserves**
- 2 **tablespoons water**
- 2 **garlic cloves, minced**
- ¼ **teaspoon ground ginger**
- 2 **medium carrots**
- 6 **green onions**
- 3 **teaspoons olive oil, divided**
- 1 **pound uncooked medium shrimp, peeled and deveined**
- 1 **large sweet red pepper, chopped**
- 2 **cups hot cooked rice**
- 8 **large lettuce leaves**

1. In a small bowl, mix the first six ingredients. Using a vegetable peeler, shave carrots lengthwise into very thin strips. Slice white parts of green onions; cut each green top in half lengthwise.

2. In a large skillet, heat 2 teaspoons oil over medium-high heat. Add shrimp; stir-fry until shrimp turn pink. Remove from pan.

3. Stir-fry pepper and carrots in remaining oil 4 minutes. Add white parts of onions; stir-fry 1-2 minutes longer or until vegetables are crisp-tender.

4. Add ⅓ cup soy sauce mixture to pan. Bring to a boil. Add shrimp; heat through. Place ¼ cup rice on each lettuce leaf; top with ½ cup shrimp mixture. Drizzle with remaining soy sauce mixture and roll up. Tie each with a green onion strip.

PER SERVING *306 cal., 5 g fat (1 g sat. fat), 138 mg chol., 777 mg sodium, 41 g carb., 3 g fiber, 23 g pro.* **Diabetic Exchanges:** *3 lean meat, 2 starch, 1 vegetable, ½ fat.*

CHICKEN-PEPPER ALFREDO

Chicken-Pepper Alfredo

When I want a lighter dinner, I use lean turkey bacon in this recipe. It gives the pasta that richness you want without all the extra fat.

—**COURTNEY HARRIS** DENTON, TX

START TO FINISH: 30 MIN.
MAKES: 4 SERVINGS

- 8 **ounces uncooked linguine**
- 1½ **pounds chicken tenderloins, cut into 1-inch cubes**
- 1 **teaspoon garlic powder**
- 1 **teaspoon pepper**
- 2 **tablespoons olive oil**
- ½ **cup sliced fresh mushrooms**
- ¼ **cup finely chopped red onion**
- 4 **turkey or pork bacon strips, chopped**
- 1 **garlic clove, minced**
- 1 **jar (15 ounces) roasted red pepper Alfredo sauce**
- ¼ **cup grated Parmesan cheese**

1. Cook linguine according to package directions. Meanwhile, sprinkle chicken with garlic powder and pepper. In a large skillet, heat oil over medium heat. Add chicken, mushrooms, onion, bacon and garlic; cook and stir 8-10 minutes or until chicken is no longer pink.

2. Drain linguine; add to skillet. Stir in Alfredo sauce; heat through. Sprinkle with cheese.

SHRIMP LETTUCE WRAPS

> My daughter's college asked parents for a favorite healthy recipe to use in the dining halls. This quinoa fit the bill.
> **—LINDSAY MCSWEENEY** WINCHESTER, MA

Black Bean & Corn Quinoa

START TO FINISH: 30 MIN.
MAKES: 4 SERVINGS

- 2 tablespoons canola oil
- 1 medium onion, finely chopped
- 1 medium sweet red pepper, finely chopped
- 1 celery rib, finely chopped
- 2 teaspoons chili powder
- ¼ teaspoon salt
- ¼ teaspoon pepper
- 2 cups vegetable stock
- 1 cup frozen corn
- 1 cup quinoa, rinsed
- 1 can (15 ounces) black beans, rinsed and drained

BLACK BEAN & CORN QUINOA

- ⅓ cup plus 2 tablespoons minced fresh cilantro, divided

1. In a large skillet, heat oil over medium-high heat. Add onion, red pepper, celery and seasonings; cook and stir 5-7 minutes or until vegetables are tender.
2. Stir in stock and corn; bring to a boil. Stir in quinoa. Reduce heat; simmer, covered, 12-15 minutes or until liquid is absorbed.
3. Add beans and ⅓ cup cilantro; heat through, stirring occasionally. Sprinkle with remaining cilantro.
NOTE *Look for quinoa in the cereal, rice or organic food aisle.*
PER SERVING *375 cal., 10 g fat (1 g sat. fat), 0 chol., 668 mg sodium, 60 g carb., 10 g fiber, 13 g pro.*

Greek Beef Pitas

A local fast-food pita restaurant inspired me to try making my own Greek-style sandwiches at home. Add olives if you like.
—NANCY SOUSLEY LAFAYETTE, IN

START TO FINISH: 25 MIN.
MAKES: 4 SERVINGS

- 1 pound lean ground beef (90% lean)
- 1 small onion, chopped
- 3 garlic cloves, minced
- 1 teaspoon dried oregano
- ¾ teaspoon salt, divided
- 1 cup reduced-fat plain Greek yogurt
- 1 medium tomato, chopped
- ½ cup chopped peeled cucumber
- 1 teaspoon dill weed
- 4 whole pita breads, warmed
  Additional chopped tomatoes and cucumber, optional

1. In a large skillet, cook beef, onion and garlic over medium heat 8-10 minutes or until beef is no longer pink and vegetables are tender, breaking up beef into crumbles; drain. Stir in oregano and ½ teaspoon salt.
2. In a small bowl, mix yogurt, tomato, cucumber, dill and remaining salt. Spoon ¾ cup beef mixture over each pita bread; top with 3 tablespoons yogurt sauce. If desired, top with additional tomatoes and cucumbers. Serve with remaining yogurt sauce.

SAGE-PECAN BUTTERNUT SQUASH RAVIOLI

Sage-Pecan Butternut Squash Ravioli

I am addicted to this ravioli recipe. The sauce is delicious with any pasta, but I like the wow factor of squash ravioli. The flavor is sweet, salty, nutty, buttery and savory all at the same time.
—BARB MILLER OAKDALE, MN

START TO FINISH: 25 MIN.
MAKES: 4 SERVINGS

- 1 package (18 ounces) frozen butternut squash ravioli or 2 packages (9 ounces each) refrigerated cheese ravioli
- ¾ cup chopped pecans or walnuts
- 3 tablespoons butter
- ¼ cup packed brown sugar
- ½ teaspoon salt
- ¼ teaspoon ground nutmeg
  Dash cayenne pepper
- ¼ cup heavy whipping cream
- 2 tablespoons minced fresh sage or 2 teaspoons rubbed sage
  Shaved or shredded Parmesan cheese

1. Cook the ravioli according to package directions.
2. Meanwhile, in a large dry skillet, toast pecans over medium-low heat 1-2 minutes or until lightly browned, stirring occasionally. Stir in butter until melted. Stir in brown sugar, salt, nutmeg and cayenne. Remove from heat; stir in cream and sage.
3. Drain ravioli; add to skillet and toss to coat. Top with cheese.

EAT SMART
Fig-Glazed Pork Tenderloin

START TO FINISH: 30 MIN.
MAKES: 4 SERVINGS

- 1 pork tenderloin (1 pound), cut into 8 slices
- ½ teaspoon salt
- ½ teaspoon pepper
- 1 tablespoon olive oil
- ⅓ cup fig preserves
- 3 tablespoons apple juice
- 2 tablespoons cider vinegar
- 1½ teaspoons Worcestershire sauce
- 1 garlic clove, minced
- ¾ teaspoon curry powder

1. Sprinkle pork with salt and pepper. In a large skillet, heat oil over medium-high heat. Brown pork on both sides; remove from pan.

2. Add preserves, juice, vinegar, Worcestershire sauce, garlic and curry powder to same pan; bring to a boil. Return pork to pan. Reduce heat; simmer, covered, 5-7 minutes or until a thermometer inserted in pork reads 145°. Let stand 5 minutes before serving.

PER SERVING *239 cal., 7 g fat (2 g sat. fat), 63 mg chol., 509 mg sodium, 20 g carb., trace fiber, 23 g pro.*

> I like to experiment with unique flavors and try to make the food look as photo-worthy as possible. But for my husband, the dish just has to taste good. Here's a supper that makes us both happy.
>
> —JEAN GOTTFRIED UPPER SANDUSKY, OH

FIG-GLAZED PORK TENDERLOIN

FREEZE IT EAT SMART
Skillet Beef Tamales

This Southwestern skillet dinner is cheesy and delicious, and it doesn't taste light at all! It's sure to become a new favorite.
—DEBORAH WILLIAMS PEORIA, AZ

START TO FINISH: 30 MIN.
MAKES: 5 SERVINGS

- 1 pound lean ground beef (90% lean)
- ⅓ cup chopped sweet red pepper
- ⅓ cup chopped green pepper
- 2 cups salsa
- ¾ cup frozen corn
- 2 tablespoons water
- 6 corn tortillas (6 inches), halved and cut into ½-inch strips
- ¾ cup shredded reduced-fat cheddar cheese
- 5 tablespoons fat-free sour cream

1. In a large nonstick skillet coated with cooking spray, cook beef and peppers over medium heat 6-8 minutes or until beef is no longer pink and vegetables are tender, breaking up beef into crumbles; drain. Stir in salsa, corn and water; bring to a boil.

2. Stir in tortilla strips. Reduce heat; simmer, covered, 10-15 minutes or until tortillas are softened. Sprinkle with cheese; cook, covered, 2-3 minutes longer or until cheese is melted. Serve with sour cream.

FREEZE OPTION *Freeze cooled meat mixture in freezer containers. To use, partially thaw in refrigerator overnight. Heat through in a saucepan, stirring occasionally and adding a little water if necessary. Serve with sour cream.*

PER SERVING *329 cal., 11 g fat (5 g sat. fat), 59 mg chol., 679 mg sodium, 28 g carb., 6 g fiber, 25 g pro.* **Diabetic Exchanges:** *3 lean meat, 1½ starch, 1 vegetable, ½ fat.*

TOP TIP

Since I love veggies, I added 1/2 cup onions. I also added 1 tablespoon taco seasoning and another 2 tablespoons water. I used lean ground turkey instead of beef. It was just as delicious!
—LONDONHAM TASTEOFHOME.COM

SKILLET BEEF TAMALES

Chicken with Mandarin Salsa

When I have leftover veggies, I dress up the salsa a little bit with some finely chopped green onions and sweet red peppers. If you like a more spicy salsa, toss in a little cayenne pepper.

—AYSHA SCHURMAN AMMON, ID

START TO FINISH: 20 MIN.
MAKES: 4 SERVINGS

- 1 can (11 ounces) mandarin oranges
- ½ cup chopped pecans
- ¼ cup finely chopped red onion
- 2 tablespoons minced fresh cilantro
- 1 pound boneless skinless chicken breasts, cut into 1-inch cubes
- ½ teaspoon salt
- ½ teaspoon pepper
- 1 tablespoon olive oil
- 2 garlic cloves, minced
- 2⅔ cups hot cooked brown rice

1. Drain oranges, reserving ¼ cup juice. For salsa, in a large bowl, combine oranges, pecans, onion and cilantro.

2. Sprinkle chicken with salt and pepper. In a large skillet, heat oil over medium-high heat. Add chicken; cook and stir 4 minutes. Add garlic; cook 1 minute longer. Stir in reserved juice. Bring to a boil. Reduce heat; simmer, uncovered, 4-6 minutes or until chicken is no longer pink. Top with salsa; serve with rice.

PER SERVING *453 cal., 18 g fat (2 g sat. fat), 63 mg chol., 362 mg sodium, 46 g carb., 5 g fiber, 28 g pro.*

SPICY TILAPIA RICE BOWL

CHICKEN WITH MANDARIN SALSA

Spicy Tilapia Rice Bowl

I love healthy living and tilapia is a staple in my kitchen. Fresh vegetables are always good but take more prep time, so I like the frozen veggie blend as a quick alternative.

—ROSALIN JOHNSON TUPELO, MS

START TO FINISH: 30 MIN.
MAKES: 4 SERVINGS

- 4 tilapia fillets (4 ounces each)
- 1¼ teaspoons Cajun seasoning
- 3 tablespoons olive oil, divided
- 1 medium yellow summer squash, halved lengthwise and sliced
- 1 package (16 ounces) frozen pepper and onion stir-fry blend
- 1 can (14½ ounces) diced tomatoes, drained
- 1 envelope fajita seasoning mix
- 1 can (15 ounces) black beans, rinsed and drained
- ⅛ teaspoon salt
- ⅛ teaspoon pepper
- 3 cups hot cooked brown rice
  Optional toppings: cubed avocado, sour cream and salsa

1. Sprinkle fillets with Cajun seasoning. In a large skillet, heat 2 tablespoons oil over medium heat. Add fillets; cook 4-6 minutes on each side or until fish just begins to flake easily with a fork. Remove and keep warm. Wipe pan clean.

2. In same skillet, heat remaining oil. Add squash; cook and stir 3 minutes. Add stir-fry blend and tomatoes; cook 6-8 minutes longer or until vegetables are tender. Stir in fajita seasoning mix; cook and stir 1-2 minutes longer or until slightly thickened.

3. In a small bowl, mix beans, salt and pepper. Divide rice among four serving bowls; layer with beans, vegetables and fillets. Serve with toppings as desired.

Tangy Turkey Tostadas

START TO FINISH: 25 MIN.
MAKES: 8 SERVINGS

- 1¼ pounds lean ground turkey
- ¾ cup sliced fresh mushrooms
- 1 medium green pepper, chopped
- 1 small onion, chopped
- 2 garlic cloves, minced
- 1 can (16 ounces) kidney beans, rinsed and drained
- 1 cup salsa
- 1 can (4 ounces) chopped green chilies
- 1 tablespoon chili powder
- 1 teaspoon ground cumin
- ½ teaspoon salt
- 4 drops hot pepper sauce
- 1½ cups (6 ounces) reduced-fat Mexican cheese blend
- ½ cup frozen corn, thawed
- 16 tostada shells
- 2 cups shredded lettuce
- 1 cup chopped tomatoes
- ¼ cup minced fresh cilantro

1. In a large skillet, cook turkey, mushrooms, pepper and onion over medium heat 6-8 minutes or until turkey is no longer pink and vegetables are tender, breaking turkey into crumbles; drain. Stir in garlic; cook 1 minute longer.

2. Stir in beans, salsa, green chilies, chili powder, cumin, salt and pepper sauce. Cook, uncovered, 4-5 minutes or until heated through. Add cheese and corn; heat through. Spread about ⅓ cup filling over each tostada shell. Sprinkle with lettuce, tomatoes and cilantro.

FREEZE OPTION *Freeze cooled meat mixture in freezer containers. To use, partially thaw in the refrigerator overnight. Heat through in a saucepan, stirring occasionally and adding a little water if necessary. Serve on tostada shells with toppings.*

I'm a fitness specialist and personal trainer, so I know how important it is to make smart food choices to fuel my day. These fast and filling tostadas are packed with lean protein, fiber and a good dose of veggies. You can have them any night of the week.
—**JULIE HUNTINGTON** MEMPHIS, TN

TANGY TURKEY TOSTADAS

RAVIOLI WITH SNAP PEAS & MUSHROOMS

> Here's a simple way to spruce up store-bought ravioli. With a tossed salad on the side, dinner's fabulous.
>
> —CHARLENE CHAMBERS
> ORMOND BEACH, FL

EAT SMART

Ravioli with Snap Peas & Mushrooms

START TO FINISH: 30 MIN.
MAKES: 8 SERVINGS

- 1 package (20 ounces) refrigerated cheese ravioli
- 1 pound fresh sugar snap peas, trimmed
- 1 tablespoon butter
- ½ pound sliced fresh mushrooms
- 3 shallots, finely chopped
- 2 garlic cloves, minced
- 2 cups fat-free evaporated milk
- 8 fresh sage leaves, thinly sliced or 2 teaspoons rubbed sage
- 1 teaspoon grated lemon peel
- 1 teaspoon lemon-pepper seasoning
- ¼ teaspoon white pepper
- ¼ cup shredded Parmesan cheese
- ¼ cup hazelnuts, coarsely chopped and toasted

1. In a large saucepan, cook ravioli according to package directions, adding snap peas during the last 3 minutes of cooking; drain.

2. Meanwhile, in a large skillet, heat butter over medium-high heat. Add mushrooms, shallots and garlic; cook and stir until mushrooms are tender. Stir in milk, sage, lemon peel, lemon-pepper and white pepper; bring to a boil. Reduce heat; simmer, uncovered, 2 minutes or until sauce is slightly thickened.

3. Add ravioli and snap peas to sauce; heat through. Sprinkle with cheese and hazelnuts.

NOTE *To toast nuts, spread in a 15x10x1-in. baking pan. Bake at 350° for 5-10 minutes or until lightly browned, stirring occasionally. Or, spread in a dry nonstick skillet and heat over low heat until lightly browned, stirring occasionally.*

PER SERVING *347 cal., 11 g fat (5 g sat. fat), 36 mg chol., 470 mg sodium, 44 g carb., 4 g fiber, 20 g pro.* **Diabetic Exchanges:** *2½ starch, 1 medium-fat meat, 1 vegetable, 1 fat.*

EAT SMART

Shrimp and Grits

For a sweet and spicy meal, I serve shrimp and veggies in a wonderful honey-kissed sauce alongside creamy grits. It's my fresh spin on the classic Southern dish.

—**JUDITH KING** MADISONVILLE, TN

START TO FINISH: 30 MIN.
MAKES: 4 SERVINGS

- 2 cups water
- 1 cup fat-free half-and-half
- 4 teaspoons butter, divided
- ¼ teaspoon salt
- ¼ teaspoon pepper
- ¾ cup quick-cooking grits
- ¼ cup ketchup
- 1 tablespoon honey
- 2 teaspoons lemon juice
- ½ to 1 teaspoon hot pepper sauce
- 3 celery ribs, chopped
- 1 medium onion, chopped
- 1 pound uncooked medium shrimp, peeled and deveined
- 1 cup (4 ounces) shredded reduced-fat cheddar cheese

1. In a large saucepan, bring water, half-and-half, 2 teaspoons butter, salt and pepper to a boil. Slowly stir in grits. Reduce heat to medium-low; cook, covered, about 5 minutes or until thickened, stirring occasionally. Remove from heat.

2. Meanwhile, in a small bowl, mix ketchup, honey, lemon juice and pepper sauce. In a large skillet, heat remaining butter over medium-high heat. Add celery and onion; cook and stir until tender. Add shrimp; cook and stir until shrimp turn pink. Stir in ketchup mixture.

3. Stir cheese into grits. Serve shrimp mixture with grits.

PER SERVING *388 cal., 11 g fat (7 g sat. fat), 198 mg chol., 823 mg sodium, 42 g carb., 3 g fiber, 30 g pro.* **Diabetic Exchanges:** *3 starch, 3 lean meat, 2 fat.*

SHRIMP AND GRITS

WHITE BEANS AND VEGGIES WITH COUSCOUS

Stir-Fry Rice Bowl

My meatless version of Korean bibimbap is tasty, pretty and easy to tweak for different spice levels. Koreans usually eat this rice dish with some beef, but I top mine with a poached egg.

—**DEVON DELANEY** WESTPORT, CT

START TO FINISH: 30 MIN.
MAKES: 4 SERVINGS

- 1 **tablespoon canola oil**
- 2 **medium carrots, julienned**
- 1 **medium zucchini, julienned**
- ½ **cup sliced baby portobello mushrooms**
- 1 **cup bean sprouts**
- 1 **cup fresh baby spinach**
- 1 **tablespoon water**
- 1 **tablespoon reduced-sodium soy sauce**
- 1 **tablespoon chili garlic sauce**
- 4 **eggs**
- 3 **cups hot cooked brown rice**
- 1 **teaspoon sesame oil**

1. In a large skillet, heat canola oil over medium-high heat. Add carrots, zucchini and mushrooms; cook and stir 3-5 minutes or until carrots are crisp-tender. Add bean sprouts, spinach, water, soy sauce and chili sauce; cook and stir just until spinach is wilted. Remove from heat; keep warm.

2. Place 2-3 in. of water in a large skillet with high sides. Bring to a boil; adjust heat to maintain a gentle simmer. Break cold eggs, one at a time, into a small bowl; holding bowl close to surface of water, slip egg into water.

3. Cook, uncovered, 3-5 minutes or until whites are completely set and yolks begin to thicken but are not hard. Using a slotted spoon, lift eggs out of water.

4. Serve rice in bowls; top with vegetables. Drizzle with sesame oil. Top each serving with a poached egg.

PER SERVING *305 cal., 11 g fat (2 g sat. fat), 186 mg chol., 364 mg sodium, 40 g carb., 4 g fiber, 12 g pro.* **Diabetic Exchanges:** *2 starch, 1 medium-fat meat, 1 vegetable, 1 fat.*

White Beans and Veggies with Couscous

We're always up for good ways to use our bumper crop of zucchini. Here's one of our favorites. I serve meatless meals two or three times a week—we can make sure we eat our veggies that way and save a little on groceries while we're at it.

—**HEATHER SAVAGE**

WOOD RIVER JUNCTION, RI

START TO FINISH: 25 MIN.
MAKES: 4 SERVINGS

- 1 **tablespoon olive oil**
- 1 **medium zucchini, quartered lengthwise and thinly sliced**
- 1 **medium onion, finely chopped**
- 4 **garlic cloves, minced**
- 1 **can (15 ounces) white kidney or cannellini beans, rinsed and drained**
- 1 **can (14½ ounces) diced tomatoes, undrained**
- ½ **teaspoon dried basil**
- ¼ **teaspoon dried rosemary, crushed**
- ¼ **teaspoon pepper**
- ⅛ **teaspoon salt**

COUSCOUS
- 1½ **cups water**
- 1 **tablespoon butter**
- ¼ **teaspoon salt**
- 1 **cup uncooked couscous**

1. In a large skillet, heat oil over medium-high heat. Add zucchini, onion and garlic; cook and stir 3-5 minutes or until the zucchini is crisp-tender.

2. Stir in beans, tomatoes and seasonings; bring to a boil. Reduce heat; simmer, uncovered, 3-4 minutes or until mixture is slightly thickened and zucchini is tender, stirring occasionally.

3. Meanwhile, in a small saucepan, combine water, butter and salt; bring to a boil. Stir in couscous. Remove from heat; let stand, covered, 5 minutes or until water is absorbed. Fluff with a fork. Serve bean mixture with couscous.

FREEZE OPTION *Freeze cooled bean mixture in freezer containers. To use, partially thaw in refrigerator overnight. Heat through in a saucepan, stirring occasionally and adding a little water if necessary.*

PER SERVING *350 cal., 8 g fat (2 g sat. fat), 8 mg chol., 521 mg sodium, 60 g carb., 9 g fiber, 13 g pro.*

TENDERLOIN STEAK DIANE

Tenderloin Steak Diane

Sometimes, I add more mushrooms to this recipe when my son's eating dinner—he loves them, and they are absolutely fantastic with the steak.

—CAROLYN TURNER RENO, NV

START TO FINISH: 30 MIN.
MAKES: 4 SERVINGS

- 4 beef tenderloin steaks (6 ounces each)
- 1 teaspoon steak seasoning
- 2 tablespoons butter
- 1 cup sliced fresh mushrooms
- ½ cup reduced-sodium beef broth
- ¼ cup heavy whipping cream
- 1 tablespoon steak sauce
- 1 teaspoon garlic salt with parsley
- 1 teaspoon minced chives

1. Sprinkle steaks with steak seasoning. In a large skillet, heat butter over medium heat. Add steaks; cook 4-5 minutes on each side or until meat reaches desired doneness (for medium-rare, a thermometer should read 145°; medium, 160°; well-done, 170°). Remove steaks from pan.
2. Add mushrooms to skillet; cook and stir over medium-high heat until tender. Add broth, stirring to loosen browned bits from pan. Stir in cream, steak sauce and garlic salt. Bring to a boil; cook and stir 1-2 minutes or until sauce is slightly thickened.
3. Return steaks to pan; turn to coat and heat through. Stir in chives.
NOTE *This recipe was tested with McCormick's Montreal Steak Seasoning. Look for it in the spice aisle.*

Linguine with Broccoli Rabe & Peppers

Broccoli rabe is one of my favorite vegetables. Because it cooks right with the pasta, you can do two things at once. Before you know it, a colorful and nutritious dinner is ready.

—GILDA LESTER MILLSBORO, DE

START TO FINISH: 25 MIN.
MAKES: 6 SERVINGS

- 1 pound broccoli rabe
- 1 package (16 ounces) linguine
- 3 tablespoons olive oil
- 2 anchovy fillets, finely chopped, optional
- 3 garlic cloves, minced
- ½ cup sliced roasted sweet red pepper
- ½ cup pitted Greek olives, halved
- ½ teaspoon crushed red pepper flakes
- ¼ teaspoon pepper
- ⅛ teaspoon salt
- ½ cup grated Romano cheese

1. Cut ½ in. off ends of broccoli rabe; trim woody stems. Cut stems and leaves into 2-in. pieces. Cook linguine according to package directions, adding broccoli rabe during the last 5 minutes of cooking. Drain, reserving ½ cup pasta water.
2. Meanwhile, in a large skillet, heat oil over medium-high heat. Add anchovies and garlic; cook and stir 1 minute. Stir in red peppers, olives, pepper flakes, pepper and salt.
3. Add linguine and broccoli rabe to skillet; toss to combine, adding reserved pasta water as desired to moisten. Serve with cheese.
PER SERVING *426 cal., 15 g fat (4 g sat. fat), 10 mg chol., 495 mg sodium, 60 g carb., 5 g fiber, 17 g pro.*

HOW TO

PREPARE MUSHROOMS

 Gently remove dirt by rubbing mushrooms with a produce brush or damp paper towel. Or quickly rinse under cold water, drain and pat dry with paper towel. Trim stems if they are tough or woody.

LINGUINE WITH BROCCOLI RABE & PEPPERS

PORK SCALLOPINI WITH MUSHROOMS

Pork Scallopini with Mushrooms

Here's a marvelous recipe for an at-home date night. I use reduced-sodium chicken broth because I add salt to season the meat and mushrooms.

—LANA DRAMSTAD HAVRE, MT

START TO FINISH: 30 MIN.
MAKES: 4 SERVINGS

- 1 **pork tenderloin (1 pound), cut into eight slices**
- 1 **teaspoon salt, divided**
- ½ **teaspoon pepper, divided**
- 4 **tablespoons butter, divided**
- ½ **pound sliced fresh mushrooms**
- 2 **celery ribs, sliced**
- 1 **cup reduced-sodium chicken broth**
- ⅓ **cup heavy whipping cream**
- 3 **tablespoons minced fresh parsley, divided**
  Hot cooked egg noodles

1. Pound pork slices with a meat mallet to ½-in. thickness; sprinkle with ½ teaspoon salt and ¼ teaspoon pepper. In a large skillet, heat 1 tablespoon butter over medium-high heat. Add pork in batches; cook 2-3 minutes on each side or until pork is golden brown, using 1 tablespoon butter as needed. Remove; keep warm.

2. In same pan, heat remaining butter over medium heat. Add mushrooms, celery, and remaining salt and pepper; cook and stir 6-8 minutes or until tender. Add broth, stirring to loosen browned bits from pan. Bring to a boil; cook 5-6 minutes or until liquid is reduced to ⅔ cup.

3. Return pork to pan. Stir in cream and 2 tablespoons parsley; heat through. Serve with noodles; sprinkle with remaining parsley.

EAT SMART
Coconut-Ginger Chickpeas & Tomatoes

This is my go-to quick dish when I'm in a hurry. When you add the tomatoes, you can also toss in some chopped green peppers to make it even more colorful.

—MALA UDAYAMURTHY SAN JOSE, CA

START TO FINISH: 30 MIN.
MAKES: 6 SERVINGS

- 2 **tablespoons canola oil**
- 2 **medium onions, chopped (about 1⅓ cups)**
- 3 **large tomatoes, seeded and chopped (about 2 cups)**
- 1 **jalapeno pepper, seeded and chopped**
- 1 **tablespoon minced fresh gingerroot**
- 2 **cans (15 ounces each) chickpeas or garbanzo beans, rinsed and drained**
- ¼ **cup water**
- 1 **teaspoon salt**
- 1 **cup light coconut milk**
- 3 **tablespoons minced fresh cilantro**
- 4½ **cups hot cooked brown rice**
  Additional minced fresh cilantro, optional

1. In a large skillet, heat oil over medium-high heat. Add onions; cook and stir until crisp-tender. Add tomatoes, jalapeno and ginger; cook and stir 2-3 minutes longer or until tender.

2. Stir in chickpeas, water and salt; bring to a boil. Reduce heat; simmer, uncovered, 4-5 minutes or until liquid is almost evaporated. Remove from heat; stir in coconut milk and cilantro.

3. Serve with rice; sprinkle with additional cilantro if desired.

NOTE *Wear disposable gloves when cutting hot peppers; the oils can burn skin. Avoid touching your face.*

PER SERVING *402 cal., 12 g fat (3 g sat. fat), 0 chol., 590 mg sodium, 65 g carb., 10 g fiber, 11 g pro.*

COCONUT-GINGER CHICKPEAS & TOMATOES

BLACKBERRY-SAUCED PORK CHOPS

My family loved these chops from the first time I fixed them. They're as tasty in a skillet as they are grilled, so you can eat them all year long. The sauce is also fantastic with chicken.

—PRISCILLA GILBERT INDIAN HARBOUR BEACH, FL

Blackberry-Sauced Pork Chops

START TO FINISH: 30 MIN.
MAKES: 4 SERVINGS

- ½ **cup seedless blackberry spreadable fruit**
- 1 **tablespoon lemon juice**
- 1 **tablespoon reduced-sodium soy sauce**
  Dash ground cinnamon
- 4 **boneless pork loin chops (5 ounces each)**
- 2 **teaspoons steak seasoning**
- 2 **teaspoons olive oil**
- 1 **cup fresh blackberries**

1. In a small saucepan, combine spreadable fruit, lemon juice, soy sauce and cinnamon. Cook and stir over low heat until spreadable fruit is melted. Remove from heat.
2. Sprinkle pork chops with steak seasoning. In a large nonstick skillet coated with cooking spray, heat oil over medium heat. Add pork chops; cook 5-7 minutes on each side or until a meat thermometer reads 145°. Let stand 5 minutes. Serve with sauce and blackberries.
PER SERVING *311 cal., 10 g fat (3 g sat. fat), 68 mg chol., 531 mg sodium, 25 g carb., 2 g fiber, 28 g pro.* **Diabetic Exchanges:** *4 lean meat, 1½ starch, ½ fat.*

Pumpkin-Chorizo Bow Ties

Chicken sausage is such a convenient way to add flavor to healthy dishes. If your family doesn't like spicy food, just skip the red pepper flakes and use a mild-flavored sausage instead.

—SHARON RICCI MENDON, NY

START TO FINISH: 25 MIN.
MAKES: 4 SERVINGS

- 3 **cups uncooked multigrain bow tie pasta**
- 1 **teaspoon canola oil**
- 1 **package (12 ounces) fully cooked chorizo chicken sausage or other spicy chicken sausage, cut into ¼-inch slices**
- 1 **cup fat-free half-and-half**
- 1 **cup canned pumpkin**
- ½ **cup shredded Mexican cheese blend**
- ⅛ **teaspoon garlic powder**
- ⅛ **teaspoon crushed red pepper flakes**
- 1 **tablespoon minced fresh cilantro**

1. Cook pasta according to package directions. Meanwhile, in a large skillet, heat oil over medium-high heat. Cook and stir sausage 4-6 minutes or until browned. Stir in half-and-half, pumpkin, cheese blend, garlic powder and pepper flakes; heat through.
2. Drain pasta. Add to sausage mixture and toss to coat. Sprinkle with cilantro.

PUMPKIN-CHORIZO BOW TIES

Beef, Rice & Pepper Skillet

START TO FINISH: 30 MIN.
MAKES: 6 SERVINGS

- 1 **pound lean ground beef (90% lean)**
- 1 **can (14½ ounces) diced tomatoes with mild green chilies, undrained**
- 1 **can (14½ ounces) beef broth**
- 1 **tablespoon chili powder**
- ¼ **teaspoon salt**
- ⅛ **teaspoon garlic powder**
- 2 **cups instant brown rice**
- 1 **medium sweet red pepper, sliced**
- 1 **medium green pepper, sliced**
- 1 **cup (4 ounces) shredded Colby-Monterey Jack cheese**

1. In a large skillet, cook beef over medium heat 6-8 minutes or until no longer pink, breaking into crumbles; drain.

2. Add tomatoes, broth, chili powder, salt and garlic powder; bring to a boil. Stir in rice and peppers. Reduce heat; simmer, covered, 8-10 minutes or until liquid is absorbed. Remove from heat; sprinkle with cheese. Let stand, covered, until cheese is melted.

> I love Mexican-inspired food and this skillet dinner definitely hits the spot. I also enjoy experimenting with dishes and making them as good for my family's health as possible. This recipe is just one example of how a light and healthy meal can still be satisfying and flavorful. **—JENNY DUBINSKY** INWOOD, WV

BEEF, RICE & PEPPER SKILLET

CHICKEN SAUSAGES WITH POLENTA

EAT SMART

Chicken Sausages with Polenta

I get a kick out of serving this dish—everyone's always on time for dinner when they know it's on the menu.

—ANGELA SPENGLER MECHANICSBURG, PA

START TO FINISH: 30 MIN.
MAKES: 6 SERVINGS

- 4 **teaspoons olive oil, divided**
- 1 **tube (1 pound) polenta, cut into ½-inch slices**
- 1 **each medium green, sweet red and yellow peppers, thinly sliced**
- 1 **medium onion, thinly sliced**
- 1 **package (12 ounces) fully cooked Italian chicken sausage links, thinly sliced**
- ¼ **cup grated Parmesan cheese**
- 1 **tablespoon minced fresh basil**

1. In a large nonstick skillet, heat 2 teaspoons oil over medium heat. Add polenta; cook 9-11 minutes on each side or until golden brown. Keep warm.

2. Meanwhile, in another large skillet, heat remaining oil over medium-high heat. Add peppers and onion; cook and stir until tender. Remove from pan.

3. Add sausages to same pan; cook and stir 4-5 minutes or until browned. Return pepper mixture to pan; heat through. Serve with polenta; sprinkle with cheese and basil.

PER SERVING *212 cal., 9 g fat (2 g sat. fat), 46 mg chol., 628 mg sodium, 19 g carb., 2 g fiber, 13 g pro.* **Diabetic Exchanges:** *2 lean meat, 1 starch, 1 vegetable, ½ fat.*

Pinto Bean Tostadas

Ready-to-go pinto beans and crispy corn tortillas prove how easy it is to make a healthy meal. Sometimes I add some chopped leftover meat to the tostadas, but they're equally satisfying just as they are.

—**LILY JULOW** LAWRENCEVILLE, GA

START TO FINISH: 30 MIN.
MAKES: 6 SERVINGS

- ¼ **cup sour cream**
- ¾ **teaspoon grated lime peel**
- ¼ **teaspoon ground cumin**
- ½ **teaspoon salt, divided**
- 2 **tablespoons canola oil, divided**
- 2 **garlic cloves, minced**
- 2 **cans (15 ounces each) pinto beans, rinsed and drained**
- 1 **to 2 teaspoons hot pepper sauce**
- 1 **teaspoon chili powder**
- 6 **corn tortillas (6 inches)**
- 2 **cups shredded lettuce**
- ½ **cup salsa**
- ¾ **cup crumbled feta cheese or queso fresco**
  Lime wedges

1. In a small bowl, mix sour cream, lime peel, cumin and ¼ teaspoon salt. In a large saucepan, heat 1 tablespoon oil over medium heat. Add the garlic; cook and stir just until fragrant, about 45 seconds. Stir in beans, pepper sauce, chili powder and remaining salt; heat through, stirring occasionally. Keep mixture warm.

2. Brush both sides of tortillas with remaining oil. Place a large skillet over medium-high heat. Add tortillas in two batches; cook 2-3 minutes on each side or until lightly browned and crisp.

3. To serve, arrange beans and lettuce over tostada shells; top with salsa, sour cream mixture and cheese. Serve with lime wedges.

SAUCY SKILLET STEAKS

PER SERVING *291 cal., 10 g fat (3 g sat. fat), 14 mg chol., 658 mg sodium, 38 g carb., 8 g fiber, 11 g pro.* **Diabetic Exchanges:** *2½ starch, 1 lean meat, 1 fat.*

Saucy Skillet Steaks

These juicy ribeye steaks couldn't be easier. I prefer steak, but I've also cooked the recipe with chicken breasts, fish, veal and hamburgers. So go ahead and use whatever meat you have in the fridge.

—**KAREN HAEN** STURGEON BAY, WI

START TO FINISH: 30 MIN.
MAKES: 4 SERVINGS

- 4 **beef ribeye steaks (¾ inch thick and 8 ounces each)**
- ¼ **cup butter**
- 1 **large onion, chopped**
- 4 **garlic cloves, minced**
- ⅓ **cup beef broth**
- 2 **tablespoons Dijon mustard**
  Salt and pepper to taste
- 1 **tablespoon minced fresh parsley**

1. Place a large nonstick skillet over medium heat. In batches, brown steaks for 1-2 minutes on each side. Remove from pan.

2. In same skillet, heat butter over medium-high heat. Add onion; cook and stir until tender. Add garlic; cook 1 minute longer. Stir in broth.

3. Return steaks to the pan; cook 4 minutes. Brush tops with mustard; turn and cook 3-6 minutes longer or until steaks reach desired doneness (for medium-rare, a thermometer should read 145°; medium, 160°; well-done, 170°). Season with salt and pepper to taste; sprinkle with parsley.

PINTO BEAN TOSTADAS

> This is one of my favorite recipes for company and potlucks. It's pure comfort food, especially during wintertime.
> —**JESSICA SILVA** NEW BERLIN, CT

GNOCCHI ALFREDO

Gnocchi Alfredo

START TO FINISH: 25 MIN.
MAKES: 5 SERVINGS

- 2 **pounds potato gnocchi**
- 3 **tablespoons butter, divided**
- 1 **tablespoon plus 1½ teaspoons all-purpose flour**
- 1½ **cups whole milk**
- ½ **cup grated Parmesan cheese Dash ground nutmeg**
- ½ **pound sliced baby portobello mushrooms Minced fresh parsley, optional**

1. Cook gnocchi according to package directions; drain. Meanwhile, in a small saucepan, melt 1 tablespoon butter. Stir in flour until smooth; gradually whisk in milk. Bring to a boil, stirring constantly; cook and stir 1-2 minutes or until thickened. Remove from heat; stir in cheese and nutmeg until blended. Keep warm.
2. In a large heavy skillet, melt remaining butter over medium heat.

Heat 5-7 minutes or until golden brown, stirring constantly. Immediately add mushrooms and gnocchi; cook and stir 4-5 minutes or until mushrooms are tender and gnocchi are lightly browned. Serve with sauce. If desired, sprinkle with fresh parsley.
NOTE *Look for potato gnocchi in the pasta or frozen foods section.*

EAT SMART
Lime-Cilantro Tilapia

I have so much fun serving this Mexican-inspired tilapia at summer parties. Finish it off with a side of rice and a salad loaded with sliced avocados and tomatoes.
—**NADINE MESCH** MOUNT HEALTHY, OH

START TO FINISH: 25 MIN.
MAKES: 4 SERVINGS

- ⅓ **cup all-purpose flour**
- ¾ **teaspoon salt**
- ½ **teaspoon pepper**
- ½ **teaspoon ground cumin, divided**
- 4 **tilapia fillets (6 ounces each)**

- 1 **tablespoon olive oil**
- ½ **cup reduced-sodium chicken broth**
- 2 **tablespoons minced fresh cilantro**
- 1 **teaspoon grated lime peel**
- 2 **tablespoons lime juice**

1. In a shallow bowl, mix flour, salt, pepper and ¼ teaspoon cumin. Dip fillets in flour mixture to coat both sides; shake off excess.
2. In a large nonstick skillet, heat oil over medium heat. Add fillets; cook, uncovered, 3-4 minutes on each side or until fish flakes easily with a fork. Remove and keep warm.
3. To the same skillet, add broth, cilantro, lime peel, lime juice and remaining cumin; bring to a boil. Reduce heat; simmer, uncovered, 2-3 minutes or until slightly thickened. Serve with tilapia.
PER SERVING *198 cal., 5 g fat (1 g sat. fat), 83 mg chol., 398 mg sodium, 6 g carb., trace fiber, 33 g pro.* **Diabetic Exchanges:** *4 lean meat, ½ starch, ½ fat.*

Turkey with Curried Cream Sauce

Give plain old turkey a brand-new spin with classic Indian spices. My version's pretty mild, but if you're in the mood for fire, add extra curry and a shake or two of cayenne pepper. This dish disappears fast, no matter who's at the table.

—**LORI LOCKREY** SCARBOROUGH, ON

START TO FINISH: 30 MIN.
MAKES: 3 SERVINGS

- 2 tablespoons butter
- 2 tablespoons all-purpose flour
- ½ teaspoon curry powder
- 1 cup chicken broth
- ¼ cup 2% milk
- 2 teaspoons canola oil
- 1 small yellow summer squash, sliced
- 1 small zucchini, sliced
- ½ small onion, thinly sliced
- 2 cups cubed cooked turkey breast
- ½ teaspoon grated lemon peel
  Hot cooked rice
- 3 tablespoons chopped cashews

1. In a small saucepan, melt butter over medium heat. Stir in flour and curry powder until smooth; gradually whisk in broth and milk. Bring to a boil, stirring constantly; cook and stir 1-2 minutes or until thickened. Remove from heat; set aside.
2. In a large skillet, heat oil over medium-high heat. Add squash, zucchini and onion; cook and stir until tender. Add turkey, lemon peel and reserved sauce; heat through. Serve with rice; sprinkle with cashews.

TURKEY WITH CURRIED CREAM SAUCE

PENNE WITH TOMATOES & WHITE BEANS

Penne with Tomatoes & White Beans

I learned how to make this tasty and simple combination of veggies, pasta and beans from friends living in Genoa, Italy. To give this dish a Greek twist, you can use feta cheese instead of Parmesan.

—**TRISHA KRUSE** EAGLE, ID

START TO FINISH: 30 MIN.
MAKES: 4 SERVINGS

- 8 ounces uncooked penne pasta
- 2 tablespoons olive oil
- 1 garlic clove, minced
- 2 cans (14½ ounces each) Italian diced tomatoes, undrained
- 1 can (15 ounces) white kidney or cannellini beans, rinsed and drained
- 1 package (10 ounces) fresh spinach, trimmed
- ¼ cup sliced ripe olives
- ½ teaspoon salt
- ¼ teaspoon pepper
- ½ cup grated Parmesan cheese

1. Cook pasta according to package directions. Meanwhile, in a large skillet, heat oil over medium-high heat. Add garlic; cook and stir 1 minute. Add tomatoes and beans. Bring to a boil. Reduce heat; simmer, uncovered, 5-7 minutes to allow flavors to blend.
2. Add spinach, olives, salt and pepper; cook and stir over medium heat until spinach is wilted. Drain pasta; top with tomato mixture and cheese.

Balsamic Chicken with Broccoli Couscous

This quick recipe is all about saving time thanks to a couple of convenience items and an ingenious shortcut: The broccoli cooks right along with the couscous. The result is pure satisfaction on a plate.

—*TASTE OF HOME* TEST KITCHEN

START TO FINISH: 30 MIN.
MAKES: 4 SERVINGS

- 4 **boneless skinless chicken breast halves (4 ounces each)**
- ½ **teaspoon salt**
- ¼ **teaspoon pepper**
- 1 **tablespoon olive oil**
- 2 **tablespoons balsamic vinegar**
- 1 **tablespoon honey**
- ¼ **teaspoon Italian seasoning**

COUSCOUS

- 1 **can (14½ ounces) chicken broth**
- ¼ **teaspoon garlic powder**
- ¼ **teaspoon pepper**
- 3 **cups frozen chopped broccoli, thawed and drained**
- 1 **cup uncooked couscous**
- ¼ **cup grated Parmesan cheese**

1. Sprinkle chicken with salt and pepper. In a large skillet, heat oil over medium heat. Add chicken; cook 4-6 minutes on each side or until a thermometer reads 165°. Stir in vinegar, honey and Italian seasoning; heat through.

2. Meanwhile, in a small saucepan, bring broth, garlic powder and pepper to a boil. Stir in broccoli and couscous. Remove from heat; let stand, covered, 5-10 minutes or until the broth is absorbed. Stir in cheese. Serve chicken with couscous.

EAT SMART
Pork Medallions with Sauteed Apples

Pork and apples are such a good match, and this down-home supper is proof. I really like that the lean cut of meat is tender and juicy, but healthy, too.

—**CLARA COULSON MINNEY**
WASHINGTON COURT HOUSE, OH

START TO FINISH: 30 MIN.
MAKES: 4 SERVINGS

- 2 **teaspoons cornstarch**
- ⅔ **cup reduced-sodium chicken broth**
- ¼ **cup apple juice**
- 1 **tablespoon butter**
- 2 **medium apples, thinly sliced**
- 2 **green onions, sliced**
- 1 **garlic clove, minced**
- ¾ **teaspoon dried thyme**
- ½ **teaspoon paprika**
- ¼ **teaspoon salt**
- ¼ **teaspoon pepper**
- 1 **pound pork tenderloin, cut into 1-inch slices**

1. Preheat broiler. In a small bowl, mix cornstarch, broth and apple juice. In a nonstick skillet, heat butter over medium-high heat. Add apples, green onions and garlic; cook and stir 2-3 minutes or until apples are crisp-tender. Stir cornstarch mixture and add to pan. Bring to a boil; cook and stir 1-2 minutes or until thickened. Keep warm.

2. Mix thyme, paprika, salt and pepper. Pound pork slices with a meat mallet to ½-in. thickness; sprinkle both sides with seasonings.

3. Place pork on a broiler pan. Broil 3 in. from heat 3-4 minutes on each side or until a thermometer reads 145°. Let stand 5 minutes before serving. Serve with apples.

PER SERVING *251 cal., 10 g fat (4 g sat. fat), 85 mg chol., 335 mg sodium, 15 g carb., 3 g fiber, 25 g pro.* **Diabetic Exchanges:** *3 lean meat, 1 fruit, ½ fat.*

PORK MEDALLIONS
WITH SAUTEED APPLES

BALSAMIC CHICKEN WITH
BROCCOLI COUSCOUS

Braised Pork Stew

Pork tenderloin becomes amazingly tender in this braised stew. It's a fantastic meal for a cold winter night.
—**NELLA PARKER** HERSEY, MI

START TO FINISH: 30 MIN.
MAKES: 4 SERVINGS

- 1 **pound pork tenderloin, cut into 1-inch cubes**
- ½ **teaspoon salt**
- ½ **teaspoon pepper**
- 5 **tablespoons all-purpose flour, divided**
- 1 **tablespoon olive oil**
- 1 **package (16 ounces) frozen vegetables for stew**
- 1½ **cups reduced-sodium chicken broth**
- 2 **garlic cloves, minced**
- 2 **teaspoons stone-ground mustard**
- 1 **teaspoon dried thyme**
- 2 **tablespoons water**

1. Sprinkle pork with salt and pepper; add 3 tablespoons flour and toss to coat. In a large skillet, heat oil over medium heat. Brown pork. Drain if necessary. Stir in vegetables, broth, garlic, mustard and thyme. Bring to a boil. Reduce heat; simmer, covered, 10-15 minutes or until pork and vegetables are tender.
2. In a small bowl, mix remaining flour and water until smooth; stir into stew. Return to a boil, stirring constantly; cook and stir 1-2 minutes or until sauce is thickened.
PER SERVING *275 cal., 8 g fat (2 g sat. fat), 63 mg chol., 671 mg sodium, 24 g carb., 1 g fiber, 26 g pro.* **Diabetic Exchanges:** *3 lean meat, 1½ starch, ½ fat.*

HOW TO

BRAISE

Season and coat the meat with flour as the recipe directs. In a Dutch oven, brown the meat in oil in batches. To ensure nice browning, do not crowd the meat.

Sausage, Spinach and Gnocchi

START TO FINISH: 30 MIN.
MAKES: 4 SERVINGS

- 1 **package (16 ounces) potato gnocchi**
- 1 **tablespoon olive oil**
- 3 **Italian turkey sausage links (4 ounces each), casings removed**
- 1 **garlic clove, minced**
- 1 **package (6 ounces) fresh baby spinach**
- 2 **medium tomatoes, coarsely chopped**
- 1½ **cups spaghetti sauce**

1. Cook gnocchi according to package directions; drain. Meanwhile, in a large skillet, heat oil over medium heat; cook sausage 5-7 minutes or until no longer pink, breaking up sausage into crumbles. Add garlic; cook 1 minute longer. Drain. Add spinach and tomatoes; cook and stir just until spinach is wilted.
2. Stir in gnocchi and spaghetti sauce; heat through.
NOTE *Look for potato gnocchi in the pasta or frozen foods section.*
FREEZE OPTION *Freeze cooled gnocchi mixture in freezer containers. To use, partially thaw in refrigerator overnight. Heat through in a skillet, stirring occasionally and adding a little water if necessary.*

I get creative in the kitchen with dishes like this when we're too busy to go to the grocery store. My daughter absolutely loves this dinner, and it's easy for little fingers to pick up while still learning how to use utensils.
—**CARLA ANDREWS** LORTON, VA

SAUSAGE, SPINACH AND GNOCCHI

HEARTY SALISBURY STEAKS

EAT SMART

Hearty Salisbury Steaks

I love serving Salisbury steak with mashed potatoes and vegetables. With its down-home taste, this meal always disappears in the blink of an eye!

—**DOROTHY BAYES** SARDIS, OH

START TO FINISH: 30 MIN.
MAKES: 5 SERVINGS

- 1 **medium onion, finely chopped**
- ½ **cup crushed saltines (about 15 crackers)**
- ¼ **cup egg substitute**
- ½ **teaspoon pepper**
- 1 **pound lean ground beef (90% lean)**
- 1 **tablespoon canola oil**
- 2 **cups water**
- 1 **envelope reduced-sodium onion soup mix**
- 2 **tablespoons all-purpose flour**

1. In a large bowl, combine onion, saltines, egg substitute and pepper. Add beef; mix lightly but thoroughly. Shape into five patties.

2. In a large skillet, heat oil over medium heat. Add patties; cook 3-4 minutes on each side or until lightly browned. Remove patties and keep warm; discard drippings.

3. Combine water, soup mix and flour; stir into skillet. Bring to a boil. Return patties to skillet. Reduce heat; simmer, covered, 5-7 minutes or until meat is no longer pink.

FREEZE OPTION *Freeze individual cooled steak with some gravy in a resealable freezer bag. To use, partially thaw in refrigerator overnight. Microwave, covered, on high in a microwave-safe dish until heated through, gently stirring and adding a little water if necessary.*

PER SERVING *233 cal., 10 g fat (3 g sat. fat), 45 mg chol., 418 mg sodium, 14 g carb., 1 g fiber, 20 g pro.* **Diabetic Exchanges:** *2 lean meat, 1 starch, 1 fat.*

Smoked Mozzarella Chicken with Pasta

Make chicken breasts extraordinary with just a few flavorful additions. Try using prosciutto instead of ham to elevate this dish even further.

—**NAYLET LAROCHELLE** MIAMI, FL

START TO FINISH: 30 MIN.
MAKES: 4 SERVINGS

- 8 **ounces uncooked angel hair pasta or thin spaghetti**
- 4 **boneless skinless chicken breast halves (6 ounces each)**
- ½ **teaspoon salt**
- ¼ **teaspoon pepper**
- ⅔ **cup seasoned bread crumbs**
- 2 **tablespoons olive oil**
- 4 **thin slices smoked deli ham**
- 4 **slices smoked mozzarella cheese**
- ½ **teaspoon dried sage leaves**
- ½ **cup prepared pesto**
  Grated Parmesan cheese, optional

1. Cook pasta according to package directions. Drain and transfer to a large bowl.

2. Meanwhile, pound chicken breasts with a meat mallet to ½-in. thickness; sprinkle with salt and pepper. Place bread crumbs in a shallow bowl. Dip chicken in bread crumbs to coat both sides; shake off excess.

3. In a large skillet, heat oil over medium-high heat. Add chicken; cook 4 minutes. Turn; cook 2 minutes longer. Top with ham and mozzarella cheese; sprinkle with sage. Cook 1-2 minutes longer or until a thermometer inserted in chicken reads 165°. Remove from heat.

4. Add pesto to pasta and toss to coat. Serve chicken with pasta. If desired, sprinkle with Parmesan cheese.

SMOKED MOZZARELLA
CHICKEN WITH PASTA

CHICKEN & PINEAPPLE STIR-FRY

We love how the snappy veggies and pineapple make this stir-fry taste fresh and bright. Add brown sugar and you get a sweet-and-sour dish that's packed with flavor.
—DEETTA RASMUSSEN
FORT MADISON, IA

Chicken & Pineapple Stir-Fry

START TO FINISH: 30 MIN.
MAKES: 4 SERVINGS

- 1 can (8 ounces) pineapple chunks
- 2 tablespoons plus 1 teaspoon cornstarch
- ¼ teaspoon ground ginger
- 1½ cups chicken broth
- 3 tablespoons brown sugar
- 1 tablespoon soy sauce
- 1 tablespoon molasses
- ½ cup all-purpose flour
- ¼ teaspoon salt
- ¼ teaspoon garlic salt
- ¼ teaspoon paprika
- ⅛ teaspoon pepper
- ¾ pound boneless skinless chicken breasts, cut into 1-inch cubes
- 5 tablespoons canola oil, divided
- 3 medium carrots, chopped
- 1 small onion, sliced
- 1 small green pepper, coarsely chopped
  Hot cooked rice

1. Drain pineapple, reserving juice; set pineapple aside. In a small bowl, mix pineapple juice, cornstarch and ginger until smooth. Stir in broth, brown sugar, soy sauce and molasses.

2. In a large resealable plastic bag, combine flour and seasonings. Add chicken, a few pieces at a time; close bag and shake to coat.

3. In a large skillet, heat 4 tablespoons oil over medium heat. Add the chicken; cook and stir until no longer pink. Remove from pan; discard cooking juices.

4. Stir-fry vegetables in remaining oil until crisp-tender. Stir cornstarch mixture and add to pan. Bring to a boil; cook and stir 1-2 minutes or until sauce is thickened. Return chicken to pan. Add reserved pineapple; heat through. Serve with rice.

EAT SMART
Easy Crab Cakes

Canned crabmeat makes these delicate and appetizing cakes ideal for dinner when you are pressed for time. You can also form the crab mixture into four thick patties instead of eight cakes.
—CHARLENE SPELOCK APOLLO, PA

START TO FINISH: 25 MIN.
MAKES: 4 SERVINGS

- 1 cup seasoned bread crumbs, divided
- 2 green onions, finely chopped
- ¼ cup finely chopped sweet red pepper
- 1 egg, lightly beaten
- ¼ cup reduced-fat mayonnaise
- 1 tablespoon lemon juice
- ½ teaspoon garlic powder
- ⅛ teaspoon cayenne pepper
- 2 cans (6 ounces each) crabmeat, drained, flaked and cartilage removed
- 1 tablespoon butter

1. In a large bowl, combine ⅓ cup bread crumbs, green onions, red pepper, egg, mayonnaise, lemon juice, garlic powder and cayenne; fold in crab.

2. Place remaining bread crumbs in a shallow bowl. Divide mixture into eight portions; shape into 2-in. balls. Gently coat in bread crumbs and shape into a ½-in.-thick patty.

3. In a large nonstick skillet, heat butter over medium-high heat. Add crab cakes; cook 3-4 minutes on each side or until golden brown.

PER SERVING *239 cal., 11 g fat (3 g sat. fat), 141 mg chol., 657 mg sodium, 13 g carb., 1 g fiber, 21 g pro.* **Diabetic Exchanges:** *3 lean meat, 2 fat, 1 starch.*

EASY CRAB CAKES

MEDITERRANEAN
SPINACH & BEANS

EAT SMART

Mediterranean Spinach & Beans

If you want to make this dish vegetarian, use soy sauce instead of Worcestershire. Warm or cold, it always hits the spot.

—**BECKY CUBA** SPOTSYLVANIA, VA

START TO FINISH: 30 MIN.
MAKES: 4 SERVINGS

- 1 tablespoon olive oil
- 1 small onion, chopped
- 2 garlic cloves, minced
- 1 can (14½ ounces) no-salt-added diced tomatoes, undrained
- 2 tablespoons Worcestershire sauce
- ¼ teaspoon salt
- ¼ teaspoon pepper
- ⅛ teaspoon crushed red pepper flakes
- 1 can (15 ounces) white kidney or cannellini beans, rinsed and drained
- 1 can (14 ounces) water-packed artichoke hearts, rinsed, drained and quartered
- 1 package (6 ounces) fresh baby spinach
  Additional olive oil, optional

1. In a large skillet, heat oil over medium-high heat. Add onion; cook and stir 3-5 minutes or until tender. Add garlic; cook 1 minute longer.
2. Stir in tomatoes, Worcestershire sauce, salt, pepper and pepper flakes. Bring to a boil. Reduce heat; simmer, uncovered, 6-8 minutes or until liquid is almost evaporated.

3. Add beans, artichoke hearts and spinach; cook and stir 3-5 minutes or until spinach is wilted. Drizzle with additional oil if desired.
PER SERVING *194 cal., 4 g fat (1 g sat. fat), 0 chol., 687 mg sodium, 31 g carb., 7 g fiber, 9 g pro.* **Diabetic Exchanges:** *2 vegetable, 1 starch, 1 lean meat, 1 fat.*

EAT SMART

Quick Turkey Scallopini

Here's one of my most-requested recipes, thanks to the special white wine and mustard sauce. It makes an ordinary weeknight feel like a little party.

—**SUSAN WARREN** NORTH MANCHESTER, IN

START TO FINISH: 25 MIN.
MAKES: 4 SERVINGS

- ⅓ cup all-purpose flour
- ¼ teaspoon dried rosemary, crushed
- ¼ teaspoon dried thyme
- ⅛ teaspoon white pepper
- 1 package (17.6 ounces) turkey breast cutlets
- 4 teaspoons canola oil
- ¼ cup white wine or reduced-sodium chicken broth
- ½ teaspoon cornstarch
- ⅓ cup reduced-sodium chicken broth
- ½ cup reduced-fat sour cream
- 1 teaspoon spicy brown mustard
  Paprika, optional

1. In a shallow bowl, mix flour and seasonings. Dip cutlets in flour mixture to coat both sides; shake off excess. In a large nonstick skillet coated with cooking spray, heat oil over medium heat. Add turkey in batches and cook 2-4 minutes on each side or until no longer pink. Remove to a serving plate; keep warm.
2. Add wine to pan; increase heat to medium-high. Cook 30 seconds, stirring to loosen browned bits from pan. In a small bowl, mix cornstarch and broth until smooth; stir into skillet. Bring to a boil; cook and stir 1-2 minutes or until slightly thickened.
3. Stir in sour cream and mustard; heat through. Pour over turkey. If desired, sprinkle with paprika.
PER SERVING *263 cal., 8 g fat (2 g sat. fat), 88 mg chol., 194 mg sodium, 11 g carb., trace fiber, 34 g pro.* **Diabetic Exchanges:** *4 lean meat, 1 starch, 1 fat.*

EAT SMART

Scallops with Linguine

A buttery garlic sauce adds zip to linguine, bay scallops and veggies. Celebrate something special or toast the end of another workday with this dish that's perfectly sized for two.

—**PAULA JONES** BROOKSVILLE, FL

START TO FINISH: 25 MIN.
MAKES: 2 SERVINGS

- 2 ounces uncooked linguine
- 1 tablespoon cornstarch
- 1 cup chicken broth
- 2 tablespoons white wine or additional chicken broth
- 1½ teaspoons butter
- 1 garlic clove, minced
- ¾ cup sliced fresh mushrooms
- 2 green onions, sliced
- ¼ cup grated carrot
- ½ pound bay scallops
- 1½ teaspoons minced fresh parsley
  Lemon wedges, optional

1. Cook linguine according to package directions; drain. Meanwhile, in a small bowl, mix cornstarch, broth and wine until smooth.
2. In a nonstick skillet, heat butter over medium heat. Add garlic; cook and stir 1 minute. Add mushrooms, green onions and carrot; stir-fry 2-3 minutes or until vegetables are crisp-tender.
3. Stir cornstarch mixture and add to pan. Bring to a boil; cook and stir 1-2 minutes or until sauce is thickened. Reduce heat. Add scallops and parsley; cook until scallops are firm and opaque. Serve with linguine and, if desired, lemon wedges.
PER SERVING *281 cal., 5 g fat (2 g sat. fat), 47 mg chol., 709 mg sodium, 32 g carb., 2 g fiber, 25 g pro.* **Diabetic Exchanges:** *3 lean meat, 2 starch, ½ fat.*

DID YOU KNOW?

Farmed scallops are becoming more common. Because scallops are filter-feeders that live on plankton, they don't require feeding. Their low environmental impact makes farmed scallops a green choice.

WASABI BEEF FAJITAS

EAT SMART
Wasabi Beef Fajitas

Beef fajitas get an Eastern spin with gingerroot, sesame oil and wasabi, a type of Japanese horseradish. You can find it in the Asian section at your supermarket.
—*TASTE OF HOME* TEST KITCHEN

START TO FINISH: 20 MIN.
MAKES: 8 SERVINGS

- 2 **teaspoons cornstarch**
- 3 **tablespoons reduced-sodium soy sauce**
- 2 **teaspoons prepared wasabi**
- 2 **teaspoons minced fresh gingerroot**
- 1 **garlic clove, minced**
- 2 **tablespoons sesame oil, divided**
- 1 **pound uncooked beef stir-fry strips**
- 12 **green onions with tops, cut in half lengthwise**
- 1 **large sweet red pepper, julienned**
- 8 **flour tortillas (8 inches), warmed**
- 1 **cup coleslaw mix**

1. In a small bowl, mix cornstarch, soy sauce, wasabi, ginger and garlic until blended. In a large skillet, heat 1 tablespoon oil over medium-high heat. Add beef; stir-fry 4-6 minutes or until no longer pink. Remove from pan.
2. Stir-fry green onions and red pepper in remaining oil 2-3 minutes or until vegetables are crisp-tender.
3. Stir cornstarch mixture and add to pan. Bring to a boil; cook and stir 1-2 minutes or until sauce is thickened. Return beef to pan; heat through. Serve with tortillas and coleslaw mix.

PER SERVING *273 cal., 9 g fat (2 g sat. fat), 23 mg chol., 533 mg sodium, 30 g carb., 1 g fiber, 18 g pro.* **Diabetic Exchanges:** *2 starch, 2 lean meat.*

Angel Hair with Chicken & Cherries

START TO FINISH: 30 MIN.
MAKES: 4 SERVINGS

- 8 **ounces uncooked multigrain angel hair pasta**
- ¾ **pound boneless skinless chicken breasts, cut into ½-inch cubes**
- 1 **tablespoon cornstarch**
- ½ **teaspoon salt**
- ⅛ **teaspoon pepper**
- 1 **tablespoon olive oil**
- 1 **package (6 ounces) fresh baby spinach**
- ½ **cup dried cherries**
- ¼ **teaspoon ground nutmeg**
- ½ **cup shredded Parmesan cheese**
- ⅓ **cup chopped pecans, toasted**
- ¼ **cup pine nuts, toasted**

1. Cook pasta according to package directions.
2. Meanwhile, in a small bowl, toss chicken with cornstarch, salt and pepper. In a large nonstick skillet, heat oil over medium-high heat. Add chicken mixture; cook and stir until no longer pink. Stir in spinach and cherries; cook 3-4 minutes longer or until spinach is wilted.
3. Drain pasta, reserving ¾ cup pasta water. Place pasta in a large bowl; sprinkle with nutmeg and toss to combine, adding enough reserved pasta water to moisten pasta. Serve with chicken mixture. Sprinkle with cheese and nuts.

NOTE *To toast nuts, spread in a 15x10x1-in. baking pan. Bake at 350° for 5-10 minutes or until lightly browned, stirring occasionally. Or, spread in a dry nonstick skillet and heat over low heat until lightly browned, stirring occasionally.*

> Nutmeg is the secret something that really makes this dish. My vegetarian friend likes it just as well without chicken. —**MARY ANN SANDER** CENTRALIA, MO

ANGEL HAIR WITH CHICKEN & CHERRIES

THAI PASTA WITH
SPICY PEANUT SAUCE

Thai Pasta with Spicy Peanut Sauce

Get ready for crunchy and colorful vegetables in a nutty sauce that packs a big punch. Some eat it hot, but my husband and I prefer to wait until it's closer to room temperature.

—DONNA MCCALLIE LAKE PARK, FL

START TO FINISH: 30 MIN.
MAKES: 6 SERVINGS

- 1 package (12 ounces) whole wheat linguine
- 1 jar (11½ ounces) Thai peanut sauce
- 2 tablespoons lime juice
- 2 cups bean sprouts
- 1 large cucumber, peeled, seeded and chopped
- 2 medium carrots, julienned
- 5 green onions, sliced
- 1 small sweet red pepper, julienned
- ½ cup minced fresh cilantro

1. Cook linguine according to package directions. Drain; return to pan.
2. In a small bowl, combine peanut sauce and lime juice. Add peanut sauce mixture, vegetables and cilantro to the pan; toss to coat.

DID YOU KNOW?

The hearty texture and slightly nutty taste of whole wheat pasta make it an ideal stand-in when you're preparing Asian recipes that call for buckwheat or soba noodles. Even if you don't enjoy the taste of whole wheat pasta in your favorite Italian recipes, don't be afraid to try it in Asian ones!

Hearty Turkey & Rice

We love this recipe, especially when we want an awesome dinner fast. The sauce is also excellent on tortilla chips, which we serve on the side.

—JOAN HALLFORD NORTH RICHLAND HILLS, TX

START TO FINISH: 25 MIN.
MAKES: 4 SERVINGS

- 1½ cups instant brown rice
- 1 pound extra-lean ground turkey
- 1 medium onion, chopped
- 1½ cups salsa
- 1 can (8 ounces) no-salt-added tomato sauce
- 1 teaspoon reduced-sodium chicken bouillon granules
- ¼ teaspoon salt
- ¼ cup shredded reduced-fat cheddar cheese
- ¼ cup reduced-fat sour cream
  Optional toppings: chopped tomatoes, baked tortilla chips and sliced ripe olives

1. Cook rice according to package directions. Meanwhile, in a large nonstick skillet coated with cooking spray, cook turkey and onion over medium heat 6-8 minutes or until turkey is no longer pink and onion is tender, breaking up turkey into crumbles. Add salsa, tomato sauce, bouillon and salt; heat through.
2. Serve with rice, cheese, sour cream and, if desired, toppings of your choice.
FREEZE OPTION *Freeze cooled turkey mixture in freezer containers. To use, partially thaw in refrigerator overnight. Heat through in a saucepan, stirring occasionally and adding a little water or broth if necessary.*
PER SERVING *354 cal., 5 g fat (2 g sat. fat), 55 mg chol., 732 mg sodium, 40 g carb., 3 g fiber, 34 g pro.* **Diabetic Exchanges:** *4 lean meat, 2 starch, 2 vegetable, ½ fat.*

HEARTY TURKEY & RICE

DIJON SHRIMP WITH PASTA

⅛ teaspoon pepper
1 package (17.6 ounces) turkey breast cutlets
2 tablespoons canola oil

LIME BUTTER SAUCE
1 green onion, chopped
2 garlic cloves, minced
¼ cup reduced-sodium chicken broth
¼ cup lime juice
½ cup butter, cubed
½ teaspoon minced chives
½ teaspoon minced fresh dill
½ teaspoon grated lime peel
Salt and pepper to taste

1. In a large resealable plastic bag, combine the first five ingredients. Add turkey, a few pieces at a time; close bag and shake to coat.
2. In a large skillet, heat oil over medium heat. Add turkey in batches and cook 1-2 minutes on each side or until no longer pink. Remove and keep warm.
3. In same skillet, cook green onion and garlic 1 minute. Add broth and lime juice, stirring to loosen browned bits from pan. Bring to a boil. Reduce heat to low; stir in remaining ingredients. Cook and stir until butter is melted. Serve turkey with lime butter sauce.

Dijon Shrimp with Pasta

I combined several family recipes to create this dish, which I like to serve when we have company. If my husband had his way, though, I'd make it every night.
—GAIL CAWSEY GENESEO, IL

START TO FINISH: 25 MIN.
MAKES: 4 SERVINGS

8 ounces uncooked angel hair pasta
¼ cup butter, cubed
2 cups sliced fresh mushrooms
⅓ cup chopped onion
4 teaspoons all-purpose flour
1¼ cups chicken broth
⅓ cup white wine or chicken broth
4 teaspoons Dijon mustard
1½ teaspoons minced fresh tarragon or ½ teaspoon dried tarragon
½ teaspoon paprika
¼ teaspoon pepper
1 pound uncooked medium shrimp, peeled and deveined
⅓ cup heavy whipping cream
¼ cup grated Parmesan cheese

1. Cook pasta according to package directions; drain.

2. Meanwhile, in a large skillet, heat butter over medium-high heat. Add mushrooms and onion; cook and stir until tender. Stir in flour until blended; gradually stir in broth, wine, mustard, tarragon, paprika and pepper. Cook and stir for 5 minutes or until sauce is thickened.
3. Reduce heat to medium; stir in shrimp and cream. Cook, covered, 2-3 minutes or until shrimp turn pink. Serve with pasta; sprinkle with cheese.

Turkey with Lime Butter Sauce

When I'm in Florida, I buy Key limes for the butter sauce, but any fresh limes will work just fine. If I'm using leftover turkey, I brown the meat a little so the sauce picks up the excellent flavor.
—PATRICIA KILE ELIZABETHTOWN, PA

START TO FINISH: 30 MIN.
MAKES: 4 SERVINGS

½ cup all-purpose flour
⅛ teaspoon salt
⅛ teaspoon Italian seasoning
⅛ teaspoon paprika

TURKEY WITH LIME BUTTER SAUCE

PENNE ALLA VODKA

This easy and impressive pasta is always on the menu when my husband and I invite first-time guests over for dinner. Many friends have asked me to make the recipe again years after they first tried it.

—**CARA LANGER** OVERLAND PARK, KS

Penne alla Vodka

START TO FINISH: 30 MIN.
MAKES: 6 SERVINGS

- 1 **package (16 ounces) penne pasta**
- 3 **tablespoons butter**
- 2 **garlic cloves, minced**
- 4 **ounces thinly sliced prosciutto, cut into strips**
- 1 **can (28 ounces) whole plum tomatoes, drained and chopped**
- ¼ **cup vodka**
- ½ **teaspoon salt**
- ½ **teaspoon crushed red pepper flakes**
- ½ **cup heavy whipping cream**
- ½ **cup shredded Parmesan cheese**

1. Cook pasta according to package directions.
2. Meanwhile, in a large skillet, heat butter over medium-high heat. Add

garlic; cook and stir 1 minute. Add prosciutto; cook 2 minutes longer. Stir in tomatoes, vodka, salt and pepper flakes. Bring to a boil. Reduce heat; simmer, uncovered, 5 minutes. Stir in cream; cook 2-3 minutes longer, stirring occasionally.
3. Drain pasta. Add pasta and cheese to sauce; toss to combine.

EAT SMART
Apple-Balsamic Pork Chops & Rice

Thanks to tangy balsamic vinegar and sweet apples, this one-pot dish lets you have a little something special anytime.
—**GREG HAGELI** ELMHURST, IL

START TO FINISH: 30 MIN.
MAKES: 4 SERVINGS

- 4 **boneless pork loin chops (6 ounces each)**
- ½ **teaspoon salt, divided**
- ½ **teaspoon pepper, divided**
- 1 **tablespoon canola oil**
- 2 **medium Gala apples, cut into ½-inch pieces**
- 2 **cups sliced fresh mushrooms**
- 1 **medium onion, chopped**
- 1½ **cups instant brown rice**
- 1 **cup reduced-sodium chicken broth**
- 2 **tablespoons balsamic vinegar**
- ¼ **teaspoon dried thyme**

1. Sprinkle pork chops with ¼ teaspoon salt and ¼ teaspoon pepper. In a large skillet, heat oil over medium heat. Brown pork chops on both sides; remove from pan.
2. To the same skillet, add apples, mushrooms and onion; cook and stir 4-5 minutes or until tender. Stir in rice, broth, vinegar, thyme, and remaining salt and pepper. Bring to a boil. Reduce heat; cook, covered, 5 minutes.
3. Place pork chops over top; cook, covered, 4-6 minutes or until a thermometer inserted in pork reads 145°. Let stand for 5 minutes before serving.
PER SERVING *454 cal., 15 g fat (4 g sat. fat), 82 mg chol., 498 mg sodium, 42 g carb., 4 g fiber, 38 g pro.* **Diabetic Exchanges:** *5 lean meat, 2 starch, 1 fat, ½ fruit.*

APPLE-BALSAMIC PORK CHOPS & RICE

I really like the rich taste of sesame oil in this Thai-inspired dish. If you don't have it, canola oil does the trick, too. To get a similar nuttiness, toss in some toasted sesame seeds or almonds before serving.

—**KELLI WHITING** FORTVILLE, IN

SESAME TURKEY STIR-FRY

EAT SMART

Sesame Turkey Stir-Fry

START TO FINISH: 25 MIN.
MAKES: 4 SERVINGS

- 1 **teaspoon cornstarch**
- ½ **cup water**
- 2 **tablespoons reduced-sodium soy sauce**
- 1 **tablespoon honey**
- 2 **teaspoons curry powder**
- ⅛ **teaspoon crushed red pepper flakes**
- 2 **teaspoons sesame or canola oil**
- 1 **medium sweet red pepper, julienned**
- 1 **small onion, cut into thin wedges**
- 1 **garlic clove, minced**
- 2 **cups shredded cooked turkey breast**
- 1 **green onion, sliced**
- 2 **cups hot cooked brown rice**
    Thinly sliced serrano pepper and toasted sesame seeds, optional

1. In a small bowl, combine the first six ingredients. In a large skillet, heat oil over medium-high heat. Add red pepper and onion; stir-fry until crisp-tender. Add garlic; cook 1 minute.

2. Stir cornstarch mixture and add to pan. Bring to a boil; cook and stir 2 minutes or until sauce is thickened. Add turkey; heat through. Stir in green onion. Serve with rice. If desired, top with serrano pepper and sesame seeds.

NOTE *Wear disposable gloves when cutting hot peppers; the oils can burn skin. Avoid touching your face.*

PER SERVING *269 cal., 4 g fat (1 g sat. fat), 60 mg chol., 349 mg sodium, 32 g carb., 3 g fiber, 25 g pro.* **Diabetic Exchanges:** *3 lean meat, 2 starch, ½ fat.*

Roasted Red Pepper Sausage Skillet

On nights when I make this dish, my two teenagers always make sure they're home. Eat it on its own, or pair it with breadsticks, a green salad and apple slices.

—**JANET TEAS** ZANESVILLE, OH

START TO FINISH: 30 MIN.
MAKES: 5 SERVINGS

- 4 cups uncooked egg noodles
- ½ pound bulk Italian sausage
- 1 small onion, chopped
- 1 small green pepper, chopped
- ½ cup chopped fresh mushrooms
- 2 jars (7½ ounces each) roasted sweet red peppers, drained and coarsely chopped
- 1 can (10¾ ounces) condensed golden mushroom soup, undiluted
- 3 ounces cream cheese, cubed
- ⅓ cup 2% milk
- ½ cup shredded smoked provolone cheese

1. Cook noodles according to package directions; drain. Meanwhile, in a large skillet, cook sausage, onion, green pepper and mushrooms over medium heat until sausage is no longer pink and the vegetables are tender, breaking up sausage into crumbles; drain.

2. Stir in red peppers, soup, cream cheese and milk; heat through. Stir noodles into sausage mixture; sprinkle with provolone cheese. Let stand, covered, for 5 minutes or until cheese is melted.

STEAK DIANE

ROASTED RED PEPPER
SAUSAGE SKILLET

Steak Diane

Whenever I want to make a memorable dinner without spending hours in the kitchen, this is the recipe I rely on.

—**PHOEBE CARRE** MULLICA HILL, NJ

START TO FINISH: 20 MIN.
MAKES: 4 SERVINGS

- 4 beef ribeye steaks (½ inch thick and 8 ounces each)
- ¼ teaspoon pepper
- ⅛ teaspoon salt
- 4 tablespoons butter, divided
- 1 green onion, finely chopped
- ½ teaspoon ground mustard
- 1 tablespoon lemon juice
- 1½ teaspoons Worcestershire sauce
- 1 tablespoon minced fresh parsley
- 1 tablespoon minced chives

1. Sprinkle the steaks with pepper and salt. In a large skillet, heat 2 tablespoons butter over medium heat. Add green onion and mustard; cook 1 minute. Add steaks; cook 2-5 minutes on each side or until meat reaches desired doneness (for medium-rare, a thermometer should read 145°; medium 160°; well-done 170°).

2. Remove steaks to a serving platter and keep warm. In same skillet, add lemon juice, Worcestershire sauce and remaining butter; cook and stir 2 minutes or until thickened. Add parsley and chives. Serve with steaks.

CHICKEN SAUSAGE & GNOCCHI SKILLET

Chicken Sausage & Gnocchi Skillet

I had a bunch of fresh veggies and combined them with sausage, gnocchi and goat cheese when I needed a quick dinner. Mix and match the ingredients you want for unique results to fit your family.
—**DAHLIA ABRAMS** DETROIT, MI

START TO FINISH: 30 MIN.
MAKES: 4 SERVINGS

- 1 package (16 ounces) potato gnocchi
- 1 tablespoon butter
- 1 tablespoon olive oil
- 2 fully cooked Italian chicken sausage links (3 ounces each), sliced
- ½ pound sliced baby portobello mushrooms
- 1 medium onion, finely chopped
- 1 pound fresh asparagus, trimmed and cut into ½-inch pieces
- 2 garlic cloves, minced
- 2 tablespoons white wine or chicken broth
- 2 ounces herbed fresh goat cheese
- 2 tablespoons minced fresh basil or 2 teaspoons dried basil
- 1 tablespoon lemon juice
- ¼ teaspoon salt
- ⅛ teaspoon pepper
  Grated Parmesan cheese

1. Cook gnocchi according to package directions; drain. Meanwhile, in a large skillet, heat butter and oil over medium-high heat. Add sausage, mushrooms and onion; cook and stir until sausage is browned and vegetables are tender. Add asparagus and garlic; cook 2-3 minutes longer.
2. Stir in wine. Bring to a boil; cook until liquid is almost evaporated. Add goat cheese, basil, lemon juice, salt and pepper. Stir in gnocchi; heat through. Sprinkle with Parmesan cheese.

DID YOU KNOW?

Using turkey kielbasa instead of traditional sausage made with pork and beef saves over 60 calories and 7 grams of fat per serving. Turkey kielbasa also contains more protein than traditional.

Simple Sesame Chicken with Couscous

I created this recipe after my three kids tried Chinese takeout and asked for more.
—**NAYLET LAROCHELLE** MIAMI, FL

START TO FINISH: 25 MIN.
MAKES: 4 SERVINGS

- 1½ cups water
- 1 cup uncooked whole wheat couscous
- 1 tablespoon olive oil
- 2 cups coleslaw mix
- 4 green onions, sliced
- 2 tablespoons plus ½ cup reduced-fat Asian toasted sesame salad dressing, divided
- 2 cups shredded cooked chicken breast
- 2 tablespoons minced fresh cilantro
  Chopped peanuts, optional

1. In a small saucepan, bring water to a boil. Stir in couscous. Remove from heat; let stand, covered, 5-10 minutes or until water is absorbed. Fluff couscous with a fork.
2. In a large nonstick skillet, heat oil over medium heat. Add coleslaw mix; cook and stir 3-4 minutes or just until tender. Add the green onions, 2 tablespoons dressing and couscous; heat through. Remove couscous from pan; keep warm.
3. To the same skillet, add chicken and remaining dressing; cook and stir over medium heat until heated through. Serve over couscous; top with cilantro and, if desired, peanuts.
PER SERVING *320 cal., 9 g fat (1 g sat. fat), 54 mg chol., 442 mg sodium, 35 g carb., 5 g fiber, 26 g pro.* **Diabetic Exchanges:** *3 lean meat, 2 starch, 1 fat.*

Confetti Kielbasa Skillet

Here's one of my husband's favorite dishes. When it's in season, substitute fresh corn for frozen.
—**SHEILA GOMEZ** SHAWNEE, KS

START TO FINISH: 30 MIN.
MAKES: 4 SERVINGS

- 1 tablespoon canola oil
- 7 ounces smoked turkey kielbasa, cut into ¼-inch slices

- 1 medium onion, halved and sliced
- ½ cup sliced baby portobello mushrooms
- 2 garlic cloves, minced
- ½ cup reduced-sodium chicken broth
- ¾ teaspoon Mrs. Dash Garlic & Herb seasoning blend
- 1 can (15 ounces) no-salt-added black beans, rinsed and drained
- 1 package (8.8 ounces) ready-to-serve brown rice
- 1 cup frozen corn
- ½ cup chopped roasted sweet red peppers
- 4 teaspoons minced fresh cilantro

1. In a large skillet, heat oil over medium-high heat. Add kielbasa, onion and mushrooms; cook and stir 4-6 minutes or until vegetables are tender. Add garlic; cook 1 minute longer.
2. Add broth and seasoning blend, stirring to loosen browned bits from pan. Bring to a boil; cook 2-3 minutes or until liquid is almost evaporated. Stir in remaining ingredients; heat through.
PER SERVING *347 cal., 9 g fat (1 g sat. fat), 31 mg chol., 692 mg sodium, 45 g carb., 7 g fiber, 18 g pro.* **Diabetic Exchanges:** *3 starch, 2 lean meat, ½ fat.*

CONFETTI KIELBASA SKILLET

**Maple Ricotta Mousse
with Candied Pecans**
PAGE 48

Give Me 5 or Fewer

Turn here for streamlined recipes that use five ingredients or less. Choose from stick to your ribs mains, savory soups and delectable sweets guaranteed to delight. (Recipes may also call for water, salt, pepper, and canola or olive oil.)

**Shrimp Tortellini
Pasta Toss**
PAGE 56

**Strawberry Sorbet
Sensation**
PAGE 54

**Spicy Pumpkin &
Corn Soup**
PAGE 58

PESTO CHICKEN TURNOVERS

Maple Ricotta Mousse with Candied Pecans

Try not to sneak too many of the maple-flavored pecans while you make dessert. They're even better with the mousse.

—**KATHLEEN GILL** PAHRUMP, NV

PREP: 25 MIN. + COOLING
MAKES: 4 SERVINGS

- ⅔ **cup maple syrup**
- ¼ **cup chopped pecans**
- ½ **cup heavy whipping cream**
- 1¼ **cups whole-milk ricotta cheese**
- ½ **cup mascarpone cheese**

1. Place syrup in a small saucepan; bring to a boil. Reduce heat; simmer, uncovered, 5 minutes. Transfer to a bowl; cool completely.
2. In a small heavy skillet, cook and stir pecans over medium heat, about 3 minutes. Drizzle with 1 tablespoon cooked syrup; cook and stir 1 minute longer. Spread on foil to cool.
3. In a small bowl, beat cream until soft peaks form. In a large bowl, beat ricotta and mascarpone cheeses until light and fluffy. Gradually beat in ⅓ cup cooled syrup; gently fold in whipped cream.
4. To serve, spoon mousse into dessert dishes. Drizzle with remaining cooled syrup; top with candied pecans.

MAPLE RICOTTA MOUSSE WITH CANDIED PECANS

FREEZE IT FAST FIX

Pesto Chicken Turnovers

When it comes to food, I'm all about anything in a pocket—pita bread, bierocks, empanadas and more. These Italian-inspired turnovers are great for dinner. You can also make 32 appetizers by using four tubes' worth of single crescent rolls with a tablespoon of filling in each.

—**GREG MUNOZ** SACRAMENTO, CA

START TO FINISH: 30 MIN.
MAKES: 4 SERVINGS

- 2 **tubes (8 ounces each) refrigerated seamless crescent dough sheets**
- 1 **package (10 ounces) frozen chopped spinach, thawed and squeezed dry**
- 1 **package (9 ounces) ready-to-use grilled Italian chicken strips**
- 1 **cup (4 ounces) shredded part-skim mozzarella cheese**
- 3 **tablespoons prepared pesto**

1. Preheat oven to 375°. Unroll both tubes of crescent dough and cut each into four rectangles.
2. In a large bowl, combine spinach, chicken, cheese and pesto; spoon ¾ cup in the center of each of four rectangles. Top with remaining rectangles; pinch seams to seal. Place on greased baking sheets; cut three slits in top of each turnover. Bake 18-22 minutes or until golden brown.
FREEZE OPTION *Freeze cooled turnovers in a resealable plastic freezer bag. To use, bake frozen turnovers on a greased baking sheet in a preheated 375° oven until heated through.*

TURKEY CUTLETS IN
LEMON WINE SAUCE

Turkey Cutlets in Lemon Wine Sauce

After I ate something similar to this at a local Italian restaurant, I figured out how to make it at home for my family. Now I serve it a lot since it's so quick to make—and they're so happy I do.

—KATHIE WILSON WARRENTON, VA

START TO FINISH: 25 MIN.
MAKES: 4 SERVINGS

- ½ cup all-purpose flour
- ½ teaspoon salt
- ½ teaspoon paprika
- ¼ teaspoon pepper
- 4 turkey breast cutlets (2½ ounces each)
- 1 tablespoon olive oil
- 1 cup white wine or chicken broth
- ¼ cup lemon juice

1. In a shallow bowl, mix flour, salt, paprika and pepper. Dip turkey in flour mixture to coat both sides; shake off excess.

2. In a large skillet, heat oil over medium heat. Add turkey and cook in batches 1-2 minutes on each side or until no longer pink. Remove turkey from pan.

3. Add wine and lemon juice to skillet, stirring to loosen browned bits. Bring to a boil; cook until liquid is reduced by half. Return cutlets to pan; turn to coat and heat through.

PER SERVING *145 cal., 4 g fat (1 g sat. fat), 44 mg chol., 110 mg sodium, 5 g carb., trace fiber, 18 g pro.* **Diabetic Exchanges:** *2 lean meat, 1 fat.*

Strawberry-Teriyaki Glazed Salmon

START TO FINISH: 25 MIN.
MAKES: 4 SERVINGS

- ¼ cup seedless strawberry jam
- 2 tablespoons reduced-sodium soy sauce
- 1 garlic clove, minced
- ½ teaspoon ground ginger
- 4 salmon fillets (4 ounces each)
- ¼ teaspoon salt
- ¼ teaspoon pepper

1. Preheat broiler. In a small saucepan, combine jam, soy sauce, garlic and ginger; cook and stir until mixture comes to a boil. Reduce heat; simmer, uncovered, 6-8 minutes or until mixture is reduced by half.

2. Sprinkle salmon with salt and pepper. Place in an ungreased 15x10x1-in. baking pan. Broil 4-6 in. from heat 8-10 minutes or until fish just begins to flake easily with a fork, brushing with 2 tablespoons jam mixture during the last 2 minutes of cooking. Just before serving, brush with remaining jam mixture.

PER SERVING *234 cal., 10 g fat (2 g sat. fat), 57 mg chol., 507 mg sodium, 14 g carb., trace fiber, 20 g pro.* **Diabetic Exchanges:** *3 lean meat, 1 starch.*

STRAWBERRY-TERIYAKI
GLAZED SALMON

I'm always up for a good salmon dinner, but this is the best recipe I've ever made. Strawberry jam might seem like a surprise in an Asian-inspired dish, but it makes a sweet-savory glaze that impresses everyone—even my boyfriend, who doesn't like fish.

—KRYSTINA CAHALAN WINTER PARK, FL

Blackberry Nectarine Pie

Blackberries are a huge crop in my area, so I've made this beautiful double-fruit pie many times. I can always tell when my husband wants me to make it because he brings home blackberries that he picked behind his office.

—**LINDA CHINN** ENUMCLAW, WA

PREP: 25 MIN. + CHILLING
MAKES: 8 SERVINGS

- ¼ **cup cornstarch**
- 1 **can (12 ounces) frozen apple juice concentrate, thawed**
- 2 **cups fresh blackberries, divided**
- 5 **medium nectarines, peeled and coarsely chopped**
- 1 **reduced-fat graham cracker crust (8 inches)**
  Reduced-fat whipped topping, optional

1. In a small saucepan, mix cornstarch and apple juice concentrate until smooth. Bring to a boil. Add ½ cup blackberries; cook and stir 2 minutes or until thickened. Remove from heat.
2. In a large bowl, toss nectarines with remaining blackberries; transfer to crust. Pour apple juice mixture over fruit (crust will be full). Refrigerate, covered, 8 hours or overnight. If desired, serve with whipped topping.
PER SERVING *240 cal., 4 g fat (1 g sat. fat), 0 chol., 106 mg sodium, 50 g carb., 4 g fiber, 3 g pro.*

BLACKBERRY NECTARINE PIE

SPICY APRICOT-GLAZED CHICKEN

Spicy Apricot-Glazed Chicken

Save yourself a trip to the store and check the fridge first. Chicken will turn sweet and hot when you pull out the chili sauce, mustard and apricot preserves.

—**SONYA LABBE** WEST HOLLYWOOD, CA

START TO FINISH: 20 MIN.
MAKES: 4 SERVINGS

- ⅓ **cup apricot preserves**
- ¼ **cup chili sauce**
- 1 **tablespoon hot mustard**
- ¼ **teaspoon salt**
- ⅛ **teaspoon pepper**
- 4 **boneless skinless chicken breast halves (4 ounces each)**

1. Preheat broiler. In a small saucepan, combine the first five ingredients; cook and stir over medium heat until heated through.
2. Place chicken in a 15x10x1-in. baking pan coated with cooking spray. Broil 3-4 in. from heat 6-8 minutes on each side or until a thermometer reads 165°. Brush occasionally with the preserves mixture during the last 5 minutes of cooking.
PER SERVING *209 cal., 3 g fat (1 g sat. fat), 63 mg chol., 476 mg sodium, 23 g carb., trace fiber, 23 g pro.*

APPLE PIE A LA MODE

Now that I have this recipe, my husband and I always look forward to wild salmon season. You can find hoisin sauce in the international foods aisle at the grocery store.

—CHERYL REIN ORLANDO, FL

EAT SMART **FAST FIX**

Hoisin & Honey Glazed Salmon

START TO FINISH: 20 MIN.
MAKES: 4 SERVINGS

- 3 tablespoons hoisin sauce
- 3 tablespoons honey
- 1 tablespoon unsweetened pineapple juice
- 4 salmon fillets (6 ounces each)

1. Preheat broiler. Mix hoisin sauce, honey and pineapple juice.
2. Place salmon in a foil-lined 15x10x1-in. baking pan. Broil 4-5 in. from heat 12-14 minutes or until fish just begins to flake easily with a fork. Baste occasionally with ¼ cup hoisin mixture during the last 6 minutes of cooking. Serve with remaining sauce.
PER SERVING *341 cal., 16 g fat (3 g sat. fat), 86 mg chol., 280 mg sodium, 19 g carb., trace fiber, 29 g pro.* **Diabetic Exchanges:** *4 lean meat, 1 starch.*

HOISIN & HONEY GLAZED SALMON

Apple Pie a La Mode

I was planning a dinner party and wanted a dessert that wowed. This caramel apple ice cream pie certainly did the trick! Now it's a family favorite.

—TRISHA KRUSE EAGLE, ID

PREP: 15 MIN. + FREEZING
MAKES: 8 SERVINGS

- 1 can (21 ounces) apple pie filling
- 1 graham cracker crust (9 inches)
- 2 cups butter pecan ice cream, softened if necessary
- 1 jar (12 ounces) hot caramel ice cream topping
- ¼ cup chopped pecans, toasted

1. Spread half of the pie filling over crust. Top with half of the ice cream; freeze 30 minutes. Drizzle with half of the caramel topping; layer with remaining pie filling. Freeze 30 minutes. Scoop remaining ice cream over top. Freeze, covered, until firm.

2. Remove from freezer 30 minutes before serving. In a microwave, warm remaining caramel topping. Serve pie with warm caramel topping; sprinkle with pecans.
NOTE *To toast nuts, spread in a 15x10x1-in. baking pan. Bake at 350° for 5-10 minutes or until lightly browned, stirring occasionally. Or, spread in a dry nonstick skillet and heat over low heat until lightly browned, stirring occasionally.*

TOP TIP

Wild salmon is 20% leaner than farm-raised fish, while being higher in heart-healthy omega-3 fatty acids. Some people prefer its flavor over farm-raised fish, too. Fresh wild salmon is available from May through October, as the different species travel upstream to spawn.

SOUTHWESTERN SCALLOPS

Southwestern Scallops

My saucy sea scallops are popular at dinner parties, and they're in my collection of easy weekday meals. The seasoning gives the sweet shellfish a pleasant kick.
—**MAGGIE FONTENOT** THE WOODLANDS, TX

START TO FINISH: 20 MIN.
MAKES: 4 SERVINGS

- 2 **teaspoons chili powder**
- ½ **teaspoon ground cumin**
- ¼ **teaspoon salt**
- ⅛ **teaspoon pepper**
- 12 **sea scallops (1 to 1½ pounds)**
- 2 **tablespoons butter, divided**
- ½ **cup white wine or chicken broth**

1. In a small bowl, combine the seasonings. Pat scallops dry with paper towels, then sprinkle with seasonings, pressing to coat.
2. In a large skillet, heat 1 tablespoon butter over medium-high heat. Add scallops; cook 2-3 minutes on each side or until golden brown and firm. Remove from pan; keep warm.
3. Add wine to pan. Cook over medium heat, stirring to loosen browned bits from pan. Bring to a boil; cook until liquid is reduced by half. Stir in remaining butter until melted. Serve with scallops.
PER SERVING *180 cal., 7 g fat (4 g sat. fat), 52 mg chol., 386 mg sodium, 4 g carb., 1 g fiber, 19 g pro.* **Diabetic Exchanges:** *3 lean meat, 1½ fat.*

Chocolate-Dipped Strawberry Meringue Roses

PREP: 25 MIN. • **BAKE:** 40 MIN. + COOLING
MAKES: 3½ DOZEN

- 3 **egg whites**
- ¼ **cup sugar**
- ¼ **cup freeze-dried strawberries**
- 1 **package (3 ounces) strawberry gelatin**
- ½ **teaspoon vanilla extract, optional**
- 1 **cup 60% cacao bittersweet chocolate baking chips, melted**

1. Place egg whites in a large bowl; let egg whites stand at room temperature 30 minutes. Preheat oven to 225°.

2. Place sugar and strawberries in a food processor; process until powdery. Add gelatin; pulse to blend.
3. Beat egg whites on medium speed until foamy, adding vanilla if desired. Gradually add the gelatin mixture, 1 tablespoon at a time, beating on high after each addition until sugar is dissolved. Continue beating until stiff glossy peaks form.
4. Cut a small hole in the tip of a pastry bag or in a corner of a food-safe plastic bag; insert a #1M star tip. Transfer meringue to bag. Pipe 2-in. roses 1½ in. apart onto parchment paper-lined baking sheets.

5. Bake 40-45 minutes or until set and dry. Turn off oven (do not open oven door); leave meringues in oven 1½ hours. Remove from oven; cool completely on baking sheets.
6. Remove meringues from paper. Dip bottoms in melted chocolate; allow excess to drip off. Place on waxed paper; let stand until set, about 45 minutes. Store in an airtight container at room temperature.
PER SERVING *33 cal., 1 g fat (1 g sat. fat), 0 chol., 9 mg sodium, 6 g carb., trace fiber, 1 g pro.* **Diabetic Exchange:** *½ starch.*

Eat these as-is, or try crushing them into a bowl of strawberries and whipped cream. Readers of my blog, utry.it, went nuts when I posted that idea!
—**AMY TONG** ANAHEIM, CA

CHOCOLATE-DIPPED STRAWBERRY MERINGUE ROSES

STRAWBERRY SORBET
SENSATION

On hot days in Colorado, we chill out with slices of this berries-and-cream dessert. The layered effect is so much fun. Use any flavor of sorbet you like.
—**KENDRA DOSS** COLORADO SPRINGS, CO

Strawberry Sorbet Sensation

PREP: 20 MIN. + FREEZING
MAKES: 8 SERVINGS

- 2 **cups strawberry sorbet, softened if necessary**
- 1 **cup cold fat-free milk**
- 1 **package (1 ounce) sugar-free instant vanilla pudding mix**
- 1 **carton (8 ounces) frozen reduced-fat whipped topping, thawed, divided**
- 1 **cup sliced fresh strawberries**

1. Line an 8x4-in. loaf pan with foil. Spread sorbet onto bottom of pan; place in freezer 15 minutes.

2. In a small bowl, whisk milk and pudding mix 2 minutes. Let stand 2 minutes or until soft-set. Reserve ½ cup whipped topping for serving; cover and refrigerate. Fold remaining whipped topping into pudding; spread over sorbet. Freeze, covered, 4 hours or overnight.

3. Remove dessert from freezer 10-15 minutes before serving. Unmold dessert onto a serving plate; remove foil. Cut into slices. Serve with strawberries and the reserved whipped topping.

PER SERVING *153 cal., 3 g fat (3 g sat. fat), 1 mg chol., 163 mg sodium, 27 g carb., 2 g fiber, 1 g pro.* **Diabetic Exchanges:** *2 starch, ½ fat.*

Pesto Fish with Pine Nuts

I love fish, and Italian flavors are a favorite of mine. This is a tasty way to get more healthy fish into your diet.
—**VALERY ANDERSON** STERLING HEIGHTS, MI

START TO FINISH: 15 MIN.
MAKES: 4 SERVINGS

- 2 **envelopes pesto sauce mix, divided**
- 4 **cod fillets (6 ounces each)**
- ¼ **cup olive oil**
- ½ **cup shredded Parmesan or Romano cheese**
- ½ **cup pine nuts, toasted**

1. Prepare one envelope pesto sauce mix according to package directions; set aside. Sprinkle fillets with remaining pesto mix, patting to help adhere.

2. In a large skillet, heat oil over medium heat. Add fillets; cook 4-5 minutes on each side or until fish just begins to flake easily with a fork. Remove from heat. Sprinkle with cheese and pine nuts. Serve with pesto sauce.

NOTE *To toast nuts, spread in a 15x10x1-in. baking pan. Bake at 350° for 5-10 minutes or until lightly browned, stirring occasionally. Or, spread in a dry nonstick skillet and heat over low heat until lightly browned, stirring occasionally.*

PESTO FISH WITH
PINE NUTS

ITALIAN MEATBALL BUNS

Italian Meatball Buns

One of the greatest gifts I love to share with my six grandkids is making special recipes just for them. The meatballs inside the rolls are a savory surprise.

—TRINA LINDER-MOBLEY CLOVER, SC

PREP: 30 MIN. + RISING • **BAKE:** 15 MIN.
MAKES: 2 DOZEN

- 12 frozen bread dough dinner rolls
- 1 package (12 ounces) frozen fully cooked Italian meatballs, thawed
- 2 tablespoons olive oil
- ¼ cup grated Parmesan cheese
- ¼ cup minced fresh basil
- 1½ cups marinara sauce, warmed

1. Let dough stand at room temperature 25-30 minutes or until softened.

2. Cut each roll in half. Wrap each portion around a meatball, enclosing meatball completely; pinch dough firmly to seal. Place on greased baking sheets, seam side down. Cover with kitchen towels; let rise in a warm place until almost doubled, about 1½ to 2 hours.

3. Preheat oven to 350°. Bake buns 12-15 minutes or until golden brown. Brush tops with oil; sprinkle with cheese and basil. Serve with marinara.

FAST FIX
Caramelized Pork Tenderloin

This zesty pork is a little bit savory and a little bit sweet. Best of all, it tastes grilled even though you cooked it on the stove.

—DEBI ARONE FORT COLLINS, CO

START TO FINISH: 20 MIN.
MAKES: 4 SERVINGS

- 1 pork tenderloin (1 pound)
- ¼ cup packed brown sugar
- 4 garlic cloves, minced
- 1 tablespoon Montreal steak seasoning
- 2 tablespoons butter

1. Cut pork into four pieces and pound with a meat mallet to ¼-in. thickness. In a shallow bowl, mix brown sugar, garlic and steak seasoning. Dip pork in sugar mixture, patting to help coating adhere.

2. In a large skillet, heat butter over medium-high heat. Add pork; cook 2-3 minutes on each side or until tender.

Honey Hoisin Chicken & Potatoes

When I was little, Tutu (my grandma) cooked up this blend of Asian and American flavors. The potatoes are delicious drizzled with pan juices.

—JANET YEE PHOENIX, AZ

PREP: 10 MIN. • **BAKE:** 50 MIN.
MAKES: 4 SERVINGS

- 4 medium Yukon Gold potatoes (about 1¾ pounds), cut into 1-inch pieces
- 1 large onion, cut into 1-inch pieces
- ½ cup hoisin sauce
- 3 tablespoons honey
- ½ teaspoon salt, divided
- ½ teaspoon pepper, divided
- 4 bone-in chicken thighs (about 1½ pounds)

1. Preheat oven to 400°. Place potatoes and onion in a greased 13x9-in. baking pan. In a small bowl, mix hoisin, honey, ¼ teaspoon salt and ¼ teaspoon pepper; add to potato mixture and toss to coat.

2. Place chicken over vegetables; sprinkle with remaining salt and pepper. Roast 50-60 minutes or until potatoes are tender and a thermometer inserted in chicken reads 170°-175°, basting occasionally with pan juices.

HONEY HOISIN CHICKEN & POTATOES

FAST FIX

Shrimp Tortellini Pasta Toss

Cheese tortellini may seem indulgent, but when you bulk it up with shrimp and frozen veggies, it becomes a fast and healthy meal.

—*TASTE OF HOME* TEST KITCHEN

START TO FINISH: 20 MIN.
MAKES: 4 SERVINGS

- 1 package (9 ounces) refrigerated cheese tortellini
- 1 cup frozen peas
- 3 tablespoons olive oil, divided
- 1 pound uncooked shrimp (31-40 per pound), peeled and deveined
- 2 garlic cloves, minced
- ¼ teaspoon salt
- ¼ teaspoon dried thyme
- ¼ teaspoon pepper

1. Cook tortellini according to package directions, adding peas during the last 5 minutes of cooking.
2. Meanwhile, in a large nonstick skillet, heat 2 tablespoons oil over medium-high heat. Add shrimp; cook and stir 2 minutes. Add garlic; cook 1-2 minutes longer or until the shrimp turn pink.
3. Drain tortellini mixture; add to skillet. Stir in salt, thyme, pepper and remaining oil; toss to coat.
PER SERVING *413 cal., 17 g fat (4 g sat. fat), 165 mg chol., 559 mg sodium, 36 g carb., 3 g fiber, 29 g pro.* **Diabetic Exchanges:** *4 lean meat, 2 starch, 2 fat.*

CHOCOLATE CARAMEL FONDUE

FAST FIX

Chocolate Caramel Fondue

I only need 10 minutes and three ingredients to whip up this instant party favorite. I serve it in punch cups so guests can carry it on a dessert plate with their choice of fruit, pretzels and other dippers.

—**CHERYL ARNOLD** LAKE ZURICH, IL

START TO FINISH: 10 MIN.
MAKES: 2½ CUPS

- 1 can (14 ounces) sweetened condensed milk
- 1 jar (12 ounces) caramel ice cream topping
- 3 ounces unsweetened chocolate, chopped
  Assorted fresh fruit and/or pretzels

In a small saucepan, combine milk, caramel topping and chocolate; cook and stir over low heat until blended and heated through. Transfer to a heated fondue pot; keep warm. Serve with fruit and/or pretzels for dipping.

TOP TIP

It's important to chop chocolate into uniform pieces to ensure even melting. Otherwise, the chocolate or chocolate mixture may burn before any large pieces of chocolate have the chance to melt.

SHRIMP TORTELLINI PASTA TOSS

Beef Teriyaki Noodles

START TO FINISH: 20 MIN.
MAKES: 4 SERVINGS

- 1 envelope (4.6 ounces) lo mein noodles and teriyaki sauce mix
- 1 pound beef flat iron steak or top sirloin steak, cut into bite-size pieces
- ¼ teaspoon salt
- ¼ teaspoon pepper
- 2 tablespoons canola oil, divided
- 2 cups frozen pepper and onion stir-fry blend
- 1 cup sliced fresh mushrooms

1. Prepare noodle mix according to package directions.
2. Meanwhile, sprinkle beef with salt and pepper. In a large skillet, heat 1 tablespoon oil over medium-high heat. Add beef; stir-fry 6-8 minutes or until no longer pink. Remove from pan; discard drippings.
3. Stir-fry vegetable blend and mushrooms in remaining oil 3-4 minutes or until vegetables are tender.
4. Return beef to pan. Stir in noodle mixture; heat through.

> At our house, we love to combine fresh ingredients with convenience products. This version starts with beef, mushrooms and stir-fry veggies since we always have them on hand, but feel free make the dish your own. Bring out your inner chef with whatever is in the pantry! —**RICHARD ROBINSON** PARK FOREST, IL

BEEF TERIYAKI NOODLES

GORGONZOLA & ORANGE CHICKEN TENDERS

Gorgonzola & Orange Chicken Tenders

My mom likes to make this for family gatherings, and we all enjoy eating it. Marmalade and Gorgonzola might sound like an unusual combo, but they actually make a great pair.

—**YVETTE GORMAN** DENVER, PA

START TO FINISH: 25 MIN.
MAKES: 4 SERVINGS

- 1 egg
- ¼ teaspoon salt
- ¾ cup seasoned bread crumbs
- 1 pound chicken tenderloins
- 2 tablespoons olive oil
- ¼ cup orange marmalade, warmed
- ¼ cup crumbled Gorgonzola cheese

1. In a shallow bowl, whisk egg and salt. Place bread crumbs in another shallow bowl. Dip chicken in egg, then in bread crumbs, patting to help coating adhere.
2. In a large skillet, heat oil over medium heat. Add chicken; cook 3-4 minutes on each side or until no longer pink. Drizzle with warm marmalade; top with cheese. Remove from heat; let stand, covered, until cheese begins to melt.

LEMON-POPPY SEED
CUTOUT COOKIES

Spicy Pumpkin & Corn Soup

A seriously quick dish, it can satisfy a hungry household in 20 minutes. My family loves sharing this soup with a hot pan of corn bread.

—**HEATHER ROREX** WINNEMUCCA, NV

START TO FINISH: 20 MIN.
MAKES: 8 SERVINGS

- 1 **can (15 ounces) solid-pack pumpkin**
- 1 **can (15 ounces) black beans, rinsed and drained**
- 1½ **cups frozen corn**
- 1 **can (10 ounces) diced tomatoes and green chilies**
- 2 **cans (14½ ounces each) reduced-sodium chicken broth**
- ¼ **teaspoon pepper**

In a large saucepan, mix all ingredients. Bring to a boil. Reduce heat; simmer, uncovered, 10-15 minutes or until slightly thickened, stirring occasionally.

FREEZE OPTION *Freeze cooled soup in freezer containers. To use, partially thaw in refrigerator overnight. Heat through in a saucepan, stirring occasionally and adding a little broth if necessary.*

PER SERVING *100 cal., trace fat (trace sat. fat), 0 chol., 542 mg sodium, 20 g carb., 5 g fiber, 6 g pro.* **Diabetic Exchange:** *1 starch.*

Lemon-Poppy Seed Cutout Cookies

Even though cake mix is one of the ingredients, this recipe produces fantastically crisp cookies, not cake-like ones. You'd never guess these treats weren't made from scratch.

—**CHARLOTTE MCDANIEL** JACKSONVILLE, AL

PREP: 30 MIN. + CHILLING
BAKE: 10 MIN./BATCH + COOLING
MAKES: 3 DOZEN

- 2 **eggs**
- ½ **cup canola oil**
- 1 **package lemon cake mix (regular size)**
- ¼ **cup poppy seeds**
- ¾ **teaspoon grated lemon peel**

1. In a large bowl, beat eggs and oil; gradually add cake mix and mix well. Stir in poppy seeds and lemon peel.

2. Divide dough in half. Shape each into a disk; wrap in plastic wrap. Refrigerate 2 hours or until firm enough to roll.

3. Preheat oven to 375°. On a lightly floured surface, roll each portion of dough to ⅛-in. thickness. Cut with a floured 2¼-in. flower-shaped cookie cutter. Place 2 in. apart on greased baking sheets.

4. Bake 9-11 minutes or until edges are lightly browned. Remove from pans to wire racks to cool completely. Store in airtight containers.

FREEZE OPTION *Freeze cookies in freezer containers. To use, thaw in covered containers before serving.*

SPICY PUMPKIN & CORN SOUP

Rosemary Marinated Pork Chops

PREP: 10 MIN. + MARINATING
BAKE: 20 MIN. • **MAKES:** 4 SERVINGS

- 1 cup reduced-sodium teriyaki sauce
- ¾ cup sweet white wine
- ¼ cup packed brown sugar
- 2 tablespoons minced fresh rosemary or 2 teaspoons dried rosemary, crushed
- 4 bone-in pork loin chops (1 inch thick and 10 ounces each)

1. In a 13x9-in. baking dish, mix teriyaki sauce, wine, brown sugar and rosemary until blended. Add pork; turn to coat. Refrigerate, covered, at least 4 hours.
2. Remove from the refrigerator 30 minutes before baking. Preheat oven to 350°.
3. Bake 20-25 minutes or until a thermometer reads 145°. Let stand 5 minutes before serving.

ROSEMARY MARINATED PORK CHOPS

EAT SMART **FAST FIX** ▶

Balsamic Chicken with Roasted Tomatoes

Here's a great way to use up fresh tomatoes. We love this dish in the summer. It's simple, but the sweet, tangy tomato glaze is just so good.
—**KAREN GEHRIG** CONCORD, NC

START TO FINISH: 25 MIN.
MAKES: 4 SERVINGS

- 2 tablespoons honey
- 2 tablespoons olive oil, divided
- 2 cups grape tomatoes
- 4 boneless skinless chicken breast halves (6 ounces each)
- ½ teaspoon salt
- ½ teaspoon pepper
- 2 tablespoons balsamic glaze

1. Preheat oven to 400°. In a small bowl, mix honey and 1 tablespoon oil. Add tomatoes and toss to coat.

Transfer to a greased 15x10x1-in. baking pan. Bake 5-7 minutes or until softened.
2. Pound chicken breasts with a meat mallet to ½-in. thickness; sprinkle with salt and pepper. In a large skillet, heat remaining oil over medium heat. Add chicken; cook 5-6 minutes on each side or until no longer pink. Serve with roasted tomatoes; drizzle with glaze.
NOTE *To make your own balsamic glaze, bring ½ cup balsamic vinegar to a boil in a small pan. Reduce heat to medium; simmer 10-12 minutes or until thickened to a glaze consistency. Makes: about 2 tablespoons.*
PER SERVING *306 cal., 11 g fat (2 g sat. fat), 94 mg chol., 384 mg sodium, 16 g carb., 1 g fiber, 35 g pro.* **Diabetic Exchanges:** *5 lean meat, 1½ fat, 1 starch.*

<FAST FIX>
Cheesy Bow Tie Chicken

START TO FINISH: 30 MIN.
MAKES: 4 SERVINGS

- 2 packages (8 ounces each) frozen spinach and artichoke cheese dip
- 3 cups uncooked bow tie pasta
- 3 cups cubed rotisserie chicken
- 1 cup chopped roasted sweet red peppers
- ⅓ cup pitted Greek olives, halved
- ½ teaspoon salt
- ¼ teaspoon pepper

1. Heat cheese dip according to package directions. Meanwhile, in a Dutch oven, cook pasta according to package directions; drain, reserving ½ cup pasta water. Return to pan.
2. Stir in chicken, cheese dip, peppers, olives, salt and pepper, adding enough reserved pasta water to achieve a creamy consistency; heat through.

CHEESY BOW TIE CHICKEN

Here's a super simple dish that tastes like it's straight from a nice Italian restaurant. Spinach-artichoke dip is usually available in supermarket delis and it comes frozen, too. Just make sure to thaw it according to the package directions before dinnertime.
—**SALLY SIBTHORPE** SHELBY TOWNSHIP, MI

Baked Italian Tilapia

This dish is so simple, you might as well add it to your list of go-to recipes.
—**KIMBERLY MCGEE** MOSHEIM, TN

PREP: 10 MIN. • **BAKE:** 40 MIN.
MAKES: 4 SERVINGS

- 4 tilapia fillets (6 ounces each)
- ¼ teaspoon pepper
- 1 can (14½ ounces) diced tomatoes with basil, oregano and garlic, drained
- 1 large onion, halved and thinly sliced
- 1 medium green pepper, julienned
- ¼ cup shredded Parmesan cheese

1. Place tilapia in a 13x9-in. baking dish coated with cooking spray; sprinkle with pepper. Spoon tomatoes over tilapia; top with onion and green pepper.
2. Cover and bake tilapia at 350° for 30 minutes. Uncover; sprinkle with cheese. Bake 10-15 minutes longer or until fish flakes easily with a fork.

<FAST FIX>
Peanut Butter Cup Trifle

Using just five ingredients makes this recipe so simple. You can add a little extra decoration with chocolate jimmies, too.
—**CHRIS NELSON** DECATUR, AR

START TO FINISH: 20 MIN.
MAKES: 12 SERVINGS

- 4 cups cold 2% milk
- 2 packages (3.9 ounces each) instant chocolate pudding mix
- 1 prepared angel food cake (8 to 10 ounces), cut into 1-inch cubes
- 1 carton (12 ounces) frozen whipped topping, thawed
- 2 packages (8 ounces each) Reese's mini peanut butter cups

In a large bowl, whisk milk and pudding mixes 2 minutes. Let stand for 2 minutes or until soft-set. In a 3-qt. trifle bowl or glass bowl, layer half of the cake cubes, pudding, whipped topping and peanut butter cups. Repeat the layers. Refrigerate until serving.

PEANUT BUTTER CUP TRIFLE

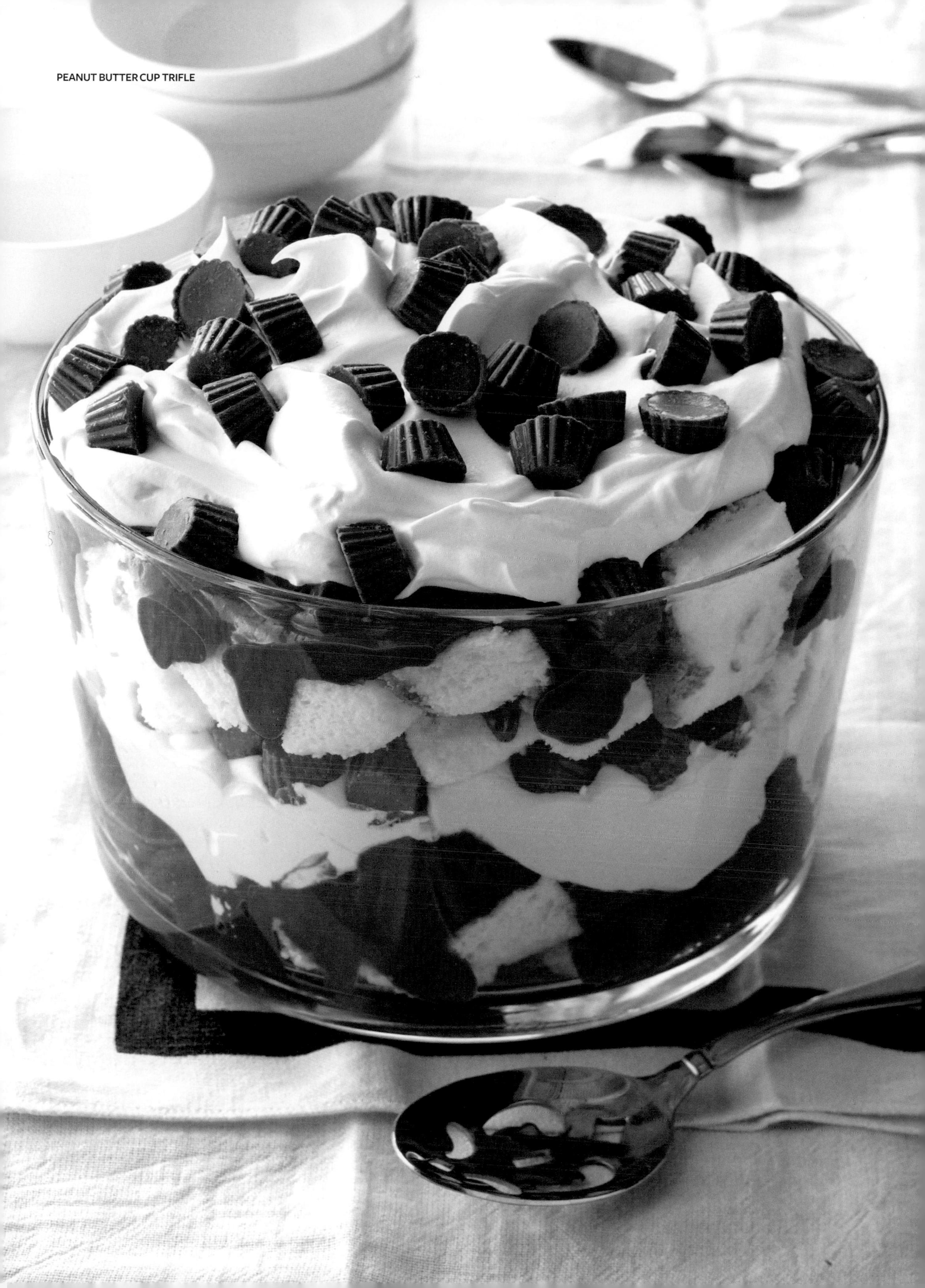

TOMATO-ARTICHOKE TILAPIA

My mom and I really like tomatoes, capers and artichokes, so I used them together in this one-pan meal. The best part is that, on a busy night, all of the ingredients are ready and waiting. **—DENISE KLIBERT** SHREVEPORT, LA

Tomato-Artichoke Tilapia

START TO FINISH: 15 MIN.
MAKES: 4 SERVINGS

- 1 tablespoon olive oil
- 1 can (14½ ounces) diced tomatoes with roasted garlic, drained
- 1 can (14 ounces) water-packed quartered artichoke hearts, drained
- 2 tablespoons drained capers
- 4 tilapia fillets (6 ounces each)

1. In a large skillet, heat oil over medium heat. Add tomatoes, artichoke hearts and capers; cook 3-5 minutes or until heated through, stirring occasionally.

2. Arrange tilapia over tomato mixture. Cook, covered, 6-8 minutes or until fish begins to flake easily with a fork.

Cherry Crumb Dessert

Here's a sweet treat that's especially good with a large dollop of whipped cream or a scoop of ice cream! The crumb topping has a wonderful nutty flavor, and no one will guess this streusel started with a handy cake mix.

—ANN EASTMAN SANTA MONICA, CA

PREP: 15 MIN. • **BAKE:** 30 MIN.
MAKES: 12-16 SERVINGS

- ½ cup cold butter
- 1 package yellow cake mix (regular size)
- 1 can (21 ounces) cherry or blueberry pie filling
- ½ cup chopped walnuts
  Whipped cream or ice cream, optional

1. In a large bowl, cut butter into cake mix until crumbly. Set aside 1 cup for topping. Pat remaining crumbs onto the bottom and ½ in. up the sides of a greased 13x9-in. baking pan.

2. Spread pie filling over crust. Combine the walnuts with reserved crumbs; sprinkle over top. Bake at 350° for 30-35 minutes. Serve warm with whipped cream or ice cream if desired.

Haddock with Lime-Cilantro Butter

In Louisiana, the good times roll when we broil fish and serve it with lots of lime juice, cilantro and butter.

—DARLENE MORRIS FRANKLINTON, LA

START TO FINISH: 15 MIN.
MAKES: 4 SERVINGS

- 4 haddock fillets (6 ounces each)
- ½ teaspoon salt
- ¼ teaspoon pepper
- 3 tablespoons butter, melted
- 2 tablespoons minced fresh cilantro
- 1 tablespoon lime juice
- 1 teaspoon grated lime peel

1. Preheat broiler. Sprinkle fillets with salt and pepper. Place on a greased broiler pan. Broil 4-5 in. from heat 5-6 minutes or until fish flakes easily with a fork.

2. In a small bowl, mix remaining ingredients. Serve over fish.

HADDOCK WITH LIME-CILANTRO BUTTER

Pork Chops with Honey-Garlic Sauce

The honey and garlic sauce is so good, I sometimes double it so we have plenty of extra sauce for dipping.

—**MICHELLE SMITH** ELDERSBURG, MD

START TO FINISH: 25 MIN.
MAKES: 4 SERVINGS

- 4 **bone-in pork loin chops (6 ounces each)**
- ¼ **cup lemon juice**
- ¼ **cup honey**
- 2 **tablespoons reduced-sodium soy sauce**
- 1 **garlic clove, minced**

1. Place a large nonstick skillet coated with cooking spray over medium heat. Add pork chops; cook 5-6 minutes on each side or until a thermometer reads 145°. Remove and keep warm.
2. In a small bowl, combine lemon juice, honey, soy sauce and garlic; add to pan. Cook over medium heat 3-4 minutes, stirring occasionally. Serve with chops.
PER SERVING *220 cal., 5 g fat (2 g sat. fat), 71 mg chol., 361 mg sodium, 20 g carb., trace fiber, 25 g pro.* **Diabetic Exchanges:** *3 lean meat, 1 starch.*

PORK CHOPS WITH
HONEY-GARLIC SAUCE

Fontina Asparagus Tart

This lemony cheese and veggie tart is easy to make but looks pretty and impressive. Be advised: your guests will be vying for the last tasty slice.

—**HEIDI MEEK** GRAND RAPIDS, MI

PREP: 15 MIN. • **BAKE:** 20 MIN.
MAKES: 24 SERVINGS

- 1 **pound fresh asparagus, trimmed**
- 1 **sheet frozen puff pastry, thawed**
- 2 **cups (8 ounces) shredded fontina cheese**
- 2 **tablespoons lemon juice**
- 1 **teaspoon grated lemon peel**
- 1 **tablespoon olive oil**
- ¼ **teaspoon salt**
- ¼ **teaspoon pepper**

1. In a large skillet, bring 1 in. of water to a boil; add asparagus. Cover and cook for 3-5 minutes or just until crisp-tender; drain.
2. On a lightly floured surface, unfold puff pastry. Roll into a 16x12-in. rectangle; transfer to a parchment paper-lined baking sheet. Bake at 400° for 10 minutes or until golden brown.
3. Sprinkle 1½ cups cheese over pastry. Arrange asparagus on top; sprinkle with remaining cheese. Combine the lemon juice, lemon peel, oil, salt and pepper; sprinkle over top. Bake 10-15 minutes longer or until asparagus is tender and cheese is melted. Serve warm.

Red Velvet Cake Bites

Everyone loves red velvet, but any cake mix will work. I've also made these bites with chopped macadamia nuts, pineapple cake and white chocolate. Whatever you do, make sure you have fun!

—**ANNE POWERS** MUNFORD, AL

PREP: 45 MIN. + CHILLING
BAKE: 25 MIN. + COOLING
MAKES: 5 DOZEN

- 1 **package red velvet cake mix (regular size)**
- 1 **can (16 ounces) cream cheese frosting**
- 1 **pound each white, milk chocolate and dark chocolate candy coating**

RED VELVET
CAKE BITES

1. Prepare and bake cake mix according to package directions, using a 13x9-in. baking pan. Cool completely.
2. Crumble cake into a large bowl. Add frosting; beat well. Refrigerate 1 hour or until easy to handle. Shape into 1-in. balls; transfer to waxed paper-lined baking sheets. Refrigerate at least 1 hour.
3. In a microwave, melt white candy coating; stir until smooth. Dip 20 cake balls in coating; allow excess to drip off. Return to baking sheets; let stand until set. Repeat with the milk chocolate and dark chocolate coatings and remaining cake balls. Store the cake bites in airtight containers.
FREEZE OPTION *Freeze uncoated cake balls in freezer containers, layered between waxed paper. To use, thaw in covered containers. Dip in coatings as directed.*

Mediterranean Pork and Orzo

All of the food groups are represented in this fresh and fabulous meal. It's one of my family's favorites.

—**MARY RELYEA** CANASTOTA, NY

START TO FINISH: 30 MIN.
MAKES: 6 SERVINGS

- 1½ **pounds pork tenderloin**
- 1 **teaspoon coarsely ground pepper**
- 2 **tablespoons olive oil**
- 3 **quarts water**
- 1¼ **cups uncooked orzo pasta**
- ¼ **teaspoon salt**
- 1 **package (6 ounces) fresh baby spinach**
- 1 **cup grape tomatoes, halved**
- ¾ **cup crumbled feta cheese**

1. Rub pork with pepper; cut into 1-in. cubes. In a large nonstick skillet, heat oil over medium heat. Add pork; cook and stir 8-10 minutes or until no longer pink.

2. Meanwhile, in a Dutch oven, bring water to a boil. Stir in orzo and salt; cook, uncovered, 8 minutes. Stir in spinach; cook 45-60 seconds longer or until orzo is tender and spinach is wilted. Drain.

3. Add tomatoes to pork; heat through. Stir in orzo mixture and cheese.

PER SERVING *372 cal., 11 g fat (4 g sat. fat), 71 mg chol., 306 mg sodium, 34 g carb., 3 g fiber, 31 g pro.* **Diabetic Exchanges:** *3 lean meat, 2 starch, 1 vegetable, 1 fat.*

DOUBLE-CHOCOLATE
TOFFEE ICEBOX CAKE

Double-Chocolate Toffee Icebox Cake

My mother-in-law gave me a cooking lesson when I first got married: "Anything tastes good if you put enough butter, chocolate or cream in it." This recipe has two out of three and proves she was right!

—**BEE ENGELHART** BLOOMFIELD TOWNSHIP, MI

PREP: 30 MIN. + CHILLING
MAKES: 8 SERVINGS

- 3 **cups 2% milk**
- 1 **package (5.9 ounces) instant chocolate pudding mix**
- 1½ **cups heavy whipping cream**
- 2 **packages (9 ounces each) chocolate wafers**
- 2 **Heath candy bars (1.4 ounces each), crushed**

1. In a large bowl, whisk milk and pudding mix 2 minutes. Let stand 2 minutes or until soft-set. In a large bowl, beat cream until stiff peaks form.

2. Arrange 20 cookies on bottom of an 8-in.-square baking dish. Spread a fourth of the chocolate pudding and a fourth of the whipped cream over cookies. Repeat layers three times. Sprinkle with crushed candy bars. Refrigerate overnight.

MEDITERRANEAN
PORK AND ORZO

MANGO CHUTNEY
CHICKEN CURRY

My father invented this recipe while we were traveling together. Adjust the amount of curry according to your taste and the level of heat desired.

—DINA MORENO SEATTLE, WA

In-a-Pinch Chicken & Spinach

I needed a fast supper while babysitting my grandchild. I used what my daughter-in-law had in the fridge and turned it into what's now one of our favorite recipes.

—SANDRA ELLIS STOCKBRIDGE, GA

START TO FINISH: 25 MIN.
MAKES: 4 SERVINGS

- 4 **boneless skinless chicken breast halves (6 ounces each)**
- 2 **tablespoons olive oil**
- 1 **tablespoon butter**
- 1 **package (6 ounces) fresh baby spinach**
- 1 **cup salsa**

1. Pound chicken with a meat mallet to ½-in. thickness. In a large skillet, heat oil and butter over medium heat. Cook chicken 5-6 minutes on each side or until no longer pink. Remove and keep warm.

2. Add spinach and salsa to pan; cook and stir 3-4 minutes or just until spinach is wilted. Serve with chicken.

PER SERVING *297 cal., 14 g fat (4 g sat. fat), 102 mg chol., 376 mg sodium, 6 g carb., 1 g fiber, 36 g pro.* **Diabetic Exchanges:** *5 lean meat, 2 fat, 1 vegetable.*

IN-A-PINCH CHICKEN & SPINACH

Mango Chutney Chicken Curry

START TO FINISH: 25 MIN.
MAKES: 4 SERVINGS

- 1 **tablespoon canola oil**
- 1 **pound boneless skinless chicken breasts, cubed**
- 1 **tablespoon curry powder**
- 2 **garlic cloves, minced**
- ¼ **teaspoon salt**
- ¼ **teaspoon pepper**
- ½ **cup mango chutney**
- ½ **cup half-and-half cream**

1. In a large skillet, heat oil over medium-high heat; brown chicken. Stir in curry powder, garlic, salt and pepper; cook 1-2 minutes longer or until aromatic.

2. Stir in chutney and cream. Bring to boil. Reduce heat; simmer, uncovered, 4-6 minutes or until chicken is no longer pink, stirring occasionally.

PARMESAN-BREADED PORK CHOPS

FAST FIX

Parmesan-Breaded Pork Chops

Shredded Parmesan and seasoned bread crumbs push the flavor of these juicy chops over the top. The whole family loves this dish that cooks hands-free while I prepare the rest of the meal.

—HAYDEN HOSICK CORONA, CA

START TO FINISH: 25 MIN.
MAKES: 4 SERVINGS

- 4 **boneless pork loin chops (6 ounces each)**
- ½ **teaspoon salt**
- ¼ **teaspoon pepper**
- ½ **cup garlic and herb bread crumbs**
- ⅓ **cup shredded Parmesan cheese**
- 2 **eggs, lightly beaten**
- 2 **tablespoons olive oil**

1. Preheat oven to 350°. Sprinkle pork chops with salt and pepper. In a shallow bowl, mix bread crumbs and cheese. Place eggs in a separate shallow bowl. Dip pork chops in eggs, then in crumb mixture, patting to help coating adhere.

2. In a 10-in. ovenproof skillet, heat oil over medium heat. Brown pork chops on both sides. Bake 12-15 minutes or until a thermometer reads 145°. Let stand 5 minutes.

FAST FIX

Fancy Fuss-Free Torte

Thanks to frozen pound cake and a can of pie filling, this torte's a cinch to make. If layers slide, keep them in place with toothpicks around the edges as you build. Just remove before serving.

—JOAN CAUSEY GREENWOOD, AR

START TO FINISH: 15 MIN.
MAKES: 10 SERVINGS

- 1 **loaf (10¾ ounces) frozen pound cake, thawed**
- 1 **can (21 ounces) cherry pie filling or flavor of your choice**
- 1 **carton (8 ounces) frozen whipped topping, thawed**
- ½ **cup chopped pecans**

Using a long serrated knife, cut cake horizontally into three layers. Place bottom cake layer on a serving plate; top with half of the pie filling. Repeat layers. Top with the remaining cake layer. Frost top and sides of the cake with whipped topping and sprinkle with pecans.

FANCY FUSS-FREE TORTE

MEDITERRANEAN STUFFED CHICKEN BREASTS

Honey-Pecan Pork Chops

These sweet and nutty chops are a favorite at our house. They're delicious with green beans, rice or sweet potatoes.
—**LINDA BOUNDS** CEDAR HILL, TX

START TO FINISH: 25 MIN.
MAKES: 2 SERVINGS

- 2 **boneless pork loin chops (about ½ inch thick and 4 ounces each)**
- 3 **tablespoons all-purpose flour**
- ¼ **teaspoon salt**
- ¼ **teaspoon pepper**
- 2 **tablespoons butter**
- 2 **tablespoons honey**
- 1 **to 2 tablespoons coarsely chopped pecans**

1. Pound pork chops with a meat mallet to flatten slightly. In a shallow bowl, mix flour, salt and pepper. Dip chops in flour mixture to coat both sides; shake off excess.
2. In a large skillet, heat butter over medium heat. Add pork chops; cook 3-4 minutes on each side or until a thermometer reads 145°. Remove from pan; keep warm.
3. Add honey and pecans to same skillet; heat through, stirring to loosen browned bits from pan. Serve with pork chops.

HONEY-PECAN PORK CHOPS

This was the first recipe I tried after moving into my first apartment after college. Enjoy it with rice pilaf and a side salad.
—**AMANDA ROCHETTE** WATERTOWN, MA

Mediterranean Stuffed Chicken Breasts

PREP: 20 MIN. • **BAKE:** 30 MIN.
MAKES: 4 SERVINGS

- 1 **cup (4 ounces) crumbled feta cheese**
- ⅓ **cup chopped oil-packed sun-dried tomatoes**
- 4 **boneless skinless chicken breast halves (6 ounces each)**
- 2 **tablespoons olive oil from sun-dried tomatoes, divided**
- 1 **teaspoon Greek seasoning**

1. Preheat oven to 375°. In a small bowl, mix cheese and tomatoes. Pound chicken breasts with a meat mallet to ¼-in. thickness. Brush with 1 tablespoon oil; sprinkle with Greek seasoning. Top with cheese mixture. Roll up chicken from a short side; secure with a toothpick.
2. Place in a greased 11x7-in. baking dish, seam side down; brush with remaining oil. Bake, uncovered, for 30-35 minutes or until a thermometer reads 165°. Discard the toothpicks before serving.

African Chicken & Sweet Potatoes

I combined some of my absolute favorite ingredients— sweet potatoes, chicken and peanut butter— to create this supper. It's a fantastic busy-day recipe.
—**DEVON DELANEY** WESTPORT, CT

PREP: 10 MIN. • **BAKE:** 40 MIN.
MAKES: 6 SERVINGS

- 6 **bone-in chicken thighs (about 2¼ pounds)**
- ½ **teaspoon salt**
- ¼ **teaspoon pepper**
- 2 **tablespoons canola oil**
- 2 **medium sweet potatoes, peeled and finely chopped (about 4 cups)**
- ½ **cup mango chutney**
- ¼ **cup creamy peanut butter**
- 1 **can (10 ounces) diced tomatoes and green chilies, undrained**

1. Preheat oven to 375°. Place chicken in a greased 13x9-in. baking dish; sprinkle with salt and pepper. Bake, uncovered, 30 minutes.

2. Meanwhile, in a large skillet, heat oil over medium-high heat. Add sweet potatoes; cook and stir 10-12 minutes or until tender. In a small bowl, mix chutney and peanut butter; stir into sweet potatoes. Add tomatoes and heat through.

3. Spoon potato mixture over chicken. Bake 10-15 minutes longer or until a thermometer inserted in chicken reads 180°.

EAT SMART

Southwest Pork Tenderloin

When living in Europe, I missed classic Southwestern flavors. Using what I had, I baked up a spicy pork tenderloin dish. It's been a regular in my repertoire ever since.
—**JOHN COX** SEGUIN, TX

PREP: 10 MIN. • **BAKE:** 25 MIN. + STANDING
MAKES: 8 SERVINGS

- 2 **pork tenderloins (1 pound each)**
- 2 **tablespoons canola oil**
- 1 **envelope taco seasoning**
- 3 **medium limes, cut into wedges**

1. Preheat oven to 425°. Rub tenderloins with oil; sprinkle with taco seasoning. Place on a rack in a shallow roasting pan.

2. Roast 25-30 minutes or until a thermometer reads 145°. Remove tenderloins from oven; tent with foil. Let stand 10 minutes before slicing. Squeeze lime wedges over pork.

PER SERVING *184 cal., 7 g fat (2 g sat. fat), 63 mg chol., 446 mg sodium, 6 g carb., 1 g fiber, 22 g pro.* **Diabetic Exchanges:** *3 lean meat, ½ starch, ½ fat.*

TOP TIP

Chutney has sweet, sour, spicy and savory flavors. It is typically fruit-flavored, with mango being the most popular. Chutney enhances savory dishes. Try mixing a little chutney into your favorite deviled egg recipe, serving it alongside curried dishes, or spooning it over cream cheese and sprinkling with green onions for an impromptu appetizer.

AFRICAN CHICKEN & SWEET POTATOES

GLAZED ROAST CHICKEN

Apple-Pecan Pork Tenderloin

PREP: 10 MIN. + MARINATING
BAKE: 25 MIN. + STANDING
MAKES: 4 SERVINGS

- 1 pork tenderloin (1 pound)
- ½ cup apple cider or juice
- 1 teaspoon salt
- ½ cup finely chopped pecans
- ¼ cup honey
- 2 tablespoons Dijon mustard
  Salt to taste

1. Preheat oven to 425°. Place pork in a large resealable plastic bag; add apple cider and 1 teaspoon salt. Seal bag and turn to coat. Refrigerate 4 hours or overnight.

2. Spread pecans on a plate. Drain pork, discarding marinade. In a small bowl, mix honey and mustard; rub over pork. Roll pork in pecans, patting to help nuts adhere.

3. Transfer to a greased 13x9-in. baking dish. Bake 25-30 minutes or until a thermometer reads 145°. Let stand 10 minutes before slicing. Cut into slices; season with salt to taste.

This recipe came about when I needed to use up some apple cider. It was so good that it's now a staple for company. I like to crush the nuts with a rolling pin, but chopping works just fine, too.
—**ELISABETH LARSEN** PLEASANT GROVE, UT

APPLE-PECAN PORK TENDERLOIN

Glazed Roast Chicken

A few pantry items inspired this recipe, which I've since made for small weeknight meals and for big parties. The quince jelly comes from my boss, who grows the fruit in his own backyard.
—**VICTORIA MILLER** SAN RAMON, CA

PREP: 15 MIN.
BAKE: 1½ HOURS + STANDING
MAKES: 6 SERVINGS

- 1 cup white wine or chicken broth
- 1 cup apricot preserves or quince jelly
- 1 tablespoon stone-ground mustard
- 1 broiler/fryer chicken (3 to 4 pounds)
- ¾ teaspoon salt
- ½ teaspoon pepper

1. Preheat oven to 375°. In a small saucepan, bring wine to a boil; cook 3-4 minutes or until wine is reduced by half. Stir in preserves and mustard. Reserve half of the glaze for basting.

2. Place chicken on a rack in a shallow roasting pan, breast side up. Sprinkle with salt and pepper. Tuck wings under chicken; tie drumsticks together. Pour remaining glaze over chicken.

3. Roast 1½ to 1¾ hours or until a thermometer inserted in thigh reads 180°, basting occasionally with reserved glaze after 45 minutes. Remove chicken from oven; tent with foil. Let stand 15 minutes before carving.

**BBQ Hot Dog &
Potato Packs**
PAGE 83

Cooking for Kids

It's child's play to serve up wholesome, home-cooked foods that kids will want to eat. These pages are brimming with tot-pleasing entrees, whimsical treats, cute sandwiches and inspiring ideas guaranteed to bring smiles to even the littlest faces.

Fluffy Scrambled Eggs
PAGE 78

Sweet 'n' Spicy Munch
PAGE 93

Snowflake Tomato Soup
PAGE 96

COCONUT-CRUSTED
TURKEY STRIPS

My granddaughter shared these baked turkey strips with me. With a plum dipping sauce, they're just the thing for a light supper.

—**AGNES WARD** STRATFORD, ON

Pigs in a Blanket

These classic baked dogs will appeal to the kid in all of us. Even my husband, Allan, admits to enjoying every bite! Serve them with ketchup and mustard alongside for delicious dipping.

—**LINDA YOUNG** LONGMONT, CO

START TO FINISH: 25 MIN.
MAKES: 4 SERVINGS

- 1 **tube (8 ounces) refrigerated crescent rolls**
- 8 **hot dogs**
- 1 **egg, lightly beaten**
- 1 **tablespoon water**
  Caraway seeds

1. Separate crescent dough into triangles. Place hot dogs at wide ends of triangles and roll up. Place on an ungreased baking sheet. Combine egg and water; brush over rolls. Sprinkle with caraway seeds and press lightly into rolls.
2. Bake at 375° for 12-15 minutes or until golden brown.

EAT SMART FAST FIX ▶

Coconut-Crusted Turkey Strips

START TO FINISH: 30 MIN.
MAKES: 6 SERVINGS

- 2 **egg whites**
- 2 **teaspoons sesame oil**
- ½ **cup flaked coconut, toasted**
- ½ **cup dry bread crumbs**
- 2 **tablespoons sesame seeds, toasted**
- ½ **teaspoon salt**
- 1½ **pounds turkey breast tenderloins, cut into ½-inch strips**
  Cooking spray

DIPPING SAUCE
- ½ **cup plum sauce**
- ⅓ **cup unsweetened pineapple juice**
- 1½ **teaspoons prepared mustard**
- 1 **teaspoon cornstarch**

1. Preheat oven to 425°. In a shallow bowl, whisk egg whites and oil. In another shallow bowl, mix coconut, bread crumbs, sesame seeds and salt. Dip turkey in egg mixture, then in coconut mixture, patting to help coating adhere.
2. Place on baking sheets coated with cooking spray; spritz turkey with cooking spray. Bake for 10-12 minutes or until turkey is no longer pink, turning once.
3. Meanwhile, in a small saucepan, mix sauce ingredients. Bring to a boil; cook and stir 1-2 minutes or until thickened. Serve turkey with sauce.

NOTE *To toast coconut, spread in a 15x10x1-in. baking pan. Bake at 350° for 5-10 minutes or until golden brown, stirring frequently.*
PER SERVING *278 cal., 8 g fat (3 g sat. fat), 56 mg chol., 519 mg sodium, 22 g carb., 1 g fiber, 30 g pro.* **Diabetic Exchanges:** *3 lean meat, 1½ starch, ½ fat.*

Hearty Beef Ravioli

In this fun family-friendly supper, we add our favorite taco toppings to beef ravioli. It's fun for kids to customize their own plates for a no-fuss meal.
—*TASTE OF HOME* TEST KITCHEN

START TO FINISH: 25 MIN.
MAKES: 6 SERVINGS

- 1   package (25 ounces) frozen beef ravioli
- ½   pound extra-lean ground beef (95% lean)
- 1   medium green pepper, chopped
- 1   can (14½ ounces) no-salt-added diced tomatoes, undrained
- 1   can (8 ounces) no-salt-added tomato sauce
- 2   tablespoons reduced-sodium taco seasoning
- ¾   cup shredded reduced-fat cheddar cheese
- 1   can (2¼ ounces) sliced ripe olives, drained

1. Cook ravioli according to the package directions.
2. Meanwhile, in a large nonstick skillet, cook beef and pepper over medium heat 4-6 minutes or until meat is no longer pink and pepper is tender, breaking up beef into crumbles. Stir in tomatoes, tomato sauce and taco seasoning. Bring to a boil. Reduce heat; simmer, uncovered, 5-7 minutes or until slightly thickened.
3. Drain ravioli. Serve with sauce; sprinkle with cheese and olives.
PER SERVING *375 cal., 10 g fat (5 g sat. fat), 44 mg chol., 695 mg sodium, 49 g carb., 4 g fiber, 21 g pro.*

TOP TIP

My girls come up with dishes we don't get a chance to make during a busy week. They also take turns looking for new recipes for me to try.
—**KRISTIN K.** LETHBRIDGE, AB

BEAN & CHEESE QUESADILLAS

HEARTY BEEF RAVIOLI

Bean & Cheese Quesadillas

My son doesn't eat meat, so I created this recipe as a way for me to cook one meal for the family instead of two. It's so easy, my toddler grandson helps me make it!
—**TINA MCMULLEN** SALINA, KS

START TO FINISH: 15 MIN.
MAKES: 6 SERVINGS

- 1   can (16 ounces) refried beans
- ½   cup canned petite diced tomatoes
- 2   green onions, chopped
- 12 flour tortillas (8 inches)
- 2   cups (8 ounces) shredded cheddar cheese
     Sour cream and salsa, optional

1. In a small bowl, mix beans, tomatoes and green onions. Spread half of the tortillas with bean mixture. Sprinkle with cheese; top with remaining tortillas.
2. Heat a griddle over medium heat. Place tortillas on griddle in batches. Cook 2-3 minutes on each side or until golden brown and cheese is melted. If desired, serve quesadillas with sour cream and salsa.

Mini Burgers with the Works

I started preparing these mini burgers several years ago as a way to use up bread crusts. Their tiny size makes them simply irresistible.

—LINDA LANE BENNINGTON, VT

START TO FINISH: 30 MIN.
MAKES: 1 DOZEN

- ¼ **pound ground beef**
- 3 **slices process American cheese**
- 4 **slices white bread (heels of loaf recommended)**
- 2 **tablespoons prepared Thousand Island salad dressing**
- 2 **pearl onions, thinly sliced**
- 4 **baby dill pickles, thinly sliced**
- 3 **cherry tomatoes, thinly sliced**

1. Shape beef into twelve 1-in. patties. Place on a microwave-safe plate lined with paper towels. Cover with another paper towel; microwave on high for 1 minute until meat is no longer pink. Cut each slice of cheese into fourths; set aside.

2. Using a 1-in. round cookie cutter, cut out six circles from each slice of bread. Spread half of the bread circles with dressing. Layer with burgers, cheese, onions, pickles and tomatoes. Top with remaining bread circles; secure with toothpicks.

NOTE *This recipe was tested in a 1,100-watt microwave.*

MINI BURGERS WITH THE WORKS

RAINBOW SPRITZER

Follow the rainbow to this sweet and fizzy treasure. Kids will love sipping their way through pretty layers of colorful fruit.
—WENDY HERR O'FALLON, MO

Rainbow Spritzer

START TO FINISH: 20 MIN.
MAKES: 4 SERVINGS

- ½ **cup fresh blueberries**
- ½ **cup chopped peeled kiwifruit**
- ½ **cup chopped fresh pineapple**
- ½ **cup sliced fresh strawberries or fresh raspberries**
- 1 **cup chilled ginger ale**
- ½ **cup chilled unsweetened pineapple juice**
- ½ **cup chilled lemonade**

In four tall glasses, layer blueberries, kiwi, pineapple and strawberries. In a 2-cup glass measure or small pitcher, mix remaining ingredients; pour over fruit. Serve immediately.

M&M Snack Mix

This fun snack mix will satisfy everyone, whether they have a sweet tooth or a salty tooth!
—BILLIE BLANTON KINGSPORT, TN

START TO FINISH: 5 MIN.
MAKES: 11 CUPS

- 2½ **cups milk chocolate M&M's**
- 2½ **cups peanut M&M's**
- 1 **package (15 ounces) golden raisins**
- 1 **can (11½ ounces) mixed nuts**
- 1 **package (11 ounces) butterscotch chips**

Combine all ingredients in a large bowl. Transfer to airtight containers; store in a cool, dry place.

Taco Spaghetti

I came up with this kid-friendly Southwestern recipe one afternoon when I was using up leftover spaghetti and ground beef. When I'm lucky enough to have extra time, I make two batches and freeze one.

—**JOHANNA VAN NESS** WICHITA, KS

PREP: 20 MIN. • **BAKE:** 25 MIN.
MAKES: 8 SERVINGS

- 12 **ounces uncooked spaghetti**
- 1 **pound ground beef**
- 1 **envelope taco seasoning**
- ¾ **cup water**
- 1 **can (15 ounces) black beans, rinsed and drained**
- 1 **can (10 ounces) diced tomatoes and green chilies, undrained**
- 2 **cups (8 ounces) shredded Mexican cheese blend, divided**
- ⅔ **cup salsa**

1. Preheat oven to 350°. Break spaghetti into thirds; cook according to package directions for al dente.
2. Meanwhile, in a Dutch oven, cook beef over medium heat 6-8 minutes or until no longer pink, breaking into crumbles; drain. Stir in taco seasoning and water; bring to a boil. Reduce heat; simmer, uncovered, for 5 minutes, stirring occasionally.

3. Stir in beans, tomatoes, 1 cup cheese and salsa. Drain spaghetti; add to beef mixture and toss to combine.
4. Transfer to a greased 13x9-in. baking dish. Bake, covered, 20 minutes. Sprinkle with remaining cheese. Bake, uncovered, 3-5 minutes longer or until cheese is melted. Let stand 5 minutes before serving.
FREEZE OPTION *Cool unbaked casserole; sprinkle with remaining cheese. Cover and freeze. To use, partially thaw in refrigerator overnight. Remove from refrigerator 30 minutes before baking. Preheat oven to 350°. Bake casserole, covered, 55-60 minutes or until heated through and a thermometer inserted into center reads 165°.*

Grilled Ham 'n' Cheese

These cute sandwich strips are an easy upgrade from the typical grilled cheese. If desired, substitute deli turkey or chicken for the ham.

—**TASTE OF HOME** TEST KITCHEN

START TO FINISH: 20 MIN.
MAKES: 4 SERVINGS

- 2 **tablespoons Dijon mustard**
- 8 **slices white bread, crusts removed**
- 8 **slices Swiss cheese**
- 4 **thin slices deli ham**
- 2 **tablespoons butter, softened**

GRILLED HAM 'N' CHEESE

1. Spread mustard over four slices of bread. Layer each with a slice of cheese, ham and another cheese slice. Top with remaining bread.
2. Butter outsides of sandwiches. In a large skillet over medium heat, toast sandwiches for 3-4 minutes on each side or until bread is lightly browned and cheese is melted. Remove to a cutting board; cut each sandwich lengthwise into thirds.

Good Green Fun

Tip your hat to St. Pat with a rainbow of crisp multicolored munchies. Toss in some cauliflower clouds for a whimsical touch. Suddenly, even the littlest leprechauns will be happy to gobble up their veggies. What luck!

* Put a pot of honey-mustard dippin' gold at the end of the arc. Hummus works, too.

⑤INGREDIENTS EAT SMART

Frozen Fruit Salad

I use this recipe to add a healthy twist to brown-bag lunches. I'm always in a hurry in the morning, so having a ready-made salad is a great help.

—**VIRGINIA POWELL** EUREKA, KS

PREP: 20 MIN. + FREEZING
MAKES: 22-24 SERVINGS

- 1 **can (16 ounces) apricot halves, drained**
- 1 **container (16 ounces) frozen sweetened sliced strawberries, thawed and drained**
- 3 **medium bananas, sliced**
- ¾ **cup pineapple tidbits**
- 1 **can (6 ounces) frozen orange juice concentrate, thawed**
- 1 **juice can water**

1. In a food processor, chop apricots. In a bowl, combine the apricots, strawberries, bananas, pineapple, orange juice and water. Ladle into muffin cups that have been sprayed with cooking spray. Freeze.
2. When frozen, quickly remove salads to freezer bags or tightly covered storage containers. When packing a lunch, place the salad in an individual storage container in a thermal lunch bag and it will thaw by lunchtime.
PER SERVING *62 cal., trace fat (trace sat. fat), 0 chol., 2 mg sodium, 16 g carb., 1 g fiber, 1 g pro.*

EAT SMART FAST FIX▸

Cinnamon-Apple Pork Chops

When I found this recipe online years ago, it quickly became a favorite. The ingredients are easy to keep on hand, and the one-pan cleanup is a bonus.

—**CHRISTINA PRICE** PITTSBURGH, PA

START TO FINISH: 25 MIN.
MAKES: 4 SERVINGS

- 2 **tablespoons reduced-fat butter, divided**
- 4 **boneless pork loin chops (4 ounces each)**
- 3 **tablespoons brown sugar**
- 1 **teaspoon ground cinnamon**
- ½ **teaspoon ground nutmeg**
- ¼ **teaspoon salt**
- 4 **medium tart apples, thinly sliced**
- 2 **tablespoons chopped pecans**

1. In a large skillet, heat 1 tablespoon butter over medium heat. Add pork chops; cook 4-5 minutes on each side or until a thermometer reads 145°. Meanwhile, in a small bowl, mix brown sugar, cinnamon, nutmeg and salt.
2. Remove chops; keep warm. Add apples, pecans, brown sugar mixture and remaining butter to pan; cook and stir until apples are tender. Serve with pork chops.
NOTE *This recipe was tested with Land O'Lakes light stick butter.*
PER SERVING *316 cal., 12 g fat (4 g sat. fat), 62 mg chol., 232 mg sodium, 31 g carb., 4 g fiber, 22 g pro.* **Diabetic Exchanges:** *3 lean meat, 1 starch, 1 fruit, 1 fat.*

TOP TIP

For a treat, I sometimes fill a short thermos with ice cream or sherbet and store it in the freezer. Packed with lunch in the morning, it'll still be thick and creamy come lunchtime!

—**LEONA L.** WEST BURLINGTON, IA

CINNAMON-APPLE PORK CHOPS

SPINACH QUESADILLAS

Sausage Pizza Pasta

It's pizza in a bowl! Here's a terrific (and tasty) way to make sure your kids get the whole grains and vegetables they need to grow up big and strong.

—**DANNA HOLT** SHOALS, IN

START TO FINISH: 30 MIN.
MAKES: 6 SERVINGS

- 1 **pound Italian turkey sausage links, casings removed**
- 2 **cups sliced fresh mushrooms**
- 1 **medium green pepper, chopped**
- 1 **medium onion, chopped**
- 3 **cups uncooked whole grain spiral pasta**
- 1 **can (15 ounces) pizza sauce**
- 1½ **cups water**
- 1½ **teaspoons Italian seasoning**
- ¼ **teaspoon salt**
- ¾ **cup shredded part-skim mozzarella cheese**

1. In a Dutch oven, cook sausage, mushrooms, green pepper and onion over medium heat 5-6 minutes or until sausage is no longer pink and vegetables are tender, breaking up sausage into crumbles; drain.

2. Stir in pasta, pizza sauce, water, Italian seasoning and salt; bring to a boil. Reduce heat; simmer, covered, 10-15 minutes or until pasta is tender. Remove from heat; sprinkle with cheese. Let stand, covered, 5 minutes or until cheese is melted.

PER SERVING *358 cal., 8 g fat (3 g sat. fat), 36 mg chol., 577 mg sodium, 52 g carb., 4 g fiber, 21 g pro.*

My family gave these cheesy quesadillas oohs and aahs. Quickly wilting the spinach means it's still a little crisp when it's tucked inside the tortillas.

—**PAM KAISER** MANSFIELD, MO

Spinach Quesadillas

START TO FINISH: 25 MIN.
MAKES: 4 SERVINGS

- 4 **cups fresh baby spinach**
- 4 **green onions, chopped**
- 1 **small tomato, chopped**
- 2 **tablespoons lemon juice**
- 1 **teaspoon ground cumin**
- ¼ **teaspoon garlic powder**
- 1 **cup (4 ounces) shredded reduced-fat Monterey Jack cheese or Mexican cheese blend**
- ¼ **cup reduced-fat ricotta cheese**
- 6 **flour tortillas (6 inches)**
- ¼ **cup fat-free sour cream**

1. Place the first six ingredients in a large nonstick skillet; cook and stir over medium heat just until spinach is wilted. Remove from the heat; stir in cheeses.

2. Top half of each tortilla with spinach mixture; fold other half over filling. Place on a griddle coated with cooking spray. Cook over medium heat 1-2 minutes on each side or until golden brown. Cut each quesadilla in half. Serve with sour cream.

PER SERVING *267 cal., 12 g fat (4 g sat. fat), 27 mg chol., 634 mg sodium, 28 g carb., 2 g fiber, 15 g pro.* **Diabetic Exchanges:** *1½ starch, 1 medium-fat meat, 1 vegetable.*

SAUSAGE PIZZA PASTA

Hop, Hop, Hooray!

Kick off Easter Sunday with a breakfast that's as tasty as it is cute. Drop pancake batter into different sizes and shapes, then let the kids help assemble some adorable bunnies. Start with a pancake mix so you can hightail it out of the kitchen in no time.

Make a tail with a dollop of whipped cream. Then fuzz it up with coconut.

⑤INGREDIENTS FAST FIX
Fluffy Scrambled Eggs

When our son, Chris, wants something other than cold cereal in the morning, he whips up these eggs. Cheese and evaporated milk make them especially good. They're easy to make when you're camping, too.

—**CHRIS PFLEGHAAR** ELK RIVER, MN

START TO FINISH: 15 MIN.
MAKES: 3 SERVINGS

- 6 **eggs**
- ¼ **cup evaporated milk or half-and-half cream**
- ¼ **teaspoon salt**
- ⅛ **teaspoon pepper**
- 1 **tablespoon canola oil**
- 2 **tablespoons process cheese sauce**

In a bowl, whisk eggs, milk, salt and pepper. In a large skillet, heat oil over medium heat. Pour in egg mixture; stir in cheese sauce. Cook and stir until eggs are thickened and no liquid egg remains.

MANGO-PEACH SMOOTHIES

EAT SMART FAST FIX
Mango-Peach Smoothies

This is my toddler son's favorite breakfast—he'll take one of these creamy smoothies over pancakes any day! Get creative when mixing fruits and fruit-flavored yogurts; we love peach yogurt with mango, strawberry yogurt with blueberries or pina colada yogurt with mango and banana.

—**DANA HERRA** DEKALB, IL

START TO FINISH: 5 MIN.
MAKES: 4 SERVINGS

- 1 **cup fat-free milk**
- 12 **ounces peach yogurt (about 1¼ cups)**
- 2½ **cups frozen mango chunks**

Place all ingredients in a blender; cover and process until smooth. Serve immediately.
PER SERVING *180 cal., 1 g fat (1 g sat. fat), 5 mg chol., 71 mg sodium, 39 g carb., 3 g fiber, 6 g pro.*

FLUFFY SCRAMBLED EGGS

Fruit Salad with Vanilla

Peach pie filling is the secret ingredient in this crowd-pleasing salad. Make it throughout the year using whatever fruits are in season.

—**NANCY DODSON** SPRINGFIELD, IL

START TO FINISH: 20 MIN.
MAKES: 10 SERVINGS

- 1 **pound fresh strawberries, quartered**
- 1½ **cups seedless red and/or green grapes, halved**
- 2 **medium bananas, sliced**
- 2 **kiwifruit, peeled, sliced and quartered**
- 1 **cup cubed fresh pineapple**
- 1 **can (21 ounces) peach pie filling**
- 3 **teaspoons vanilla extract**

In a large bowl, combine the strawberries, grapes, bananas, kiwi and pineapple. Fold in pie filling and vanilla. Chill until serving.

PER SERVING *126 cal., trace fat (trace sat. fat), 0 chol., 12 mg sodium, 30 g carb., 3 g fiber, 2 g pro.* **Diabetic Exchange:** *2 fruit.*

Berry Granola Pancakes

My son and I like to make this breakfast favorite together. You can leave the berries out of the mix and sprinkle them on top, or sub in chocolate chips or nuts instead.

—**ELIZABETH STEWART** CRAB ORCHARD, WV

PREP: 15 MIN. • **COOK:** 5 MIN./BATCH
MAKES: 1½ DOZEN

- 2 **cups whole wheat flour**
- 3 **tablespoons sugar**
- 4 **teaspoons baking powder**
- ½ **teaspoon salt**
- 2 **eggs**
- 2 **cups fat-free milk**
- ⅓ **cup unsweetened applesauce**
- 1 **tablespoon canola oil**
- ½ **teaspoon vanilla extract**

BERRY GRANOLA PANCAKES

- 1 **cup granola with fruit and nuts**
- 1 **cup fresh or frozen blueberries**
- ½ **cup fresh or frozen blackberries or raspberries**

1. In a large bowl, whisk flour, sugar, baking powder and salt. In another bowl, whisk eggs, milk, applesauce, oil and vanilla until blended. Add to the dry ingredients, stirring just until moistened. Fold in granola and berries.
2. Heat a griddle coated with cooking spray on medium heat. Pour batter by ¼ cupfuls onto griddle. Cook until bubbles on top begin to pop and bottoms are golden brown. Turn; cook until second side is golden brown.
NOTE *If using frozen blueberries, use without thawing to avoid discoloring the batter.*
FREEZE OPTION *Freeze cooled pancakes between layers of waxed paper in a resealable plastic freezer bag. To use, place pancakes on an ungreased baking sheet, cover with foil and reheat in a preheated 375° oven 6-10 minutes. Or, place a stack of three pancakes on a microwave-safe plate and microwave on high for 1¼ to 1½ minutes or until heated through.*
PER SERVING *3 pancakes equals 321 cal., 8 g fat (1 g sat. fat), 72 mg chol., 543 mg sodium, 54 g carb., 7 g fiber, 12 g pro.*

FRUIT SALAD WITH VANILLA

ULTIMATE CANDY
BAR COOKIES

I created these after Halloween, when I had way too much candy left over. You can make them with any kind of little candy bars or chocolate candies that you have on hand.

—TARA JOHN PLYMOUTH, MN

FREEZE IT
Ultimate Candy Bar Cookies

PREP: 30 MIN. • **BAKE:** 10 MIN./BATCH
MAKES: 4½ DOZEN

- 7 **Butterfinger candy bars (2.1 ounces each), coarsely chopped**
- 1 **cup butter, softened**
- 2 **eggs**
- 3 **cups all-purpose flour**
- 1 **teaspoon baking powder**
- ½ **teaspoon salt**
- 27 **Reese's mini peanut butter cups**
- 27 **miniature Snickers candy bars**

1. Preheat oven to 375°. Place Butterfinger candy bars in a food processor; process until ground. In a large bowl, cream butter and 2 cups ground candy bars until blended. Beat in eggs. In another bowl, whisk flour, baking powder and salt; gradually beat into creamed mixture.

2. Shape into 1-in. balls; roll in remaining ground candy bars. Place 2 in. apart on parchment paper-lined baking sheets. Bake 8-10 minutes or until tops are cracked.

3. Immediately press a piece of candy into the center of each cookie. Cool on pans 2 minutes. Remove to wire racks to cool.

FREEZE OPTION *Freeze cookies, layered between waxed paper, in freezer containers. To use, thaw before serving.*

⑤INGREDIENTS **EAT SMART** **FAST FIX**
Roasted Carrot Fries

Turn carrot sticks into crispy baked fries with a happier health profile than the old familiar ones. These are delicious with sweet and spicy ketchup.

—TASTE OF HOME TEST KITCHEN

START TO FINISH: 20 MIN.
MAKES: 5 SERVINGS

- 1 **pound fresh carrots, cut into ½-inch sticks**
- 2 **teaspoons olive oil**
- ½ **teaspoon salt**

Place carrots in a greased 15x10x1-in. baking pan. Drizzle with oil and sprinkle with salt; toss to coat. Bake, uncovered, at 450° for 10-12 minutes or until crisp-tender.

PER SERVING *53 cal., 2 g fat (trace sat. fat), 0 chol., 299 mg sodium, 9 g carb., 3 g fiber, 1 g pro.* **Diabetic Exchange:** *2 vegetable.*

Microwave Beef & Cheese Enchiladas

Every time I make these enchiladas, they disappear fast. Fix them for a speedy weeknight meal, a neighborhood potluck, even a tailgate.

—**KAREN MOORE** JACKSONVILLE, FL

START TO FINISH: 25 MIN.
MAKES: 3 SERVINGS

- ½ **pound ground beef**
- 2 **tablespoons chopped onion**
- 2 **cups (8 ounces) shredded cheddar cheese, divided**
- 1 **can (10 ounces) enchilada sauce, divided**
- 1 **tablespoon canned chopped green chilies**
- 6 **corn tortillas (6 inches), warmed Shredded lettuce and sour cream, optional**

1. Crumble beef into a 2-qt. microwave-safe dish; add onion. Microwave, covered, on high for 2-3 minutes or until beef is no longer pink; drain. Stir in 1 cup cheese, ¼ cup enchilada sauce and green chilies.
2. Place about ½ cup beef mixture off center on each tortilla. Roll up and place in a greased 11x7-in. microwave-safe dish, seam side down. Top with remaining enchilada sauce.
3. Microwave, covered, on high for 5-6 minutes or until heated through. Sprinkle with remaining cheese. Cook, uncovered, 1-2 minutes longer or until cheese is melted. If desired, serve with lettuce and sour cream.
NOTE *This recipe was tested in a 1,100-watt microwave.*

GARLIC TOAST PIZZAS

Garlic Toast Pizzas

These quick little pizzas pack a huge amount of flavor. That's a win-win for a busy mom like me.

—**AMY GRIM** CHILLICOTHE, OH

START TO FINISH: 15 MIN.
MAKES: 8 SLICES

- 1 **package (11¼ ounces) frozen garlic Texas toast**
- ½ **cup pizza sauce**
- 1 **package (3½ ounces) sliced regular or turkey pepperoni**
- 2 **cups (8 ounces) shredded part-skim mozzarella cheese**

1. Preheat oven to 425°. Place Texas toast in a 15x10x1-in. baking pan. Bake 5 minutes.
2. Spread toast with pizza sauce; top with pepperoni and cheese. Bake 4-5 minutes longer or until the cheese is melted.

TOP TIP

These pizzas are a great way to let kids help make dinner. They work well on the grill, too, so you don't have to turn on the oven in the summer.
—**CHICKLUVS2COOK**
TASTEOFHOME.COM

MICROWAVE BEEF & CHEESE ENCHILADAS

My husband and I had just moved to Dallas when I first made this recipe. Everything was new—new city, new home—but this dish felt familiar and comforting.
—**DARLA ANDREWS** LEWISVILLE, TX

APPLE BARBECUE CHICKEN

FAST FIX ▶
Apple Barbecue Chicken

START TO FINISH: 30 MIN.
MAKES: 6 SERVINGS

- 12 **chicken drumsticks**
- ¼ **teaspoon pepper**
- 1 **tablespoon olive oil**
- 1 **bottle (18 ounces) sweet and spicy barbecue sauce**
- 2 **cups applesauce**
- ⅓ **cup packed brown sugar**
- 1 **tablespoon chili powder**

1. Sprinkle drumsticks with pepper. In a Dutch oven, heat oil over medium heat. Brown drumsticks in batches; drain. Remove from pan.
2. Add remaining ingredients to pan, stirring to combine.
3. Return chicken to the pan and bring to a boil. Reduce heat; simmer, covered, for 20-25 minutes or until chicken is tender.

FAST FIX ▶
Swiss Ham Kabobs

With warm cheese, juicy pineapple and salty ham, these kabobs are my daughter's birthday dinner request every May. What a fantastic way to kick off grilling season .
—**HELEN PHILLIPS** HORSEHEADS, NY

START TO FINISH: 20 MIN.
MAKES: 4 SERVINGS

- 1 **can (20 ounces) pineapple chunks**
- ½ **cup orange marmalade**
- 1 **tablespoon prepared mustard**
- ¼ **teaspoon ground cloves**
- 1 **pound fully cooked ham, cut into 1-inch cubes**
- ½ **pound Swiss cheese, cut into 1-inch cubes**
- 1 **medium green pepper, cut into 1-inch pieces, optional**

1. Drain the pineapple, reserving 2 tablespoons juice; set pineapple aside. In a small bowl, mix marmalade, mustard, cloves and reserved pineapple juice. On eight metal or soaked wooden skewers, alternately thread ham, cheese, pineapple and, if desired, green pepper.
2. Moisten a paper towel with cooking oil; using long-handled tongs, rub on grill rack to coat lightly. Grill kabobs, uncovered, over medium heat or broil 4 in. from heat 5-7 minutes or until heated through, turning and basting frequently with marmalade sauce. Serve with remaining sauce.

Starry Bites

Eyes light up when my firecracker fruit pops hit the scene. Graduated cookie cutters make watermelon and lime juice-dipped apples the stars of the show. Try any hardy fruit here. I've even cut bright red strawberries into shapes and stuffed them into star fruit slices.

—**NAOMI R.** BAKERSROYALE.COM

✳ Cut a thin slice from the end of the watermelon so it doesn't rock 'n' roll all over the place.

Make-Ahead S'mores

These are perfect little desserts to keep on hand for when unexpected company drops in. Young people especially like these.

—**ANNE SHERMAN** ORANGEBURG, SC

START TO FINISH: 20 MIN.
MAKES: 16 S'MORES

- 8 ounces semisweet chocolate, chopped
- 1 can (14 ounces) sweetened condensed milk
- 1 teaspoon vanilla extract
- 16 whole graham crackers, halved
- 2 cups miniature marshmallows

1. In a heavy saucepan, melt chocolate over low heat. Add milk; cook and stir until smooth. Stir in vanilla. Spread 1 tablespoon chocolate mixture over each of two graham cracker halves. Place eight or nine marshmallows on one cracker; gently press the other cracker on top. Repeat.
2. Wrap s'mores in plastic wrap; store at room temperature.

TOP TIP

For a deluxe s'more sundae, top vanilla ice cream with hot fudge sauce, mini marshmallows, whipped cream and Teddy Grahams or graham cracker crumbs.

BBQ HOT DOG & POTATO PACKS

Lemony Fruit Dip

I make this fluffy dip several times a month to encourage my kids to eat more fruit. It's a special treat in summer, when local produce is at its best.

—**SONJA WHITCHURCH** ST. THOMAS, ON

PREP: 10 MIN. + CHILLING
MAKES: 12 SERVINGS (¼ CUP EACH)

- ½ cup confectioners' sugar
- 1½ teaspoons grated lemon peel
- 3 tablespoons lemon juice
- 1 carton (8 ounces) frozen whipped topping, thawed
- 4 to 5 drops yellow food coloring, optional
  Assorted fresh fruit

In a bowl, mix confectioners' sugar, lemon peel and lemon juice until blended. Stir in whipped topping and, if desired, food coloring. Refrigerate, covered, at least 4 hours before serving. Serve with fruit.
PER SERVING *73 cal., 3 g fat (3 g sat. fat), 0 chol., trace sodium, 10 g carb., trace fiber, trace pro.* **Diabetic Exchanges:** *½ starch, ½ fat.*

BBQ Hot Dog & Potato Packs

The kids will have fun helping to assemble these nifty foil packs, then savoring the tasty results in short order. They're perfect for camping, or just camping in the backyard.

—**KELLY WESTPHAL** WIND LAKE, WI

START TO FINISH: 20 MIN.
MAKES: 4 SERVINGS

- 1 package (20 ounces) refrigerated red potato wedges
- 4 hot dogs
- 1 small onion, cut into wedges
- ¼ cup shredded cheddar cheese
- ½ cup barbecue sauce

1. Divide potato wedges among four pieces of heavy-duty foil (about 18 in. square). Top each with a hot dog, onion wedges and cheese. Drizzle with barbecue sauce. Fold foil around mixture, sealing tightly.
2. Grill, covered, over medium heat 10-15 minutes or until heated through. Open foil carefully to allow steam to escape.

MAKE-AHEAD S'MORES

STAR SANDWICHES

(5) INGREDIENTS FAST FIX
Stovetop Macaroni and Cheese

When I was a girl, Mama used Texas longhorn cheese in this recipe. After it melted all over the macaroni, I loved to dig in and see how many strings of cheese would follow my spoonful.

—**IMOGENE HUTTON** BROWNWOOD, TX

START TO FINISH: 25 MIN.
MAKES: 6 SERVINGS

- 1 package (7 ounces) elbow macaroni
- ¼ cup butter, cubed
- ¼ cup all-purpose flour
- ½ teaspoon salt
- Dash pepper
- 2 cups whole milk
- 2 cups (8 ounces) shredded cheddar cheese
- Paprika, optional

1. Cook macaroni according to package directions. Meanwhile, in a large saucepan, melt butter over medium heat. Stir in flour, salt and pepper until smooth; gradually whisk in milk. Bring to a boil, stirring constantly; cook and stir 1-2 minutes longer or until thickened.

2. Stir in cheese until melted. Drain macaroni; add to cheese sauce and stir to coat. If desired, sprinkle with paprika.

(5) INGREDIENTS FAST FIX
Star Sandwiches

A simple, well-seasoned egg salad makes these star-shaped sandwiches a hit, especially during the holidays. You can use whatever bread you like, but I prefer yellow egg bread.

—**PAM LANCASTER** WILLIS, VA

START TO FINISH: 25 MIN.
MAKES: 8 SANDWICHES

- 4 hard-cooked eggs, diced
- ½ cup mayonnaise
- 1 teaspoon Dijon mustard
- ¼ teaspoon dill weed
- ⅛ teaspoon salt
- ⅛ teaspoon pepper
- 16 slices egg bread or white bread

1. In a small bowl, combine the diced eggs, mayonnaise, mustard, dill, salt and pepper.

2. Using a large star-shaped cookie cutter, cut out 16 stars from bread.

3. Spread half of bread slices with egg salad and top with remaining bread slices.

STOVETOP MACARONI AND CHEESE

Strawberry Surprise Cupcakes

PREP: 25 MIN. • **BAKE:** 25 MIN. + COOLING
MAKES: 2 DOZEN

- 1 package strawberry cake mix (regular size)
- 2 cups (16 ounces) sour cream
- 2 eggs
- ¼ cup strawberry preserves
- 1 can (16 ounces) vanilla frosting
  Halved fresh strawberries

1. Preheat the oven to 350°. Line 24 muffin cups with paper liners. In a large bowl, combine cake mix, sour cream and eggs. Beat on low speed for 30 seconds. Beat on medium speed for 2 minutes.

2. Fill prepared cups half full. Drop about ½ teaspoon preserves into center of each cupcake; cover with remaining batter.

3. Bake 22-27 minutes or until a toothpick inserted into the cake portion comes out clean. Cool in pans 10 minutes before removing to wire racks to cool completely.

4. Pipe frosting over cupcakes and top each with a strawberry half.

FAST FIX
Kid-Pleasing Taco Pizza

Kids will love this quick-and-easy take on both tacos and pizza. And you'll love that it uses healthier ingredients!
—**KIMBERLY THEOBALD** GALESBURG, IL

START TO FINISH: 30 MIN.
MAKES: 10 PIECES

- 1 tube (13.8 ounces) refrigerated pizza crust
- 1 pound lean ground turkey
- ¾ cup water
- 1 envelope reduced-sodium taco seasoning

KID-PLEASING TACO PIZZA

- 1 can (16 ounces) fat-free refried beans
- 1½ cups (6 ounces) shredded pizza cheese blend
- 3 medium tomatoes, chopped
- 7 cups shredded lettuce
- 2 cups crushed baked tortilla chip scoops

1. Unroll crust into a 15x10x1-in. baking pan coated with cooking spray; flatten dough and build up edges slightly. Bake at 425° for 8-10 minutes or until edges are lightly browned.

2. Meanwhile, in a large nonstick skillet, cook turkey over medium heat until no longer pink; drain. Stir in water and taco seasoning. Bring to a boil. Reduce heat; simmer, uncovered, for 5 minutes. Stir in refried beans until blended.

3. Spread turkey mixture over crust; sprinkle with cheese. Bake at 425° for 5-7 minutes or until cheese is melted. Top with tomatoes, lettuce and chips. Serve immediately.

DID YOU KNOW?

Lean ground turkey (93% lean) contains 53% less fat and 38% less saturated fat than regular ground turkey (85% lean). It works great in casseroles, tacos and other dishes that use crumbled meat. Higher-fat meat works better for burgers or meat loaf.

Kids get a thrill when they discover the fruity surprise tucked inside these cupcakes. They really wow at parties, bake sales and snack time.
—**MARGARET WILSON** SUN CITY, CA

STRAWBERRY SURPRISE CUPCAKES

PRETTY PENNE HAM SKILLET

FAST FIX ▶
Pretty Penne Ham Skillet

I'm a busy nurse, so fast meals are a must. Here's a tasty change of pace from the typical potato-ham casserole.
—**KATHY STEPHAN** WEST SENECA, NY

START TO FINISH: 30 MIN.
MAKES: 6 SERVINGS

- 1 **package (16 ounces) penne pasta**
- ¼ **cup olive oil**
- 3 **tablespoons butter**
- 3 **cups cubed fully cooked ham**
- 1 **large sweet red pepper, finely chopped**
- 1 **medium onion, chopped**
- 2 **garlic cloves, minced**
- ¼ **cup minced fresh parsley**
- 1½ **teaspoons minced fresh basil or ½ teaspoon dried basil**
- 1½ **teaspoons minced fresh oregano or ½ teaspoon dried oregano**
- 1 **can (14½ ounces) chicken broth**
- 1 **tablespoon lemon juice**
- ½ **cup shredded Parmesan cheese**

1. Cook pasta according to package directions; drain. Meanwhile, in a large skillet, heat oil and butter over medium-high heat. Add ham, red pepper and onion; cook and stir 4-6 minutes or until ham is browned and vegetables are tender. Add garlic and herbs; cook 1-2 minutes longer.
2. Stir in broth and lemon juice. Bring to a boil. Reduce heat; simmer, uncovered, 10-15 minutes or until liquid is reduced by half. Add pasta; toss to combine. Sprinkle with cheese.

TOP TIP

We loved this recipe! Definitely quick and easy. The only changes that I made were to use tri-color penne and to double the lemon juice. I served this with Greek salad and garlic bread.—**KATLAYDEE3**
TASTEOFHOME.COM

FAST FIX ▶
Sweet-and-Sour Beef

This healthful stir-fry recipe is a family favorite. I've used a variety of meats and apples and sometimes replace the green onion with yellow onion. It always tastes great!
—**BRITTANY MCCLOUD** KENYON, MN

START TO FINISH: 30 MIN.
MAKES: 4 SERVINGS

- 1 **tablespoon cornstarch**
- 2 **tablespoons cold water**
- 1 **pound beef top sirloin steak, cut into ½-inch cubes**
- 1 **teaspoon salt**
- ½ **teaspoon pepper**
- 3 **teaspoons canola oil, divided**
- 1 **large green pepper, cut into ½-inch pieces**
- 1 **large sweet red pepper, cut into ½-inch pieces**
- 2 **medium tart apples, chopped**
- ½ **cup plus 2 tablespoons thinly sliced green onions, divided**
- ⅔ **cup packed brown sugar**
- ½ **cup cider vinegar**
  Hot cooked rice, optional

1. In a small bowl, mix cornstarch and water until smooth. Sprinkle beef with salt and pepper. In a large nonstick skillet or wok coated with cooking spray, heat 2 teaspoons oil over medium-high heat. Add beef; stir-fry 2-3 minutes or until no longer pink. Remove from pan.
2. In same skillet, stir-fry peppers and apples in remaining oil for 2 minutes. Add ½ cup green onions; stir-fry 1-3 minutes longer or until peppers are crisp-tender. Remove from pan.
3. Add brown sugar and vinegar to skillet; bring to a boil, stirring to dissolve sugar. Stir cornstarch mixture and add to pan. Return to a boil; cook and stir 1-2 minutes or until thickened.
4. Return beef and pepper mixture to pan; heat through. If desired, serve with rice. Sprinkle with remaining green onion.

SWEET-AND-SOUR BEEF

NEAPOLITAN CRISPY BARS

Neapolitan Crispy Bars

The multicolored layers in these goodies create quite the buzz. Just wait until people take a bite. The chocolate and strawberry really pop.

—TASTE OF HOME TEST KITCHEN

PREP: 10 MIN. • **COOK:** 30 MIN. + COOLING
MAKES: 1 DOZEN

- 1 **package (10 ounces) large marshmallows, divided**
- 3 **tablespoons butter, divided**
- 2 **cups Cocoa Krispies**
- ½ **cup miniature semisweet chocolate chips**
- 4 **cups Rice Krispies, divided**
- ¼ **cup strawberry preserves**
- 5 **drops red food coloring, optional**

1. In a large saucepan, combine a third of the marshmallows (about 2 cups) and 1 tablespoon butter. Cook and stir over medium-low heat until melted. Remove from heat; stir in Cocoa Krispies and chocolate chips. Press into a greased 11x7-in. dish.
2. In a saucepan, combine a third of the marshmallows and 1 tablespoon butter. Cook and stir over medium-low

heat until melted. Remove from heat; stir in 2 cups Rice Krispies. Press into dish over chocolate layer.
3. In a saucepan, combine remaining marshmallows and butter. Cook and stir over medium-low heat until melted. Remove from heat; stir in preserves and, if desired, food coloring. Stir in remaining Rice Krispies. Press into dish; cool. Cut into bars.

Bumblebee Banana Cupcakes

Those who love sweets will make a beeline for these cute-as-a-bug cupcakes. They're wonderful for school treats, kids' parties, or even outdoor summer events.

—BEATRICE RICHARD POSEN, MI

PREP: 35 MIN. • **BAKE:** 15 MIN.
MAKES: 1 DOZEN

- 1 **package (14 ounces) banana quick bread and muffin mix**
- 1 **cup milk**
- ½ **cup canola oil**
- 2 **eggs**
- 1 **can (16 ounces) vanilla frosting**
- 5 **drops yellow food coloring**

- 12 **large yellow gumdrops**
- ½ **cup chocolate frosting**
- 12 **semisweet chocolate chips**
- 24 **miniature semisweet chocolate chips**
- 12 **large white gumdrops**
  Black shoestring licorice, cut into 1-inch pieces

1. In a large bowl, combine the muffin mix, milk, oil and eggs. Fill 12 greased or paper-lined muffin cups two-thirds full with batter.
2. Bake at 375° for 15-18 minutes or until a toothpick inserted near the center comes out clean. Cool for 5 minutes before removing from pan to a wire rack to cool completely.
3. In a small bowl, combine vanilla frosting and food coloring. Frost cupcakes. Cut yellow gumdrops in half widthwise. Use the rounded tops for heads. Flatten remaining portions into ovals for bodies. Place one head and one body on each cupcake.
4. Place chocolate frosting in a resealable plastic bag; cut a small hole in a corner of the bag. Pipe stripes on gumdrop bodies to resemble a bumblebee. For the stinger, place one chocolate chip at the end of body with pointed end facing out.
5. Pipe two eyes with chocolate frosting or position two mini chocolate chips in front of head for eyes. Cut white gumdrops in half lengthwise; position next to bodies for wings. Insert two licorice pieces for antennae.

BUMBLEBEE BANANA CUPCAKES

Take a Dip

Roll the classic ice cream sandwich into any sweet treat you like, such as jimmies, sprinkles, Teddy Grahams, toasted coconut, Swedish fish or crushed candy bars or Oreos. This slam-dunk of an ice cream treat will have the whole gang screaming for seconds.

Before you decorate, let the ice cream get a little soft so goodies stick. Refreeze if needed.

Easy Cake Mix Bars

PREP: 5 MIN. • **BAKE:** 20 MIN. + COOLING
MAKES: 3 DOZEN

- 1 **yellow cake mix (regular size)**
- 1 **egg**
- ½ **cup 2% milk**
- ⅓ **cup canola oil**
- 1 **cup white baking chips**
- ⅓ **cup jimmies**

1. Preheat oven to 350°. In a large bowl, combine cake mix, egg, milk and oil (mixture will be thick). Stir in baking chips and jimmies. Spread into a greased 15x10x1-in. baking pan.

2. Bake 18-20 minutes or until a toothpick inserted into center comes out clean. Cool completely in pan on a wire rack. Cut into bars.

FREEZE OPTION *Freeze bars in freezer containers. To use, thaw in covered containers before serving.*

I take these bars to work for Friday pick-me-ups. I love to share them because they're so easy to eat, easy to make and easy on the wallet.
—**AMY ROSE** BALLWIN, MO

EASY CAKE MIX BARS

Orange Chicken Pasta Salad

Refreshing fruit teams up with chicken, pasta and crispy veggies for the perfect single-serving salad. It makes an ideal hot-weather lunch.
—**MARY LEWIS** NORMAN, OK

START TO FINISH: 20 MIN.
MAKES: 1 SERVING.

- ½ **cup uncooked spiral pasta**
- ½ **cup cubed cooked chicken breast**
- ¼ **cup mandarin oranges**
- ¼ **cup chopped cucumber**
- ¼ **cup halved seedless red grapes**
- 1 **green onion, sliced**

ORANGE VINAIGRETTE

- 3 **tablespoons orange juice concentrate**
- 1 **tablespoon white vinegar**
- 1 **tablespoon olive oil**

1. Cook pasta according to package directions; drain and rinse in cold water. In a small bowl, combine the pasta, chicken, oranges, cucumber, grapes and onion.

2. In another bowl, whisk the vinaigrette ingredients. Drizzle over the pasta salad and toss to coat. Refrigerate until serving.

PER SERVING *529 cal., 17 g fat (3 g sat. fat), 54 mg chol., 52 mg sodium, 67 g carb., 2 g fiber, 28 g pro.*

Pizzeria Salad

If your family loves pizza, let it inspire you to make a tempting salad! Be sure to include everyone's favorite pizza toppings.

—*TASTE OF HOME* COOKING SCHOOL

START TO FINISH: 25 MIN.
MAKES: 4 MAIN-DISH SERVINGS; 8 SIDE SALADS

- 2 **prebaked mini pizza crusts**
- ½ **cup Western, Catalina or French salad dressing**
- 1 **tablespoon minced fresh basil or oregano**
- 1 **package (10 ounces) torn romaine lettuce (8 cups)**
- 1 **cup sliced pepperoni or chopped Canadian bacon**
- 1 **cup (4 ounces) shredded part-skim mozzarella cheese or cheese blend**
- 1 **can (2¼ ounces) sliced ripe olives, drained**

1. Bake pizza crusts at 400° for 8-10 minutes or grill over medium heat until desired crispness. When cool enough to handle, tear into bite-size pieces; set aside.

2. In a small bowl, combine salad dressing and basil; set aside. In a salad bowl, combine the lettuce, pizza crusts, pepperoni, cheese and olives. Toss to mix ingredients. Drizzle each serving with dressing.

EASY MEATBALL STROGANOFF

PIZZERIA SALAD

This recipe has fed not only my own family, but many neighborhood kids! They come running when I make this supper. It's one of those things you throw together after work on a busy day because you know it works.

—**JULIE MAY** HATTIESBURG, MS

Easy Meatball Stroganoff

START TO FINISH: 30 MIN.
MAKES: 4 SERVINGS

- 3 **cups uncooked egg noodles**
- 1 **tablespoon olive oil**
- 1 **package (12 ounces) frozen fully cooked Italian meatballs, thawed**
- 1½ **cups beef broth**
- 1 **teaspoon dried parsley flakes**
- ¾ **teaspoon dried basil**
- ½ **teaspoon salt**
- ½ **teaspoon dried oregano**
- ¼ **teaspoon pepper**
- 1 **cup heavy whipping cream**
- ¾ **cup sour cream**

1. Cook egg noodles according to package directions for al dente; drain.

2. Meanwhile, in a large skillet, heat oil over medium-high heat. Brown meatballs; remove from pan. Add broth, stirring to loosen browned bits from pan. Add seasonings. Bring to a boil; cook 5-7 minutes or until liquid is reduced to ½ cup.

3. Add meatballs, noodles and whipping cream. Bring to a boil. Reduce heat; simmer, uncovered, 3-5 minutes or until slightly thickened. Stir in sour cream; heat through.

S'more Ice Cream Pie

Our pretty s'more pie will make you glad you're not camping! Boys and girls will adore the hot toasty marshmallows atop rocky road ice cream.

—*TASTE OF HOME* TEST KITCHEN

PREP: 20 MIN. + FREEZING
MAKES: 4 SERVINGS

- ⅔ **cup graham cracker crumbs**
- 2 **tablespoons sugar**
- 3 **tablespoons butter, melted**
- 2½ **cups rocky road ice cream, softened**
- ⅔ **cup marshmallow creme**
- ¾ **cup miniature marshmallows**

1. Preheat oven to 325°. In a small bowl, combine cracker crumbs and sugar; stir in butter. Press onto the bottom and up the sides of a 7-in. pie plate coated with cooking spray. Bake 7-9 minutes or until lightly browned. Cool on a wire rack.

2. Carefully spread ice cream into crust; freeze until firm. Spread marshmallow creme over ice cream.

Top with marshmallows; gently press into creme. Cover and freeze 4 hours or overnight.

3. Just before serving, broil 6 in. from the heat for 1-2 minutes or until marshmallows are golden brown.

Sweet & Spicy Chicken Drummies

We were on a camping trip, and a young bachelor brought these glazed drumsticks for dinner. They were fabulous! I was so impressed, I asked him for the recipe.

—**LYNETTE HANUS** FAYETTEVILLE, GA

PREP: 15 MIN. + CHILLING • **BAKE:** 50 MIN.
MAKES: 10 SERVINGS

- 2 **cups sugar**
- ¼ **cup paprika**
- 2 **tablespoons salt**
- 2 **teaspoons pepper**
- 1 **teaspoon garlic powder**
- 1 **teaspoon chili powder**
- ½ **teaspoon cayenne pepper**
- 20 **chicken drumsticks (about 5 pounds)**

1. In a large resealable plastic bag, combine the sugar, paprika, salt, pepper, garlic powder, chili powder and cayenne. Add drumsticks, a few at a time; seal bag and shake to coat.

2. Place chicken in two greased 15x10x1-in. baking pans. Cover and refrigerate for 8 hours or overnight. (A small amount of meat juices will form in the pan.)

3. Bake, uncovered, at 325° for 50-60 minutes or until chicken juices run clear and a thermometer reads 170°-175°.

TOP TIP

My husband has asked me to make this four times already, he totally loves this recipe. I use chicken legs and thighs. I add a little more cayenne pepper to spice it up to his liking. I also substitute Splenda for half of the sugar.

—**KAREN.BUSKE** TASTEOFHOME.COM

SWEET & SPICY CHICKEN DRUMMIES

With three kids at home and a full-time job, I always needed dinners that were extra quick and easy. This peanutty stir-fry is still a favorite after 15 years.
—**CHERYL MURPHY** DELTA, BC

GRAND PRIZE

FAST FIX
Simple Chicken Stir-Fry

START TO FINISH: 25 MIN.
MAKES: 4 SERVINGS

- 2 **tablespoons canola oil, divided**
- 1 **pound boneless skinless chicken breasts, cut into 1-inch cubes**
- 1 **medium green pepper, chopped**
- 3 **garlic cloves, minced**
- 2 **teaspoons minced fresh gingerroot**
- 1½ **cups salsa**
- ½ **cup creamy peanut butter**
- 2 **tablespoons reduced-sodium soy sauce**
  Hot cooked rice

CRISPY BARBECUE
CHICKEN TENDERS

1. In a large skillet, heat 1 tablespoon oil over medium-high heat. Add chicken; stir-fry 4-6 minutes or until no longer pink. Remove from pan. In same skillet, heat remaining oil. Add pepper; cook and stir 2-3 minutes or until crisp-tender. Add garlic and ginger; cook 1 minute longer. Add salsa, peanut butter and soy sauce; stir until peanut butter is blended. Stir in chicken; heat through. Serve with rice.

SIMPLE CHICKEN STIR-FRY

FAST FIX
Crispy Barbecue Chicken Tenders

These crunchy potato chip-coated chicken tenders are a little sweet, a little tangy and a whole lot of fun. In half an hour, your family's new favorite dish is ready to eat. When I have extra time, I roast garlic and add it to the sauce.
—**ANDREANN GEISE** MYRTLE BEACH, SC

START TO FINISH: 30 MIN.
MAKES: 6 SERVINGS

- 1 **cup (8 ounces) sour cream**
- ¼ **cup minced fresh chives**
- 2 **garlic cloves, minced**
- ½ **teaspoon salt**

CHICKEN
- ¼ **cup all-purpose flour**
- 2 **tablespoons light brown sugar**
- 1 **teaspoon ground mustard**
- ¾ **teaspoon pepper**
- ½ **teaspoon salt**
- ¼ **teaspoon cayenne pepper**
- 2 **eggs, lightly beaten**
- 2 **cups coarsely crushed barbecue potato chips**
- 1½ **pounds chicken tenderloins**
  Oil for frying

1. In a small bowl, mix sour cream, chives, garlic and salt. In a shallow bowl, mix flour, brown sugar and seasonings. Place eggs and potato chips in separate shallow bowls. Dip chicken in flour mixture to coat both sides; shake off excess. Dip in eggs, then in potato chips, patting to help coating adhere.
2. In a deep skillet, heat ¼ in. oil to 375°. Fry chicken, a few strips at a time, 2-3 minutes on each side or until golden brown. Drain on paper towels. Serve with sauce.

Sweet 'n' Spicy Munch

Kids of all ages love the sweet and salty blend in this fast-to-fix snack mix. Wrap it up in colored paper cones so kids can enjoy it on the go.

—SHANA REILEY THERESA, NY

START TO FINISH: 5 MIN.
MAKES: 2 QUARTS

- 1 **pound spiced gumdrops**
- 1 **pound candy corn**
- 1 **can (16 ounces) salted peanuts**

In a large bowl, combine the gumdrops, candy corn and peanuts. Store in an airtight container.

SWEET 'N' SPICY MUNCH

Peanut Butter Popcorn Balls

Trick-or-treaters are always happy to receive these tasty popcorn balls. I love making them as well as eating them!

—BETTY CLAYCOMB ALVERTON, PA

PREP: 20 MIN. + STANDING
MAKES: 10 POPCORN BALLS

- 5 **cups popped popcorn**
- 1 **cup dry roasted peanuts**
- ½ **cup sugar**
- ½ **cup light corn syrup**
- ½ **cup chunky peanut butter**
- ½ **teaspoon vanilla extract**
- 10 **lollipop sticks**

PEANUT BUTTER POPCORN BALLS

1. Place popcorn and peanuts in a large bowl; set aside. In a large heavy saucepan over medium heat, bring sugar and corn syrup to a rolling boil, stirring occasionally. Remove from the heat; stir in peanut butter and vanilla. Quickly pour over popcorn mixture and mix well.

2. When cool enough to handle, quickly shape into ten 2½-in. balls; insert a lollipop stick into each ball. Let stand at room temperature until firm; wrap in plastic wrap.

Yummy Mummies

Raid your fridge for condiments that turn everyday chicken strips into spooktacular mummies. Ranch dressing bandages and glowing mustard eyes make these cuties an instant Halloween hit. Dinner is so simple it's scary!

✳ Fill a squirt bottle with ranch dressing while the chicken strips bake. Drizzle in zigzags to make the mummies' wraps.

FAVORITE SKILLET LASAGNA

Favorite Skillet Lasagna

Whole wheat noodles and zucchini pump up the nutrition in this easy dinner, while fat-free ricotta cheese makes it look and feel indulgent.

—**LORIE MINER** KAMAS, UT

START TO FINISH: 30 MIN.
MAKES: 5 SERVINGS

- ½ **pound Italian turkey sausage links, casings removed**
- 1 **small onion, chopped**
- 1 **jar (14 ounces) spaghetti sauce**
- 2 **cups uncooked whole wheat egg noodles**
- 1 **cup water**
- ½ **cup chopped zucchini**
- ½ **cup fat-free ricotta cheese**
- 2 **tablespoons grated Parmesan cheese**
- 1 **tablespoon minced fresh parsley or 1 teaspoon dried parsley flakes**
- ½ **cup shredded part-skim mozzarella cheese**

1. In a large nonstick skillet, cook sausage and onion over medium heat until no longer pink, breaking up sausage into crumbles; drain. Stir in spaghetti sauce, egg noodles, water and zucchini. Bring to a boil. Reduce heat; simmer, covered, 8-10 minutes or until the noodles are tender, stirring occasionally.

2. In a small bowl, combine ricotta cheese, Parmesan cheese and parsley. Drop by tablespoonfuls over pasta mixture. Sprinkle with mozzarella cheese; cook, covered, 3-5 minutes longer or until cheese is melted.

PER SERVING *250 cal., 10 g fat (3 g sat. fat), 41 mg chol., 783 mg sodium, 24 g carb., 3 g fiber, 17 g pro.* **Diabetic Exchanges: 2 lean meat, 1½ starch, 1 fat.**

Layered Taco Salad

I came up with this fun taco salad to make my kids happy. Make it with ground beef, turkey or chicken...they all work well.

—**BETTY NICKELS** TAMPA, FL

START TO FINISH: 25 MIN.
MAKES: 6 SERVINGS

- 1 **pound lean ground beef (90% lean)**
- 2 **tablespoons reduced-sodium taco seasoning**
- 1 **cup salsa**
- 1 **tablespoon lime juice**
- 6 **ounces baked tortilla chips (about 70 chips)**
- 12 **cups chopped iceberg lettuce**
- 6 **plum tomatoes, seeded and chopped**
- 1 **can (15 ounces) black beans, rinsed and drained**
- 1½ **cups (6 ounces) shredded reduced-fat Mexican cheese blend**
- 1 **large sweet yellow or red pepper, thinly sliced**
- 1 **medium red onion, thinly sliced**
- ⅓ **cup fat-free sour cream**

1. In a large nonstick skillet, cook beef over medium heat 6-8 minutes or until no longer pink, breaking meat into crumbles; drain. Sprinkle the taco seasoning over the beef and stir to combine.

2. In a small bowl, mix the salsa and lime juice.

3. Arrange tortilla chips on a serving platter; layer with lettuce, tomatoes, beans, cheese, yellow pepper, beef mixture, onion, salsa mixture and sour cream. Serve immediately.

LAYERED TACO SALAD

CHERRY-CHICKEN LETTUCE WRAPS

Coney Dogs

My mom and I always make these top dogs for get-togethers. Leftovers are no problem—there never are any!

—**DONNA STERNTHAL** SHARPSVILLE, PA

PREP: 15 MIN. • **COOK:** 45 MIN.
MAKES: 24 SERVINGS

- 2 **pounds ground beef**
- 3 **small onions, chopped**
- 3 **cups water**
- 1 **can (12 ounces) tomato paste**
- 5 **teaspoons chili powder**
- 2 **teaspoons rubbed sage**
- 2 **teaspoons salt**
- 1 **teaspoon pepper**
- ½ **teaspoon garlic salt**
- ½ **teaspoon dried oregano**
- ¼ **teaspoon cayenne pepper**
- 24 **hot dogs, cooked**
- 24 **hot dog buns**
  Shredded cheddar cheese, optional

1. In a Dutch oven, cook beef and onions over medium heat until meat is no longer pink; drain. Stir in the water, tomato paste and seasonings.
2. Cover and simmer for 30 minutes, stirring occasionally. Serve on hot dogs; sprinkle with cheese if desired.

I came up with this amazing recipe when I had a load of cherries on hand. You could use chopped water chestnuts or cashews instead of almonds, or dried cherries instead of fresh. These wraps—including the lettuce—would also taste fab rolled up in tortillas!

—**MELISSA BARLOW** FRUIT HEIGHTS, UT

Cherry-Chicken Lettuce Wraps

START TO FINISH: 25 MIN.
MAKES: 4 SERVINGS

- ¾ **pound boneless skinless chicken breasts, cut into ¾-inch cubes**
- 1 **teaspoon ground ginger**
- ¼ **teaspoon salt**
- ¼ **teaspoon pepper**
- 2 **teaspoons olive oil**
- 1½ **cups shredded carrots**
- 1¼ **cups coarsely chopped pitted fresh sweet cherries**
- 4 **green onions, chopped**
- ⅓ **cup coarsely chopped almonds**
- 2 **tablespoons rice vinegar**
- 2 **tablespoons reduced-sodium teriyaki sauce**
- 1 **tablespoon honey**
- 8 **Bibb or Boston lettuce leaves**

1. Sprinkle chicken with ginger, salt and pepper. In a large nonstick skillet coated with cooking spray, heat oil over medium-high heat. Add chicken; cook and stir 3-5 minutes or until no longer pink.
2. Remove from heat. Stir in carrots, cherries, green onions and almonds. In a small bowl, mix vinegar, teriyaki sauce and honey; stir into chicken mixture. Divide among lettuce leaves; fold lettuce over filling.
PER SERVING *257 cal., 10 g fat (1 g sat. fat), 47 mg chol., 381 mg sodium, 22 g carb., 4 g fiber, 21 g pro.* **Diabetic Exchanges:** *3 lean meat, 1 vegetable, ½ fruit, ½ fat.*

CONEY DOGS

Winter Wonderland

Grow your own enchanted forest with your family's most-requested Christmas sweets—no green thumb necessary. Shredded coconut makes the perfect snowy backdrop. Just see if the resident elves can keep from snacking on this sparkling display!

Icing is the sweet glue that holds together a tree of sugar cookies and halved gumdrops. Use a Rolo for a tasty trunk.

FAST FIX

ABC Soup

Instead of opening a can of alphabet soup, why not make some from scratch? Kids of all ages love this traditional soup with a tomato base, beef and alphabet pasta.

—**SHARON BROCKMAN** APPLETON, WI

START TO FINISH: 30 MIN.
MAKES: 11 SERVINGS (2¾ QUARTS)

- 1 **pound ground beef**
- 1 **medium onion, chopped**
- 2 **quarts tomato juice**
- 1 **can (15 ounces) mixed vegetables, undrained**
- 1 **cup water**
- 2 **beef bouillon cubes**
- 1 **cup uncooked alphabet pasta**
  Salt and pepper to taste

1. In a large saucepan, cook beef and onion over medium heat until meat is no longer pink; drain. Add tomato juice, vegetables, water and bouillon; bring to a boil.

2. Stir in pasta. Cook, uncovered, for 6-8 minutes or until pasta is tender, stirring frequently. Season with salt and pepper.

FAST FIX

Snowflake Tomato Soup

Our sensational soup packs lots of pleasing ingredients, and is extra fun to eat when decorated with a pretty snowflake.

—**TASTE OF HOME** TEST KITCHEN

START TO FINISH: 25 MIN.
MAKES: 8-10 SERVINGS

- 2 **cans (28 ounces each) crushed tomatoes**
- 1 **can (14½ ounces) chicken broth**
- 2 **tablespoons minced fresh oregano or 2 teaspoons dried oregano**
- 1 **to 2 tablespoons sugar**
- 1 **cup heavy whipping cream**
- ⅓ **cup sour cream**

1. In a blender, process tomatoes, one can at a time, until smooth. Transfer to a large saucepan. Stir in the broth; bring to a boil. Reduce heat; cover and simmer for 10 minutes. Stir in the oregano and sugar.

2. Add a small amount of hot tomato mixture to whipping cream; return all to the saucepan. Cook until slightly thickened (do not boil).

3. Cut a small hole in the corner of a pastry or plastic bag; fill with sour cream. Pipe a snowflake on each bowl of soup.

SNOWFLAKE TOMATO SOUP

PEPPERMINT TAFFY

(5) INGREDIENTS

Peppermint Taffy

Get the whole family together for an old-fashioned taffy pull, then reward them with a big batch of these minty sweets. The recipe brings back many memories of my grandmother. I used to help her pull this taffy every Christmas Eve.
—**SUZETTE JURY** KEENE, CA

PREP: 1½ HOURS
COOK: 20 MIN. + COOLING
MAKES: 1¾ POUNDS

- 1 tablespoon plus ¼ cup butter, cubed
- 2 cups light corn syrup
- 1½ cups sugar
- 2 teaspoons peppermint extract
- ½ teaspoon salt
- 6 drops red food coloring, optional

1. Grease a 15x10x1-in. pan with 1 tablespoon butter; set aside.
2. In a heavy small saucepan, combine corn syrup and sugar. Bring to a boil over medium heat. Add remaining butter; stir until melted. Cook and stir until a candy thermometer reads 250° (hard-ball stage).

3. Remove from the heat; stir in the peppermint extract, salt and food coloring if desired. Pour into prepared pan. Let stand for 5-10 minutes or until cool enough to handle. Divide into four portions.
4. With well-buttered fingers, quickly pull one portion of candy until firm but pliable (color will become light pink). Pull into a ½-in.-wide rope. Repeat with remaining candy. Cut into 1-in. pieces. Wrap each in waxed paper.
NOTE *We recommend that you test your candy thermometer before each use by bringing water to a boil; the thermometer should read 212°. Adjust your recipe temperature up or down based on your test.*

DID YOU KNOW?

Saltwater taffy originated at a candy store in the popular vacation spot Atlantic City in the 1880s. The original version may have contained a small amount of salt water. Today, saltwater taffy recipes may or may not contain salt and water.

(5) INGREDIENTS EAT SMART FAST FIX

Oven-Fried Fish Nuggets

My husband and I love fried fish, but we're both trying to cut back on dietary fat. I made up this recipe and it's a hit with us both. He says he likes it as much as deep-fried fish, and that's saying a lot!
—**LADONNA REED** PONCA CITY, OK

START TO FINISH: 25 MIN.
MAKES: 4 SERVINGS

- ⅓ cup seasoned bread crumbs
- ⅓ cup crushed cornflakes
- 3 tablespoons grated Parmesan cheese
- ½ teaspoon salt
- ¼ teaspoon pepper
- 1½ pounds cod fillets, cut into 1-inch cubes
  Butter-flavored cooking spray

1. In a shallow bowl, combine the bread crumbs, cornflakes, Parmesan cheese, salt and pepper. Coat fish with butter-flavored spray, then roll in crumb mixture.
2. Place on a baking sheet coated with cooking spray. Bake at 375° for 15-20 minutes or until fish flakes easily with a fork.
PER SERVING *171 cal., 2 g fat (1 g sat. fat), 66 mg chol., 415 mg sodium, 7 g carb., trace fiber, 29 g pro.* **Diabetic Exchanges:** *5 lean meat, ½ starch.*

OVEN-FRIED FISH NUGGETS

FREEZE IT FAST FIX
Sweet BBQ Meatballs

These sauced-up meatballs have lots of Asian flair. If your family likes sweet-and-sour chicken, the beefy version is bound to hit the spot. It's good over rice noodles, too.

—*TASTE OF HOME* TEST KITCHEN

START TO FINISH: 25 MIN.
MAKES: 6 SERVINGS

- 2 **teaspoons olive oil**
- ½ **pound sliced fresh mushrooms**
- 1 **medium green pepper, cut into 1-inch pieces**
- 1 **medium onion, cut into 1-inch pieces**
- 1 **package (12 ounces) frozen fully cooked Italian meatballs, thawed**
- 1 **bottle (18 ounces) barbecue sauce**
- 1 **jar (10 ounces) apricot preserves**
- 1 **cup unsweetened pineapple chunks**
- ½ **cup water**
- ¾ **teaspoon ground mustard**
- ⅛ **teaspoon ground allspice**
  Hot cooked rice

1. In a Dutch oven, heat oil over medium-high heat. Add mushrooms, pepper and onion; cook and stir 7-9 minutes or until tender.

2. Stir in meatballs, barbecue sauce, preserves, pineapple, water, mustard and allspice. Reduce heat to medium; cook and stir 6-8 minutes or until meatballs are heated through. Serve with rice.

FREEZE OPTION *Freeze cooled meatball mixture in freezer containers. To use, partially thaw in refrigerator overnight. Heat through in a covered saucepan, stirring and adding a little water if necessary. Serve as directed.*

BLT WRAPS

FAST FIX
BLT Wraps

My mom used to make these delicious wraps for all of the kids and grandkids on summer days at the lake. Nowadays, we love to pack them along for picnics and days in the park.

—**SHELLY BURKS** BRIGHTON, MO

START TO FINISH: 15 MIN.
MAKES: 8 SERVINGS

- 16 **ready-to-serve fully cooked bacon strips, warmed if desired**
- 8 **flour tortillas (8 inches), room temperature**
- 4 **cups chopped lettuce**
- 2 **cups chopped tomatoes (3 small tomatoes)**
- 2 **cups (8 ounces) shredded cheddar cheese**
- ½ **cup ranch salad dressing**

1. Place two bacon strips across the center of each tortilla. Top with lettuce, tomatoes and cheese; drizzle with salad dressing.

2. Fold bottom and sides of tortilla over filling and roll up.

SWEET BBQ MEATBALLS

Bistro Mac & Cheese

START TO FINISH: 25 MIN.
MAKES: 8 SERVINGS

- 1 **package (16 ounces) uncooked elbow macaroni**
- 5 **tablespoons butter, divided**
- 3 **tablespoons all-purpose flour**
- 2½ **cups 2% milk**
- 1 **teaspoon salt**
- ½ **teaspoon onion powder**
- ½ **teaspoon pepper**
- ¼ **teaspoon garlic powder**
- 1 **cup (4 ounces) shredded part-skim mozzarella cheese**
- 1 **cup (4 ounces) shredded cheddar cheese**
- ½ **cup crumbled Gorgonzola cheese**
- 3 **ounces cream cheese, softened**
- ½ **cup sour cream**
- ½ **cup seasoned bread crumbs**

1. Cook macaroni according to package directions; drain. Meanwhile, in a Dutch oven, melt 3 tablespoons butter over low heat. Stir in flour until smooth; gradually whisk in milk and seasonings. Bring to a boil, stirring constantly; cook and stir 2 minutes or until thickened.

2. Reduce heat; stir in cheeses until melted. Stir in sour cream. Add macaroni; toss to coat. In a small skillet, heat remaining butter over medium heat. Add bread crumbs; cook and stir until golden brown. Sprinkle over the top.

I like to serve this mac & cheese with a salad and crusty bread. It's a satisfying meal that feels upscale, but will fit just about any budget. And because the Gorgonzola is so mild in this dish, even the kiddos will go for it. —**CHARLOTTE GILTNER** MESA, AZ

BISTRO MAC & CHEESE

Muffin-Cup Cheddar Beef Pies

My kids love these beef rolls so much that I always make extra. I give them their choice of dipping sauces—spaghetti sauce and ranch dressing are the top picks.
—**KIMBERLY FARMER** WICHITA, KS

PREP: 25 MIN. + STANDING • **BAKE:** 20 MIN.
MAKES: 20 MEAT PIES

- 2 **loaves (1 pound each) frozen bread dough**
- 2 **pounds ground beef**
- 1 **can (8 ounces) mushroom stems and pieces, drained**
- 1¼ **cups (5 ounces) shredded cheddar cheese**
- 1½ **teaspoons Italian seasoning**
- 1 **teaspoon garlic powder**
- ½ **teaspoon salt**
- ¼ **teaspoon pepper**
  Spaghetti sauce, warmed

1. Let the dough stand at room temperature 30 minutes or until softened. Preheat oven to 350°. Meanwhile, in a Dutch oven, cook beef over medium heat 12-15 minutes or until no longer pink, breaking into crumbles; drain. Stir in mushrooms, cheese and seasonings.

2. Divide each loaf into 10 portions; roll each into a 4-in. circle. Top with ¼ cup filling; bring edges of dough up over filling and pinch to seal.

3. Place meat pies in greased muffin cups, seam side down. Bake 20-25 minutes or until golden brown. Serve with spaghetti sauce.

FREEZE OPTION *Freeze cooled beef pies in a resealable plastic freezer bag. To use, reheat beef pies on greased baking sheets in a preheated 350° oven until heated through.*

TOP TIP

I didn't have any frozen bread dough so I rolled out individual Grands biscuits and wrapped them around the filling. Yummy. I made them as mini bacon cheeseburgers the second time. A big hit.
—**SHOPPERMOM1** TASTEOFHOME.COM

Zucchini Egg Skillet
PAGE 113

Breakfast & Brunch Favorites

These easy, eye-opening specialties are sure to set the perfect tone for a bright and satisfying day. Whether you're looking for tasteful brunch dishes, healthy on-the-go breakfasts or a lazy Saturday meal, you'll find it in this sun-kissed chapter.

**Fruit-Filled
Puff Pancake**
PAGE 102

**On-the-Go
Breakfast Muffins**
PAGE 105

**Smoked Salmon
Bagel Sandwiches**
PAGE 109

Spinach Quiche with Potato Crust

PREP: 25 MIN. • **BAKE:** 55 MIN. + STANDING
MAKES: 8 SERVINGS

- 1 package (24 ounces) refrigerated mashed potatoes
- 2 tablespoons olive oil, divided
- 8 ounces sliced fresh mushrooms
- 2 garlic cloves, minced
- 5 ounces frozen chopped spinach, thawed and squeezed dry (about ½ cup)
- 6 bacon strips, cooked and crumbled
- 2 teaspoons minced fresh rosemary or ½ teaspoon dried rosemary, crushed
- 4 eggs
- 1 cup 2% milk
- ¼ teaspoon pepper
- 1 cup (4 ounces) shredded cheddar cheese

1. Preheat oven to 350°. Press mashed potatoes onto bottom and up sides of a greased 9-in. deep-dish pie plate. Brush with 1 tablespoon oil. Bake potatoes for 30 minutes or until edges are golden brown.

2. Meanwhile, in a large skillet, heat remaining oil over medium-high heat. Add mushrooms; cook and stir 3-4 minutes or until tender. Add garlic; cook 1 minute longer. Remove from heat. Stir in spinach, bacon and rosemary; spoon over crust. In a small bowl, whisk eggs, milk and pepper until blended; stir in cheese. Pour over mushroom mixture.

3. Bake 25-30 minutes longer or until golden brown and a knife inserted near the center comes out clean. Let stand 10 minutes before cutting.

Here's a smart way to use up leftover potatoes and veggies, if you have them. Use 2½ cups leftover mashed potatoes and whatever cooked vegetables you have on hand. You can also use ½ pound of Italian sausage instead of bacon. —**HEATHER KING** FROSTBURG, MD

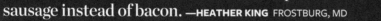

SPINACH QUICHE WITH POTATO CRUST

FRUIT-FILLED PUFF PANCAKE

Fruit-Filled Puff Pancake

This fruity puff pancake is a top breakfast request at my house. The bright combo of cinnamon, blueberries and bananas really wakes you up.

—**LEANNE SENGER** OREGON CITY, OR

START TO FINISH: 25 MIN.
MAKES: 4 SERVINGS

- 3 eggs
- ½ cup 2% milk
- ⅓ cup all-purpose flour
- ¼ teaspoon salt
- 3 tablespoons sugar, divided
- 1 tablespoon butter
- 1½ cups fresh or frozen blueberries, thawed
- 1 medium ripe banana, sliced
- ¼ teaspoon ground cinnamon

1. Preheat oven to 400°. In a large bowl, whisk eggs, milk, flour, salt and 1 tablespoon sugar until smooth. Place butter in a 9-in. pie plate. Place in oven 2-3 minutes or until melted.

2. Tilt pie plate to coat evenly with butter. Pour batter into hot plate. Bake 10-12 minutes or until sides are puffed and golden brown.

3. Meanwhile, in a bowl, combine blueberries and banana. Remove pancake from oven. Top with fruit. Mix cinnamon and remaining sugar; sprinkle over top. Cut into wedges; serve immediately.

PER SERVING *232 cal., 8 g fat (4 g sat. fat), 171 mg chol., 240 mg sodium, 34 g carb., 2 g fiber, 8 g pro.* **Diabetic Exchanges:** *1 starch, 1 medium-fat meat, 1 fruit, ½ fat.*

Asparagus Cream Cheese Omelet

When asparagus is in season, it makes an appearance at almost all of my meals. It tastes fantastic in this omelet, and it looks pretty, too.
—**JANE CAIN** JUNCTION CITY, OH

START TO FINISH: 20 MIN.
MAKES: 2 SERVINGS

- 4 **fresh asparagus spears, trimmed and cut into 1-inch pieces**
- 4 **eggs**
- ¼ **cup sour cream**
- 2 **teaspoons dried minced onion**
- ¼ **teaspoon salt**
- ¼ **teaspoon crushed red pepper flakes**
- 2 **teaspoons butter**
- 2 **ounces cream cheese, cubed and softened**

1. Fill a small saucepan three-fourths full with water; bring to a boil. Add asparagus; cook, uncovered, 2-4 minutes or until crisp-tender. Remove and immediately drop into ice water. Drain and pat dry.
2. In a small bowl, whisk eggs, sour cream, onion, salt and pepper flakes.

In a large nonstick skillet, heat butter over medium-high heat. Pour in egg mixture. Mixture should set immediately at edge. As eggs set, push cooked portions toward the center, letting uncooked eggs flow underneath.
3. When eggs are thickened and no liquid egg remains, top one side with cream cheese and asparagus. Fold omelet in half. Reduce heat to low; let stand, covered, 1-2 minutes or until cream cheese is melted. Cut omelet in half before serving.

Multigrain Pancakes

My husband and I love foods prepared with whole grains. But our children prefer white bread. So I created this recipe to appeal to their love of pancakes while giving them a taste of whole grains.
—**ANN HARRIS** LANCASTER, CA

START TO FINISH: 20 MIN.
MAKES: 8 PANCAKES

- ½ **cup all-purpose flour**
- ¼ **cup whole wheat flour**
- ¼ **cup cornmeal**
- 2 **tablespoons sugar**
- ½ **teaspoon baking soda**
- ½ **teaspoon salt**
- 1 **egg**
- 1 **cup buttermilk**
- 2 **tablespoons butter, melted**
  Maple syrup

1. In a large bowl, combine the first six ingredients. In a small bowl, whisk the egg, buttermilk and butter. Stir into dry ingredients just until moistened.
2. Pour batter by ¼ cupfuls onto a greased hot griddle; turn when bubbles form on top. Cook until the second side is golden brown. Serve with syrup.
PER SERVING *231 cal., 8 g fat (4 g sat. fat), 70 mg chol., 575 mg sodium, 33 g carb., 2 g fiber, 7 g pro.* **Diabetic Exchanges:** *2 starch, 1½ fat.*

DID YOU KNOW?

Instead of buying buttermilk, you can place 1 tablespoon of white vinegar or lemon juice in a liquid measuring cup and add enough milk to measure 1 cup. Stir, then let stand for 5 minutes. Or you can substitute 1 cup of plain yogurt for the buttermilk.

ASPARAGUS CREAM CHEESE OMELET

Overnight Maple Oatmeal

I tasted muesli on a trip to Switzerland, and when I came home, I made it my way. Keep things interesting (and avoid the mid-morning munchies) by adding different fruits and nuts every day.

—MADDIE KIRK SPRINGFIELD, PA

PREP: 10 MIN. + CHILLING
MAKES: 6 SERVINGS

- 2 **cups old-fashioned oats**
- 1 **cup fat-free milk**
- ¼ **cup maple syrup**
- 2 **teaspoons vanilla extract**
- 1 **cup vanilla yogurt**
- ½ **cup chopped walnuts, toasted**
  Assorted fresh fruit

1. In a large bowl, combine oats, milk, syrup and vanilla. Refrigerate, covered, overnight.

2. Just before serving, stir in yogurt. Top with walnuts and fruit.

NOTE *To toast nuts, spread in a 15x10x1-in. baking pan. Bake at 350° for 5-10 minutes or until lightly browned, stirring occasionally. Or, spread in a dry nonstick skillet and heat over low heat until lightly browned, stirring occasionally.*

PER SERVING *249 cal., 9 g fat (1 g sat. fat), 3 mg chol., 46 mg sodium, 36 g carb., 3 g fiber, 9 g pro.* **Diabetic Exchanges:** *2½ starch, 1 fat.*

OVERNIGHT MAPLE OATMEAL

MUSHROOM BROCCOLI QUICHE

Mushroom Broccoli Quiche

I take this dish to many of my family's picnics because it's always such a hit. Serve it at any time of day. Quiche makes a great meatless main dish—and, of course, it's a tasty attraction at any brunch.

—EDIE DESPAIN LOGAN, UT

PREP: 30 MIN. • **BAKE:** 1 HOUR
MAKES: 8 SERVINGS

- **Pastry for single-crust pie (9 inches)**
- 3 **eggs**
- 2 **cups 2% milk**
- 1 **tablespoon Worcestershire sauce**
- ½ **teaspoon salt**
- ⅛ **teaspoon cayenne pepper**
- 1 **cup chopped fresh broccoli**
- ½ **cup sliced fresh mushrooms**
- 2 **green onions, chopped**
- 1 **cup (4 ounces) shredded Swiss cheese**

1. Preheat oven to 425°. On a floured surface, roll pastry dough to fit a 9-in. pie plate. Trim and flute.

2. Line unpricked pastry with a double thickness of foil. Fill with pie weights. Bake 15-20 minutes or until light golden brown. Remove foil and weights; bake 3-5 minutes or until golden brown. Cool. Reduce oven setting to 350°.

3. In a large bowl, whisk eggs, milk, Worcestershire sauce, salt and cayenne. Stir in broccoli, mushrooms and green onions. Sprinkle cheese over crust; pour egg mixture over cheese. Bake 60-65 minutes or until a knife inserted near the center comes out clean.

FREEZE OPTION *Securely wrap baked and cooled quiche in plastic wrap and foil; freeze. To use, partially thaw in refrigerator overnight. Remove from refrigerator 30 minutes before baking. Preheat oven to 350°. Unwrap quiche; reheat in oven until heated through and a thermometer inserted in center reads 165°.* **Pastry for single-crust pie (9 inches)**: *Combine 1¼ cups all-purpose flour and ¼ tsp. salt; cut in ½ cup cold butter until crumbly. Gradually add 3-5 Tbsp. ice water, tossing with a fork until dough holds together when pressed. Wrap in plastic wrap and refrigerate 1 hour.*

Fruity Frappe

START TO FINISH: 10 MIN.
MAKES: 4 SERVINGS

- 1 cup water
- 1 cup fat-free milk
- ⅔ cup thawed orange juice concentrate
- 3 tablespoons honey
- ½ teaspoon vanilla extract
- 1 cup ice cubes
- 1 cup frozen unsweetened mixed berries

Place all ingredients in a blender; cover and process until blended. Serve immediately.
PER SERVING *166 cal., trace fat (trace sat. fat), 1 mg chol., 28 mg sodium, 39 g carb., 1 g fiber, 3 g pro.*

Making a taste-alike of a restaurant drink is fun, but better yet, I know exactly what's in this one. My frappe gets all of its sweetness from berries, juice and honey.
—**PATRICIA CROUSE** WARREN, PA

FRUITY FRAPPE

On-the-Go Breakfast Muffins

Family members frequently request that I make these muffins. I usually prepare them on Sunday night so when we're running late on weekday mornings, the kids can grab these to eat on the bus.
—**IRENE WAYMAN** GRANTSVILLE, UT

PREP: 30 MIN. • **BAKE:** 15 MIN.
MAKES: 1½ DOZEN

- 1 pound bulk Italian sausage
- 7 eggs
- 2 cups all-purpose flour
- ⅓ cup sugar
- 3 teaspoons baking powder
- ½ teaspoon salt
- ½ cup 2% milk
- ½ cup canola oil
- 1 cup (4 ounces) shredded cheddar cheese, divided

1. Preheat oven to 400°. In a large nonstick skillet, cook sausage over medium heat 6-8 minutes or until no longer pink, breaking into crumbles. Remove with a slotted spoon; drain on paper towels. Wipe skillet clean.
2. In a small bowl, whisk five eggs. Pour into same skillet; cook and stir over medium heat until thickened and no liquid egg remains. Remove from the heat.
3. In a large bowl, whisk flour, sugar, baking powder and salt. In another bowl, whisk remaining eggs, milk and oil until blended. Add to flour mixture; stir just until moistened. Fold in ⅔ cup cheese, sausage and the scrambled eggs.
4. Fill greased or paper-lined muffin cups three-fourths full. Sprinkle tops with remaining cheese. Bake muffins for 12-15 minutes or until a toothpick inserted in center comes out clean. Cool 5 minutes before removing from pans to wire racks. Serve warm.
FREEZE OPTION *Freeze cooled muffins in resealable plastic freezer bags. To use, microwave each muffin on high for 45-60 seconds or until heated through.*

Maple-Bacon French Toast

PREP: 20 MIN. + CHILLING • **BAKE:** 30 MIN.
MAKES: 8 SERVINGS

- 6 **eggs**
- 2 **cups half-and-half cream**
- 1 **cup 2% milk**
- ¼ **cup maple syrup**
- 2 **tablespoons sugar**
- ¼ **teaspoon ground cinnamon**
  Dash salt
- 16 **slices French bread (1 inch thick)**
- 10 **bacon strips, cooked and crumbled**
  Additional maple syrup

1. In a shallow bowl, whisk eggs, cream, milk, syrup, sugar, cinnamon and salt. Dip both sides of bread in the egg mixture. Arrange the bread slices into two shingled rows in a greased 13x9-in. baking dish. Pour remaining egg mixture over top. Refrigerate, covered, overnight.

2. Preheat oven to 350°. Remove French toast from refrigerator while oven heats. Bake, covered, 25 minutes.

Sprinkle with bacon. Bake, uncovered, 5-10 minutes longer or until a knife inserted near the center comes out clean. Let stand 5 minutes before serving. Serve with additional syrup.

Potato-Cheddar Frittata

I like to serve this protein-packed frittata with toasted rustic bread. You can also use leftovers instead of the refrigerated potatoes with onions.
—**DONNA MARIE RYAN** TOPSFIELD, MA

START TO FINISH: 30 MIN.
MAKES: 4 SERVINGS

- 8 **egg whites**
- 4 **eggs**
- ½ **cup shredded cheddar cheese**
- ½ **cup fat-free milk**
- 2 **green onions, chopped**
- 2 **teaspoons minced fresh parsley**
- ¼ **teaspoon salt**
- ¼ **teaspoon pepper**
- 1 **tablespoon canola oil**
- 1½ **cups refrigerated diced potatoes with onion**

1. Preheat broiler. In a large bowl, whisk the first eight ingredients. In a 10-in. ovenproof skillet, heat oil over medium-high heat. Add potatoes with onion; cook and stir 3-4 minutes or until tender. Reduce heat; pour in egg mixture. Cook, covered, 5-7 minutes or until nearly set.

2. Broil 3-4 in. from heat 2-3 minutes or until eggs are completely set. Let stand 5 minutes. Cut into wedges.
PER SERVING *241 cal., 13 g fat (5 g sat. fat), 201 mg chol., 555 mg sodium, 11 g carb., 1 g fiber, 19 g pro.* **Diabetic Exchanges:** *2 medium-fat meat, 1 starch, 1 fat.*

Salsa & Scrambled Egg Sandwiches

Power up with a breakfast that keeps you going all morning long. In my humble opinion, these quick sandwiches taste so much better than anything that comes from a drive-thru!
—**MARCIA CONLON** TRAVERSE CITY, MI

START TO FINISH: 25 MIN.
MAKES: 4 SERVINGS

- 8 **eggs**
- ½ **teaspoon salt**
- ¼ **teaspoon pepper**
- 1 **cup salsa, divided**
- ½ **cup shredded cheddar cheese**
- 4 **whole wheat English muffins, split and toasted**
- ¼ **cup reduced-fat spreadable cream cheese**
- 1 **medium ripe avocado, peeled and cubed**
- ½ **small limevReduced-fat sour cream, optional**

1. In a large bowl, whisk eggs, salt and pepper. Place a large nonstick skillet coated with cooking spray over medium-high heat. Pour in egg mixture; cook and stir until eggs are thickened and no liquid egg remains. Add ½ cup salsa and cheese; stir gently until cheese is melted.

2. Spread cut sides of English muffins with cream cheese and remaining salsa. Top with scrambled eggs and avocado. Squeeze lime juice over tops. If desired, serve with sour cream.

This is my favorite Sunday breakfast. It's easy to put together Saturday night and pop in the fridge until morning. It gives me more time for enjoying family on Sundays. Plus, we all get to sit down to a wonderful breakfast together! —**ERIN WRIGHT** WALLACE, KS

MAPLE-BACON FRENCH TOAST

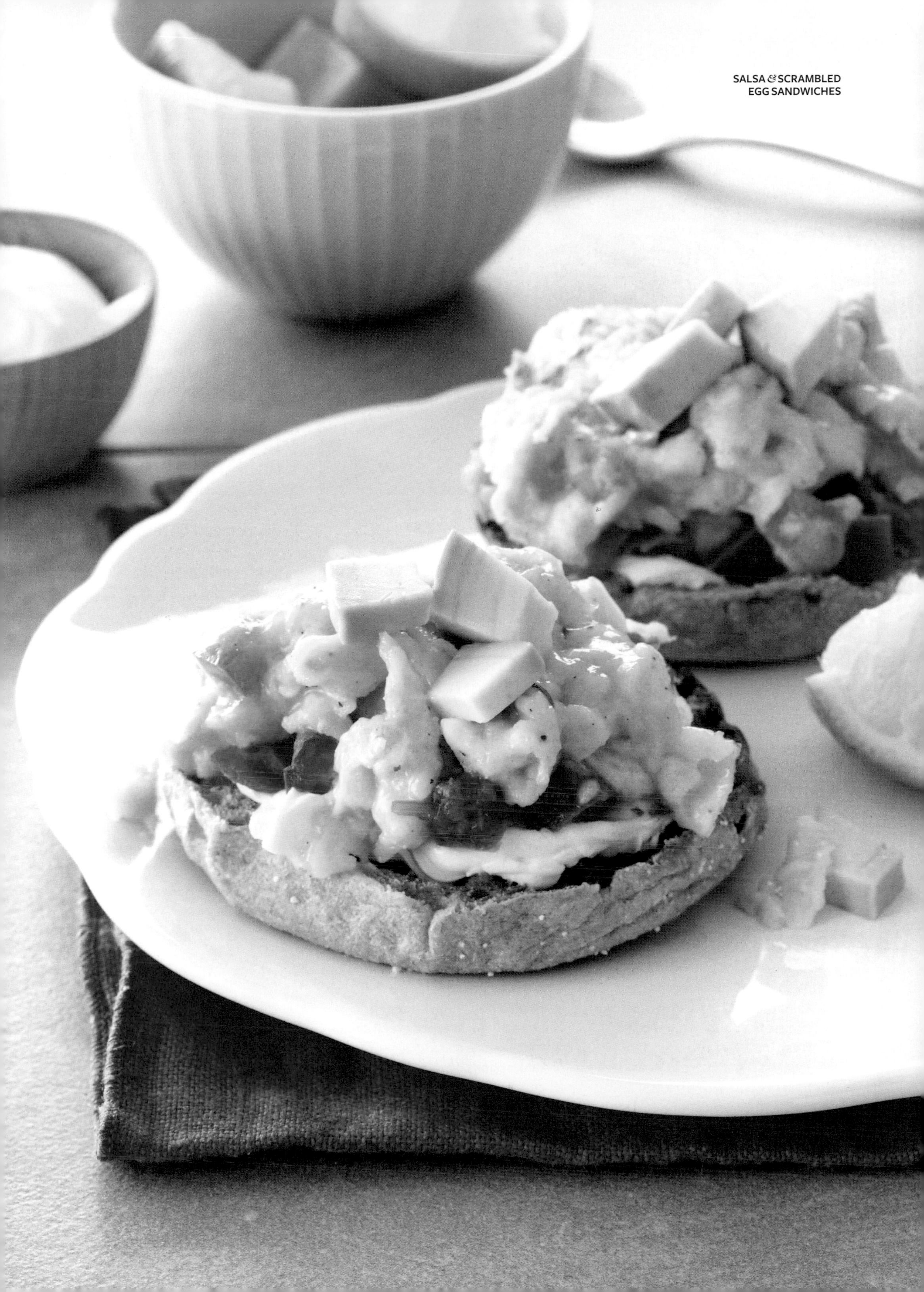

SALSA & SCRAMBLED
EGG SANDWICHES

FULL GARDEN FRITTATA

Full Garden Frittata

I was cooking for a health-conscious friend, and wanted to serve a frittata. To brighten it up, I added classic bruschetta toppings. This has become a flavorful staple in my recipe book.

—**MELISSA ROSENTHAL** VISTA, CA

PREP: 25 MIN. • **BAKE:** 10 MIN.
MAKES: 2 SERVINGS

- 4 **eggs**
- ⅓ **cup 2% milk**
- ¼ **teaspoon salt, divided**
- ⅛ **teaspoon coarsely ground pepper**
- 2 **teaspoons olive oil**
- ½ **medium zucchini, chopped**
- ½ **cup chopped baby portobello mushrooms**
- ¼ **cup chopped onion**
- 1 **garlic clove, minced**
- 2 **tablespoons minced fresh basil**
- 1 **teaspoon minced fresh oregano**
- 1 **teaspoon minced fresh parsley**
  Optional toppings: halved grape tomatoes, small fresh mozzarella cheese balls and thinly sliced fresh basil

1. Preheat oven to 375°. In a bowl, whisk eggs, milk, ⅛ teaspoon salt and pepper. In an 8-in. ovenproof skillet, heat oil over medium-high heat. Add zucchini, mushrooms and onion; cook and stir until tender. Add garlic, herbs

and remaining salt; cook 1 minute longer. Pour in egg mixture.
2. Bake, uncovered, 10-15 minutes or until eggs are set. Cut into four wedges. If desired, serve with toppings.

FAST FIX
Spicy Hash Brown Waffles with Fried Eggs

By using ready-to-go hash browns, you can make quick work of these crunchy waffles. Let guests customize their waffles with the toppings of their choice.

—**NANCY JUDD** ALPINE, UT

START TO FINISH: 30 MIN.
MAKES: 4 SERVINGS

- 5 **eggs, divided**
- ½ **teaspoon salt**
- ½ **teaspoon ground cumin**
- ½ **teaspoon pepper**
- ¼ **teaspoon chili powder**
- 1¾ **cups refrigerated shredded hash brown potatoes**
- 1 **small onion, finely chopped**
- ¼ **cup canned chopped green chilies**
- 2 **tablespoons salsa**
- 2 **tablespoons canola oil**
- ½ **cup shredded cheddar-Monterey Jack cheese**
  Optional toppings: salsa, guacamole, sour cream and minced fresh cilantro

1. In a large bowl, whisk 1 egg, salt, cumin, pepper and chili powder. Stir in potatoes, onion, green chilies and salsa. Bake in a preheated waffle iron coated with cooking spray until golden brown and potatoes are tender, about 8-12 minutes.
2. In a large skillet, heat oil over medium-high heat. Break remaining eggs, one at a time, into pan. Reduce heat to low. Cook until desired doneness, turning after whites are set if desired. Remove from heat. Sprinkle with cheese; cover and let stand for 3 minutes or until melted.
3. Serve eggs with waffles and toppings of your choice.

⑤INGREDIENTS FAST FIX
Cherry Cinnamon Cobbler

It's not a misprint—there really are just two ingredients in this spiced cherry treat. It's a good brunch offering for those who love morning sweets.

—**TERRI ROBINSON** MUNCIE, IN

START TO FINISH: 25 MIN.
MAKES: 8 SERVINGS

- 1 **can (21 ounces) cherry pie filling**
- 1 **tube (12.4 ounces) refrigerated cinnamon rolls with icing**

Preheat oven to 375°. Spread pie filling into a greased 8-in.-square baking dish. Separate cinnamon rolls; reserve icing. Place rolls in baking dish, cinnamon side up. Bake 15-20 minutes or until rolls are golden and filling is bubbly. Spread icing over rolls. Serve warm.

CHERRY CINNAMON COBBLER

BREAKFAST BREAD BOWLS

These bread bowls are so elegant, tasty and simple, you'll wonder why you haven't been making them for years. My wife loves when I make these for her in the morning!
—**PATRICK LAVIN, JR.** BIRDSBORO, PA

⑤INGREDIENTS
Breakfast Bread Bowls

PREP: 20 MIN. • **BAKE:** 20 MIN.
MAKES: 4 SERVINGS

- ½ **cup chopped pancetta**
- 4 **crusty hard rolls (4 inches wide)**
- ½ **cup finely chopped fresh mushrooms**
- 4 **eggs**
- ⅛ **teaspoon salt**
- ⅛ **teaspoon pepper**
- ¼ **cup shredded Gruyere or fontina cheese**

1. Preheat oven to 350°. In a small skillet, cook pancetta over medium heat until browned, stirring occasionally. Remove with a slotted spoon; drain on paper towels.
2. Meanwhile, cut a thin slice off top of each roll. Hollow out bottom of roll, leaving a ½-in.-thick shell (save removed bread for another use); place shells on an ungreased baking sheet.

3. Add mushrooms and pancetta to bread shells. Carefully break an egg into each; sprinkle eggs with salt and pepper. Sprinkle with cheese. Bake 18-22 minutes or until egg whites are completely set and yolks begin to thicken but are not hard.

⑤INGREDIENTS FAST FIX ▶
Mimosa

A standard beverage at brunch, mimosas are as pretty as they are tasty. Make sure the wine you use is labeled extra-dry or dry (not brut), so it doesn't overpower the orange juice.
—*TASTE OF HOME* TEST KITCHEN

START TO FINISH: 5 MIN.
MAKES: 1 SERVING.

- 2 **ounces champagne or other sparkling wine, chilled**
- ½ **ounce Triple Sec**
- 2 **ounces orange juice**

GARNISH
- **Orange slice**

Pour champagne into a champagne flute or wine glass. Pour the Triple Sec and orange juice into the glass. Garnish as desired.

NOTE *To make a batch of mimosas (12 servings), slowly pour one bottle (750 ml) chilled champagne into a pitcher. Stir in 3 cups orange juice and ¾ cup Triple Sec.*

FAST FIX ▶
Smoked Salmon Bagel Sandwiches

A memorable pesto salmon I tried in Hawaii inspired these super-convenient sandwiches. Pack them in a lunch, or serve them on a brunch buffet.
—**SHERRYL VERA** HURLBURT FIELD, FL

START TO FINISH: 10 MIN.
MAKES: 2 SERVINGS

- 2 **tablespoons prepared pesto**
- 2 **whole wheat bagels, split and toasted**
- ⅛ **teaspoon coarsely ground pepper**
- 4 **to 5 ounces smoked salmon or lox**
- 2 **slices tomato**
- 2 **Bibb or Boston lettuce leaves**

Spread pesto over bagel bottoms; sprinkle with pepper. Layer with salmon, tomato and lettuce leaves. Replace tops.

SMOKED SALMON BAGEL SANDWICHES

RHUBARB COMPOTE WITH
YOGURT & ALMONDS

(5) INGREDIENTS **EAT SMART**

Rhubarb Compote with Yogurt & Almonds

My grandma Dot used to make rhubarb compote and always had some in the freezer when I came to visit. This breakfast is a tribute to her. No two stalks of rhubarb are exactly alike, so make sure to taste your compote before you chill it. It should be tart, but sometimes needs a little extra sugar.

—MICHAEL HOFFMAN BROOKLYN, NY

PREP: 10 MIN. • **COOK:** 15 MIN. + CHILLING
MAKES: 6 SERVINGS

- 2 **cups finely chopped fresh rhubarb**
- ¼ **cup sugar**
- 2 **tablespoons water**
- 3 **cups reduced-fat plain Greek yogurt**
- 2 **tablespoons honey**
- ¾ **cup sliced almonds, toasted**

1. In a small saucepan, combine rhubarb, sugar and water. Bring to a boil. Reduce heat; simmer, uncovered, 10-15 minutes or until rhubarb is tender, stirring occasionally. Transfer to a bowl; cool slightly. Refrigerate until cold.

2. In a small bowl, whisk yogurt and honey until blended. Spoon into serving dishes. Top with compote; sprinkle with almonds.

NOTE *To toast nuts, spread in a 15x10x1-in. baking pan. Bake at 350°* *for 5-10 minutes or until lightly browned, stirring occasionally. Or, spread in a dry nonstick skillet and heat over low heat until lightly browned, stirring occasionally.*

PER SERVING *218 cal., 8 g fat (2 g sat. fat), 7 mg chol., 49 mg sodium, 23 g carb., 2 g fiber, 14 g pro.* **Diabetic Exchanges:** *1 starch, 1 reduced-fat milk, 1 fat.*

TOP TIP

I like to add sliced bananas to cooled rhubarb sauce. The bananas do not turn brown, and the sauce will keep for a few days in the refrigerator.

—DONNA T. ROARING SPRING, PA

My mom loves quiche, so for Mother's Day one year I created my own quiche recipe just for her. I've been making it ever since. All it takes is a trip to the farmers market. If you have the time, make the pie pastry from scratch. —YANIQUE DOUGLAS
WAYNESBORO, PA

Asparagus & Corn Quiche

PREP: 30 MIN. • **BAKE:** 35 MIN. + STANDING
MAKES: 6 SERVINGS

- 2 teaspoons olive oil
- 2 cups cut fresh asparagus (½-inch pieces)
- 1 small onion, finely chopped
- ¼ teaspoon salt
- ⅛ teaspoon cayenne pepper
- 3 eggs
- ½ cup heavy whipping cream
- 1 tablespoon cornstarch
- 3 medium ears sweet corn
- 1 cup (4 ounces) shredded sharp white or yellow cheddar cheese
- 1 refrigerated pie pastry

1. Preheat oven to 350°. In a large nonstick skillet, heat oil over medium heat. Add asparagus and onion; cook and stir 4-5 minutes or just until tender. Stir in salt and cayenne; remove from heat.
2. In a bowl, whisk eggs, cream and cornstarch until blended. Using a large-hole grater, remove corn from cobs; add to egg mixture. Stir in cheese.
3. Unroll pastry sheet into a 9-in. pie plate; flute edge. Add asparagus mixture; pour egg mixture over top.
4. Bake on a lower oven rack for 35-40 minutes or until a knife inserted near the center comes out clean. Let stand 10 minutes before cutting.
FREEZE OPTION *Securely wrap and freeze cooled, baked quiche in plastic wrap and foil. To use, partially thaw in refrigerator overnight. Remove from refrigerator 30 minutes before baking. Preheat oven to 350°. Unwrap the quiche; reheat on a lower oven rack for 35-40 minutes or until heated through and a thermometer inserted in center reads 165°.*

Berry Best Smoothies

This fun recipe is a wonderful way to use up over-ripened bananas and to help my family get their five daily servings of fruits and veggies. It's so quick and easy —and my kids absolutely love it!
—**PAMELA KLIM** BETTENDORF, IA

START TO FINISH: 10 MIN.
MAKES: 3 SERVINGS

- 3 tablespoons orange juice concentrate
- 3 tablespoons fat-free half-and-half
- 12 ice cubes
- 1 cup fresh strawberries, hulled
- 1 medium ripe banana, cut into chunks
- ½ cup fresh or frozen blueberries
- ½ cup fresh or frozen raspberries

In a blender, combine all ingredients; cover and process for 30-45 seconds or until smooth. Stir if necessary. Pour into chilled glasses; serve immediately.
PER SERVING *108 cal., 1 g fat (trace sat. fat), 0 chol., 14 mg sodium, 26 g carb., 4 g fiber, 2 g pro.* **Diabetic Exchange:** *1½ fruit.*

Savory Apple-Chicken Sausage

These easy, healthy sausages make a great-tasting brunch dish. The recipe is also quite versatile. You can double or triple it for a crowd, and the sausage freezes well either cooked or raw.
—**ANGELA BUCHANAN** LONGMONT, CO

START TO FINISH: 25 MIN.
MAKES: 8 PATTIES

- 1 large tart apple, peeled and diced
- 2 teaspoons poultry seasoning
- 1 teaspoon salt
- ¼ teaspoon pepper
- 1 pound ground chicken

1. In a large bowl, combine the apple, poultry seasoning, salt and pepper. Crumble chicken over mixture and mix well. Shape into eight 3-in. patties.
2. In a large skillet coated with cooking spray, cook patties over medium heat for 5-6 minutes on each side or until no longer pink.
PER SERVING *92 cal., 5 g fat (1 g sat. fat), 38 mg chol., 328 mg sodium, 4 g carb., 1 g fiber, 9 g pro.* **Diabetic Exchange:** *1 medium-fat meat.*

ASPARAGUS & CORN QUICHE

SAVORY APPLE-CHICKEN SAUSAGE

Breakfast Bundles

Getting kids to eat breakfast is a breeze when you serve these tasty little bundles packed with hearty ingredients. The recipe is so simple, kids of all ages will enjoy helping you make them.

—**BERNICE WILLIAMS** NORTH AURORA, IL

START TO FINISH: 30 MIN.
MAKES: 2 DOZEN

- ½ cup butter, softened
- 2 tablespoons orange juice concentrate
- 1 egg, lightly beaten
- 1½ cups all-purpose flour
- ⅔ cup sugar
- ½ cup Grape-Nuts cereal
- 1 teaspoon baking powder
- ½ pound sliced bacon, cooked and crumbled

1. Preheat oven to 350°. In a bowl, beat butter and orange juice. Add egg; mix well. Combine flour, sugar, cereal and baking powder; stir into butter mixture. Fold in bacon.
2. Drop by rounded tablespoonfuls onto ungreased baking sheets. Bake 11-13 minutes or until edges are lightly brown. Store in the refrigerator.
FREEZE OPTION *Freeze cooled bundles in resealable plastic freezer bags. To use, bake bundles on an ungreased baking sheet in a preheated 350° oven until heated through.*

Asparagus Frittata

You would never guess that egg substitute is used in this fun variation on the classic frittata. I loaded it with fresh asparagus in honor of springtime.

—**JAMES BATES** HERMISTON, OR

START TO FINISH: 25 MIN.
MAKES: 4 SERVINGS

- ⅔ pound fresh asparagus, trimmed and cut into 1-inch pieces
- 1½ cups egg substitute
- 5 tablespoons shredded Parmesan cheese, divided
- ¼ teaspoon salt
- ⅛ teaspoon pepper
- 2 teaspoons olive oil
- 1 medium onion, chopped
- 2 tablespoons minced fresh parsley
- ¼ cup shredded reduced-fat cheddar cheese

1. Preheat broiler. In a large saucepan, bring 4 cups water to a boil. Add asparagus; cook, uncovered, for 2-4 minutes or just until crisp-tender. Drain asparagus and immediately drop into ice water. Drain and pat dry.
2. In a small bowl, whisk egg substitute, 3 tablespoons Parmesan cheese, salt and pepper.
3. In a 10-in. ovenproof skillet, heat oil over medium-high heat. Add onion; cook and stir until tender. Stir in asparagus and parsley. Pour in egg mixture. Reduce heat to medium; cook, covered, 8-10 minutes or until eggs are nearly set. Uncover; sprinkle with remaining Parmesan cheese.
4. Broil 5-6 in. from heat 2-3 minutes or until eggs are completely set. Sprinkle with cheddar cheese. Cut into quarters.
NOTE *To use whole eggs, omit the egg substitute and use 6 eggs.*
PER SERVING *146 cal., 5 g fat (2 g sat. fat), 8 mg chol., 533 mg sodium, 9 g carb., 2 g fiber, 16 g pro. **Diabetic Exchanges:** 2 lean meat, 1 vegetable, ½ fat.*

Blueberry Muffin French Toast

My 13-year-old daughter and her friends asked for French toast at a sleepover, but we were out of bread. I used muffins instead, and they loved it. Double or triple this recipe for a holiday brunch.

—**BONNIE GEAVARAS-BOOTZ**
SCOTTSDALE, AZ

START TO FINISH: 25 MIN.
MAKES: 6 SERVINGS

- 4 day-old jumbo blueberry muffins
- 3 eggs
- ¾ cup refrigerated French vanilla nondairy creamer
- ¼ teaspoon ground cinnamon
- 3 tablespoons butter
  Confectioners' sugar, optional

1. Trim rounded tops off muffins (save for another use). Cut remaining muffins crosswise into ½-in. slices.
2. In a shallow bowl, whisk eggs, creamer and cinnamon.
3. In a large skillet, heat butter over medium heat. Dip both sides of muffin slices in egg mixture. Place in skillet; toast 2-3 minutes on each side or until golden brown. If desired, dust French toast with confectioners' sugar.

BREAKFAST BUNDLES

SOUTHWEST HASH WITH
ADOBO-LIME CREMA

EAT SMART

Southwest Hash with Adobo-Lime Crema

If you have leftover pulled pork, it's delicious tossed into this satisfying hash. For a bit more decadence, add lime juice and adobo sauce to a traditional hollandaise instead of the sour cream. Perfect for brunch guests!

—BROOKE KELLER LEXINGTON, KY

PREP: 20 MIN. • BAKE: 25 MIN.
MAKES: 4 SERVINGS

- 3 medium sweet potatoes (about 1½ pounds), cubed
- 1 medium onion, chopped
- 1 medium sweet red pepper, chopped
- 1 tablespoon canola oil
- 1 teaspoon garlic powder
- 1 teaspoon smoked paprika
- ¾ teaspoon ground chipotle pepper
- ½ teaspoon salt
- ¼ teaspoon pepper
- ⅔ cup canned black beans, rinsed and drained
- 4 eggs
- ½ cup reduced-fat sour cream
- 2 tablespoons lime juice
- 2 teaspoons adobo sauce
- ½ medium ripe avocado, peeled and sliced, optional
- 2 tablespoons minced fresh cilantro

1. Preheat oven to 400°. Place sweet potatoes, onion and red pepper in a 15x10x1-in. baking pan coated with cooking spray. Drizzle with oil; sprinkle with seasonings. Toss to coat. Roast 25-30 minutes or until potatoes are tender, adding beans during the last 10 minutes of cooking time.
2. Place 2-3 in. of water in a large saucepan or skillet with high sides. Bring to a boil; adjust heat to maintain a gentle simmer. Break cold eggs, one at a time, into a small bowl; holding bowl close to surface of water, slip egg into water.
3. Cook, uncovered, 3-5 minutes or until whites are completely set and yolks begin to thicken but are not hard. Using a slotted spoon, lift eggs out of the water.
4. In a small bowl, mix sour cream, lime juice and adobo sauce. Serve sweet potato mixture with egg, sour cream mixture and, if desired, avocado. Sprinkle with cilantro.

PER SERVING *304 cal., 12 g fat (3 g sat. fat), 222 mg chol., 520 mg sodium, 37 g carb., 6 g fiber, 13 g pro.* **Diabetic Exchanges:** *2 starch, 1½ fat, 1 medium-fat meat.*

FAST FIX

Zucchini Egg Skillet

My neighbor shared more zucchini from his garden than I knew what to do with. But creating new dishes proved to be a delicious, healthy way to give back the fruit of his labor. He loved this recipe. It's great for brunch or a special breakfast.

—DARCY KENNEDY NEW WINDSOR, NY

START TO FINISH: 30 MIN.
MAKES: 4 SERVINGS

- 2 tablespoons olive oil
- 2 medium red potatoes (about 8 ounces), cut into ¼-inch cubes
- 1 medium onion, chopped
- 2 small zucchini, shredded (about 3 cups)
- 4 frozen fully cooked breakfast sausage links, thawed and cut into ½-inch slices
- ½ cup chopped roasted sweet red peppers
- 6 cherry tomatoes, quartered
- ¼ teaspoon salt
- ⅛ teaspoon pepper
- ½ cup shredded cheddar cheese
- 4 eggs

1. In a large skillet, heat oil over medium-high heat. Add potatoes and onion; cook and stir 4-6 minutes or until potatoes are crisp-tender. Stir in zucchini and sausage; cook 4-6 minutes longer or until vegetables are tender.
2. Gently stir in red peppers, tomatoes, salt and pepper; sprinkle with cheese. With back of spoon, make four wells in potato mixture; break an egg into each well. Reduce heat to medium. Cook, covered, 4-6 minutes or until egg whites are completely set and yolks begin to thicken but are not hard.

ZUCCHINI EGG SKILLET

Greek Stuffed Mini Potatoes
PAGE 119

Swift Snacks & Appetizers

When the time is right for light, irresistible bites, turn here for crowd-pleasing appetizers, fabulously cheesy hot dips, crunchy snacks and more. Tide guests over till dinner, serve up after-school delights or make it a meal with a festive array of these simple munchies.

**Tangy Glazed
Meatballs**
PAGE 122

**Herb-Roasted
Olives & Tomatoes**
PAGE 127

**Cranberry-Brie
Tartlets**
PAGE 125

SMOKED SALMON
CHEESE SPREAD

FAST FIX
Island Vacation Party Mix

What's not to love about this taste of the tropics? Because this snack mix uses a simple no-bake method, you'll be munching on it in no time flat.

—MELISSA TALBOTT PEORIA, IL

START TO FINISH: 15 MIN.
MAKES: 3 QUARTS

- 2½ cups Corn Chex
- 2½ cups Rice Chex
- 2 cups macadamia nuts
- ¼ cup butter, cubed
- 2 tablespoons sugar
- 2 tablespoons corn syrup
- 1 cup flaked coconut
- 1 package (6 ounces) chopped dried pineapple
- 1 cup white baking chips

1. In a large microwave-safe bowl, combine cereals and nuts; set aside. In a small microwave-safe bowl, combine the butter, sugar and corn syrup. Microwave, uncovered, on high for 2 minutes, stirring once. Pour over cereal mixture and toss to coat.
2. Cook cereal mixture, uncovered, on high for 2 minutes, stirring once. Add coconut; cook 2 minutes longer, stirring once. Spread onto waxed paper to cool. Stir in pineapple and chips. Store in an airtight container.
NOTE *This recipe was tested in a 1,100-watt microwave.*

ISLAND VACATION
PARTY MIX

FAST FIX
Smoked Salmon Cheese Spread

Pretzels, chips and veggies would all make delicious dippers for this creamy salmon dip. It's wonderful during the holidays with crackers and wine.

—JILL CAMPBELL HUNTSVILLE, TX

START TO FINISH: 15 MIN.
MAKES: 2½ CUPS

- 2 packages (8 ounces each) cream cheese, softened
- 1 package (4 ounces) smoked salmon or lox
- 3 tablespoons horseradish sauce
- 1 tablespoon lemon juice
- 1 tablespoon Worcestershire sauce
- ¼ teaspoon Creole seasoning
- ¼ teaspoon coarsely ground pepper
  Chopped walnuts and snipped fresh dill
  Assorted crackers

Place the first seven ingredients in a food processor; process until blended. Transfer to a serving dish; sprinkle with walnuts and dill. Refrigerate, covered, until serving. Serve with crackers.
NOTE *The following spices may be substituted for 1 teaspoon Creole seasoning: ¼ teaspoon each salt, garlic powder and paprika; and a pinch each of dried thyme, ground cumin and cayenne pepper.*

PORK & CHIVE POT STICKERS

Here's my top make-ahead appetizer. My three kids are old enough to cook these themselves, right from the freezer. The hidden veggies in mine make them better than the restaurant's!

—MARISA RAPONI VAUGHAN, ON

FREEZE IT
Pork & Chive Pot Stickers

PREP: 1 HOUR • **COOK:** 5 MIN./BATCH
MAKES: 5 DOZEN

- 2 medium carrots, finely chopped
- 1 small onion, finely chopped
- ½ cup finely chopped water chestnuts
- ⅓ cup minced fresh chives
- 1 egg white, lightly beaten
- 3 tablespoons reduced-sodium soy sauce
- ½ teaspoon pepper
- 1 pound ground pork
- 60 pot sticker or gyoza wrappers
- 3 tablespoons canola oil, divided
- 1 cup chicken broth, divided
  Additional reduced-sodium soy sauce, optional

1. In a large bowl, combine the first seven ingredients. Add pork; mix lightly but thoroughly. Place a scant tablespoon filling in center of each wrapper. (Keep wrappers covered with a damp paper towel until ready to use.)

2. Moisten wrapper edges with water. Fold wrapper over filling; seal edges, pleating the front side several times to form a pleated pouch. Stand pot stickers on a work surface to flatten bottoms; curve slightly to form crescent shapes, if desired.

3. In a large nonstick skillet, heat 1 tablespoon oil over medium-high heat. Arrange a third of the pot stickers in concentric circles in pan, flat side down; cook 1-2 minutes or until bottoms are golden brown. Carefully add ⅓ cup broth (broth may spatter); reduce heat to medium-low. Cook, covered, 2-3 minutes or until broth is almost absorbed and filling is cooked through.

4. Cook, uncovered, until bottoms are crisp and broth is completely evaporated, about 1 minute. Repeat with remaining oil, pot stickers and broth. If desired, serve with additional soy sauce.

NOTE *Wonton wrappers may be substituted for pot sticker and gyoza wrappers. Stack two or three wonton wrappers on a work surface; cut into circles with a 3½-in. biscuit or round cookie cutter. Fill and wrap as directed.*
FREEZE OPTION *Place uncooked pot stickers on waxed paper-lined baking sheets; freeze until firm. Transfer to resealable plastic freezer bags; return to freezer. To use, cook frozen pot stickers as directed, increasing broth to ½ cup and simmering time to 4-6 minutes when cooking each batch.*

(5) INGREDIENTS
Cheese-Stuffed Jalapenos

A few years ago, I saw a man in the grocery store buying a big bag full of jalapeno peppers. I asked him what he planned to do with them, and he shared this amazing recipe with me right there in the store!

—JANICE MONTIVERDI SUGAR LAND, TX

PREP: 30 MIN. • **BAKE:** 5 MIN.
MAKES: 4 DOZEN

- 24 medium fresh jalapeno peppers
- 1 package (8 ounces) cream cheese, softened
- 3 cups (12 ounces) finely shredded cheddar cheese
- 1½ teaspoons Worcestershire sauce
- 4 bacon strips, cooked and crumbled

1. Cut jalapenos in half lengthwise; remove seeds and membranes. In a large saucepan, boil peppers in water for 5-10 minutes (the longer you boil the peppers, the milder they become). Drain and rinse in cold water; set aside.

2. In a small bowl, beat the cream cheese, cheddar cheese and Worcestershire sauce until smooth. Spoon 2 teaspoonfuls into each jalapeno half; sprinkle with bacon.

3. Place on a greased baking sheet. Bake at 400° for 5-10 minutes or until cheese is melted. Serve warm.

NOTE *Wear disposable gloves when cutting hot peppers; the oils can burn skin. Avoid touching your face.*

(5) INGREDIENTS
Ham & Pickle Wraps

I decided to try this dish with my card club, and they loved it. The recipe can be swapped around and changed in so many different ways, and it always turns out. What an easy, great-tasting centerpiece over a hand of cards.

—DETRA LITTLE MOULTRIE, GA

PREP: 10 MIN. + CHILLING
MAKES: 1 DOZEN

- 2 ounces cream cheese, softened
- 1½ teaspoons spicy ranch salad dressing mix
- 2 slices deli ham
- 2 whole dill pickles

In a small bowl, combine cream cheese and dressing mix. Spread over ham slices. Place a pickle on each ham slice. Roll up tightly; wrap in plastic wrap. Refrigerate for at least 1 hour or until firm. Cut each wrap into six slices.

HAM & PICKLE WRAPS

FAST FIX ▶
Blue Cheese Onion Dip

I decided to tweak the onion soup dip you see at every gathering, and everyone seems to be glad I did. Serve with crisp veggies or potato chips, and you're set.

—**VICKI DESY** TUCSON, AZ

PREP: 10 MIN. + CHILLING
MAKES: 12 SERVINGS (¼ CUP EACH)

- 2 cups (16 ounces) sour cream
- 1 cup (4 ounces) crumbled blue cheese
- ⅔ cup mayonnaise
- 2 tablespoons onion soup mix
- 1 garlic clove, minced
- ⅓ cup chopped walnuts, toasted
  Assorted fresh vegetables

In a small bowl, mix the first five ingredients until blended. Refrigerate, covered, at least 2 hours to allow flavors to blend. Just before serving, top with walnuts. Serve with fresh vegetables.

NOTE *To toast nuts, spread in a 15x10x1-in. baking pan. Bake at 350° for 5-10 minutes or until lightly browned, stirring occasionally. Or, spread in a dry nonstick skillet and heat over low heat until lightly browned, stirring occasionally.*

SESAME CHICKEN BITES

BLUE CHEESE ONION DIP

FAST FIX ▶
Sesame Chicken Bites

These bites have been a party favorite at our house for many years. You can make the sauce the night before so the prep is even easier.

—**KATHY GREEN** LAYTON, NJ

START TO FINISH: 30 MIN.
MAKES: ABOUT 2½ DOZEN (¾ CUP SAUCE)

SAUCE
- ¾ cup mayonnaise
- 4 teaspoons honey
- 1½ teaspoons Dijon mustard

CHICKEN
- ½ cup dry bread crumbs
- ¼ cup sesame seeds
- 2 teaspoons minced fresh parsley
- ½ cup mayonnaise
- 1 teaspoon onion powder
- 1 teaspoon ground mustard
- ¼ teaspoon pepper
- 1 pound boneless skinless chicken breasts, cut into 1-inch cubes
- 2 to 4 tablespoons canola oil

1. In a small bowl, mix sauce ingredients. Refrigerate until serving.
2. In a shallow bowl, mix bread crumbs, sesame seeds and parsley. In a separate shallow bowl, mix mayonnaise and seasonings. Dip chicken in mayonnaise mixture, then in crumb mixture, patting to help coating adhere to all sides.
3. In a large skillet, heat 2 tablespoons oil over medium-high heat. Add chicken in batches; cook until chicken is no longer pink, turning occasionally and adding additional oil as needed. Serve with sauce.

TOP TIP

Instead of cutting these into little bites, I cooked four chicken breast halves for my family as a dinner meal. They loved it! One of their favorites!

—**KNITWIT84** TASTEOFHOME.COM

Greek Stuffed Mini Potatoes

PREP: 25 MIN. • **BAKE:** 45 MIN.
MAKES: 16 APPETIZERS

- 8 **small red potatoes, halved**
- 2 **tablespoons olive oil**
- 1 **tablespoon snipped fresh dill**
- ½ **teaspoon salt**
- ¼ **teaspoon pepper**
- ½ **medium ripe avocado, peeled**
- 16 **marinated quartered artichoke hearts, drained**
- 16 **pitted Greek olives**
- ⅓ **cup crumbled feta cheese**

1. Preheat oven to 350°. Place potatoes in a large bowl. Add oil, dill, salt and pepper; toss to coat. Transfer to a greased 15x10x1-in. baking pan. Roast 40-50 minutes or until tender.
2. Cut avocado half into eight slices; halve crosswise. When cool enough to handle, scoop out 1 tablespoon pulp from each potato half (save for another use). Fill each half with avocado, artichoke, olive and cheese.

> I love this recipe because whether you serve it warm or cold, you can't go wrong. I usually make it ahead of time and serve it chilled with a tzatziki sauce.
> —**DEE GUELCHER** ACWORTH, GA

GREEK STUFFED
MINI POTATOES

WHITE CHOCOLATE
BRIE CUPS

(5) INGREDIENTS FAST FIX ▶

White Chocolate Brie Cups

Try these unique little tarts as an appetizer before a special meal, or save them for a surprisingly different dinner finale. They're sweet, creamy and crunchy—and extremely addictive!

—**ANGELA VITALE** DELAWARE, OH

START TO FINISH: 25 MIN.
MAKES: 15 APPETIZERS

- 1 **package (1.9 ounces) frozen miniature phyllo tart shells**
- 1½ **ounces white baking chocolate, chopped**
- 2 **ounces Brie cheese, chopped**
- ⅓ **cup orange marmalade**
  Kumquat slices, optional

1. Fill each tart shell with chocolate, then cheese. Place on an ungreased baking sheet. Top with marmalade.
2. Bake at 350° for 6-8 minutes or until golden brown. Serve warm. If desired, top with kumquat.

ARTICHOKE &
SPINACH DIP PIZZA

Artichoke & Spinach Dip Pizza

Whenever I happen to have it in my pantry, I swap out garlic oil for regular olive oil. It adds a little something without totally overpowering the toppings.

—SHELLY BEVINGTON HERMISTON, OR

START TO FINISH: 20 MIN.
MAKES: 24 PIECES

- 1 **pre-baked 12-inch pizza crust**
- 1 **tablespoon olive oil**
- 1 **cup spinach dip**
- 1 **cup (4 ounces) shredded part-skim mozzarella cheese**
- 1 **jar (7½ ounces) marinated quartered artichoke hearts, drained**
- ½ **cup oil-packed sun-dried tomatoes, patted dry and chopped**
- ¼ **cup chopped red onion**

1. Preheat oven to 450°. Place crust on an ungreased pizza pan; brush with oil. Spread spinach dip over top. Sprinkle with cheese, artichokes, tomatoes and onion.
2. Bake 8-10 minutes or until cheese is melted and edges are lightly browned. Cut into squares.

EAT SMART FAST FIX

Makeover Cheesy Bean Dip

This reworked version of a party dip favorite has all the great taste of the original, but it contains less fat and fewer calories.

—TASTE OF HOME TEST KITCHEN

START TO FINISH: 30 MIN.
MAKES: 32 SERVINGS
(2 TABLESPOONS EACH)

- 1½ **cups (6 ounces) shredded reduced-fat Mexican cheese blend**
- 1½ **cups (6 ounces) shredded reduced-fat cheddar cheese**
- 1 **can (16 ounces) fat-free refried beans**
- 1 **can (10 ounces) diced tomatoes and green chilies**
- 1 **package (8 ounces) reduced-fat cream cheese, cubed**
- ½ **cup reduced-fat sour cream**
- 1 **tablespoon taco seasoning**
  Tortilla chips and assorted fresh vegetables

1. In a large bowl, combine cheeses; set aside 1 cup for topping. Add the beans, tomatoes, cream cheese, sour cream and taco seasoning to the remaining cheeses; stir until blended. Transfer mixture to a greased 2-qt. baking dish; sprinkle with reserved cheeses.
2. Bake dip, uncovered, at 350° for 20-25 minutes or until bubbly around the edges. Serve warm with tortilla chips and vegetables.
PER SERVING *61 cal., 3 g fat (2 g sat. fat), 10 mg chol., 177 mg sodium, 4 g carb., 1 g fiber, 5 g pro.* **Diabetic Exchanges:** *½ starch, ½ lean meat.*

⑤ INGREDIENTS FAST FIX

Barbecued Chicken Egg Rolls

These egg rolls are delicious and ideal if you're cooking for one or two. You may like to add more barbecue sauce or cheese, depending on your taste. Also enjoy them for dinner alongside garlic mashed potatoes!

—ERIN STROUD STERLING, IL

START TO FINISH: 20 MIN.
MAKES: 2 SERVINGS

- 1 **cup shredded cooked chicken**
- ½ **cup shredded cheddar-Monterey Jack cheese**
- ⅓ **cup honey barbecue sauce**
- 4 **egg roll wrappers**
  Oil for frying

1. In a small bowl, combine the chicken, cheese and barbecue sauce. Place about ¼ cup in the center of each egg roll wrapper. Fold bottom corner over filling; fold sides over filling. Moisten remaining corner with water; roll up tightly to seal.
2. In an electric skillet, heat 1 in. of oil to 375°. Fry egg rolls, two at a time, for 30 seconds on each side or until golden brown. Drain on paper towels. Serve warm.

Pecan-Date Cheese Ball

This lightly sweet cheese ball is great to have on hand when company drops by or if you're just craving something creamy. It's even nice enough to serve at holiday work parties.

—SUE BROYLES CHEROKEE, TX

PREP: 20 MIN. + CHILLING
MAKES: 3½ CUPS (4-INCH BALL)

- 1 **teaspoon ground mustard**
- 1 **teaspoon water**
- 2 **packages (8 ounces each) cream cheese, softened**
- ¼ **cup mayonnaise**
- ¼ **teaspoon ground nutmeg**
- 2 **cups (8 ounces) shredded cheddar cheese**
- 1 **cup chopped dates**
- 1 **cup chopped pecans**
  Crackers

In a small bowl, dissolve the mustard in water; let stand for 10 minutes. In a bowl, beat cream cheese and mayonnaise until smooth. Add nutmeg and mustard mixture. Stir in cheese and dates. Chill for 15 minutes. Shape into a ball; roll in pecans. Chill. Serve with crackers.

BARBECUED CHICKEN EGG ROLLS

> The slightly sweet sauce on these meatballs has such a great zing to it. Use a little more or less hot sauce depending on what you're in the mood for.
>
> —JOHN SLIVON MILTON, FL

TANGY GLAZED MEATBALLS

peaks form. Gradually add sugar, beating until stiff peaks form. Fold in cinnamon and almonds; pour over butter and toss to coat. Bake at 325° for 40 minutes or until almonds are crisp, stirring every 10 minutes.

Smoky Chicken Spread

The unique smoky flavor in this spread comes from smoked almonds. It makes a hearty snack on your favorite crackers.

—MARY BETH WAGNER RIO, WI

PREP: 10 MIN. + CHILLING
MAKES: 4 CUPS

- 3 **cups finely chopped cooked chicken**
- ½ **cup finely chopped celery**
- ½ **cup coarsely chopped smoked almonds**
- ¾ **cup mayonnaise**
- ¼ **cup finely chopped onion**
- 1 **tablespoon honey**
- ½ **teaspoon seasoned salt**
- ⅛ **teaspoon pepper**
  Crackers

In a large bowl, combine the first eight ingredients. Cover and chill for at least 2 hours. Serve with crackers.

FAST FIX
Tangy Glazed Meatballs

START TO FINISH: 25 MIN.
MAKES: ABOUT 5 DOZEN

- 1 **jar (9 ounces) mango chutney**
- ¾ **cup A.1. steak sauce**
- ½ **cup chili sauce**
- ½ **cup ketchup**
- 2 **tablespoons Worcestershire sauce**
- 1 **teaspoon hot pepper sauce**
- 1 **package (32 ounces) frozen fully cooked homestyle meatballs, thawed**

In a large saucepan, mix the first six ingredients; cook and stir over medium heat until blended. Add the meatballs; cook, covered, for 15-20 minutes or until heated through, stirring occasionally.

⑤ INGREDIENTS
Presidential Cinnamon-Glazed Almonds

For his 1993 inauguration, President Bill Clinton ordered a half ton of these sweet and crunchy almonds! They were later nicknamed the president's snack of choice. You and your family will likely find them irresistible as well.

—ALMOND BOARD OF CALIFORNIA

PREP: 10 MIN. • **BAKE:** 40 MIN.
MAKES: 3 CUPS

- ⅓ **cup butter, cubed**
- 2 **egg whites**
  Pinch salt
- 1 **cup sugar**
- 4 **teaspoons ground cinnamon**
- 3 **cups whole almonds**

Place butter in a 15x10x1-in. baking pan. Bake at 325° until melted, about 5-7 minutes. Meanwhile, in a bowl, beat egg whites with salt until soft

SMOKY CHICKEN SPREAD

BACON-CHEESE
APPETIZER PIE

Lightly prick the bottom. Bake at 450° for 8-10 minutes or until lightly browned. Cool slightly.

2. In a large bowl, beat cream cheese until fluffy. Add eggs and milk; beat until smooth. Add cheese, onions, bacon, salt, pepper and cayenne; mix well. Pour into the crust.

3. Bake at 350° for 40-45 minutes or until a knife inserted near the center comes out clean. Cool 20 minutes. Remove sides of pan. Cut into thin slices; serve warm with crackers.

Fresh Vegetable Dip

This cool and creamy dip is a family favorite for snacking. Kids are all smiles while they munch their fresh veggies.
—**DENISE GOEDEKEN** PLATTE CENTER, NE

PREP: 10 MIN. + CHILLING
MAKES: 2¼ CUPS

1½ cups (12 ounces) sour cream
¾ cup mayonnaise
1 tablespoon dried minced onion
1 teaspoon garlic salt
1 teaspoon dill weed
1 teaspoon dried parsley flakes
Dash Worcestershire sauce
Fresh vegetables

In a small bowl, mix the first seven ingredients. Refrigerate, covered, at least 1 hour. Serve with vegetables.

Bacon-Cheese Appetizer Pie

I first made this for an open house several years ago and everybody enjoyed it. Cheesecake is popular in these parts—and this recipe makes it fun to serve as an appetizer instead of the typical dessert.
—**JOANIE ELBOURN** GARDNER, MA

PREP: 25 MIN. • **BAKE:** 40 MIN. + COOLING
MAKES: 20 SERVINGS

Pastry for a single-crust pie
3 packages (8 ounces each) cream cheese, softened
4 eggs, lightly beaten
¼ cup milk
1 cup (4 ounces) shredded Swiss cheese
½ cup sliced green onions
6 bacon strips, cooked and crumbled
½ teaspoon salt
⅛ teaspoon pepper
⅛ teaspoon cayenne pepper
Assorted crackers

1. Roll the pastry into a 13½ in. circle. Fit into the bottom and up the sides of an ungreased 9-in. springform pan.

FRESH VEGETABLE DIP

SHRIMP SPREAD

FAST FIX

Shrimp Spread

This tasty appetizer spread is always a crowd-pleaser. People will never know that you used lower-fat ingredients.
—**NORENE WRIGHT** MANILLA, IN

START TO FINISH: 15 MIN.
MAKES: 20 SERVINGS
(3 TABLESPOONS EACH)

- 1 **package (8 ounces) reduced-fat cream cheese**
- ½ **cup reduced-fat sour cream**
- ¼ **cup reduced-fat mayonnaise**
- 1 **cup seafood cocktail sauce**
- 2 **cups (8 ounces) shredded part-skim mozzarella cheese**
- 1 **can (6 ounces) small shrimp, rinsed and drained**
- 3 **green onions, sliced**
- 1 **medium tomato, finely chopped**
  Sliced Italian bread or assorted crackers

1. In a small bowl, beat the cream cheese, sour cream and mayonnaise until smooth. Spread onto a 12-in. round serving plate; top with cocktail sauce. Sprinkle with cheese, shrimp, onions and tomato.

2. Chill until serving. Serve with bread or crackers.

FREEZE IT (5)**INGREDIENTS** **EAT SMART**

Rosy Applesauce

Each summer I always end up with more rhubarb than I know what to do with, but many rhubarb recipes I find use a lot of sugar. This one relies mostly on fruit to sweeten up the rhubarb instead. I recommend refrigerating the sauce overnight to help the flavors blend.
—**AMY NELSON** WESTON, WI

PREP: 25 MIN. • **COOK:** 25 MIN.
MAKES: 6 CUPS

- 5 **large Red Delicious apples, peeled and finely chopped**
- 4 **cups finely chopped fresh or thawed frozen rhubarb (about 8 stalks)**
- 4 **cups fresh strawberries, hulled and halved**
- ½ **cup sugar**
- ¼ **cup water**
- 1 **teaspoon vanilla extract**

1. In a Dutch oven, bring apples, rhubarb, strawberries, sugar and water to a boil. Reduce heat; simmer, covered, 18-22 minutes or until the fruit is tender, stirring occasionally.

2. Remove from heat; stir in vanilla. If a smoother consistency is desired, cool slightly and, in batches, process in a blender. Serve warm or cold.

FREEZE OPTION *Freeze cooled applesauce in freezer containers. To use, thaw in refrigerator overnight. Serve cold or heat through in a saucepan, stirring occasionally.*

PER (½-CUP) SERVING *93 cal., trace fat (trace sat. fat), 0 chol., 2 mg sodium, 23 g carb., 3 g fiber, 1 g pro.* ***Diabetic Exchanges:*** *1 fruit, ½ starch.*

DID YOU KNOW?

Most vanilla comes from Madagascar and Reunion Island—formerly known as the Bourbon Islands—off the southeast coast of Africa. Bourbon vanilla is celebrated for its strong, clear vanilla flavor and creamy finish.

My family hosts a holiday drop-in each year, and that's where these tartlets made their first appearance. They're easy to make, but they look like a gourmet treat.

—**CINDY DAVIS** BONITA SPRINGS, FL

⑤INGREDIENTS FAST FIX

Cranberry-Brie Tartlets

PREP: 30 MIN. • **BAKE:** 10 MIN.
MAKES: 4 DOZEN

- 2 **tubes (8 ounces each) refrigerated crescent rolls**
- 6 **ounces Brie cheese, rind removed**
- 1 **cup whole-berry cranberry sauce**
- ½ **cup chopped pecans**

1. Preheat oven to 375°. Unroll one tube of crescent dough into one long rectangle; press perforations to seal. Cut into 24 pieces; lightly press each piece onto the bottom and up sides of an ungreased mini-muffin cup. Repeat with remaining crescent dough.
2. Place about 1 rounded teaspoon cheese in each cup; top with cranberry sauce and sprinkle with pecans. Bake 10-15 minutes or until golden brown. Serve warm.

CRANBERRY-BRIE TARTLETS

BACON-PECAN STUFFED MUSHROOMS

FAST FIX

Bacon-Pecan Stuffed Mushrooms

When I had my kitchen remodeled, I lost the recipe for these mushrooms. But I'd shared it so many times, I had no trouble finding someone to "lend" it back to me.
—**BEVERLY PIERCE** INDIANOLA, MS

START TO FINISH: 30 MIN.
MAKES: 1 DOZEN

- 4 **tablespoons butter, divided**
- 2 **tablespoons canola oil**
- 12 **large fresh mushrooms (about 1 pound), stems removed**
- ¼ **teaspoon salt**
- 2 **tablespoons finely chopped onion**
- 1 **cup soft bread crumbs**
- 6 **bacon strips, cooked and crumbled**
- 2 **tablespoons chopped pecans**
- 2 **tablespoons sherry or beef broth**
- 2 **tablespoons sour cream**
- 2 **tablespoons minced fresh chives**

1. Preheat broiler. In a large skillet, heat 2 tablespoons butter and oil over medium-high heat. Add mushroom caps; cook 2 minutes on each side. Sprinkle with salt. Remove with tongs; drain on paper towels, stem side down.
2. In same pan, heat remaining butter over medium-high heat. Add onion; cook and stir until tender. Remove from heat; stir in the remaining ingredients. Spoon into mushroom caps.
3. Place on a broiler pan. Broil 5 in. from heat 2-3 minutes or until filling is browned.
NOTE *To make soft bread crumbs, tear bread into pieces and place in a food processor or blender. Cover and pulse until crumbs form. One slice of bread yields ½ to ¾ cup crumbs.*

FREEZE IT (5) INGREDIENTS EAT SMART

Spicy Applesauce

Every year, we have an apple-picking party and end up with loads of apples. This is one of the recipes I always look forward to making with our harvest.

—MARIAN PLATT SEQUIM, WA

PREP: 25 MIN. • **COOK:** 30 MIN.
MAKES: 8 CUPS

- 5 **pounds tart apples (about 16 medium), peeled and sliced**
- 1 **cup apple juice**
- 1 **teaspoon ground cinnamon**
- ½ **teaspoon ground allspice**
- ½ **teaspoon ground cloves**

In a Dutch oven, combine all ingredients; bring to a boil. Reduce heat; simmer, covered, 25-35 minutes or until apples are tender, stirring occasionally. Remove from heat; mash apples to desired consistency. Serve warm or cold.

FREEZE OPTION *Freeze cooled applesauce in freezer containers. To use, thaw in refrigerator overnight. Serve cold or heat through in a saucepan, stirring occasionally.*

PER (½-CUP) SERVING *94 cal., 1 g fat (trace sat. fat), 0 chol., 1 mg sodium, 24 g carb., 3 g fiber, trace pro.* **Diabetic Exchange:** *1½ fruit.*

CHILAQUILAS APPETIZER

SPICY APPLESAUCE

Chilaquilas Appetizer

I learned how to make this recipe when I was attending high school in California. It's been a family favorite for years.

—JOY FROST WOOD RIVER, IL

PREP: 10 MIN. • **COOK:** 30 MIN.
MAKES: 8-10 SERVINGS

- 1 **pound ground beef**
- 1 **can (16 ounces) chili beans, undrained**
- 1 **can (14½ ounces) diced tomatoes, undrained**
- 1 **can (6 ounces) pitted ripe olives, drained and sliced**
- 6 **green onions, sliced**
- 1 **to 2 tablespoons chili powder**
  Salt and pepper to taste
- 1 **package (20 ounces) tortilla or corn chips**
- 1 **to 2 cups (4 to 8 ounces) shredded cheddar cheese**

1. In a large skillet, cook beef over medium heat until no longer pink; drain. Add the beans, tomatoes, olives, onions, chili powder, salt and pepper.

2. Bring to a boil. Reduce heat; simmer, uncovered, for 20 minutes or until thickened. Arrange chips on a platter; top with meat mixture and sprinkle with cheese.

Basil White Bean Dip

START TO FINISH: 15 MIN.
MAKES: 6 SERVINGS

- 1 **can (15 ounces) white kidney or cannellini beans, rinsed and drained**
- 2 **tablespoons lemon juice**
- 1 **garlic clove, halved**
- ½ **teaspoon salt**
- ⅛ **teaspoon pepper**
- ¼ **cup olive oil**
- 1 **plum tomato, seeded and chopped**
- ⅔ **cup loosely packed basil leaves, coarsely chopped**
  Baked pita chips

Place the first five ingredients in a food processor; pulse until beans are coarsely chopped. Add oil; process until blended. Add the tomato and basil; pulse to combine. Serve with pita chips.

> We're big fans of hummus, but my son is allergic. I came up with a similar dip that uses cannellini beans, and it has turned out to be a great alternative.
> —ERIN BOSCO CARLTON, WA

HERB-ROASTED OLIVES & TOMATOES

Herb-Roasted Olives & Tomatoes

Eat these roasted veggies with a crunchy baguette or a couple of cheeses. You can also double or even triple the amounts and have tasty leftovers to toss with spaghetti the next day.
—ANNDREA BAILEY
HUNTINGTON BEACH, CA

START TO FINISH: 20 MIN.
MAKES: 4 CUPS

- 2 **cups cherry tomatoes**
- 1 **cup garlic-stuffed olives**
- 1 **cup Greek olives**
- 1 **cup pitted ripe olives**
- 8 **garlic cloves, peeled**
- 3 **tablespoons olive oil**
- 1 **tablespoon herbes de Provence**
- ¼ **teaspoon pepper**

Preheat oven to 425°. Combine the first five ingredients on a greased 15x10x1-in. baking pan. Add oil and seasonings; toss to coat. Roast 15-20 minutes or until tomatoes are softened, stirring occasionally.
NOTE *Look for herbes de Provence in the spice aisle.*

TOP TIP

To quickly seed a tomato, cut it into wedges. Swipe your index finger over each wedge to remove the gel pocket and its seeds. Then chop the tomato as desired. This is a nice technique for when you don't need perfectly seeded tomatoes.

BASIL WHITE BEAN DIP

Seafood Soup
PAGE 144

Quick Soups & Sandwiches

For classic mealtime comfort, you just can't beat a big bowlful of soup and a freshly made sandwich. For fiery chili, cool gazpacho, crowd-size heroes and lunch box-friendly wraps—and everything in between—turn here.

Salsa Bean Burgers
PAGE 132

Weeknight Taco Soup
PAGE 155

Summer Sub Sandwich
PAGE 137

FREEZE IT EAT SMART
Turkey Gnocchi Soup

PREP: 15 MIN. • **COOK:** 25 MIN.
MAKES: 6 SERVINGS (2 QUARTS)

- 1 **tablespoon butter**
- 3 **medium carrots, chopped**
- 4 **garlic cloves, minced**
- 6 **cups water**
- 3 **teaspoons reduced-sodium chicken base**
- ¾ **teaspoon Italian seasoning**
- 1 **package (16 ounces) potato gnocchi**
- 2 **cups cubed cooked turkey breast**
- 1 **cup frozen peas**
- ½ **teaspoon pepper**
- ½ **cup shredded Parmesan cheese**

1. In a Dutch oven, heat butter over medium heat. Add carrots; cook and stir 8-10 minutes or until crisp-tender. Add garlic; cook 1 minute longer.

2. Stir in water, chicken base and Italian seasoning; bring to a boil. Add gnocchi. Reduce heat; simmer, uncovered, 3-4 minutes or until gnocchi float. Stir in turkey, peas and pepper; heat through. Top servings with cheese.

FREEZE OPTION *Freeze cooled soup in freezer containers. To use, partially thaw in refrigerator overnight. Heat through in a saucepan, stirring occasionally and adding a little water if necessary.*

PER SERVING *307 cal., 6 g fat (3 g sat. fat), 55 mg chol., 782 mg sodium, 39 g carb., 4 g fiber, 24 g pro.* **Diabetic Exchanges:** *3 lean meat, 2 starch, ½ fat.*

CHICKEN PITA POCKETS

TURKEY GNOCCHI SOUP

While trying to find an interesting use for leftover turkey, we decided to add gnocchi instead of noodles. My 8-year-old daughter always asks for more. If you don't have leftover turkey, a rotisserie chicken works just as well. —**AMY BABINES** VIRGINIA BEACH, VA

FAST FIX
Chicken Pita Pockets

If everybody's hungry and you're crunched for time, reach for pita pockets. Just fill them up and go. Save even more time with chicken tenders.

—**JACQUELINE PARKER**
COLORADO SPRINGS, CO

START TO FINISH: 25 MIN.
MAKES: 6 SERVINGS

- 2 **tablespoons olive oil**
- 1 **teaspoon dried thyme**
- 1 **teaspoon paprika**
- 1 **garlic clove, minced**
- ¾ **teaspoon salt, divided**
- 1½ **pounds boneless skinless chicken breasts, cut into 1-inch strips**
- 1 **package (14 ounces) coleslaw mix**
- ⅔ **cup mayonnaise**
- 12 **whole wheat pita pocket halves**

1. In a large bowl, mix oil, thyme, paprika, garlic and ½ teaspoon salt until blended. Add chicken; toss to coat. Let stand 10 minutes.

2. Meanwhile, in a large bowl, combine coleslaw mix, mayonnaise and remaining salt; spoon into pita halves. Place chicken on an ungreased baking sheet. Broil 3-4 in. from heat 3-4 minutes on each side or until no longer pink. Fill pita pockets with chicken strips.

FREEZE IT
Hearty Beef & Bean Soup

PREP: 15 MIN. • **COOK:** 30 MIN.
MAKES: 10 SERVINGS (4 QUARTS)

- 1 **pound lean ground beef (90% lean)**
- 1 **large onion, chopped**
- 1 **small green pepper, chopped**
- 1 **can (28 ounces) petite diced tomatoes, undrained**
- 1 **can (16 ounces) chili beans, undrained**
- 1 **can (15 ounces) white kidney or cannellini beans, rinsed and drained**
- 1 **can (15 ounces) black beans, rinsed and drained**

HEARTY BEEF & BEAN SOUP

- 1 **package (13½ ounces) beef smoked sausage, sliced**
- 2 **serrano peppers, seeded and chopped**
- 2 **teaspoons chili powder**
- 1 **teaspoon salt**
- 1 **carton (32 ounces) beef broth**
- 2 **cups water**

1. In a Dutch oven, cook beef, onion and green pepper over medium heat 8-10 minutes or until the meat is no longer pink, breaking up beef into crumbles. Drain.
2. Stir in remaining ingredients; bring to a boil. Reduce heat; simmer, uncovered, 15-20 minutes or until flavors are blended.
FREEZE OPTION *Freeze cooled soup in freezer containers. To use, partially thaw in refrigerator overnight. Heat through in a saucepan, stirring occasionally.*

EAT SMART
Shrimp Gazpacho

This refreshing take on the classic chilled tomato soup features shrimp, lime and plenty of avocado.
—TASTE OF HOME TEST KITCHEN

PREP: 15 MIN. + CHILLING
MAKES: 12 SERVINGS (ABOUT 3 QUARTS)

- 6 **cups Spicy Hot V8 juice**
- 2 **cups cold water**
- 1 **pound peeled and deveined cooked shrimp (31-40 per pound)**
- 2 **medium tomatoes, seeded and diced**
- 1 **medium cucumber, seeded and diced**
- 2 **medium ripe avocados, diced**
- ½ **cup lime juice**
- ½ **cup minced fresh cilantro**
- ½ **teaspoon salt**
- ¼ **to ½ teaspoon hot pepper sauce**

In a large bowl, combine all of the ingredients. Cover and refrigerate for 1 hour. Serve cold.
NOTE *This recipe is best served the same day it's made.*
PER SERVING *128 cal., 6 g fat (1 g sat. fat), 57 mg chol., 551 mg sodium, 10 g carb., 2 g fiber, 10 g pro.* **Diabetic Exchanges:** *2 vegetable, 1 lean meat, 1 fat.*

ITALIAN STEAK SANDWICHES

FREEZE IT | FAST FIX ▶
Italian Steak Sandwiches

My sister came up with these quick sandwiches packed with Italian seasonings like basil, oregno and garlic. Add some carrot sticks or a tomato salad for a fantastic lunch in minutes.
—MARIA REGAKIS SAUGUS, MA

START TO FINISH: 15 MIN.
MAKES: 4 SERVINGS

- 2 **tablespoons olive oil**
- 2 **garlic cloves, minced**
- ⅛ **teaspoon crushed red pepper flakes**
- ½ **pound sliced deli roast beef**
- ½ **cup beef broth**
- 2 **tablespoons red wine or additional beef broth**
- 2 **teaspoons dried parsley flakes**
- 2 **teaspoons dried basil**
- ¼ **teaspoon salt**
- ¼ **teaspoon dried oregano**
- ⅛ **teaspoon pepper**
- 4 **sandwich rolls, split**
- 4 **slices provolone cheese**

In a large skillet, heat oil over medium-high heat. Add garlic and pepper flakes; cook and stir 1 minute. Add roast beef, broth, wine and seasonings; heat through. Place beef slices on rolls; drizzle with the broth mixture. Top with cheese.
FREEZE OPTION *Freeze cooled meat mixture and juices in freezer container. To use, partially thaw in refrigerator overnight. Heat through in a saucepan, stirring occasionally and adding a little broth if necessary.*

SALSA BEAN BURGERS

Turkey & Noodle Tomato Soup

START TO FINISH: 25 MIN.
MAKES: 6 SERVINGS (2 QUARTS)

- 1 pound ground turkey
- 1 envelope reduced-sodium onion soup mix
- 1 package (3 ounces) beef ramen noodles
- 1½ teaspoons sugar
- ¾ teaspoon pepper
- ¼ teaspoon salt
- 1 bottle (46 ounces) reduced-sodium V8 juice
- 1 package (16 ounces) frozen mixed vegetables

1. In a Dutch oven, cook turkey over medium heat 6-8 minutes or until no longer pink, breaking into crumbles; drain. Stir in soup mix, 1½ teaspoons seasoning from the noodles, sugar, pepper and salt. Add V8 juice and vegetables; bring to a boil. Reduce heat; simmer, uncovered, 5 minutes.

2. Break noodles into small pieces; add to soup (discard remaining seasoning or save for another use). Cook 3-5 minutes longer or until the noodles are tender, stirring soup occasionally.

FREEZE OPTION *Freeze cooled soup in freezer containers. To use, partially thaw in refrigerator overnight. Heat through in a saucepan, stirring occasionally and adding a little reduced-sodium broth or water if necessary.*

TOP TIP

Easily upgrade instant ramen by stirring in some peanut butter, chopped green onion or sliced boiled egg. Or stir a beaten egg into ramen during the last 30 seconds of cooking. Cook and stir until egg is firm.

EAT SMART
Salsa Bean Burgers

I came up with these based on a turkey burger recipe because I wanted to make them even healthier. Don't skimp on salsa, and be sure to use your favorite, since it's such an important part of the recipe.
—**JENNY LEIGHTY** WEST SALEM, OH

PREP: 15 MIN. + CHILLING • **COOK:** 10 MIN.
MAKES: 4 SERVINGS

- 1 can (15 ounces) black beans, rinsed and drained
- ¾ cup panko (Japanese) bread crumbs
- 1 cup salsa, divided
- 1 egg, lightly beaten
- 2 tablespoons minced fresh cilantro
- 1 garlic clove, minced
- 2 teaspoons canola oil
- 4 whole wheat hamburger buns, split

1. In a large bowl, mash beans. Mix in bread crumbs, ½ cup salsa, egg, cilantro and garlic. Shape bean mixture into four patties; refrigerate 30 minutes.

2. In a large skillet, heat oil over medium heat. Cook burgers 3-5 minutes on each side or until a thermometer reads 160°. Serve on buns with remaining salsa.

PER SERVING *299 cal., 6 g fat (1 g sat. fat), 53 mg chol., 696 mg sodium, 49 g carb., 8 g fiber, 12 g pro.* **Diabetic Exchanges:** *3 starch, 1 lean meat, ½ fat.*

Turn V8 juice, ramen and frozen veggies into a wonderful soup that really satisfies. I like to serve it with biscuits.
—**JENNIFER BRIDGES** LOS ANGELES, CA

TURKEY & NOODLE TOMATO SOUP

MUSHROOM TORTELLINI SOUP

Tomato Bisque

A rich and satisfying bisque is perfect for winter weather. I love to serve it with a slice of homemade bread.

—B.B. MALLORY IRVING, TX

PREP: 25 MIN. • **COOK:** 35 MIN.
MAKES: 8 SERVINGS (2 QUARTS)

- 2 **cans (14½ ounces each) diced tomatoes, undrained**
- 2 **teaspoons beef bouillon granules**
- 1 **tablespoon sugar**
- 1 to 2 **teaspoons salt**
- 1 **teaspoon onion powder**
- 1 **bay leaf**
- ¼ **teaspoon dried basil**
- ¼ **teaspoon white pepper**
- ½ **cup butter, cubed**
- ⅓ **cup all-purpose flour**
- 4 **cups milk**

1. In a saucepan, combine the first eight ingredients; bring to a boil. Reduce heat; simmer, uncovered, for 30 minutes.

2. Discard bay leaf; press mixture through a sieve and set aside. In a large saucepan, melt butter over medium heat; stir in flour until smooth. Gradually stir in milk. Bring to a boil, stirring constantly; cook and stir for 2 minutes. Reduce heat. Gradually stir in tomato mixture and heat through.

TOMATO BISQUE

FAST FIX
Mushroom Tortellini Soup

This nutritious veggie soup is practically a meal thanks to the cheese tortellini. It's a real comfort on a cold or rainy day.

—JEN LUCAS BALDWINVILLE, MA

START TO FINISH: 25 MIN.
MAKES: 6 SERVINGS

- 2 **tablespoons olive oil**
- ½ **pound sliced fresh mushrooms**
- 2 **garlic cloves, minced**
- 4 **cups vegetable broth**
- 1 **can (14½ ounces) diced tomatoes with basil, oregano and garlic, undrained**
- 1 **package (19 ounces) frozen cheese tortellini**
- 2 **cups fresh baby spinach, coarsely chopped**
- ⅛ **teaspoon pepper**
  Shredded Parmesan cheese, optional

1. In a Dutch oven, heat oil over medium-high heat. Add mushrooms; cook and stir until tender. Add garlic; cook 1 minute longer.

2. Add broth and tomatoes; bring to a boil. Add tortellini; cook, uncovered, 3-4 minutes or just until tortellini float (do not boil). Stir in spinach and pepper; cook just until spinach is wilted. If desired, serve with cheese.

SMOKED GOUDA VEGGIE MELT

Smoked Gouda Veggie Melt

After a long day of teaching, I like to make these open-faced sandwiches. My 8-year-old daughter is a big fan, too.

—**CHARLIE HERZOG** WEST BROOKFIELD, VT

START TO FINISH: 25 MIN.
MAKES: 4 SERVINGS

- 1 cup chopped fresh mushrooms
- 1 cup chopped fresh broccoli
- 1 medium sweet red pepper, chopped
- 1 small onion, chopped
- 2 tablespoons olive oil
- 8 slices Italian bread (½ inch thick)
- ½ cup mayonnaise
- 1 garlic clove, minced
- 1 cup (4 ounces) shredded smoked Gouda cheese

1. Preheat oven to 425°. Place mushrooms, broccoli, pepper and onion in a greased 15x10x1-in. baking pan. Drizzle with oil; toss to coat. Roast 10-12 minutes or until tender.
2. Meanwhile, place bread slices on a baking sheet. Mix mayonnaise and garlic; spread over bread slices.
3. Change oven setting to broil. Spoon vegetables over bread slices; sprinkle with cheese. Broil 3-4 in. from heat 2-3 minutes or until cheese is melted.

Turkey Pitas with Creamy Slaw

Pack these easy pockets for school, work or a weekend picnic—or just enjoy them at home. Toss in some red bell pepper for added crunch.

—*TASTE OF HOME* TEST KITCHEN

START TO FINISH: 10 MIN.
MAKES: 4 SERVINGS

- 3 cups coleslaw mix
- ¼ cup golden raisins
- 3 tablespoons chopped red onion
- ⅓ cup reduced-fat mayonnaise
- 3 tablespoons mango chutney
- 8 pita pocket halves
- ½ pound sliced deli turkey
- 8 pieces ready-to-serve fully cooked bacon, warmed
- 1 medium cucumber, thinly sliced

In a large bowl, combine coleslaw mix, raisins and onion. Add mayonnaise and chutney; toss to coat. Line pita halves with turkey, bacon and cucumber; fill with coleslaw mixture.

Broccoli-Chicken Rice Soup

I transformed leftover chicken and rice into this tasty soup. It even passed the company test.

—**KAREN REED** MIDDLETOWN, OH

START TO FINISH: 30 MIN.
MAKES: 6 SERVINGS (2½ QUARTS)

- 4 cups whole milk
- 2 cans (14½ ounces each) chicken broth
- 1 envelope ranch salad dressing mix
- 2 cups fresh broccoli florets
- ½ pound process cheese (Velveeta), cubed
- 3 cups cooked rice
- 2 cups cubed cooked chicken

In a Dutch oven, combine milk, broth and dressing mix; bring to a boil. Add broccoli; cook, uncovered, 3-5 minutes or until tender. Stir in the process cheese until melted. Add rice and chicken; heat through, stirring soup occasionally.

GRAND PRIZE

FREEZE IT
Moroccan Apple Beef Stew

I love the mix of sweet and savory flavors in this stew. It's the perfect blend of adventurous and comforting, and it makes a fun dish to share with guests.

—**TRISHA KRUSE** EAGLE, ID

PREP: 20 MIN. • **COOK:** 2 HOURS
MAKES: 8 SERVINGS (2 QUARTS)

- 1¼ teaspoons salt
- ½ teaspoon ground cinnamon
- ½ teaspoon pepper
- ¼ teaspoon ground allspice
- 2½ pounds beef stew meat, cut into 1-inch pieces
- 2 to 3 tablespoons olive oil
- 1 large onion, chopped (about 2 cups)
- 3 garlic cloves, minced
- 1 can (15 ounces) tomato sauce
- 1 can (14½ ounces) beef broth
- 1 cup pitted dried plums, coarsely chopped
- 1 tablespoon honey
- 2 medium Fuji or Gala apples, peeled and cut into 1½-inch pieces
  Hot cooked rice or couscous, optional

1. Mix salt, cinnamon, pepper and allspice; sprinkle over beef and toss to coat. In a Dutch oven, heat 2 tablespoons oil over medium heat. Brown beef in batches, adding additional oil as necessary. Remove beef with a slotted spoon.
2. Add onion to same pan; cook and stir 6-8 minutes or until tender. Add garlic; cook 1 minute longer. Stir in tomato sauce, broth, dried plums and honey. Return beef to pan; bring to a boil. Reduce heat; simmer, covered, 1½ hours.
3. Add apples; cook, covered, 30-45 minutes longer or until beef and apples are tender. Skim fat. If desired, serve stew with rice.
FREEZE OPTION *Freeze cooled stew in freezer containers. To use, partially thaw in refrigerator overnight. Heat through in a saucepan, stirring occasionally and adding a little broth if necessary.*

MOROCCAN APPLE BEEF STEW

WEST COAST
SNAPPY JOES

Meet my California-inspired sloppy joe.
Load it up with whatever taco toppings
you like. It's also incredible served over mac
and cheese.
—**DEVON DELANEY** WESTPORT, CT

FREEZE IT | **EAT SMART** | **FAST FIX**
West Coast Snappy Joes

START TO FINISH: 30 MIN.
MAKES: 6 SERVINGS

- 1 **pound lean ground beef (90% lean)**
- 1 **medium onion, chopped**
- 1 **garlic clove, minced**
- 1 **can (8 ounces) tomato sauce**
- ⅓ **cup soft sun-dried tomato halves (not packed in oil), chopped**
- ⅓ **cup chopped roasted sweet red peppers**
- 2 **tablespoons chopped pickled jalapeno peppers**
- 2 **tablespoons tomato paste**
- 1 **tablespoon brown sugar**
- 1 **tablespoon balsamic vinegar**
- ½ **teaspoon Montreal steak seasoning**
- ½ **teaspoon pepper**
- 6 **hamburger buns, split**
  Optional toppings: chopped avocado, sour cream, shredded cheddar cheese and chopped green onions

1. In a large skillet, cook beef, onion and garlic over medium heat 6-8 minutes or until beef is no longer pink, breaking up meat into crumbles; drain.
2. Stir in tomato sauce, sun-dried tomatoes, roasted peppers, jalapenos, tomato paste, brown sugar, vinegar, steak seasoning and pepper. Bring to a boil. Reduce heat; simmer, uncovered, 4-6 minutes or until thickened, stirring occasionally. Serve on buns with toppings as desired.

NOTE *This recipe was tested with sun-dried tomatoes that are ready to use without soaking. When using other sun-dried tomatoes that are not oil-packed, cover with boiling water and let stand until soft. Drain tomatoes before using.*

FREEZE OPTION *Freeze cooled meat mixture in freezer containers. To use, partially thaw in refrigerator overnight. Heat through in a saucepan, stirring occasionally and adding a little water if necessary.*

PER SERVING *288 cal., 8 g fat (3 g sat. fat), 47 mg chol., 575 mg sodium, 32 g carb., 3 g fiber, 20 g pro.* **Diabetic Exchanges:** *2 starch, 2 lean meat.*

Comforting Beef Stew

The aroma of slow-simmered stew that's loaded with root vegetables just says fall comfort food to me. Even my toddlers love this dish!
—**COURTNEY PERCY** BROOKSVILLE, FL

PREP: 20 MIN. • **COOK:** 2½ HOURS
MAKES: 6 SERVINGS

- 2 **pounds beef stew meat**
- 1 **teaspoon salt**
- ¾ **teaspoon pepper**
- 3 **tablespoons canola oil**
- 1 **tablespoon butter**
- 1 **medium onion, chopped**
- 2 **garlic cloves, minced**
- ¼ **cup tomato paste**
- 4 **cups beef broth**
- 3 **tablespoons all-purpose flour**
- 3 **tablespoons water**
- 5 **medium carrots, cut into ½-inch pieces**
- 3 **medium turnips, peeled and cubed**
- 2 **tablespoons minced fresh parsley**

1. Sprinkle beef with salt and pepper. In a Dutch oven, heat oil over medium-high heat. Brown beef in batches. Remove with a slotted spoon.
2. In same pan, heat butter over medium heat. Add onion; cook and stir 2-3 minutes or until tender. Add garlic; cook 1 minute longer. Stir in tomato paste. Gradually stir in broth until blended. Return beef to pan; bring to a boil. Reduce heat; simmer, covered, 1½ hours.
3. In a small bowl, mix flour and water until smooth; gradually stir into stew. Add carrots and turnips; cook, covered, 30-40 minutes longer or until stew is thickened and beef and vegetables are tender. Stir in parsley.

COMFORTING
BEEF STEW

SUMMER SUB SANDWICH

FAST FIX ▶

Summer Sub Sandwich

We were raised in the Northeast, so we've always loved submarine sandwiches. I put together this hearty ham and cheese combo as a nod to our roots. It's good either hot or cold, and it's so quick to make.
—**JENNIFER BECK** CONCORD, OH

START TO FINISH: 15 MIN.
MAKES: 4 SERVINGS

- 1 loaf (1 pound) unsliced French bread
- 3 ounces cream cheese, softened
- ½ pound sliced deli ham
- 6 slices provolone cheese
- 1 jar (4 ounces) sliced mushrooms, drained
- 1½ cups shredded lettuce
- 2 medium tomatoes, thinly sliced
- 1 small onion, thinly sliced
- 2 banana peppers, thinly sliced

1. Split bread lengthwise; spread bread bottom with cream cheese and layer with ham, provolone cheese and mushrooms. Replace top. Cut sandwich crosswise in half.
2. On a microwave-safe plate, microwave each half, covered, on high for 15-30 seconds or until cheese is melted. Remove bread tops and layer with lettuce, tomatoes, onion and peppers. Close sandwiches; cut each in half.
NOTE *This recipe was tested in a 1,100-watt microwave.*

EAT SMART
Turkey-Sweet Potato Soup

This satisfying soup has all the heartwarming flavors and nostalgic feel of the holiday season. It makes the whole house smell cozy.
—**RADINE KELLOGG** FAIRVIEW, IL

PREP: 20 MIN. • **COOK:** 30 MIN.
MAKES: 4 SERVINGS

- 2 medium sweet potatoes, peeled and cubed
- 2 cups water
- 2 teaspoons sodium-free chicken bouillon granules
- 1 can (14¾ ounces) cream-style corn
- 1 tablespoon minced fresh sage
- ¼ teaspoon pepper
- 1 tablespoon cornstarch
- 1 cup 2% milk
- 2 cups cubed cooked turkey breast

1. In a large saucepan, combine potatoes, water and bouillon; bring to a boil. Reduce heat; cook, covered, 10-15 minutes or until the potatoes are tender.
2. Stir in corn, sage and pepper; heat through. In a small bowl, mix the cornstarch and milk until smooth; stir into soup. Bring to a boil; cook and stir 1-2 minutes or until thickened. Stir in turkey; heat through.
PER SERVING *275 cal., 3 g fat (1 g sat. fat), 65 mg chol., 374 mg sodium, 39 g carb., 3 g fiber, 26 g pro.* **Diabetic Exchanges:** *3 lean meat, 2½ starch.*

TOP TIPS

I thickened this recipe a little bit by adding less liquid, then placed a crust on top and baked it like a potpie. It was a big hit!
—**ASKFOR SECONDS** TASTEOFHOME.COM

I added a little butter since I didn't have 2% milk and used skim instead. I also used fresh rosemary instead of the sage. It was very yummy!
—**COOGIRL80** TASTEOFHOME.COM

TURKEY-SWEET POTATO SOUP

DILLED SEAFOOD
SALAD SANDWICHES

Hearty Sausage Minestrone

As a teacher, I appreciate quick and easy recipes. If I make this for just my husband and me, we have leftovers for lunches. But when there are more people at the table, every bit of it disappears.

—**TAMI STOUDT** EVANS, CO

START TO FINISH: 30 MIN.
MAKES: 8 SERVINGS (3½ QUARTS)

- 1 **pound bulk Italian sausage**
- 1 **medium onion, chopped**
- 2 **celery ribs, chopped**
- 2 **medium carrots, chopped**
- 3 **cans (14½ ounces each) diced tomatoes with basil, oregano and garlic, undrained**
- 2 **cans (16 ounces each) kidney beans, rinsed and drained**
- 2 **cans (14½ ounces each) chicken broth**
- ¼ **teaspoon garlic powder**
- ¼ **teaspoon pepper**
- 1 **cup ditalini or other small pasta**

1. In a Dutch oven, cook sausage, onion, celery and carrots over medium heat 8-10 minutes or until sausage is no longer pink and onion is tender, breaking up sausage into crumbles; drain.

2. Stir in tomatoes, beans, broth, garlic powder and pepper; bring to a boil. Add pasta; cook, covered, 6-8 minutes or until pasta is tender.

FREEZE OPTION *Freeze cooled minestrone in freezer containers. To use, partially thaw in refrigerator overnight. Heat through in a saucepan, stirring occasionally and adding a little broth if necessary.*

HEARTY SAUSAGE
MINESTRONE

Dilled Seafood Salad Sandwiches

Living in California, we fell in love with a local deli's seafood salad. After we moved away, I went to work re-creating it.

—**TANNA RICHARD** CEDAR RAPIDS, IA

START TO FINISH: 15 MIN.
MAKES: 4 SERVINGS

- 8 **ounces imitation crabmeat (flake-style)**
- ⅔ **cup reduced-fat mayonnaise**
- 1 **can (2¼ ounces) sliced ripe olives, drained**
- 1 **celery rib, chopped**
- 2 **green onions, chopped**
- 1 **tablespoon snipped fresh dill**
- 1 **tablespoon lemon juice**
- ¾ **teaspoon salt**
- ½ **teaspoon sugar**
- ½ **teaspoon garlic powder**
- ½ **teaspoon lemon-pepper seasoning**
- 4 **whole wheat hamburger buns, split**

In a small bowl, mix the first 11 ingredients, breaking up crab into bite-size pieces. Serve on buns.

I recently made this recipe for one of my cooking classes, and the students loved that they could have a taste of Greece on a budget. I like to serve it with kale chips on the side. —KIZMET BYRD FORT WAYNE, IN

WARM GREEK
CHICKEN WRAPS

FAST FIX
Warm Greek
Chicken Wraps

START TO FINISH: 20 MIN.
MAKES: 6 SERVINGS

- 2½ cups frozen grilled chicken breast strips
- 1 cup (4 ounces) crumbled feta cheese
- 1 small sweet red pepper, chopped
- ½ cup soft sun-dried tomato halves (not packed in oil), chopped
- ½ cup fat-free zesty Italian salad dressing
- ½ cup chopped ripe olives
- 2 cups fresh baby spinach
- 6 whole wheat tortillas (8 inches), warmed

1. Prepare chicken according to package directions. Cut chicken into ½-in. pieces; place in a large bowl. Add cheese, red pepper, tomatoes, salad dressing and olives; toss to combine.

2. Place spinach down center of tortillas; top with chicken mixture. Roll up tightly and serve.

FREEZE IT
Apple Squash Soup

I add a little ginger and sage to apples and squash to make this creamy soup. My family loves it when autumn rolls around.
—CRYSTAL RALPH-HAUGHN
BARTLESVILLE, OK

PREP: 10 MIN. • **COOK:** 35 MIN.
MAKES: 5 SERVINGS

- 2 tablespoons butter
- 1 large onion, chopped
- ½ teaspoon rubbed sage
- 1 can (14½ ounces) chicken or vegetable broth
- 2 medium tart apples, peeled and finely chopped
- ¾ cup water
- 1 package (12 ounces) frozen cooked winter squash, thawed
- 1 teaspoon ground ginger
- ½ teaspoon salt
- ½ cup fat-free milk

1. In a large saucepan, heat butter over medium-high heat. Add onion and sage; cook and stir 2-4 minutes or until tender. Add broth, apples and water; bring to a boil. Reduce heat; simmer, covered, 12 minutes.

2. Add squash, ginger and salt; return to a boil. Reduce heat; simmer mixture, uncovered, for 10 minutes to allow flavors to blend. Remove from heat; cool slightly.

3. Process in batches in a blender until smooth; return to pan. Add milk; heat through, stirring occasionally (do not allow to boil).

FREEZE OPTION *Freeze cooled soup in freezer containers. To use, partially thaw in refrigerator overnight. Heat through in a saucepan, stirring occasionally and adding a little broth if necessary.*

For these wraps, I combined a traditional Southern appetizer of jam and cream cheese on crackers with the turkey sandwiches we ate at my bridal luncheon. I like to sneak fresh baby spinach into all sorts of recipes because it has such a nice crunch and fresh flavor.

—KIM BEAVERS NORTH AUGUSTA, SC

⑤INGREDIENTS | **EAT SMART** | **FAST FIX**
Turkey & Apricot Wraps

START TO FINISH: 15 MIN.
MAKES: 4 SERVINGS

- ½ cup reduced-fat cream cheese
- 3 tablespoons apricot preserves
- 4 whole wheat tortillas (8 inches), room temperature
- ½ pound sliced reduced-sodium deli turkey
- 2 cups fresh baby spinach or arugula

In a small bowl, mix cream cheese and preserves. Spread about 2 tablespoons over each tortilla to within ½ in. of edges. Layer with turkey and spinach. Roll up tightly; wrap in plastic wrap. Refrigerate until serving.

TURKEY & APRICOT WRAPS

PER SERVING *312 cal., 10 g fat (4 g sat. fat), 41 mg chol., 655 mg sodium, 33 g carb., 2 g fiber, 20 g pro.* **Diabetic Exchanges:** *2 starch, 2 lean meat, 1 fat.*

FREEZE IT | **EAT SMART**
Guilt-Free Chicken Chili
This lightened-up chili is a keeper. Make it on Sunday and you get lunch for the rest of the week, too.

—AMY CHALMERS POUGHKEEPSIE, NY

PREP: 20 MIN. • **COOK:** 25 MIN.
MAKES: 8 SERVINGS

- 1 pound lean ground chicken
- 1 medium onion, chopped
- 1 medium sweet red pepper, chopped
- 4 garlic cloves, minced
- 2 cans (15 ounces each) pinto beans, rinsed and drained
- 1 can (28 ounces) diced tomatoes, undrained
- 1 cup water
- 1 tablespoon tomato paste
- 2 tablespoons baking cocoa
- 2 tablespoons chili powder
- 1 tablespoon ground cumin
- ½ teaspoon coarsely ground pepper
- ¼ teaspoon salt
- 4 cups hot cooked brown rice
  Optional toppings: Greek yogurt, reduced-fat shredded cheddar cheese and/or sliced jalapeno peppers

1. In a Dutch oven, cook chicken, onion, red pepper and garlic over medium heat 6-8 minutes or until chicken is no longer pink and vegetables are tender, breaking up chicken into crumbles; drain.
2. Add the beans, tomatoes, water, tomato paste, cocoa and seasonings. Bring to a boil. Reduce heat; simmer, uncovered, 15-20 minutes or until flavors are blended.
3. Serve with rice and, if desired, toppings of your choice.
FREEZE OPTION *Freeze cooled chili in freezer containers. To use, partially thaw in refrigerator overnight. Heat through in a saucepan, stirring occasionally and adding a little water or reduced-sodium broth if necessary. Serve with brown rice and toppings as directed.*

PER SERVING *326 cal., 5 g fat (1 g sat. fat), 41 mg chol., 411 mg sodium, 50 g carb., 10 g fiber, 21 g pro.*

FREEZE IT | **EAT SMART** | **FAST FIX**
Buffalo Turkey Burgers
Celery and blue cheese dressing help tame the hot sauce in these juicy burgers. For an even lighter version, pass on the buns and serve with lettuce leaves, sliced onion and chopped tomato.

—MARY PAX-SHIPLEY BEND, OR

START TO FINISH: 25 MIN.
MAKES: 4 SERVINGS

- 2 tablespoons Louisiana-style hot sauce, divided
- 2 teaspoons ground cumin
- 2 teaspoons chili powder
- 2 garlic cloves, minced
- ½ teaspoon salt
- ⅛ teaspoon pepper
- 1 pound lean ground turkey
- 4 whole wheat hamburger buns, split
- 1 cup shredded lettuce
- 2 celery ribs, chopped
- 2 tablespoons fat-free blue cheese salad dressing

1. In a large bowl, combine 1 tablespoon hot sauce, cumin, chili powder, garlic, salt and pepper. Add turkey; mix lightly but thoroughly. Shape into four ½-in.-thick patties.
2. In a large nonstick skillet coated with cooking spray, cook burgers over medium heat 4-6 minutes on each side or until a thermometer reads 165°.
3. Serve burgers on buns with lettuce, celery, salad dressing and remaining hot sauce.
FREEZE OPTION *Place patties on a plastic wrap-lined baking sheet; wrap and freeze until firm. Remove from pan and transfer to a large resealable plastic bag; return to freezer. To use, cook frozen patties as directed, increasing time as necessary for a thermometer to read 165°.*

PER SERVING *312 cal., 12 g fat (3 g sat. fat), 90 mg chol., 734 mg sodium, 28 g carb., 5 g fiber, 24 g pro.* **Diabetic Exchanges:** *3 lean meat, 2 starch, ½ fat.*

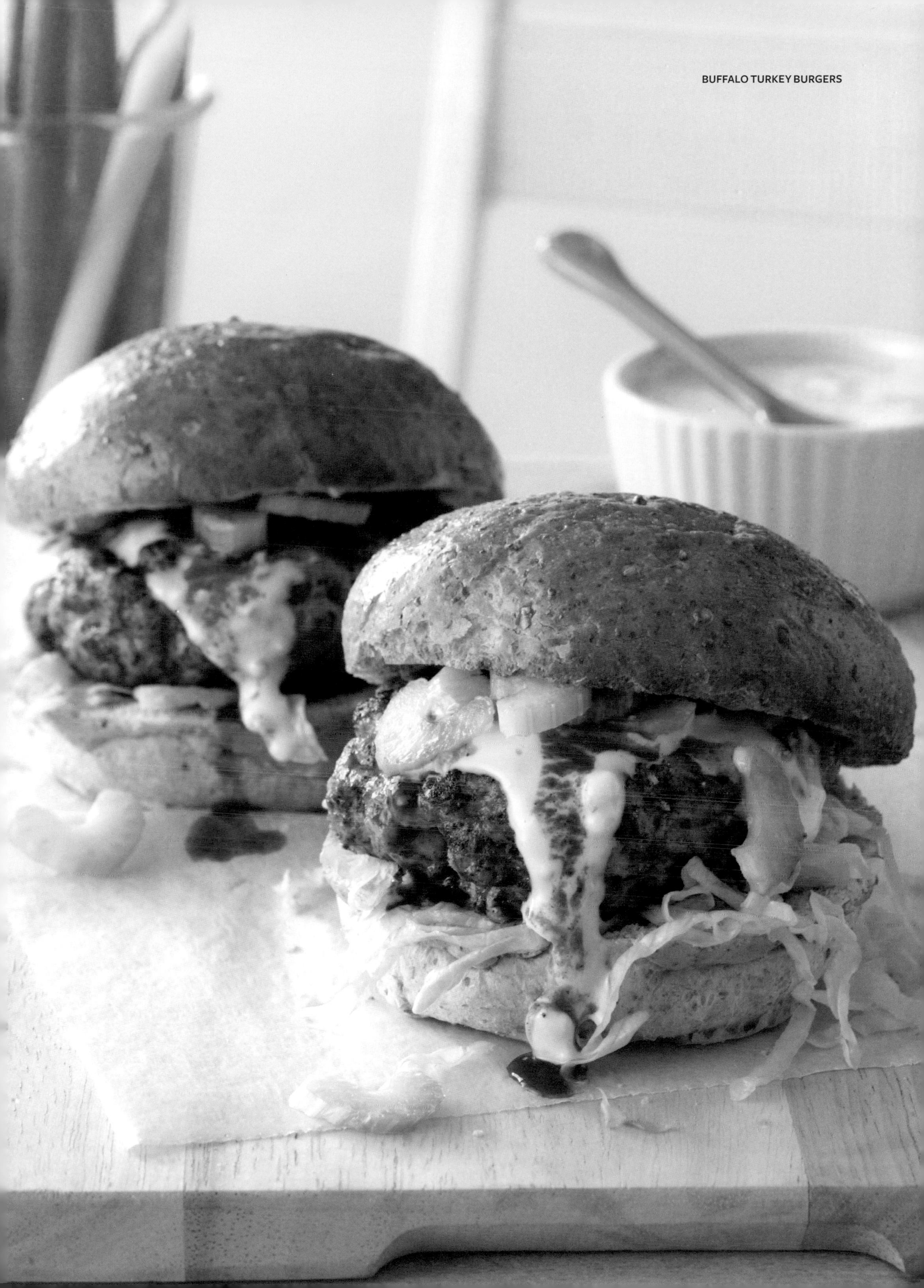

I made a pot of this soup when visiting my sister and her family. Now I bring it along when I stop by, or I pack up a few containers for my nephew, who appreciates a home-cooked meal while he's away at college. —**TIFFANY IHLE** BRONX, NY

**SAUSAGE, KALE &
LENTIL STEW**

FREEZE IT
Sausage, Kale &
Lentil Stew

PREP: 15 MIN. • **COOK:** 45 MIN.
MAKES: 6 SERVINGS (2 QUARTS)

- 1 **pound bulk pork sausage**
- 10 **baby carrots, chopped (about ¾ cup)**
- 1 **small onion, finely chopped**
- 4 **garlic cloves, minced**
- 4 **plum tomatoes, halved**
- ¾ **cup roasted sweet red peppers**
- 1 **cup dried lentils, rinsed**
- 2 **cans (14½ ounces each) vegetable broth**
- 1 **bay leaf**
- ½ **teaspoon ground cumin**
- ¼ **teaspoon pepper**
- 2 **cups coarsely chopped fresh kale**

1. In a Dutch oven, cook sausage, carrots and onion over medium-high heat 8-10 minutes or until sausage is no longer pink, breaking up sausage into crumbles. Stir in garlic; cook 2 minutes longer. Drain.

2. Place tomatoes and red peppers in a food processor; process until finely chopped. Add to sausage mixture; stir in lentils, broth and seasonings. Bring mixture to a boil. Reduce heat and simmer, covered, for 20 minutes, stirring occasionally.

3. Stir in kale; cook 10-15 minutes longer or until lentils and kale are tender. Remove bay leaf.

FREEZE OPTION *Freeze cooled stew in freezer containers. To use, partially thaw in refrigerator overnight. Heat through in a saucepan, stirring occasionally.*

DID YOU KNOW?

Kale is a member of the cabbage family. The nutritious greens require long cooking to become tender. You can substitute collards, the leaves from Swiss chard or mustard greens.

FAST FIX ▶
Quick Taco Wraps

I was running late one night, so I shopped in my own fridge and came up with these taco wraps. Everyone at the table was happy.

—**KATIE MITSCHELEN** LA PORTE, IN

START TO FINISH: 15 MIN.
MAKES: 4 SERVINGS

- ½ **cup cream cheese, softened**
- ¼ **cup canned chopped green chilies**
- ¼ **cup sour cream**
- 2 **tablespoons taco seasoning**
- ½ **cup bean dip**
- 4 **flour tortillas (10 inches)**
- ½ **cup guacamole dip**
- 1 **small onion, chopped**
- 1 **small sweet red pepper, chopped**
- ½ **cup shredded cheddar cheese**
- 1 **can (2¼ ounces) sliced ripe olives, drained**

1. In a small bowl, beat cream cheese until smooth. Stir in green chilies, sour cream and taco seasoning.
2. Spread bean dip over tortillas to within ½ in. of edges. Layer with guacamole dip, cream cheese mixture, onion, pepper, cheese and olives. Roll up tightly and serve.

QUICK TACO WRAPS

EAT SMART   FAST FIX ▶
Asian-Style Turkey Pitas

A neighbor gave me this recipe years ago. It's been my most popular day-after turkey dish ever since.

—**BEVERLY GRAML** YORKTOWN, VA

START TO FINISH: 20 MIN.
MAKES: 4 SERVINGS

- 1 **tablespoon canola oil**
- 1 **medium sweet red pepper, julienned**
- 3 **green onions, sliced**
- 3 **garlic cloves, minced**
- ½ **teaspoon cornstarch**
- ½ **to 1 teaspoon curry powder**
- ¼ **teaspoon cayenne pepper**
- ⅓ **cup water**
- 2 **tablespoons reduced-sodium soy sauce**
- 1 **tablespoon honey**
- 1 **teaspoon sesame oil**
- 3 **cups shredded cooked turkey**
- 8 **whole wheat pita pocket halves**

1. In a large nonstick skillet, heat canola oil over medium-high heat. Add red pepper and green onions; cook and stir until tender. Add garlic; cook 2 minutes longer.
2. Sprinkle with cornstarch, curry powder and cayenne; stir until blended. Stir in water, soy sauce, honey and sesame oil. Add turkey; bring to a boil. Cook and stir 1-2 minutes or until slightly thickened. Spoon into pita halves.
PER SERVING *396 cal., 10 g fat (2 g sat. fat), 106 mg chol., 646 mg sodium, 40 g carb., 5 g fiber, 37 g pro.* **Diabetic Exchanges:** *3 lean meat, 2½ starch.*

EAT SMART
Seafood Soup

Salmon, shrimp and loads of veggies make this a flavorful, hearty main dish.

—**VALERIE BRADLEY** BEAVERTON, OR

PREP: 20 MIN. • **COOK:** 50 MIN.
MAKES: 6 SERVINGS

- 1 tablespoon olive oil
- 1 small onion, chopped
- 1 small green pepper, chopped
- 2 medium carrots, chopped
- 1 garlic clove, minced
- 1 can (15 ounces) tomato sauce
- 1 can (14½ ounces) diced tomatoes, undrained
- ¾ cup white wine or chicken broth
- 1 bay leaf
- ½ teaspoon dried oregano
- ¼ teaspoon dried basil
- ¼ teaspoon pepper
- ¾ pound salmon fillets, skinned and cut into ¾-inch cubes
- ½ pound uncooked medium shrimp, peeled and deveined
- 3 tablespoons minced fresh parsley

1. In a large saucepan, heat oil over medium heat. Add onion and green pepper; cook and stir until tender. Add carrots and garlic; cook 3 minutes longer. Stir in tomato sauce, tomatoes, wine and seasonings. Bring to a boil. Reduce heat; simmer, covered, for 30 minutes.

2. Stir in salmon, shrimp and parsley. Cook, covered, 7-10 minutes longer or until fish flakes easily with a fork and shrimp turn pink. Discard bay leaf.

PER SERVING *212 cal., 9 g fat (2 g sat. fat), 87 mg chol., 620 mg sodium, 13 g carb., 3 g fiber, 19 g pro.* **Diabetic Exchanges:** *3 lean meat, 2 vegetable.*

SEAFOOD SOUP

TOASTED REUBENS

New Yorkers say my Reubens taste like those served in the famous delis there. For a milder flavor, you can omit the horseradish.

—**PATRICIA KILE** ELIZABETHTOWN, PA

FAST FIX ▶
Toasted Reubens

START TO FINISH: 20 MIN.
MAKES: 4 SERVINGS

- 4 teaspoons prepared mustard
- 8 slices rye bread
- 4 slices Swiss cheese
- 1 pound thinly sliced deli corned beef
- 1 can (8 ounces) sauerkraut, rinsed and well drained
- ½ cup mayonnaise
- 3 tablespoons ketchup
- 2 tablespoons sweet pickle relish
- 1 tablespoon prepared horseradish
- 2 tablespoons butter

1. Spread mustard over four slices of bread. Layer with cheese, corned beef and sauerkraut. In a small bowl, mix mayonnaise, ketchup, relish and horseradish; spread over remaining bread. Place over sauerkraut. Spread outsides of sandwiches with butter.

2. In a large skillet, toast sandwiches over medium heat 3-4 minutes on each side or until golden brown and cheese is melted.

Oh-So-Good Chicken Soup

FREEZE IT **FAST FIX**

I came up with this soup one weekend when my wife and I were hungry for something better than the standard. The first attempt was pretty fantastic, and now I've got the recipe down to half an hour.

—CHRIS DALTON MUNDELEIN, IL

START TO FINISH: 30 MIN.
MAKES: 6 SERVINGS

- 4 cans (14½ ounces each) reduced-sodium chicken broth
- 2 cups uncooked bow tie pasta
- 1 tablespoon olive oil
- 1 pound boneless skinless chicken breasts, cut into ½-inch strips
- 4 green onions, chopped
- 1 pound fresh asparagus, cut into 1-inch pieces
- 1½ cups sliced fresh shiitake mushrooms
- 1 garlic clove, minced
- ⅛ teaspoon pepper
- 6 tablespoons shredded Parmesan cheese

1. In a large saucepan, bring broth to a boil. Stir in pasta; return to a boil. Reduce heat; simmer, covered, 8-10 minutes or until pasta is tender, stirring occasionally.

2. Meanwhile, in a large skillet, heat oil over medium-high heat. Add chicken and green onions; cook and stir 5 minutes. Add asparagus, mushrooms and garlic; cook and stir 2-3 minutes or until chicken is no longer pink and asparagus is crisp-tender. Sprinkle with pepper.

3. Add chicken mixture to pasta mixture; heat through. Sprinkle with cheese.

FREEZE OPTION *Before adding cheese, cool soup. Freeze soup and cheese separately in freezer containers. To use, partially thaw soup in refrigerator overnight. Heat through in a saucepan, stirring occasionally and adding a little broth if necessary. Sprinkle with cheese.*

Warm Turkey & Tomato Wraps

FAST FIX

When my wife was out and about one day, I invented these wraps to surprise her when she came home. Sometimes I substitute cranberry sauce for the chutney, or use mascarpone cheese instead of cream cheese.

—ALFRED LESTER MILLSBORO, DE

START TO FINISH: 30 MIN.
MAKES: 4 SERVINGS

- 3 plum tomatoes, thinly sliced
- ½ cup julienned roasted sweet red peppers
- 4 green onions, thinly sliced
- ½ cup olive oil vinaigrette
- 1 package (8 ounces) cream cheese, softened
- ¼ cup chutney
- ½ teaspoon curry powder
- 1¼ pounds turkey breast cutlets, cut into ½-inch strips
- 1 tablespoon olive oil
- ½ teaspoon salt
- ½ teaspoon ground cumin
- ½ teaspoon pepper
- 4 flour tortillas (10 inches), warmed
- 4 lettuce leaves

1. In a small bowl, combine tomatoes, red peppers and green onions; add vinaigrette and toss to coat. In another bowl, beat cream cheese, chutney and curry powder until blended.

2. In a small bowl, combine turkey, oil and seasonings; toss to coat. In a large skillet, cook turkey mixture in batches for 1-2 minutes or until no longer pink. Remove from heat; keep warm.

3. Spread ¼ cup cream cheese mixture over each tortilla. Near center of tortilla, layer lettuce, tomato mixture and turkey. Fold bottom and sides of tortilla over filling and roll up. Serve immediately.

Cucumber Chicken Croissants

FAST FIX

When my friends and I were new moms, we started organizing lunchtime play groups for our kids. Here's one of the recipes I made for them. It's their hands-down favorite.

—SHANNON BROWN OMAHA, NE

START TO FINISH: 15 MIN.
MAKES: 4 SERVINGS

- 2 tablespoons mayonnaise
- ¼ to ½ teaspoon dill weed
- 4 croissants, split
- 4 lettuce leaves
- 4 slices provolone cheese
- 1 medium cucumber, thinly sliced
- ½ pound thinly sliced deli chicken

In a small bowl, mix mayonnaise and dill. Spread over croissant bottoms. Top with lettuce, cheese, cucumber and chicken; replace tops.

OH-SO-GOOD
CHICKEN SOUP

This winter warmer has become a favorite because it uses kitchen staples, it's packed with healthy ingredients and it's a cinch to prepare. If I can't find escarole, I just sub fresh spinach. —GINA SAMOKAR NORTH HAVEN, CT

WHITE BEAN SOUP WITH ESCAROLE

FREEZE IT **EAT SMART**
White Bean Soup with Escarole

PREP: 15 MIN. • **COOK:** 35 MIN.
MAKES: 8 SERVINGS (2 QUARTS)

- 1 tablespoon olive oil
- 1 small onion, chopped
- 5 garlic cloves, minced
- 3 cans (14½ ounces each) reduced-sodium chicken broth
- 1 can (14½ ounces) diced tomatoes, undrained
- ½ teaspoon Italian seasoning
- ¼ teaspoon crushed red pepper flakes
- 1 cup uncooked whole wheat orzo pasta
- 1 bunch escarole or spinach, coarsely chopped (about 8 cups)
- 1 can (15 ounces) white kidney or cannellini beans, rinsed and drained
- ¼ cup grated Parmesan cheese

1. In a Dutch oven, heat oil over medium heat. Add onion and garlic; cook and stir until tender. Add broth, tomatoes, Italian seasoning and pepper flakes; bring to a boil. Reduce heat; simmer, uncovered, 15 minutes.
2. Stir in orzo and escarole. Return to a boil; cook 12-14 minutes or until orzo is tender. Add beans; heat through, stirring occasionally. Sprinkle servings with cheese.

FREEZE OPTION *Freeze cooled soup in freezer containers. To use, partially thaw in refrigerator overnight. Heat through in a saucepan, stirring occasionally and adding a little broth if necessary.*

PER SERVING *174 cal., 3 g fat (1 g sat. fat), 2 mg chol., 572 mg sodium, 28 g carb., 8 g fiber, 9 g pro.* **Diabetic Exchanges:** *1 starch, 1 lean meat, 1 vegetable, ½ fat.*

FAST FIX
Easy Chicken Corn Chowder

I play around with ingredients in my pantry instead of running to the store when I don't know what's for dinner. Here's a happy experiment. Cut some fat by leaving out the bacon—it's still tasty.
—BARBARA BANSKI FENTON, MI

START TO FINISH: 30 MIN.
MAKES: 4 SERVINGS

- 2 tablespoons butter
- 1 small onion, finely chopped
- 1 celery rib, finely chopped
- 1 small sweet red pepper, finely chopped
- 2 cans (14¾ ounces each) cream-style corn
- 1½ cups chopped cooked chicken
- 1 can (12 ounces) reduced-fat evaporated milk
- 1 teaspoon chicken bouillon granules
- ½ teaspoon pepper
- 8 bacon strips, cooked and crumbled

1. In a large saucepan, heat butter over medium-high heat. Add onion, celery and red pepper; cook and stir 6-8 minutes or until tender.
2. Stir in corn, chicken, milk, bouillon and pepper; heat through, stirring occasionally (do not boil). Top servings with bacon.

EASY CHICKEN CORN CHOWDER

SUPER SUPPER HERO

FAST FIX

Super Supper Hero

Eat this hearty hand-held meal on the go or pack it for a picnic. Kids love to get in on the action by layering up all the fixings.

—**MARIBETH EDWARDS** FOLLANSBEE, WV

START TO FINISH: 30 MIN.
MAKES: 6 SERVINGS

- ¼ cup olive oil
- 2½ cups cubed eggplant
- 1 each medium green, sweet yellow and red peppers, julienned
- 1 large red onion, thinly sliced
- 1 medium tomato, chopped
- 1 teaspoon dried oregano
- ½ teaspoon salt
- ¼ teaspoon pepper
- 1 loaf (1 pound) unsliced Italian bread
  Lettuce leaves
- ½ pound sliced fully cooked ham
- ½ pound sliced cooked turkey breast
- ¼ pound sliced hard salami
- 8 slices part-skim mozzarella cheese

1. In a large skillet, heat oil over medium-high heat. Add eggplant, peppers and onion; cook and stir 4-6 minutes or until vegetables are crisp-tender. Add tomato, oregano, salt and pepper. Remove from heat.

2. Cut bread in half lengthwise; hollow out bottom of loaf, leaving a ¾-in. shell (save removed bread for another use). Layer with lettuce, ham, turkey, salami and cheese; top with vegetable mixture. Replace top. Secure with toothpicks; cut crosswise into six slices.

⑤ INGREDIENTS FAST FIX

Portobello-Gouda Grilled Cheese

Take a simple sandwich to the next level with portobello mushrooms and Gouda cheese. Serve with a side of tomato soup for what just might be the best combination on earth.

—**SHERYL BERGMAN** SHADY SIDE, MD

START TO FINISH: 20 MIN.
MAKES: 2 SERVINGS

- 1 cup sliced baby portobello mushrooms
- 1 tablespoon plus 4 teaspoons butter, divided
- 4 ounces smoked Gouda cheese, sliced
- 4 slices rye bread
- 1 plum tomato, sliced

1. In a large skillet, saute mushrooms in 1 tablespoon butter until tender. Place cheese on two bread slices; top with mushrooms, tomato and remaining bread. Spread outsides of sandwiches with remaining butter.

2. In a small skillet over medium heat, toast sandwiches for 2-3 minutes on each side or until cheese is melted.

DID YOU KNOW?

When smoked, Gouda's exterior becomes dark brown, while the interior remains pale. Hickory is typically used in Dutch Gouda, but U.S. producers make many variations of the cheese.

CHUNKY BEEF & VEGETABLE SOUP

Chunky Beef & Vegetable Soup

Nothing cures the winter blahs like wonderful soup, including this beefy one I first cooked up on a snowy day. Serve with crusty bread or rolls.

—**BILLY HENSLEY** MOUNT CARMEL, TN

PREP: 25 MIN. • **COOK:** 2¾ HOURS
MAKES: 8 SERVINGS (3 QUARTS)

- 1½ pounds beef stew meat, cut into ½-inch pieces
- 1 teaspoon salt, divided
- 1 teaspoon salt-free seasoning blend, divided
- ¾ teaspoon pepper, divided
- 2 tablespoons olive oil, divided
- 4 large carrots, sliced
- 1 large onion, chopped
- 1 medium sweet red pepper, chopped
- 1 medium green pepper, chopped
- 2 garlic cloves, minced
- 1 cup Burgundy wine or additional reduced-sodium beef broth
- 4 cups reduced-sodium beef broth
- 1 can (14½ ounces) diced tomatoes, undrained
- 2 tablespoons tomato paste
- 2 tablespoons Worcestershire sauce
- 1 bay leaf
- 4 medium potatoes (about 2 pounds), cut into ½-inch cubes

1. Sprinkle beef with ½ teaspoon each salt, seasoning blend and pepper. In a Dutch oven, heat 1 tablespoon oil over medium heat. Brown beef in batches. Remove from pan.
2. In same pan, heat remaining oil over medium heat. Add carrots, onion and peppers; cook and stir until carrots are crisp-tender. Add garlic; cook 1 minute longer.
3. Add wine, stirring to loosen browned bits from pan. Stir in the broth, tomatoes, tomato paste, Worcestershire sauce, bay leaf and remaining seasonings. Return beef to pan; bring to a boil. Reduce heat; simmer, covered, 2 hours.
4. Add the potatoes; cook 30-40 minutes longer or until beef and potatoes are tender. Skim fat and discard the bay leaf.

PER SERVING *312 cal., 10 g fat (3 g sat. fat), 55 mg chol., 695 mg sodium, 31 g carb., 5 g fiber, 21 g pro.* **Diabetic Exchanges:** *2 starch, 2 lean meat, ½ fat.*

Hearty Italian White Bean Soup

A bowlful of this soup is so satisfying. With lots of filling beans, veggies and potato, the vegetarian recipe even hits the spot with meat lovers.

—**TINA KRUMMEL** ELKINS, AR

START TO FINISH: 30 MIN.
MAKES: 6 SERVINGS

- 1 tablespoon olive oil
- 1 medium potato, peeled and cut into ½-inch cubes
- 2 medium carrots, chopped
- 1 medium onion, chopped
- 2 celery ribs, chopped
- 1 medium zucchini, chopped
- 1 teaspoon finely chopped seeded jalapeno pepper
- 1 can (15½ ounces) navy beans, rinsed and drained
- 2 to 2½ cups vegetable or chicken broth
- 1 can (8 ounces) tomato sauce
- 2 tablespoons minced fresh parsley or 2 teaspoons dried parsley flakes
- 1½ teaspoons minced fresh thyme or ½ teaspoon dried thyme

1. In a Dutch oven, heat oil over medium-high heat. Add potato and carrots; cook and stir 3 minutes. Add onion, celery, zucchini and jalapeno; cook and stir 3-4 minutes or until vegetables are crisp-tender.
2. Stir in remaining ingredients; bring to a boil. Reduce heat; simmer, covered, 12-15 minutes or until vegetables are tender.
NOTE *Wear disposable gloves when cutting hot peppers; the oils can burn skin. Avoid touching your face.*
FREEZE OPTION *Freeze cooled soup in freezer containers. To use, partially thaw in refrigerator overnight. Heat through in a saucepan, stirring occasionally and adding a little broth or water if necessary.*

Grilled Beef & Blue Cheese Sandwiches

START TO FINISH: 25 MIN.
MAKES: 4 SERVINGS

- 2 ounces cream cheese, softened
- 2 ounces crumbled blue cheese
- 8 slices sourdough bread
- ¾ pound thinly sliced deli roast beef
- ½ small red onion, thinly sliced
- ¼ cup olive oil

1. In a small bowl, mix cream cheese and blue cheese until blended. Spread over bread slices. Layer four of the slices with roast beef and onion; top with remaining bread slices.
2. Brush outsides of sandwiches with oil. In a large skillet, toast sandwiches over medium heat 4-5 minutes on each side or until golden brown.

Roast beef, blue cheese and red onion really amp up this deluxe grilled cheese. If you like a little heat, mix some horseradish into the spread.

—**BONNIE HAWKINS** ELKHORN, WI

GRILLED BEEF & BLUE CHEESE SANDWICHES

HAM & CHICKEN ROLLS

EAT SMART
Corn Chowder

I combined two soup recipes I liked to come up with my own low-calorie favorite. It turned out so well that I decided to enter it into competition at my county fair—and came home with a blue ribbon.

—**ALYCE WYMAN** PEMBINA, ND

PREP: 15 MIN. • **COOK:** 30 MIN.
MAKES: 6 SERVINGS

- 1 **small onion, chopped**
- 1 **garlic clove, minced**
- 1½ **cups cubed peeled potatoes**
- ¼ **cup shredded carrot**
- 2 **cups water**
- 2 **teaspoons dried parsley flakes**
- 2 **teaspoons reduced-sodium chicken bouillon granules**
- ¼ **teaspoon salt**
- ⅛ **teaspoon pepper**
- 1 **can (14¾ ounces) cream-style corn**
- 1½ **cups fat-free milk, divided**
- 3 **bacon strips, cooked and crumbled**
- 3 **tablespoons all-purpose flour**
- ½ **cup cubed reduced-fat process cheese (Velveeta)**
- ½ **cup beer or nonalcoholic beer**
- ½ **teaspoon liquid smoke, optional**

1. Place a large saucepan coated with cooking spray over medium heat. Add onion and garlic; cook and stir until tender. Add potatoes, carrot, water, parsley and seasonings. Bring to a boil. Reduce heat; cook, covered, 15-20 minutes or until potatoes are tender.
2. Stir in corn, 1¼ cups milk and bacon. In a small bowl, mix flour and remaining milk until smooth; stir into soup. Bring to a boil; cook and stir 2 minutes or until thickened. Add cheese; stir until melted. Stir in beer and, if desired, liquid smoke; heat through.

PER SERVING *179 cal., 3 g fat (1 g sat. fat), 9 mg chol., 681 mg sodium, 31 g carb., 2 g fiber, 8 g pro.*

FAST FIX
Ham & Chicken Rolls

My family is so crazy about these rolls, we serve them at dinner, snack time, cocktail parties—even breakfast. You can make them the day before and refrigerate them until needed.

—**EVELYN STOCKS** WINTERVILLE, NC

START TO FINISH: 30 MIN.
MAKES: 6 SERVINGS

- ¼ **cup butter, cubed**
- 2 **tablespoons finely chopped onion**
- 1 **cup finely chopped cooked chicken**
- 1 **cup finely chopped fully cooked ham**
- 1 **tablespoon Worcestershire sauce**
- 1 **tablespoon prepared mustard**
- ¼ **teaspoon poppy seeds**
- 12 **brown-and-serve rolls**
- 1 **tablespoon butter, melted**

1. Preheat oven to 425°. In a large skillet, heat butter over medium heat. Add onion; cook and stir until tender. Stir in chicken, ham, Worcestershire sauce, mustard and poppy seeds.
2. Without separating rolls, split rolls in half with a serrated knife. Spread chicken mixture over cut sides of roll bottoms; replace tops. Place on an ungreased baking sheet; brush with melted butter. Bake 5-10 minutes or until lightly browned.

CORN CHOWDER

Homey Chicken Noodle Soup

PREP: 15 MIN. • **COOK:** 50 MIN.
MAKES: 6 SERVINGS (ABOUT 2½ QUARTS)

- ¼ cup butter, cubed
- 1 medium onion, chopped
- 2 celery ribs, chopped
- 2 medium carrots, chopped
- ¾ cup coarsely chopped fresh mushrooms
- 1 garlic clove, minced
- ¼ cup all-purpose flour
- 1½ teaspoons dried basil
- ½ teaspoon salt
- 2 cartons (32 ounces each) reduced-sodium chicken broth
- 1 package (12 ounces) frozen home-style egg noodles
- 4 cups chopped fresh kale
- 2 cups shredded cooked chicken

1. In a Dutch oven, heat butter over medium heat. Add onion, celery, carrots and mushrooms; cook and stir 8-10 minutes or until crisp-tender. Add garlic; cook 1 minute longer.

2. Stir in flour, basil and salt until blended; gradually stir in broth. Bring to a boil. Reduce heat; simmer, covered, 10 minutes.

3. Return to a boil; add noodles. Reduce heat; simmer, covered, 15 minutes. Stir in kale and chicken; cook, covered, 6-8 minutes longer or until kale and noodles are tender.

FREEZE OPTION *Freeze cooled soup in freezer containers. To use, partially thaw in refrigerator overnight. Heat through in a saucepan, stirring occasionally and adding a little broth if necessary.*

Chicken noodle soup brings back warm childhood memories. This version adds a healthy twist with kale. It's a favorite at my house, especially after a cool day spent outside. —**CYNTHIA LAFOURCADE** SALMON, ID

HOMEY CHICKEN NOODLE SOUP

TURKEY-CRANBERRY BAGELS

⑤ INGREDIENTS **FAST FIX**

Turkey-Cranberry Bagels

Take care of that Thanksgiving bird in a way your family loves. It's good with all sorts of cranberry sauces and chutneys, so have fun playing around.
—*TASTE OF HOME* TEST KITCHEN

START TO FINISH: 10 MIN.
MAKES: 4 SERVINGS

- 4 plain bagels, split and toasted
- 8 ounces thinly sliced cooked turkey
- ½ cup whole-berry cranberry sauce
- 8 slices provolone cheese

Preheat broiler. Place bagel halves on a baking sheet; layer with turkey, cranberry sauce and cheese. Broil 4-6 in. from heat 1-2 minutes or until cheese is melted.

TOP TIP

Use frozen egg noodles to give homemade soup extra flair. They're thicker, chewier and more rustic than dried noodles and require a bit more cooking time. Look for them with the frozen pasta.

SPRING SALMON CHOWDER

Spring Salmon Chowder

This creamy soup really hits the spot. Have it with a side salad and oven-fresh bread for a memorable meal.

—PAT WAYMIRE YELLOW SPRINGS, OH

START TO FINISH: 30 MIN.
MAKES: 8 SERVINGS

- 2 cups cauliflowerets
- 1 tablespoon water
- 2 tablespoons butter
- 2 celery ribs, thinly sliced
- 8 green onions, thinly sliced
- 2 tablespoons all-purpose flour
- ½ teaspoon salt
- ½ teaspoon dill weed
- 4 cups 2% milk
- 1 can (14¾ ounces) salmon, drained, skin and bones removed
- 1 package (9 ounces) frozen peas, thawed
- ½ cup shredded Swiss cheese
- ½ cup shredded cheddar cheese

1. In a microwave-safe bowl, combine cauliflower and water. Microwave, covered, on high for 4-5 minutes or until tender, stirring once.

2. In a large saucepan, heat butter over medium-high heat. Add celery and green onions; cook and stir until tender. Stir in flour, salt and dill until blended; gradually whisk in milk. Bring to a boil, stirring constantly; cook and stir for 2 minutes or until soup is thickened.

3. Stir in salmon, peas and cauliflower; heat through. Stir in the cheeses until melted. Serve immediately.

Cajun Crab Burgers

START TO FINISH: 30 MIN.
MAKES: 4 SERVINGS

- 1 egg, lightly beaten
- ¾ cup mayonnaise
- 3 green onions, thinly sliced
- 1¼ teaspoons Cajun seasoning
- 1 teaspoon Worcestershire sauce
- ¾ teaspoon ground mustard
- 1¾ cups dry bread crumbs, divided
- 3 cans (6½ ounces each) lump crabmeat, drained
- ¼ cup canola oil
- 4 kaiser rolls, split
- 4 lettuce leaves
- 4 slices tomato
  Tartar sauce, optional

1. In a large bowl, combine the first six ingredients; stir in ¾ cup bread crumbs. Fold in crab. Shape into four ½-in.-thick patties. Place remaining bread crumbs in a shallow bowl. Coat patties with crumbs.

2. In a large skillet, heat oil over medium heat. Add burgers; cook 4-5 minutes on each side or until golden brown. Drain on paper towels. Serve burgers on rolls with lettuce, tomato and, if desired, tartar sauce.

CAJUN CRAB BURGERS

Here's my take on the traditional crab cake. I like to top my sandwiches with Cajun remoulade and pile spicy baked sweet potato fries on the side.

—ATHENA RUSSELL FLORENCE, SC

TOMATO & AVOCADO
SANDWICHES

Tomato & Avocado Sandwiches

I'm a vegetarian, and I could eat this tasty, quick and healthy sandwich for every meal. At my house, we call these sandwiches HATS: hummus, avocado, tomato and shallots. They're all ingredients I regularly keep in stock.

—**SARAH JARAHA** MOORESTOWN, NJ

START TO FINISH: 10 MIN.
MAKES: 2 SERVINGS

- ½ medium ripe avocado, peeled and mashed
- 4 slices whole wheat bread, toasted
- 1 medium tomato, sliced
- 2 tablespoons finely chopped shallot
- ¼ cup hummus

Spread avocado over two slices of toast. Top with tomato and shallot. Spread hummus over remaining toasts; place over tops.
PER SERVING *278 cal., 11 g fat (2 g sat. fat), 0 chol., 379 mg sodium, 35 g carb., 9 g fiber, 11 g pro.* **Diabetic Exchanges:** *2 starch, 2 fat.*

Creamless Creamy Squash Soup

Here's my top recipe for get-togethers with family and friends. Everyone loves it, even people who aren't normally interested in vegetarian food. It's also great for those sensitive to dairy—just eliminate the Parmesan garnish.

—**SHARON VEREA** THOMASVILLE, GA

PREP: 20 MIN. • **COOK:** 35 MIN.
MAKES: 8 SERVINGS (2 QUARTS)

- 2 tablespoons olive oil
- 2 small onions, chopped
- 2 celery ribs, chopped
- 2 medium carrots, chopped
- 1 medium butternut squash (3 pounds), peeled, seeded and cut into 1-inch cubes
- 1 medium sweet potato (about 8 ounces), peeled and cut into 1-inch cubes
- 1 yellow summer squash, halved lengthwise and sliced
- 4 garlic cloves, minced
- 4 cups vegetable broth
- 2 teaspoons dried savory or herbes de Provence
- ¼ teaspoon pepper
  Grated Parmesan cheese, optional

1. In a Dutch oven, heat oil over medium heat. Add onions, celery and carrots; cook and stir 6-8 minutes or until onion is tender. Stir in butternut squash, sweet potato and summer squash. Cook and stir 5-7 minutes or until squash and potato are lightly browned. Add garlic; cook 1 minute longer.
2. Add broth, savory and pepper; bring to a boil. Reduce heat; simmer, uncovered, 20-25 minutes or until vegetables are tender.
3. Puree soup using an immersion blender, or cool slightly and, in batches, puree in a blender and return to pan; heat through. If desired, serve with cheese.
FREEZE OPTION *Freeze cooled soup in freezer containers. To use, partially thaw in refrigerator overnight. Heat through in a saucepan, stirring occasionally and adding a little broth if necessary.*
PER SERVING *138 cal., 4 g fat (1 g sat. fat), 0 chol., 497 mg sodium, 27 g carb., 7 g fiber, 2 g pro.* **Diabetic Exchanges:** *1½ starch, 1 vegetable, ½ fat.*

CREAMLESS CREAMY
SQUASH SOUP

TURKEY SALAD ON WHEAT BREAD

> When one of my favorite lunch spots closed, this recipe let me hold on to more than just good memories. The peas, bacon and cheese are such a fun and springy combo. I make big batches of the salad for parties—turns out I'm not the only fan!
>
> —**MERRIJANE RICE** KAYSVILLE, UT

FAST FIX
Turkey Salad on Wheat Bread

START TO FINISH: 15 MIN.
MAKES: 2 SERVINGS

- ⅔ cup chopped romaine
- ½ cup finely chopped cooked turkey
- 2 bacon strips, cooked and crumbled
- 1 green onion, thinly sliced
- 2 tablespoons frozen peas, thawed
- 2 tablespoons shredded Swiss cheese
- 3 tablespoons mayonnaise
  Dash pepper
- 4 slices whole wheat bread

In a small bowl, combine the first six ingredients. Stir in mayonnaise and pepper. Spread over two slices of bread; top with remaining bread.

FAST FIX
Hot Tuna Heroes

Make tuna salad special with this great sub sandwich. Peas and celery give it crunch and color, while Swiss cheese adds rich, distinctive flavor. Consider mixing the tuna filling ahead of time so you can just assemble, heat and enjoy!

—**CAROLE LANTHIER** COURTICE, ON

START TO FINISH: 30 MIN.
MAKES: 6 SERVINGS

- 2 pouches (7.06 ounces each) light water-packed tuna
- 1 cup chopped celery
- 1 cup frozen peas, thawed
- ¾ cup mayonnaise
- 4 slices Swiss cheese, cut into ½-inch strips
- ¼ cup minced fresh parsley
- ¼ cup butter, melted
- 6 hoagie buns, split

1. In a large bowl, combine the first six ingredients. Brush butter over cut sides of buns. Spoon tuna mixture onto bun bottoms; replace tops.

2. Place each sandwich on a piece of heavy-duty foil (about 12 in. square). Fold foil around sandwich and seal tightly. Bake at 400° for 15-20 minutes or until heated through.

HOW TO

MINCE PARSLEY, MESS-FREE

Skip the cutting board with this technique. Place parsley in a small glass container and snip sprigs with kitchen shears until minced. No green cutting board and no mess!

WEEKNIGHT TACO SOUP

FREEZE IT FAST FIX
Tangy Barbecued Beef Sandwiches

Every year for our church ice cream social, we'd fill six roaster ovens with these ingredients and let them simmer all day. Boy, did that barbecue smell good.

—**JANET SIPES** MONMOUTH, IL

START TO FINISH: 25 MIN.
MAKES: 6 SERVINGS

- 1½ pounds ground beef
- 1 large onion, chopped
- ¾ cup ketchup
- 2 tablespoons brown sugar
- 2 tablespoons water
- 2 tablespoons Worcestershire sauce
- 2 tablespoons prepared mustard
- 2 teaspoons white vinegar
- ¼ teaspoon salt
- 6 hamburger buns, split

In a Dutch oven, cook beef and onion over medium heat 6-8 minutes or until beef is no longer pink, breaking up beef into crumbles; drain. Stir in ketchup, brown sugar, water, Worcestershire sauce, mustard, vinegar and salt; heat through. Serve on buns.

FREEZE OPTION *Place cooled beef mixture in freezer containers. To use, partially thaw in refrigerator overnight. Microwave, covered, on high in a microwave-safe dish until heated through, gently stirring and adding a little water or broth if necessary.*

TANGY BARBECUED BEEF SANDWICHES

FREEZE IT FAST FIX
Weeknight Taco Soup

This soup turned out delicious on the first try, when I was working without a recipe. You could also add cooked ground beef or cubed stew meat dredged in seasoned flour and browned for a heartier meal.

—**AMANDA SWARTZ** GODERICH, ON

START TO FINISH: 30 MIN.
MAKES: 6 SERVINGS (2½ QUARTS)

- 1 tablespoon canola oil
- 1 large onion, chopped
- 1 medium sweet red pepper, chopped
- 1 medium green pepper, chopped
- 1 can (28 ounces) diced tomatoes, undrained
- 3 cups vegetable broth
- 1 can (15 ounces) pinto beans, rinsed and drained
- 1½ cups frozen corn
- 1 envelope taco seasoning
- ¼ teaspoon salt
- ¼ teaspoon pepper
- 1 package (8.8 ounces) ready-to-serve long grain rice
- 1 cup (8 ounces) sour cream
  Optional toppings: shredded cheddar cheese, crushed tortilla chips and additional sour cream

1. In a Dutch oven, heat oil over medium heat. Add onion and peppers; cook and stir 3-5 minutes or until crisp-tender.

2. Add tomatoes, broth, beans, corn, taco seasoning, salt and pepper; bring to a boil. Reduce heat; simmer, uncovered, 10-15 minutes or until vegetables are tender. Reduce heat. Stir in rice and sour cream; heat through. Serve with toppings as desired.

FREEZE OPTION *Freeze cooled soup in freezer containers. To use, partially thaw in refrigerator overnight. Heat through in a saucepan, stirring occasionally and adding a little broth if necessary.*

Reuben Bread Pudding
PAGE 160

Casseroles & Oven Dinners

Nothing draws a hungry family to the dinner table like a bubbling casserole, flavorful meat loaf or steaming potpie. What sets these hot-from-the-oven specialties apart? Smart shortcuts that make them a cinch to prepare! Warm your heart and home with these cozy fresh-baked dinners.

Fish & Vegetable Packets
PAGE 158

Lime Chicken with Salsa Verde Sour Cream
PAGE 171

Provolone Beef Pastry Pockets
PAGE 174

Fish & Vegetable Packets

Try this traditional cooking technique to keep the fish fillets moist while sealing in the vegetables' vitamins. I like to serve the fish still wrapped in parchment for each person to open.

—JILL ANDERSON SLEEPY EYE, MN

START TO FINISH: 25 MIN.
MAKES: 4 SERVINGS

- 1½ cups julienned carrots
- 1½ cups fresh snow peas
- 2 green onions, cut into 2-inch pieces
- 4 cod fillets (6 ounces each)
- 2 teaspoons lemon juice
- ¼ teaspoon salt
- ¼ teaspoon dried thyme
- ¼ teaspoon crushed red pepper flakes
- ¼ teaspoon pepper
- 4 teaspoons butter

1. Preheat oven to 450°. In a small bowl, combine carrots, snow peas and green onions. Cut parchment paper or heavy-duty foil into four 18x12-in. pieces; place a fish fillet off center on each. Drizzle with lemon juice and top with carrot mixture. Sprinkle with seasonings; dot with butter.

2. Fold parchment paper over fish. Bring edges of paper together on all sides and crimp to seal, forming a large packet. Repeat for remaining packets. Place on baking sheets.

3. Bake 10-15 minutes or until fish just begins to flake easily with a fork. Open packets carefully to allow steam to escape.

PER SERVING *206 cal., 5 g fat (3 g sat. fat), 75 mg chol., 301 mg sodium, 10 g carb., 3 g fiber, 29 g pro.* **Diabetic Exchanges:** *3 lean meat, 1 vegetable, 1 fat.*

FISH & VEGETABLE PACKETS

CHICKEN CORDON BLEU CRESCENT RING

Chicken Cordon Bleu Crescent Ring

A classic Cordon Bleu has chicken, cheese and ham. To change it up, roll everything inside crescent dough for a speedy meal nobody can get enough of.

—STELLA CULOTTA PASADENA, MD

START TO FINISH: 30 MIN.
MAKES: 6 SERVINGS

- 1 tube (8 ounces) refrigerated crescent rolls
- 2 cups (8 ounces) shredded Swiss cheese
- 2 cups cubed cooked chicken
- ¾ cup mayonnaise
- ½ cup cubed fully cooked ham
- 2 tablespoons honey mustard

1. Preheat oven to 375°. Unroll crescent dough and separate into triangles. On an ungreased 12-in. pizza pan, arrange triangles in a ring with points toward the outside and wide ends overlapping. Press overlapping dough to seal.

2. In a large bowl, mix the remaining ingredients. Spoon across wide ends of triangles. Fold pointed end of triangles over filling, tucking points under to form a ring (filling will be visible).

3. Bake 15-20 minutes or until golden brown and heated through.

TOP TIP

Experiment with the crescent ring to create your own flavors. For chicken club, try cubed cooked chicken, crispy bacon, shredded Swiss and your favorite seasoned mayonnaise.

Sloppy Joe Pasta

Since I found this recipe a few years ago, it's become a regular part of my menu plans. Everyone loves the combination of sloppy joe ingredients, shell pasta and cheddar cheese.

—LYNNE LEIH IDYLLWILD, CA

PREP: 20 MIN. • **BAKE:** 30 MIN.
MAKES: 4-6 SERVINGS

- 1 **pound ground beef**
- 1 **envelope sloppy joe mix**
- 1 **cup water**
- 1 **can (8 ounces) tomato sauce**
- 1 **can (6 ounces) tomato paste**
- 1 **package (7 ounces) small shell pasta, cooked and drained**
- 1 **cup (8 ounces) 4% cottage cheese**
- ½ **cup shredded cheddar cheese**

1. In a Dutch oven, cook beef over medium heat until no longer pink; drain. Stir in the sloppy joe mix, water, tomato sauce and paste; heat through. Remove from the heat; stir in pasta.

2. Spoon half into a greased 2½-qt. baking dish. Top with cottage cheese and remaining pasta mixture. Sprinkle with cheddar cheese.

3. Bake, uncovered, at 350° for 30-35 minutes or until casserole is bubbly and cheese is melted.

FREEZE IT FAST FIX
Muffin-Pan Meat Loaves

START TO FINISH: 30 MIN.
MAKES: 6 SERVINGS

- 2 **eggs, lightly beaten**
- ¾ **cup shredded Mexican cheese blend**
- 1 **tablespoon chili powder**
- 1 **tablespoon Worcestershire sauce**
- 2 **garlic cloves, minced**
- 1½ **teaspoons hot pepper sauce**
- 1 **teaspoon dried parsley flakes**
- ½ **teaspoon salt**
- ¼ **teaspoon pepper**
- ¾ **pound lean ground beef (90% lean)**
- ¾ **pound ground turkey**

TOPPING
- ½ **cup ketchup**
- 3 **tablespoons brown sugar**
- 1 **teaspoon prepared mustard**

1. Preheat oven to 375°. In a large bowl, combine the first nine ingredients. Add beef and turkey; mix lightly but thoroughly. Place ⅓ cup mixture into each of 12 ungreased muffin cups, pressing lightly.

2. In a small bowl, mix topping ingredients; spoon over meat loaves. Bake, uncovered, 15-20 minutes or until a thermometer reads 165°.

FREEZE OPTION *Bake meat loaves without topping. Cool meat loaves and freeze, covered, on a waxed paper-lined baking sheet until firm. Transfer meat loaves to resealable plastic freezer bags; return to freezer. To use, partially thaw in refrigerator overnight. Place meat loaves on a greased shallow baking pan. Prepare topping as directed; spread over tops. Bake in a preheated 350° oven until heated through.*

I used to have a catering business, and my specialty was comfort food. I once needed a gluten-free meat loaf and my clients went nuts over this recipe. I often use an 8x8 pan or a loaf pan, but a muffin tin really cuts the cooking time. **—VANGIE PANAGOTOPULOS** MOORESTOWN, NJ

MUFFIN-PAN MEAT LOAVES

Our Aunt Renee always brought this casserole to family picnics in Chicago. It became so popular that she started bringing two or three. I have also used dark rye bread or marbled rye and ham instead of corned beef.

—JOHNNA JOHNSON SCOTTSDALE, AZ

Reuben Bread Pudding

PREP: 20 MIN. • **BAKE:** 35 MIN.
MAKES: 6 SERVINGS

- 4 cups cubed rye bread (about 6 slices)
- 2 tablespoons butter, melted
- 2 cups cubed or shredded cooked corned beef (about ½ pound)
- 1 can (14 ounces) sauerkraut, rinsed and well drained
- 1 cup (4 ounces) shredded Swiss cheese, divided
- 3 eggs
- 1 cup 2% milk
- ⅓ cup prepared Thousand Island salad dressing
- 1½ teaspoons prepared mustard
- ¼ teaspoon pepper

1. Preheat oven to 350°. In a large bowl, toss bread cubes with butter. Stir in corned beef, sauerkraut and ½ cup cheese; transfer to a greased 11x7-in. baking dish.
2. In same bowl, whisk eggs, milk, salad dressing, mustard and pepper; pour over top. Bake, uncovered, 30 minutes. Sprinkle with remaining cheese. Bake 5-7 minutes longer or until golden and a knife inserted near the center comes out clean.

Chili Beef Corn Bread Casserole

This recipe is my potluck standby. And when I hear that someone needs an authentic home-cooked meal, I bring them this casserole.

—LORRAINE ESPENHAIN CORPUS CHRISTI, TX

PREP: 25 MIN. • **BAKE:** 25 MIN.
MAKES: 6 SERVINGS

- 1 pound ground beef
- 1 tablespoon cornstarch
- 1 tablespoon dried minced onion
- 1 teaspoon chili powder
- ½ teaspoon garlic powder

CHILI BEEF CORN BREAD CASSEROLE

- 1 can (15 ounces) tomato sauce
- ¾ cup all-purpose flour
- ¾ cup yellow cornmeal
- 3 tablespoons sugar
- 2 teaspoons baking powder
- 2 eggs
- ½ cup 2% milk
- 3 tablespoons canola oil
- 1 can (8¼ ounces) cream-style corn
- 1 cup (4 ounces) shredded cheddar cheese
  Sour cream and salsa, optional

1. Preheat oven to 375°. In a large skillet, cook beef over medium heat 6-8 minutes or until no longer pink, breaking into crumbles; drain. Stir in cornstarch, onion, chili powder and garlic powder. Stir in tomato sauce. Cook and stir 2 minutes or until thickened. Remove from heat.
2. In a large bowl, whisk flour, cornmeal, sugar and baking powder. In another bowl, whisk eggs, milk and oil until blended; stir in corn. Add to flour mixture; stir just until moistened. Stir in cheese.
3. Spread half of the batter into a greased 2-qt. baking dish. Top with beef mixture. Spread remaining batter over filling.
4. Bake, uncovered, 25-30 minutes or until a toothpick inserted into corn bread portion comes out clean. Let stand 5 minutes before serving. If desired, serve with sour cream and salsa.

REUBEN BREAD PUDDING

Sunday Chops and Stuffing

My family likes to make these chops for Sunday dinner. The recipe lets us spend more time having fun together and less time cooking.

—GEORGIANN FRANKLIN CANFIELD, OH

PREP: 30 MIN. • **BAKE:** 25 MIN.
MAKES: 6 SERVINGS

- 2 cups water
- 2 celery ribs, chopped (about 1 cup)
- 7 tablespoons butter, divided
- ¼ cup dried minced onion
- 6 cups seasoned stuffing cubes
- 1 tablespoon canola oil
- 6 bone-in pork loin chops (¾ inch thick and 7 ounces each)
- ¼ teaspoon salt
- ¼ teaspoon pepper
- 2 medium tart apples, sliced
- ¼ cup packed brown sugar
- ⅛ teaspoon pumpkin pie spice

1. Preheat oven to 350°. In a large saucepan, combine water, celery, 6 tablespoons butter and onion. Bring to a boil. Remove from heat; stir in stuffing cubes. Spoon into a greased 13x9-in. baking dish.

2. In a large skillet, heat oil over medium heat. Brown pork chops on both sides. Arrange over stuffing. Sprinkle with salt and pepper. In a small bowl, toss apples with brown sugar and pie spice; place over pork chops. Dot with remaining butter.

3. Bake, uncovered, 25-30 minutes or until a thermometer inserted in pork reads 145°. Let stand 5 minutes before serving.

SUNDAY CHOPS AND STUFFING

STEAK & BLUE CHEESE PIZZA

FAST FIX
Steak & Blue Cheese Pizza

Even my hubby who doesn't normally like blue cheese adores this scrumptious pizza! If time allows, cook the onion until it's rich and caramelized for a simply unbeatable flavor.

—KADIJA BRIDGEWATER DEERFIELD BEACH, FL

START TO FINISH: 30 MIN.
MAKES: 6 SERVINGS

- ½ pound beef top sirloin steak, thinly sliced
- ¼ teaspoon salt
- ¼ teaspoon pepper
- 2 tablespoons olive oil, divided
- 2 cups sliced baby portobello mushrooms
- 1 large onion, sliced
- ½ cup heavy whipping cream
- ¼ cup crumbled blue cheese
- 1 prebaked 12-inch pizza crust
- 2 teaspoons minced fresh parsley

1. Preheat oven to 450°. Sprinkle beef with salt and pepper. In a large skillet, heat 1 tablespoon oil over medium heat. Add beef and mushrooms; cook 3-4 minutes or until beef is no longer pink. Remove from pan.

2. Cook onion in remaining oil 2-3 minutes or until tender. Add cream and blue cheese; cook 3-5 minutes longer or until slightly thickened.

3. Place crust on a 12-in. pizza pan or baking sheet. Spread with cream mixture; top with beef mixture. Sprinkle with parsley. Bake 10-12 minutes or until sauce is bubbly and crust is lightly browned.

TOP TIP

For a healthy dinner variation, pile the pizza high with spinach or watercress that you've tossed with a little balsamic or red wine vinaigrette.

TURKEY CORDON BLEU
CASSEROLE

Turkey Cordon Bleu Casserole

We love the flavors of traditional Cordon Bleu, and this variation is so easy to make. It's a delicious way to use up holiday ham and turkey.

—KRISTINE BLAUERT WABASHA, MN

PREP: 20 MIN. • **BAKE:** 25 MIN.
MAKES: 8 SERVINGS

- 2 **cups uncooked elbow macaroni**
- 2 **cans (10¾ ounces each) condensed cream of chicken soup, undiluted**
- ¾ **cup 2% milk**
- ¼ **cup grated Parmesan cheese**
- 1 **teaspoon prepared mustard**
- 1 **teaspoon paprika**
- ½ **teaspoon dried rosemary, crushed**
- ¼ **teaspoon garlic powder**
- ⅛ **teaspoon rubbed sage**
- 2 **cups cubed cooked turkey**
- 2 **cups cubed fully cooked ham**
- 2 **cups (8 ounces) shredded part-skim mozzarella cheese**
- ¼ **cup crushed Ritz crackers**

1. Preheat oven to 350°. Cook macaroni according to package directions.
2. Meanwhile, in a large bowl, whisk soup, milk, Parmesan cheese, mustard and seasonings. Stir in turkey, ham and mozzarella cheese.
3. Drain macaroni; add to soup mixture and toss to combine. Transfer to eight greased 8-oz. ramekins. Sprinkle with crushed crackers. Bake, uncovered, 25-30 minutes or until bubbly.

FREEZE OPTION *Cover and freeze unbaked casserole. To use, partially thaw in refrigerator overnight. Remove from refrigerator 30 minutes before baking. Preheat oven to 350°. Bake as directed, increasing time as necessary to heat through and for a thermometer inserted into center to read 165°.*

Italian Crumb-Crusted Beef Roast

Italian-style panko crumbs and seasoning give this beef a special touch. It's a nice, effortless roast that's special enough for company.

—MARIA REGAKIS SAUGUS, MA

PREP: 10 MIN.
BAKE: 1¾ HOURS + STANDING
MAKES: 8 SERVINGS

- 1 **beef sirloin tip roast (3 pounds)**
- ¼ **teaspoon salt**
- ¾ **cup Italian-style panko (Japanese) bread crumbs**
- ¼ **cup mayonnaise**
- 3 **tablespoons dried minced onion**
- ½ **teaspoon Italian seasoning**
- ¼ **teaspoon pepper**

1. Preheat oven to 325°. Place roast on a rack in a shallow roasting pan; sprinkle with salt. In a small bowl, mix remaining ingredients; press onto top and sides of roast.
2. Roast 1¾ to 2¼ hours or until meat reaches desired doneness (for medium-rare, a thermometer should read 145°; medium, 160°; well-done, 170°). Remove roast from oven; tent with foil. Let roast stand 10 minutes before slicing.

PER SERVING *319 cal., 15 g fat (3 g sat. fat), 111 mg chol., 311 mg sodium, 7 g carb., trace fiber, 35 g pro.* **Diabetic Exchanges:** *5 lean meat, 1 fat, ½ starch.*

Creamy Buffalo Chicken Enchiladas

I'm big on spicy food, but the creamy topping makes these enchiladas easy to love for all sorts of eaters.

—CRYSTAL SCHLUETER NORTHGLENN, CO

PREP: 15 MIN. • **BAKE:** 25 MIN.
MAKES: 6 SERVINGS

- 3 **cups shredded rotisserie chicken**
- 1 **can (10 ounces) enchilada sauce**
- ¼ **cup Buffalo wing sauce**
- 1¼ **cups (5 ounces) shredded Monterey Jack or cheddar cheese, divided**
- 12 **corn tortillas (6 inches), warmed**
- 1 **can (10¾ ounces) condensed cream of celery soup, undiluted**
- ½ **cup blue cheese salad dressing**
- ¼ **cup 2% milk**
- ¼ **teaspoon chili powder**
  Optional toppings: sour cream, thinly sliced green onions and additional Buffalo wing sauce

1. Preheat oven to 350°. In a large bowl, mix chicken, enchilada sauce and wing sauce. Stir in ¾ cup cheese.
2. Place ¼ cup chicken mixture off center on each tortilla. Roll up and place in a greased 13x9-in. baking dish, seam side down.
3. In a small bowl, mix soup, salad dressing and milk; pour over enchiladas. Sprinkle with remaining cheese; top with chili powder.
4. Bake, uncovered, 25-30 minutes or until heated through. Add toppings as desired.

CREAMY BUFFALO
CHICKEN ENCHILADAS

FISH & CHIPS WITH
DIPPING SAUCE

Fish & Chips with Dipping Sauce

My husband and I really like fish and chips, but not all the grease that typically comes along with it. I decided to give the classic dinner a makeover. Turns out that we actually prefer my lightened-up pickle dip over tartar sauce!

—**MICHELLE LUCAS** COLD SPRING, KY

PREP: 30 MIN. • **BAKE:** 30 MIN.
MAKES: 4 SERVINGS

- ½ cup reduced-fat sour cream
- 2 tablespoons chopped dill pickle
- 1 tablespoon dill pickle juice
- ⅛ teaspoon pepper

FRIES

- 4 large potatoes (about 2 pounds)
- 2 tablespoons olive oil
- ½ teaspoon salt
- ¼ teaspoon pepper

FISH

- 1½ cups panko (Japanese) bread crumbs
- 1 teaspoon garlic powder
- 1 teaspoon onion powder
- ½ teaspoon salt
- ½ teaspoon pepper
- 2 egg whites, beaten
- 4 cod fillets (4 ounces each)
  Cooking spray
  Lemon wedges

1. Arrange one oven rack at lowest rack setting; place second rack in middle of oven. Preheat oven to 425°. In a small bowl, mix sour cream, chopped pickle, pickle juice and pepper. Refrigerate mixture, covered, until serving.

2. Cut potatoes into ¼-in. julienne strips. Rinse well and pat dry. In a large bowl, toss with oil, salt and pepper; transfer to a baking sheet coated with cooking spray. Bake on bottom oven rack 30-35 minutes or until golden brown and tender, turning once.

3. For fish, in a shallow bowl, mix bread crumbs, garlic powder, onion powder, salt and pepper. Place egg whites in a separate shallow bowl. Dip fish fillets in egg whites, then in crumb mixture, patting to help coating adhere.

4. Transfer to a baking sheet coated with cooking spray. Spritz fish with cooking spray. Bake on top oven rack 14-16 minutes or until fish just begins to flake easily with a fork. Serve fillets with fries, sour cream mixture and lemon wedges.

PER SERVING *402 cal., 11 g fat (3 g sat. fat), 53 mg chol., 667 mg sodium, 48 g carb., 4 g fiber, 27 g pro.* **Diabetic Exchanges:** *3 starch, 3 lean meat, 2 fat.*

Louisiana Shrimp

This is a Lenten favorite at our home. I serve it right out of the roaster with corn on the cob and boiled potatoes, to which I've added a little crab boil spice. Enjoyment guaranteed!

—**SUNDRA HAUCK** BOGALUSA, LA

PREP: 15 MIN. + SIMMERING • **BAKE:** 20 MIN.
MAKES: 10 SERVINGS

- 1 pound butter, cubed
- 3 medium lemons, sliced
- 2 tablespoons plus 1½ teaspoons coarsely ground pepper
- 2 tablespoons Worcestershire sauce
- 2 garlic cloves, minced
- ½ teaspoon salt
- ½ teaspoon hot pepper sauce
- 2½ pounds uncooked shell-on medium shrimp

1. In a large saucepan, combine the first seven ingredients. Bring to a boil. Reduce heat; cover and simmer for 30 minutes, stirring occasionally.

2. Place shrimp in a large roasting pan; pour butter mixture over top. Bake, uncovered, at 375° for 20-25 minutes or until shrimp turn pink, stirring once. Serve warm with a slotted spoon.

Ham and Leek Pies

PREP: 40 MIN. • **BAKE:** 20 MIN.
MAKES: 4 SERVINGS

- ¼ cup butter, cubed
- 4 cups sliced leeks (white portion only)
- ½ pound sliced fresh mushrooms
- 3 medium carrots, sliced
- ½ cup all-purpose flour
- 1¼ cups 2% milk
- 1¼ cups vegetable broth
- 1¾ cups cubed fully cooked ham
- 2 tablespoons minced fresh parsley
- ¼ to ½ teaspoon ground nutmeg
  Dash pepper
- 1 sheet frozen puff pastry, thawed
- 1 egg, lightly beaten

1. Preheat oven to 425°. In a large saucepan, heat butter over medium-high heat. Add leeks, mushrooms and carrots; cook and stir until tender.
2. Stir in flour until blended. Gradually stir in milk and broth. Bring to a boil over medium heat, stirring constantly; cook and stir 2 minutes or until thickened. Remove from the heat; stir in ham, parsley, nutmeg and pepper.
3. On a lightly floured surface, unfold puff pastry; roll to ¼-in. thickness. Using a 10-oz. ramekin as a template, cut out four tops for pies. Fill four greased 10-oz. ramekins with leek mixture; top with pastry. Cut slits in pastry. Brush tops with egg.
4. Bake 18-22 minutes or until golden brown. Let pies stand 5 minutes before serving.

TOP TIP

If you don't have 10-oz. ramekins, you can bake the mixture in a deep-dish pie plate or round casserole dish. Simply increase the bake time until filling is bubbly and the crust is golden brown.

MUSHROOM CHICKEN WITH WILD RICE

Mushroom Chicken with Wild Rice

Fix chicken dinner in a snap with this simple recipe. It warms you up, head to toe.
—CINDY COTHERN NAMPA, ID

PREP: 10 MIN. • **BAKE:** 35 MIN.
MAKES: 6 SERVINGS

- 2 packages (8.8 ounces each) ready-to-serve long grain and wild rice
- 6 boneless skinless chicken breast halves (4 ounces each)
- 1 can (10¾ ounces) condensed cream of mushroom soup, undiluted
- 1 cup (8 ounces) sour cream
- ½ cup water
- 2 tablespoons sherry or chicken broth
- 1 can (7 ounces) mushroom stems and pieces, drained
- ½ cup grated Parmesan cheese

1. Preheat oven to 375°. Spread rice in a greased 13x9-in. baking dish. Place chicken over rice.
2. In a small bowl, whisk soup, sour cream, water and sherry until blended; stir in mushrooms. Pour over chicken. Bake, covered, 30 minutes.
3. Sprinkle cheese over top. Bake, uncovered, 5-10 minutes longer or until light golden brown and a thermometer inserted into chicken reads 165°.

HAM AND LEEK PIES

PINWHEEL STEAK POTPIE

Pinwheel Steak Potpie

On cool nights, nothing hits the spot like a steaming homemade potpie—especially one you can get on the table so quickly. The pinwheel design on top has become my signature.

—**KRISTIN SHAW** CASTLETON, NY

PREP: 25 MIN. • **BAKE:** 20 MIN.
MAKES: 6 SERVINGS

- 2 **tablespoons butter**
- 1¼ **pounds beef top sirloin steak, cut into ½-inch cubes**
- ¼ **teaspoon pepper**
- 1 **package (16 ounces) frozen vegetables for stew**
- 2 **tablespoons water**
- ½ **teaspoon dried thyme**
- 1 **jar (12 ounces) mushroom or beef gravy**
- 1 **tube (8 ounces) refrigerated crescent rolls**

1. Preheat oven to 375°. In a 10-in. ovenproof skillet, heat butter over medium-high heat. Brown beef in batches; remove from pan. Sprinkle with pepper; keep warm.

2. In same skillet, combine vegetables, water and thyme; stir in gravy. Bring to a boil. Reduce heat; simmer, uncovered, until vegetables are thawed. Stir in beef; remove from heat.

3. Unroll crescent dough and separate into eight triangles. Starting from the wide end of each triangle, roll up a third of the length and place over beef mixture with pointed ends toward the center.

4. Bake, uncovered, 16-18 minutes or until golden brown.

Curried Chicken Turnovers

Whenever I have leftover chicken, these turnovers are on the menu. The tasty secret is in the curry.

—**LAVERNE KOHUT** MANNING, AB

PREP: 30 MIN. • **BAKE:** 15 MIN.
MAKES: 8 SERVINGS

- 1 **cup finely chopped cooked chicken**
- 1 **medium apple, peeled and finely chopped**
- ½ **cup mayonnaise**
- ¼ **cup chopped cashews or peanuts**
- 1 **green onion, finely chopped**
- 1 **to 2 teaspoons curry powder**
- ¼ **teaspoon salt**
- ¼ **teaspoon pepper**
  Pastry for double-crust pie
- 1 **egg, lightly beaten**

1. Preheat oven to 425°. In a small bowl, combine the first eight ingredients. Divide the dough into eight portions.

2. On a lightly floured surface, roll each portion into a 5-in. circle. Place about ¼ cup filling on one side. Moisten edges of pastry with water. Fold dough over filling; press edges with a fork to seal.

3. Place on greased baking sheets. Brush with egg. Cut ½-in. slits in top of each. Bake 15-20 minutes or until golden brown.

PASTRY FOR DOUBLE-CRUST PIE (9 INCHES) *Combine 2½ cups all-purpose flour and ½ tsp. salt; cut in 1 cup cold butter until crumbly. Gradually add ⅓ to ⅔ cup ice water, tossing with a fork until dough holds together when pressed. Wrap in plastic wrap and refrigerate 1 hour.*

CURRIED CHICKEN TURNOVERS

Italian Sausage-Stuffed Zucchini

I've always had to be creative when getting my family to eat vegetables, so I decided to make stuffed zucchini using the pizza flavors that everyone loves. It worked! We like to include sausage for a main dish, but it could be a meatless side dish, too.

—**DONNA MARIE RYAN** TOPSFIELD, MA

PREP: 35 MIN. • **BAKE:** 20 MIN.
MAKES: 6 SERVINGS

- 6 medium zucchini (about 8 ounces each)
- 1 pound Italian turkey sausage links, casings removed
- 2 medium tomatoes, seeded and chopped
- 1 cup panko (Japanese) bread crumbs
- ⅓ cup grated Parmesan cheese
- ⅓ cup minced fresh parsley
- 2 tablespoons minced fresh oregano or 2 teaspoons dried oregano
- 2 tablespoons minced fresh basil or 2 teaspoons dried basil
- ¼ teaspoon pepper
- ¾ cup shredded part-skim mozzarella cheese

1. Preheat oven to 350°. Cut each zucchini lengthwise in half. Scoop out pulp, leaving a ¼-in. shell; chop pulp. Place zucchini shells in a large microwave-safe dish. In batches, microwave, covered, on high 2-3 minutes or until crisp-tender.

2. In a large skillet, cook sausage and zucchini pulp over medium heat 6-8 minutes or until sausage is no longer pink, breaking sausage into crumbles; drain. Stir in tomatoes, bread crumbs, Parmesan cheese, herbs and pepper. Spoon into zucchini shells.

3. Place in two ungreased 13x9-in. baking dishes. Bake, covered, 15-20 minutes or until zucchini is tender. Sprinkle with mozzarella cheese. Bake, uncovered, 5-8 minutes longer or until cheese is melted.

PER SERVING *206 cal., 9 g fat (3 g sat. fat), 39 mg chol., 485 mg sodium, 16 g carb., 3 g fiber, 17 g pro. **Diabetic Exchanges:** 2 lean meat, 2 vegetable, ½ starch.*

ITALIAN SAUSAGE-
STUFFED ZUCCHINI

Cheddar Shrimp and Penne

My wife and I take turns in the kitchen. When I created this creamy dish, it quickly became one of our favorites.

—**BRAD WALKER** HOLT, MI

PREP: 20 MIN. • **BAKE:** 35 MIN.
MAKES: 4-6 SERVINGS

- 2 cups uncooked penne pasta
- 2 garlic cloves, minced
- 2 tablespoons butter
- 2 tablespoons all-purpose flour
- ½ teaspoon salt
- ¼ teaspoon pepper
- 2 cups 2% milk
- 1½ cups (6 ounces) shredded cheddar cheese, divided
- 1 pound peeled and deveined cooked medium shrimp
- 1 can (15¼ ounces) whole kernel corn, drained

1. Cook pasta according to package directions. Meanwhile, in a large saucepan, cook the garlic in butter over medium heat for 1 minute. Stir in the flour, salt and pepper until blended. Gradually add milk. Bring to a boil; cook and stir for 2 minutes or until thickened. Reduce heat; stir in 1 cup of cheese until melted. Remove from the heat.

2. Drain pasta; add the pasta, shrimp and corn to cheese sauce. Transfer to a greased 2-qt. baking dish.

3. Bake, casserole, covered, at 350° for 25 minutes. Uncover; sprinkle with remaining cheese. Bake 10-15 minutes longer or until bubbly.

⑤ INGREDIENTS **EAT SMART**

Beef Brisket Marinara

Tender beef in marinara sauce is real comfort food to me. Serve the brisket with mashed potatoes, rice or pasta.

—**DONNA MARIE RYAN** TOPSFIELD, MA

PREP: 10 MIN. • **COOK:** 3¾ HOURS
MAKES: 10 SERVINGS

- 1 fresh beef brisket (4 pounds)
- ½ teaspoon salt
- ¼ teaspoon pepper
- 2 tablespoons olive oil
- 2 celery ribs, finely chopped
- 1 medium carrot, finely chopped
- ½ cup dry red wine or beef broth
- 1 jar (24 ounces) marinara sauce

1. Sprinkle brisket with salt and pepper. In a Dutch oven, heat oil over medium heat. Brown brisket on both sides. Remove from pan.
2. Add celery and carrot to same pan; cook and stir 2-3 minutes or until crisp-tender. Add wine; cook, stirring to loosen browned bits from pan. Stir in marinara sauce.
3. Return brisket to pan; bring to a boil. Reduce heat; simmer, covered, 3½ to 4 hours or until meat is tender.
4. Remove brisket from pan. Skim fat from sauce. Cut brisket diagonally across the grain into thin slices; serve with sauce.
PER SERVING *295 cal., 11 g fat (3 g sat. fat), 77 mg chol., 307 mg sodium, 9 g carb., 1 g fiber, 38 g pro.* **Diabetic Exchanges:** *5 lean meat, ½ starch, ½ fat.*

BEEF BRISKET MARINARA

EASY CHICKEN AND POTATOES

Since returning to work after having my daughter, I've had a lot on my plate. To make life easier, I came up with this time-saving recipe. I make it once a week now.
—**LISA TURCO** CUMBERLAND, RI

Easy Chicken and Potatoes

PREP: 20 MIN. • **BAKE:** 35 MIN.
MAKES: 4 SERVINGS

- 4 bone-in chicken thighs (about 1½ pounds)
- ¾ teaspoon salt, divided
- ¼ teaspoon plus ⅛ teaspoon pepper, divided
- 2 tablespoons olive oil, divided
- 1 pound red potatoes (about 4 medium), cut into ½-inch cubes
- 4 medium carrots, sliced
- 1 medium onion, chopped
- 3 garlic cloves, minced
- 1 teaspoon dried rosemary, crushed

1. Preheat oven to 350°. Sprinkle chicken with ½ teaspoon salt and ¼ teaspoon pepper. In an ovenproof Dutch oven, heat 1 tablespoon oil over medium-high heat. Brown chicken on both sides. Remove chicken from pan; discard drippings.
2. In same pan, combine potatoes, carrots, onion, garlic, rosemary and remaining oil, salt and pepper; return chicken to pan.
3. Bake, covered, 35-40 minutes or until thermometer inserted in chicken reads 170°-175° and vegetables are tender.

Quick & Easy Deep-Dish Pizza

I was trying to impress my boyfriend with my cooking, so I made this meaty pizza. I think it worked. Here we are 17 years later, and I still make it for our family at least once a month, if not more!

—**STACEY WHITE** FUQUAY-VARINA, NC

PREP: 30 MIN. • **BAKE:** 30 MIN.
MAKES: 8 SERVINGS

- 1 **pound ground beef**
- 1 **medium green pepper, chopped**
- 1 **small onion, chopped**
- 1 **jar (14 ounces) pizza sauce**
- 10 **slices Canadian bacon (about 6 ounces), coarsely chopped**
- 2 **packages (6½ ounces each) pizza crust mix**
- 2 **cups (8 ounces) shredded part-skim mozzarella cheese**
- 4 **ounces sliced pepperoni**

1. Preheat oven to 425°. In a large skillet, cook beef, pepper and onion over medium heat 8-10 minutes or until meat is no longer pink, breaking up beef into crumbles; drain. Stir in pizza sauce and Canadian bacon; remove from heat.

2. Prepare dough for pizza crust according to package directions. Press dough to fit bottom and 1 in. up sides of a greased 13x9-in. baking pan.

3. Spoon meat sauce into crust. Sprinkle with cheese; top with pepperoni. Bake, covered, 25 minutes. Uncover; bake 5-10 minutes longer or until the crust and cheese are golden brown.

FREEZE OPTION *Cool meat sauce before assembling pizza. Securely cover and freeze unbaked pizza. To use, bake frozen pizza, covered with foil, in a preheated 425° oven 25 minutes. Uncover; bake 15-20 minutes longer or until pizza is golden brown and heated through.*

DID YOU KNOW?

You can easily turn pizza crust mix into irresistible cheesy breadsticks. Prepare mix as package directs, adding 1½ teaspoons garlic powder. Pat into an 8-in. square on a greased pan and brush with olive oil. Sprinkle with your favorite cheeses and Italian seasonings; bake at 450° until golden brown. Cut into sticks.

QUICK & EASY DEEP-DISH PIZZA

Puffy Chile Rellenos Casserole

Here's a wonderfully zesty casserole that's much lower in fat and easier to assemble than traditional chiles rellenos. I don't remember where I got the recipe, but I've enjoyed this entree for years.

—**MARILYN MOREY** MALLARD, IA

PREP: 20 MIN. • **BAKE:** 40 MIN. + STANDING
MAKES: 12 SERVINGS

- 4 **cans (7 ounces each) whole green chilies, drained**
- 8 **flour tortillas (6 inches), cut into 1-inch strips**
- 2 **cups (8 ounces) shredded part-skim mozzarella cheese**
- 2 **cups (8 ounces) shredded reduced-fat cheddar cheese**
- 3 **cups egg substitute**
- ¾ **cup fat-free milk**
- ½ **teaspoon garlic powder**
- ½ **teaspoon ground cumin**
- ½ **teaspoon pepper**
- ¼ **teaspoon salt**
- 1 **teaspoon paprika**
- 1 **cup salsa**

1. Cut along one side of each pepper and open to lie flat. Coat a 13x9-in. baking dish with cooking spray. Layer half of the chilies, tortilla strips, mozzarella and cheddar cheeses in prepared dish. Repeat layers.

2. In a small bowl, beat the egg substitute, milk, garlic powder, cumin, pepper and salt. Pour over cheese. Sprinkle with paprika.

3. Bake, uncovered, at 350° for 40-45 minutes or until puffy and a knife inserted 2 in. from the edge of the pan comes out clean. Let stand for 10 minutes before cutting. Serve with salsa.

NOTE *Wear disposable gloves when cutting hot peppers; the oils can burn skin. Avoid touching your face.*

PER SERVING *213 cal., 9 g fat (5 g sat. fat), 25 mg chol., 690 mg sodium, 14 g carb., 1 g fiber, 18 g pro.* **Diabetic Exchanges:** *2 lean meat, 1 starch, 1 vegetable.*

SPINACH-PESTO
WHITE PIZZA

LIME CHICKEN WITH SALSA
VERDE SOUR CREAM

Spinach-Pesto White Pizza

When my kids were really small, they tried to avoid veggies and I had to get creative. I figured that because pesto is already green, it would be the perfect place to add some spinach. The recipe gained a following right away.

—**JANET BURBACH** NORTH PLATTE, NE

START TO FINISH: 30 MIN.
MAKES: 6 SLICES

- 1 teaspoon olive oil
- 3 cups fresh baby spinach
- ¼ cup plus 1 tablespoon prepared pesto, divided
- 1 package (6 ounces) ready-to-use grilled chicken breast strips
- 1 prebaked 12-inch pizza crust
- 2 cups (8 ounces) shredded part-skim mozzarella cheese
- 5 bacon strips, cooked and crumbled
- ½ cup part-skim ricotta cheese
- ¼ cup shredded Parmesan cheese

1. Preheat oven to 450°. In a large skillet, heat oil over medium-high heat. Add spinach; cook and stir just until wilted. Remove from heat; stir in ¼ cup pesto. In a small bowl, toss chicken with remaining pesto.
2. Place crust on an ungreased baking sheet. Spread with spinach mixture; top with chicken, mozzarella cheese and bacon.
3. Drop ricotta cheese by rounded teaspoonfuls over top; sprinkle with Parmesan cheese. Bake 8-10 minutes or until cheese is melted.

TOP TIP

A simple and quick recipe that really delivers the flavor. We loved this pizza and will be making it again. I didn't use the olive oil but just wilted the spinach in the bacon drippings.
—**CONSERVATIVEGRANNY**
TASTEOFHOME.COM

Lime Chicken with Salsa Verde Sour Cream

Whenever I'm in a crunch, this dish comes to the rescue. Mexican spices and salsa verde give broiled chicken a big pick-me-up. My friends are always asking me for the recipe.

—**ELLEN FOWLER** SEATTLE, WA

START TO FINISH: 20 MIN.
MAKES: 4 SERVINGS

- ¾ teaspoon ground coriander
- ¼ teaspoon salt
- ¼ teaspoon ground cumin
- ¼ teaspoon pepper
- 4 boneless skinless chicken thighs (about 1 pound)
- ⅓ cup reduced-fat sour cream
- 2 tablespoons salsa verde
- 2 tablespoons minced fresh cilantro, divided
- 1 medium lime

1. Preheat broiler. Mix seasonings; sprinkle over chicken. Place chicken on a broiler pan. Broil 4 in. from heat 6-8 minutes on each side or until a thermometer reads 170°.
2. Meanwhile, in a small bowl, mix sour cream, salsa and 1 tablespoon cilantro. Cut lime in half. Squeeze juice from one lime half into sour cream mixture; stir to combine. Cut remaining lime half into four wedges. Serve chicken with sauce and lime wedges. Sprinkle with remaining cilantro.

PER SERVING *199 cal., 10 g fat (3 g sat. fat), 82 mg chol., 267 mg sodium, 4 g carb., 1 g fiber, 23 g pro.* **Diabetic Exchanges:** *3 lean meat, 1 fat.*

Biscuit Turkey Bake

As a college student, I go for stick-to-your-ribs foods that are also easy on the budget. Here's one that fits the bill. I like to bake this casserole for friends' birthdays.

—**STEPHANIE DENNING** MOUNT PLEASANT, IA

START TO FINISH: 30 MIN.
MAKES: 5 SERVINGS

- 1 can (10¾ ounces) condensed cream of chicken soup, undiluted
- 1 cup chopped cooked turkey or chicken
- 1 can (4 ounces) mushroom stems and pieces, drained
- ½ cup frozen peas
- ¼ cup 2% milk
  Dash each ground cumin, dried basil and thyme
- 1 tube (12 ounces) refrigerated buttermilk biscuits

1. Preheat oven to 350°. In a large bowl, combine the soup, turkey, mushrooms, peas, milk and seasonings. Pour into a greased 8-in.-square baking dish; arrange biscuits over top.
2. Bake, uncovered, 20-25 minutes or until biscuits are golden brown.

FAVORITE CHEESEBURGER PIZZA

My sister-in-law used to own a pizza restaurant. I was so happy when she shared this recipe, which piles on ground beef, cheddar, Thousand Island dressing and pickles. You just have to try it.

—**KATIE BUCKLEY** WYOMING, DE

FAST FIX

Favorite Cheeseburger Pizza

START TO FINISH: 25 MIN.
MAKES: 8 SLICES

- 1 pound ground beef
- ¼ teaspoon salt
- 1 prebaked 12-inch thin pizza crust
- ½ cup Thousand Island salad dressing
- 1 small onion, chopped
- 2 cups (8 ounces) shredded cheddar cheese
- 2 cups shredded lettuce
- ½ cup sliced dill pickles

1. Preheat oven to 450°. In a large skillet, cook beef over medium heat 6-8 minutes or until no longer pink, breaking into crumbles; drain. Sprinkle beef with salt.

2. Place crust on an ungreased pizza pan or baking sheet; spread with salad dressing. Top with beef, onion and cheddar cheese.

3. Bake 6-8 minutes or until cheese is melted. Top with lettuce and pickles just before serving.

Broccoli Scalloped Potatoes

The combination of ham and Swiss creates a wonderfully rich, smoky flavor. I also love that I can cook an entire meal—veggie and all—in one standout dish.
—**DENELL SYSLO** FULLERTON, NE

PREP: 25 MIN. • **BAKE:** 1 HOUR
MAKES: 8 SERVINGS

- ¼ cup butter, cubed
- 2 tablespoons chopped onion
- 4 garlic cloves, minced
- 5 tablespoons all-purpose flour
- ¼ teaspoon white pepper
- ⅛ teaspoon salt
- 2½ cups whole milk
- 2 cups (8 ounces) shredded Swiss cheese, divided
- 2 pounds potatoes, peeled and thinly sliced (about 4 cups)
- 2 cups julienned fully cooked ham
- 2 cups frozen broccoli florets, thawed and patted dry

1. Preheat oven to 350°. In a Dutch oven, heat butter over medium-high heat. Add onion and garlic; cook and stir 2-3 minutes or until tender. Stir in flour, white pepper and salt until blended; gradually whisk in milk. Bring to a boil, stirring constantly; cook and stir 2 minutes or until mixture is thickened.

2. Stir in 1 cup cheese. Reduce heat; cook 1-2 minutes or until cheese is melted (sauce will be thick). Remove from heat.

3. Add potatoes, ham and broccoli to sauce; stir gently to coat. Transfer to eight greased 8-oz. ramekins.

4. Bake, covered, 40 minutes. Sprinkle with remaining cheese. Bake, uncovered, 20-25 minutes longer or until potatoes are tender and the cheese is melted.

BROCCOLI SCALLOPED POTATOES

Barbecue Shepherd's Pie

Have a wholesome meal even on hectic nights. I like to add leftover veggies, such as green beans, sweet potatoes or corn, and zip it up with chipotle powder.
—**ANGELA BUCHANAN** LONGMONT, CO

PREP: 15 MIN. • **BAKE:** 30 MIN.
MAKES: 6 SERVINGS

- 1 tablespoon olive oil
- 1 pound ground turkey
- 1 medium onion, chopped
- 2 medium carrots, thinly sliced
- ½ cup frozen peas
- ½ cup honey barbecue sauce
- ⅓ cup ketchup
- 1 package (24 ounces) refrigerated mashed potatoes
- ½ teaspoon paprika

1. Preheat oven to 350°. In a large skillet, heat oil over medium heat. Add turkey and onion; cook 6-8 minutes or until turkey is no longer pink, breaking up turkey into crumbles; drain. Stir in the carrots, peas, barbecue sauce and ketchup.
2. Transfer to a greased 1½-qt. baking dish. Spread mashed potatoes over top; sprinkle with paprika. Bake, uncovered, 30-35 minutes or until filling is bubbly.
FREEZE OPTION *Cool unbaked casserole; cover and freeze. To use, partially thaw in refrigerator overnight. Remove from refrigerator 30 minutes before baking. Preheat oven to 350°. Bake casserole as directed, increasing time as necessary to heat through and for a thermometer inserted into center to read 165°.*

Fontina Chicken & Pasta Bake

This pasta is so good, we adjusted the recipe to make two casseroles. Eat one tonight and freeze one for later. It's awesome anytime!
—*TASTE OF HOME* TEST KITCHEN

PREP: 25 MIN. • **BAKE:** 15 MIN.
MAKES: 2 CASSEROLES (4 SERVINGS EACH)

- 1 package (16 ounces) uncooked spiral pasta
- 4 teaspoons olive oil, divided
- 2 pounds boneless skinless chicken breasts, cut into ¾-inch cubes
- ½ pound sliced fresh mushrooms
- 4 garlic cloves, minced
- 3 cans (10¾ ounces each) condensed cream of mushroom soup, undiluted
- 1½ cups chicken broth
- 1½ cups (6 ounces) shredded fontina cheese, divided
- 4 teaspoons minced fresh oregano or 1¼ teaspoons dried oregano
- ½ teaspoon pepper
- 2 packages (6 ounces each) fresh baby spinach, coarsely chopped
- 2 medium tomatoes, chopped

1. Preheat oven to 350°. Cook pasta according to package directions for al dente.
2. Meanwhile, heat 3 teaspoons oil in a Dutch oven over medium-high heat. Add chicken in batches; cook and stir 3-5 minutes or until no longer pink. Remove from pan.
3. In same pan, add mushrooms to remaining oil; cook and stir over medium-high heat 3-5 minutes or until tender. Add garlic; cook 1 minute longer. Stir in soup, broth, 1 cup cheese, oregano and pepper. Add spinach and tomatoes; return chicken to pan.
4. Drain pasta; add to soup mixture and toss to combine. Divide between two greased 8-in.-square baking dishes. Sprinkle with remaining cheese. Bake, covered, 15-20 minutes or until heated through.
FREEZE OPTION *Cool unbaked casseroles; cover and freeze. To use, partially thaw in refrigerator overnight. Remove from refrigerator 30 minutes before baking. Preheat oven to 350°. Cover casseroles with foil; bake as directed, increasing baking time to 1¼ hours or until heated through and a thermometer inserted into center reads 165°.*

FONTINA CHICKEN
& PASTA BAKE

FAST FIX
Speedy Hummus Pizza

START TO FINISH: 20 MIN.
MAKES: 6 SLICES

- 1 **prebaked 12-inch pizza crust**
- 1 **cup hummus**
- ¾ **teaspoon dried oregano**
- ¼ **teaspoon crushed red pepper flakes**
- ½ **cup crumbled feta cheese**
- ½ **cup oil-packed sun-dried tomatoes, chopped**
- ½ **cup pitted Greek olives, chopped**
- 1 **tablespoon olive oil**

1. Preheat oven to 450°. Place crust on an ungreased baking sheet or 12-in. pizza pan.
2. In a small bowl, mix hummus, oregano and pepper flakes; spread over crust. Sprinkle with cheese, tomatoes and olives. Bake 8-10 minutes or until heated through. Drizzle with oil.

FREEZE IT
Provolone Beef Pastry Pockets

My children always make sure they're home when they find out we're having these pockets for dinner. It's also a smart way to use leftover pot roast.
—**KAREN BURKETT** RESEDA, CA

PREP: 25 MIN. • **BAKE:** 20 MIN.
MAKES: 6 SERVINGS

- 1 **tablespoon butter**
- 2 **cups finely chopped fresh mushrooms**
- 1 **small onion, finely chopped**
- 1 **package (17 ounces) refrigerated beef roast au jus**
- 1 **egg**
- 1 **tablespoon water**
- 1 **package (17.3 ounces) frozen puff pastry, thawed**
- 6 **slices provolone cheese**

1. Preheat oven to 425°. In a large skillet, heat butter over medium-high heat. Add mushrooms and onion; cook and stir 5-7 minutes or until tender and liquid is evaporated. Remove from pan; cool completely.
2. Drain beef, discarding sauce or saving for another use. Coarsely chop beef. In a small bowl, whisk egg and water.
3. Unfold one sheet of puff pastry. On a lightly floured surface, roll pastry into a 15x9-in. rectangle; cut crosswise into thirds, making three 5-in.-wide rectangles.
4. Place a cheese slice on one half of each rectangle, trimming cheese to fit. Top each with a rounded tablespoon of mushroom mixture and scant 3 tablespoons beef. Lightly brush edges of pastry with egg mixture. Fold pastry over filling; press edges with a fork to seal. Transfer to a parchment paper-lined baking sheet. Repeat with remaining pastry sheet and filling.
5. Brush tops with egg mixture. Bake 17-20 minutes or until golden brown. Serve warm.

FREEZE OPTION *Freeze unbaked pastries on a waxed paper-lined baking sheet until firm. Transfer to a resealable plastic freezer bag; return to freezer. To use, bake pastries on a parchment paper-lined baking sheet in a preheated 400° oven 20-25 minutes or until they are golden brown and heated through.*

PROVOLONE BEEF PASTRY POCKETS

What started as an appetizer is now one of my favorite Mediterranean meals. I make sure I always have the ingredients so I can whip it up anytime. I like to use fresh tomatoes instead of sun-dried ones when they're in season, and sometimes I throw in chopped artichoke hearts, too. —**NIKKI HADDAD** GERMANTOWN, MD

SPEEDY HUMMUS PIZZA

Tina's Pot Roast

Tender pot roast is hearty, feel-good food at its best. It's also kid-friendly. Even fussy eaters will gobble it up. The last time I made this for my family, the gravy was so tasty that we poured it over the entire meal—meat, carrots and potatoes!

—TINA MEYER LAKE ORION, MI

PREP: 10 MIN. • **BAKE:** 2¾ HOURS
MAKES: 8 SERVINGS

- 1 tablespoon canola oil
- 1 boneless beef chuck roast (3 pounds)
- 1½ cups water
- 1 envelope brown gravy mix
- 1 envelope Italian salad dressing mix
- 1 envelope onion soup mix
- ½ teaspoon garlic powder
- ½ teaspoon pepper
- 3 pounds potatoes (about 9 medium), peeled and quartered
- 1 pound carrots, cut into 2-inch pieces

1. Preheat oven to 325°. In a Dutch oven, heat oil over medium heat. Brown roast on all sides. In a small bowl, whisk water, gravy mix, dressing mix, soup mix, garlic powder and pepper until blended; add to pan. Bring to a boil. Bake, covered, for 1½ hours.

2. Add the vegetables; cook 1¼ to 1½ hours longer or until meat and vegetables are tender. Skim fat if necessary.

TINA'S POT ROAST

LEMON-PARSLEY
BAKED COD

EAT SMART FAST FIX
Lemon-Parsley Baked Cod

This is the first fish recipe that got two thumbs up from my picky "meat-only" eaters. The tangy lemon gives the cod some oomph. Thanks to this recipe, my family will eat healthy fish more often. I've also used tilapia or snapper—adjust the cook time according to the thickness of the fish.

—TRISHA KRUSE EAGLE, ID

START TO FINISH: 30 MIN.
MAKES: 4 SERVINGS

- 3 tablespoons lemon juice
- 3 tablespoons butter, melted
- ¼ cup all-purpose flour
- ½ teaspoon salt
- ¼ teaspoon paprika
- ¼ teaspoon lemon-pepper seasoning
- 4 cod fillets (6 ounces each)
- 2 tablespoons minced fresh parsley
- 2 teaspoons grated lemon peel

1. Preheat oven to 400°. In a shallow bowl, mix lemon juice and butter. In a separate shallow bowl, mix flour and seasonings. Dip fillets in lemon juice mixture, then in flour mixture to coat both sides; shake off excess.

2. Place in a 13x9-in. baking dish coated with cooking spray. Drizzle with remaining lemon juice mixture. Bake 12-15 minutes or until fish just begins to flake easily with a fork. Mix parsley and lemon peel; sprinkle over fish.

PER SERVING *232 cal., 10 g fat (6 g sat. fat), 87 mg chol., 477 mg sodium, 7 g carb., trace fiber, 28 g pro.* **Diabetic Exchanges:** *4 lean meat, 2 fat, ½ starch.*

**Tex-Mex Shredded
Beef Sandwiches**
PAGE 193

Slow-Cooked Sensations

With a little advance planning and your trusty slow cooker, you win! Come home to a hot and satisfying meal, no matter how busy your day has been. You can enjoy such down-home favorites as pizza hot dish, BBQ chicken, Swedish meatballs and loaded potato soup.

Meat-Lover's Pizza Hot Dish
PAGE 184

Sunday Chicken Supper
PAGE 190

Warm Rocky Road Cake
PAGE 191

Comforting Cheesy Potatoes

As fourth-generation Idahoans, we love our potatoes and cook with them in every way possible. I have served this for weddings, family dinners and more. Leftovers are great out of the microwave.
—**KARLA KIMBALL** EMMETT, ID

PREP: 10 MIN. • **COOK:** 4 HOURS
MAKES: 8 SERVINGS

- 1 can (10¾ ounces) condensed cream of chicken soup, undiluted
- 1 cup (8 ounces) sour cream
- 1 small onion, finely chopped
- ¼ cup butter, melted
- ¾ teaspoon salt
- ¼ teaspoon pepper
- 1 package (32 ounces) frozen cubed hash brown potatoes, thawed
- 2 cups (8 ounces) shredded cheddar cheese, divided

In a 4-qt. slow cooker, combine the first six ingredients. Stir in hash browns and 1½ cups cheese. Cook, covered, on low 4-5 hours or until potatoes are tender, sprinkling with remaining cheese during the last 5 minutes.

TURKEY SAUSAGE SOUP WITH FRESH VEGETABLES

COMFORTING CHEESY POTATOES

We're big on soup. This favorite is quick to make, very tasty and gives me plenty of time to have fun with my children and grandchildren while it simmers away.
—**NANCY HEISHMAN** LAS VEGAS, NV

FREEZE IT **EAT SMART**

Turkey Sausage Soup with Fresh Vegetables

PREP: 30 MIN. • **COOK:** 6 HOURS
MAKES: 10 SERVINGS (3½ QUARTS)

- 1 package (19½ ounces) Italian turkey sausage links, casings removed
- 3 large tomatoes, chopped
- 1 can (15 ounces) garbanzo beans or chickpeas, rinsed and drained
- 3 medium carrots, thinly sliced
- 1½ cups cut fresh green beans (1-inch pieces)
- 1 medium zucchini, quartered lengthwise and sliced
- 1 large sweet red or green pepper, chopped
- 8 green onions, chopped
- 4 cups chicken stock
- 1 can (12 ounces) tomato paste
- ½ teaspoon seasoned salt
- ⅓ cup minced fresh basil

1. In a large skillet, cook sausage over medium heat 8-10 minutes or until no longer pink, breaking into crumbles. Drain sausage and transfer to a 6-qt. slow cooker.

2. Add tomatoes, beans, carrots, green beans, zucchini, pepper and green onions. In a large bowl, whisk stock, tomato paste and seasoned salt; pour over vegetables.

3. Cook, covered, on low 6-8 hours or until vegetables are tender. Just before serving, stir in basil.

FREEZE OPTION *Freeze cooled soup in freezer containers. To use, partially thaw in refrigerator overnight. Heat through in a saucepan, stirring occasionally and adding a little stock if necessary.*

PER SERVING *167 cal., 5 g fat (1 g sat. fat), 20 mg chol., 604 mg sodium, 21 g carb., 5 g fiber, 13 g pro.* **Diabetic Exchanges:** *2 lean meat, 2 vegetable, ½ starch.*

Ginger Country-Style Pork Ribs

Finally, a rib recipe where you get to taste the meat instead of the sauce. The orange and ginger add a nice flavor while letting the ribs be the star.

—**GILDA LESTER** MILLSBORO, DE

PREP: 15 MIN. • **COOK:** 4¼ HOURS
MAKES: 8 SERVINGS

- 4 **pounds boneless country-style pork ribs**
- ½ **teaspoon salt**
- ¼ **teaspoon pepper**
- 1 **cup orange juice**
- ½ **cup balsamic vinegar**
- ¼ **cup reduced-sodium soy sauce**
- 2 **tablespoons minced fresh gingerroot**
- 2 **tablespoons honey**
- 3 **garlic cloves, minced**
- ¼ **teaspoon crushed red pepper flakes**
- 2 **tablespoons cornstarch**
- 2 **tablespoons cold water**

1. Sprinkle ribs with salt and pepper; place in a 5-qt. slow cooker. In a small bowl, whisk orange juice, vinegar, soy sauce, ginger, honey, garlic and pepper flakes; pour over ribs. Cook, covered, on low for 4-5 hours or until the meat is tender.

2. Remove ribs to a serving platter; keep warm. Transfer cooking juices to a small saucepan; skim fat. Bring cooking juices to a boil. In a small bowl, mix cornstarch and water until smooth; stir into cooking juices. Return to a boil; cook and stir until thickened. Spoon over ribs.

DID YOU KNOW?

Country-style ribs come from the loin end close to the shoulder. They're generally considered the meatiest type of rib. Country-style ribs are sold in a bone-in rack form, as single ribs similar to pork chops, and boneless.

GINGER COUNTRY-STYLE PORK RIBS

SAUCY BBQ
CHICKEN THIGHS

FREEZE IT **EAT SMART**
Saucy BBQ Chicken Thighs

Barbecued chicken gets a makeover in this recipe. The combination of ingredients makes for a mellow, not-too-sweet flavor that's more grown-up than the original. It's great over rice, pasta or potatoes.
—**SHARON FRITZ** MORRISTOWN, TN

PREP: 15 MIN. • **COOK:** 5 HOURS
MAKES: 6 SERVINGS

- 6 **boneless skinless chicken thighs (about 1½ pounds)**
- ½ **teaspoon poultry seasoning**
- 1 **medium onion, chopped**
- 1 **can (14½ ounces) diced tomatoes, undrained**
- 1 **can (8 ounces) tomato sauce**
- ½ **cup barbecue sauce**
- ¼ **cup orange juice**
- 1 **teaspoon garlic powder**
- ¾ **teaspoon dried oregano**
- ½ **teaspoon hot pepper sauce**
- ¼ **teaspoon pepper**
  Hot cooked brown rice, optional

1. Place chicken in a 3-qt. slow cooker; sprinkle with poultry seasoning. Top with onion and tomatoes. In a small bowl, mix tomato sauce, barbecue sauce, orange juice and seasonings; pour over top.
2. Cook, covered, on low 5-6 hours or until chicken is tender. If desired, serve with rice.
FREEZE OPTION *Place cooked chicken mixture in freezer containers. Cool and freeze. To use, partially thaw in refrigerator overnight. Microwave, covered, on high in a microwave-safe dish until heated through, gently stirring and adding a little water if necessary.*
PER SERVING *221 cal., 9 g fat (2 g sat. fat), 76 mg chol., 517 mg sodium, 12 g carb., 2 g fiber, 23 g pro.* **Diabetic Exchanges:** *3 lean meat, 2 starch.*

EAT SMART
Warm 'n' Fruity Breakfast Cereal

Sleepyheads will love the heartiness of this nutritious cooked cereal with cinnamon. It's loaded with chopped fruit and nuts. Eat it with a dollop of plain yogurt and sliced bananas or blueberries.
—**JOHN VALE** LONG BEACH, WA

PREP: 10 MIN. • **COOK:** 6 HOURS
MAKES: 10 SERVINGS

- 2 **cups seven-grain cereal**
- 1 **medium apple, peeled and chopped**
- ¼ **cup dried apricots, chopped**
- ¼ **cup dried cranberries**
- ¼ **cup raisins**
- ¼ **cup chopped dates**
- 5 **cups water**
- 1 **cup unsweetened apple juice**
- ¼ **cup maple syrup**
- 1 **teaspoon ground cinnamon**
- ½ **teaspoon salt**
  Chopped walnuts, optional

In a 4- or 5-qt. slow cooker, combine the first 11 ingredients. Cook, covered, on low 6-7 hours or until cereal and fruit are tender. If desired, top with chopped walnuts.
NOTE *This recipe was tested with Bob's Red Mill 7-Grain Hot Cereal.*
PER (1-CUP) SERVING *185 cal., 3 g fat (trace sat. fat), 0 chol., 120 mg sodium, 37 g carb., 5 g fiber, 5 g pro.* **Diabetic Exchanges:** *1 starch, 1 fruit, ½ fat.*

WARM 'N' FRUITY BREAKFAST CEREAL

SLOW-COOKED
LOADED POTATO SOUP

> I like to put a twist on my grandmother's recipes. I look forward to passing my own delicious comfort food recipes down to my kids. —JAMIE CHASE RISING SUN, IN

Slow-Cooked Loaded Potato Soup

PREP: 30 MIN. • **COOK:** 8¼ HOURS
MAKES: 12 SERVINGS (4 QUARTS)

- 5 **pounds potatoes, peeled and cubed (about 10 cups)**
- 1 **medium onion, finely chopped**
- 5 **cans (14½ ounces each) chicken broth**
- 1 **garlic clove, minced**
- 1½ **teaspoons salt**
- ¼ **teaspoon pepper**
- 2 **packages (8 ounces each) cream cheese, softened and cubed**
- 1 **cup half-and-half cream**
- ¼ **cup butter, cubed**

TOPPINGS

- 1 **pound bacon strips, cooked and crumbled**
- ¾ **cup shredded sharp cheddar cheese**
- ¼ **cup minced chives**

1. Place potatoes and onion in a 6-qt. slow cooker; add broth, garlic, salt and pepper. Cook, covered, on low 8-10 hours or until potatoes are tender.
2. Mash potatoes to desired consistency. Stir in cream cheese, cream and butter. Cook, covered, 15 minutes longer or until heated through. Just before serving, whisk soup to combine. Top servings with bacon, cheese and chives.

TOP TIP

Potatoes and other dense foods can take a long time to cook in the slow cooker. They are often layered in the bottom of the slow cooker, where they can be closer to the heat than an item that is layered on top. For best results, always follow any layering instructions that a recipe provides.

Meat Loaf with Chili Sauce

I used to serve this meat loaf in my cafe. Many customers asked for the recipe. I adapted it for home with my slow cooker, where it's quite popular, too.
—**ROBERT COX** LAS CRUCES, NM

PREP: 20 MIN.
COOK: 3 HOURS + STANDING
MAKES: 8 SERVINGS

- 1 **large onion, finely chopped**
- ½ **cup seasoned bread crumbs**
- 1 **small green pepper, chopped**
- 2 **eggs, lightly beaten**
- ½ **cup chili sauce**
- 2 **tablespoons spicy brown mustard**
- 3 **to 4 garlic cloves, minced**
- ¾ **teaspoon salt**
- ¼ **teaspoon dried oregano**
- ¼ **teaspoon dried basil**
- 2 **pounds lean ground beef (90% lean)**
  Additional chili sauce, optional

1. Cut four 20x3-in. strips of heavy-duty foil; crisscross so they resemble spokes of a wheel. Place strips on bottom and up sides of a 5-qt. slow cooker. Coat strips with cooking spray.
2. In a large bowl, combine the first 10 ingredients. Add beef; mix lightly but thoroughly. Shape into a 9-in. round loaf. Place loaf in center of strips in slow cooker.
3. Cook, covered, on low 3-4 hours or until a thermometer reads at least 160°. If desired, spoon additional chili sauce over meat loaf; let stand for 10 minutes. Using foil strips as handles, remove meat loaf to a platter.
FREEZE OPTION *Securely wrap and freeze cooled meat loaf in plastic wrap and foil. To use, partially thaw in refrigerator overnight. Unwrap meat loaf; reheat on a greased shallow baking pan in a preheated 350° oven until heated through and a thermometer inserted into the center reads 165°.*
PER SERVING *253 cal., 11 g fat (4 g sat. fat), 123 mg chol., 686 mg sodium, 12 g carb., 1 g fiber, 25 g pro.* **Diabetic Exchanges:** *3 lean meat, 1 starch.*

SWEDISH MEATBALLS
ALFREDO

ginger, allspice and cloves on a double thickness of cheesecloth; bring up corners of cloth and tie with string to form a bag. Place in slow cooker.

2. Cover and cook on high for 2-3 hours or until heated through. Discard tea bags and spice bag. Serve warm in mugs.

EAT SMART

Sunday Pot Roast

With the help of a slow cooker, you can prepare a down-home dinner any day of the week, not just on Sundays. The roast turns out tender and savory every time.

—**BRANDY SCHAEFER** GLEN CARBON, IL

PREP: 10 MIN. + CHILLING • **COOK:** 8 HOURS
MAKES: 14 SERVINGS

- 1 teaspoon dried oregano
- ½ teaspoon onion salt
- ½ teaspoon caraway seeds
- ½ teaspoon pepper
- ¼ teaspoon garlic salt
- 1 boneless pork loin roast (3½ to 4 pounds), trimmed
- 6 medium carrots, peeled and cut into 1½-inch pieces
- 3 large potatoes, peeled and quartered
- 3 small onions, quartered
- 1½ cups beef broth
- ⅓ cup all-purpose flour
- ⅓ cup cold water
- ¼ teaspoon browning sauce, optional

1. In a small bowl, combine the first five ingredients; rub over roast. Wrap in plastic wrap and refrigerate overnight.

2. Place carrots, potatoes and onions in a 6-qt. slow cooker; add broth. Unwrap roast; place in slow cooker. Cook, covered, on low 8-10 hours or until meat and vegetables are tender.

3. Transfer roast and vegetables to a serving platter; tent with foil. Pour cooking juices into a small saucepan. In a small bowl, mix flour and water until smooth; stir into pan. Bring to a boil; cook and stir 2 minutes or until thickened. If desired, add browning sauce. Serve roast with gravy.

PER SERVING *233 cal., 5 g fat (2 g sat. fat), 56 mg chol., 249 mg sodium, 21 g carb., 2 g fiber, 24 g pro.* **Diabetic Exchanges:** *3 lean meat, 1½ starch.*

I'm a big fan of this potluck-perfect dish. It only takes a few hours, unlike many other slow-cooker recipes. Plus, it's easy. I'm all for the easy!

—**CAROLE BESS WHITE** PORTLAND, OR

Swedish Meatballs Alfredo

PREP: 10 MIN. • **COOK:** 2 HOURS
MAKES: 10 SERVINGS

- 2 jars (15 ounces each) roasted garlic Alfredo sauce
- 2 cups heavy whipping cream
- 2 cups (16 ounces) sour cream
- ¾ teaspoon hot pepper sauce
- ½ teaspoon garlic powder
- ½ teaspoon dill weed
- ⅛ teaspoon pepper
- 1 package (32 ounces) frozen fully cooked Swedish meatballs, thawed
  Paprika
  Hot cooked egg noodles

1. In a 5-qt. slow cooker, combine the first seven ingredients. Stir in meatballs. Cook, covered, on low 2-3 hours or until the meatballs are heated through.

2. Sprinkle with paprika. Serve with egg noodles.

Spicy Apple Tea

This recipe has a permanent home in our slow cooker during the cold winter months! Sometimes I'll leave the appliance on the "keep warm" setting and enjoy the drink with breakfast, brunch or on a cozy evening.

—**KAREN LARA** KAMLOOPS, BC

PREP: 15 MIN. • **COOK:** 2 HOURS
MAKES: 21 SERVINGS (¾ CUP EACH)

- 2 quarts water
- 2 quarts unsweetened apple juice
- 1 cup packed brown sugar
- 4 individual black tea bags
- 4 cinnamon sticks (3 inches)
- 1 tablespoon minced fresh gingerroot
- 1 tablespoon whole allspice
- 1 tablespoon whole cloves

1. In a 6-qt. slow cooker, combine the water, apple juice, brown sugar and tea bags. Place the cinnamon sticks,

SUNDAY POT ROAST

Slow-Cooked Stuffed Peppers

I use the slow cooker more than anyone I know. I love the convenience of walking in the door and having a meal ready to go. My stuffed red peppers are a favorite because they're healthy and easy; no need to parboil the peppers, as with many other recipes.

—MICHELLE GURNSEY LINCOLN, NE

PREP: 15 MIN. • **COOK:** 3 HOURS
MAKES: 4 SERVINGS

- 4 **medium sweet red peppers**
- 1 **can (15 ounces) black beans, rinsed and drained**
- 1 **cup (4 ounces) shredded pepper jack cheese**
- ¾ **cup salsa**
- 1 **small onion, chopped**
- ½ **cup frozen corn**
- ⅓ **cup uncooked converted long grain rice**
- 1¼ **teaspoons chili powder**
- ½ **teaspoon ground cumin**
  Reduced-fat sour cream, optional

1. Cut and discard tops from peppers; remove seeds. In a large bowl, mix beans, cheese, salsa, onion, corn, rice, chili powder and cumin; spoon into peppers. Place in a 5-qt. slow cooker coated with cooking spray.
2. Cook, covered, on low 3-4 hours or until peppers are tender and filling is

MEAT-LOVER'S
PIZZA HOT DISH

heated through. If desired, serve with sour cream.
PER SERVING *317 cal., 10 g fat (5 g sat. fat), 30 mg chol., 565 mg sodium, 43 g carb., 8 g fiber, 15 g pro.* **Diabetic Exchanges:** *2 starch, 2 lean meat, 2 vegetable, 1 fat.*

Meat-Lover's Pizza Hot Dish

I make this hearty casserole for the men who help us out during harvest time. Every year they say it's the best, hands down. Throw in any pizza toppings your family likes—Canadian bacon, black olives and green peppers are some of our picks.

—BROOK BOTHUN CANBY, MN

PREP: 25 MIN. • **COOK:** 3¼ HOURS
MAKES: 10 SERVINGS

- 1 **pound ground beef**
- 1 **pound bulk Italian sausage**
- 1 **medium onion, chopped**
- 1 **cup sliced fresh mushrooms**
- 4 **cans (8 ounces each) no-salt-added tomato sauce**
- 2 **cans (15 ounces each) pizza sauce**
- 1 **package (16 ounces) penne pasta**
- 1 **cup water**
- 1 **can (6 ounces) tomato paste**
- 1 **package (3½ ounces) sliced pepperoni**
- 1 **teaspoon Italian seasoning**
- 2 **cups (8 ounces) shredded part-skim mozzarella cheese, divided**
- 2 **cups (8 ounces) shredded cheddar cheese, divided**

1. In a large skillet, cook beef, sausage, onion and mushrooms over medium heat 10-12 minutes or until meat is no longer pink and vegetables are tender, breaking up meat into crumbles; drain.
2. Transfer meat mixture to a greased 6-qt. slow cooker. Stir in tomato sauce, pizza sauce, pasta, water, tomato paste, pepperoni and Italian seasoning. Cook, covered, on low 3-4 hours or until pasta is tender.
3. Stir thoroughly; mix in 1 cup mozzarella cheese and 1 cup cheddar cheese. Sprinkle remaining cheese over top. Cook, covered, 15-20 minutes longer or until cheese is melted.

TOP TIP

Beans pack a nutritional one-two punch of protein and fiber. They're a great choice for vegetarians and meat-eaters alike. Use economical beans to stretch or replace the meat in a recipe.

SLOW-COOKED
STUFFED PEPPERS

Mexican Fondue

This irresistible fondue has become such a favorite with family and friends, I make it often for all kinds of occasions. It's fun to serve with fondue forks if you have them.

—NELLA PARKER HERSEY, MI

PREP: 15 MIN. • **COOK:** 1½ HOURS
MAKES: 4½ CUPS

- 1 can (14¾ ounces) cream-style corn
- 1 can (14½ ounces) diced tomatoes, drained
- 3 tablespoons chopped green chilies
- 1 teaspoon chili powder
- 1 package (16 ounces) process cheese (Velveeta), cubed
  French bread cubes

1. In a small bowl, combine the corn, tomatoes, green chilies and chili powder. Stir in cheese. Pour mixture into a 1½-qt. slow cooker coated with cooking spray.

2. Cover and cook on high for 1½ hours, stirring every 30 minutes or until cheese is melted. Serve warm with bread cubes.

FREEZE IT
Slow-Cooked Split Pea Soup

PREP: 15 MIN. • **COOK:** 7 HOURS
MAKES: 8 SERVINGS (ABOUT 3 QUARTS)

- 1 meaty ham bone or 2 pounds smoked ham hocks
- 1 package (16 ounces) dried green split peas
- 1 pound potatoes, peeled and cubed (about 3 cups)
- 1 large onion, chopped
- 2 medium carrots, chopped
- 1 tablespoon dried celery flakes
- ½ teaspoon garlic powder
- ½ teaspoon dried thyme
- ½ teaspoon dried basil
- ¼ teaspoon lemon-pepper seasoning
- ⅛ teaspoon dried marjoram
- 1 bay leaf
- 6 cups reduced-sodium chicken broth

1. In a 4- or 5-qt. slow cooker, combine all ingredients. Cook, covered, on low 7-9 hours or until peas are tender.

2. Remove ham bone from soup. When cool enough to handle, remove meat from bone; discard bone. Cut meat into cubes and return to soup or save meat for another use. Remove bay leaf.

FREEZE OPTION *Freeze cooled soup in freezer containers. To use, partially thaw in refrigerator overnight. Heat through in a saucepan, stirring occasionally and adding a little broth if necessary.*

I've been making this soup for years. After every holiday when ham is served, the hostess sends me home with the ham bone and a bag of peas so I can cook up this family favorite.
—SUSAN SIMONS EATONVILLE, WA

SLOW-COOKED SPLIT PEA SOUP

SLOW-SIMMERED MEAT RAGU

Slow-Simmered Meat Ragu

After a day of simmering in the slow cooker, this ragu is not your typical spaghetti sauce. It's so hearty, it's almost like a stew.

—**LAURIE LACLAIR** NORTH RICHLAND HILLS, TX

PREP: 30 MIN. • **COOK:** 6 HOURS
MAKES: 10 SERVINGS

- 1 jar (24 ounces) tomato basil pasta sauce
- 1 can (14½ ounces) Italian diced tomatoes, undrained
- 2 jars (6 ounces each) sliced mushrooms, drained
- 1 can (8 ounces) tomato sauce
- 1 jar (3½ ounces) prepared pesto
- 1½ pounds chicken tenderloins
- 1 medium sweet red pepper, chopped
- ½ cup chopped pepperoni
- ½ cup pitted ripe olives, halved
- 1 teaspoon dried oregano
- ½ teaspoon hot pepper sauce
- 1 pound Italian sausage links, cut into 1-inch pieces
- 1 medium onion, chopped
  Hot cooked angel hair pasta

1. In a 5- or 6-qt. slow cooker, combine the first 11 ingredients. Heat a large skillet over medium heat. Add sausage and onion; cook and stir until sausage is no longer pink and onion is tender. Drain. Add to slow cooker.

2. Cook, covered, on low 6-8 hours or until chicken is tender. Serve the ragu with pasta.

FREEZE OPTION *Do not cook or add pasta. Freeze cooled ragu in freezer containers. To use, partially thaw in refrigerator overnight. Cook pasta according to package directions. Place meat mixture in a large saucepan; heat through, stirring occasionally and adding a little water if necessary. Proceed as directed.*

Vegetarian Stew in Bread Bowls

PREP: 30 MIN. • **COOK:** 8½ HOURS
MAKES: 10 SERVINGS

- 3 cups cubed red potatoes (about 4 medium)
- 2 cups chopped celery (about 4 ribs)
- 2 medium leeks (white portion only), cut into ½-inch pieces
- 1¾ cups coarsely chopped peeled parsnips (about 2 medium)
- 1½ cups chopped carrots (about 3 medium)
- 1 can (28 ounces) Italian crushed tomatoes
- 1 can (14½ ounces) vegetable broth
- 2 teaspoons sugar
- ½ teaspoon salt
- ½ teaspoon dried thyme
- ½ teaspoon dried rosemary, crushed
- 3 tablespoons cornstarch
- 3 tablespoons cold water
- 8 large sourdough rolls

1. In a 4- or 5-qt. slow cooker, combine the first 11 ingredients. Cook, covered, on low 8-9 hours or until vegetables are tender.

2. In a small bowl, mix cornstarch and water until smooth. Stir into stew. Cook, covered, on high 30 minutes or until thickened.

3. Cut a thin slice off the top of each roll. Hollow out rolls, leaving ½-in.-thick shells (save removed bread for another use). Serve the stew in bread bowls.

> Shortly before we had our third child, my husband wisely got our first slow cooker. This was the first recipe I tried on a cool day. It felt great to take care of the kids and still provide a hot homemade meal at the end of the day. —**MARIA KELLER** ANTIOCH, IL

VEGETARIAN STEW IN BREAD BOWLS

SLOW COOKER
POTATO & HAM SOUP

Slow Cooker Potato & Ham Soup

In our house, this recipe is a win-win. It's easy for me to whip up and easy for my family to devour. Serve crusty bread for dipping alongside.

—LINDA HAGLUND BUFFALO, MN

PREP: 10 MIN. • **COOK:** 6¼ HOURS
MAKES: 8 SERVINGS (2½ QUARTS)

- 1 carton (32 ounces) chicken broth
- 1 package (30 ounces) frozen shredded hash brown potatoes, thawed
- 1 small onion, finely chopped
- ¼ teaspoon pepper
- 4 ounces cream cheese, softened and cubed
- 1 cup cubed deli ham
- 1 can (5 ounces) evaporated milk
  Sour cream and chopped green onions, optional

1. In a 4- or 5-qt. slow cooker, combine broth, potatoes, onion and pepper. Cook, covered, on low for 6-8 hours or until the vegetables are tender.
2. Mash potatoes to desired consistency. Whisk in cream cheese until melted. Stir in ham and milk. Cook, covered, 15-20 minutes longer or until heated through. Top with sour cream and green onions if desired.

⑤ INGREDIENTS
Party Sausages

Don't want any leftovers from your party? Serve these tempting sausages in a sweet and savory sauce. I've never had even one piece go uneaten.

—JO ANN RENNER XENIA, OH

PREP: 15 MIN. • **COOK:** 1 HOUR
MAKES: 16 SERVINGS

- 2 pounds smoked sausage links
- 1 bottle (8 ounces) Catalina salad dressing
- 1 bottle (8 ounces) Russian salad dressing
- ½ cup packed brown sugar
- ½ cup pineapple juice

1. Cut sausages diagonally into ½-in. slices; cook in a skillet over medium heat until lightly browned. Transfer the sausages to a 3-qt. slow cooker; discard drippings.
2. Add dressings, brown sugar and juice to skillet; cook and stir over medium-low heat until sugar is dissolved. Pour over sausages. Cover and cook on low for 1-2 hours or until heated through.
NOTE *French salad dressing may be substituted for one or both dressings.*

Saucy Cocktail Meatballs

I received this appetizer recipe from my grandmother many years ago. She would serve it every year at Christmas while I was growing up, and now I serve it every year.

—SUSIE SNYDER BOWLING GREEN, OH

PREP: 10 MIN. • **COOK:** 3 HOURS
MAKES: ABOUT 5 DOZEN

- 1 package (32 ounces) frozen fully cooked homestyle meatballs, thawed
- 1 can (10¾ ounces) condensed tomato soup, undiluted
- ⅓ cup chopped onion
- ⅓ cup chopped green pepper
- 2 tablespoons brown sugar
- 4 teaspoons Worcestershire sauce
- 1 tablespoon white vinegar
- 1 tablespoon prepared mustard

1. Place meatballs in a 3-qt. slow cooker. In a small bowl, combine the remaining ingredients. Pour over meatballs.
2. Cover and cook on low for 3-4 hours or until heated through.

GULF COAST JAMBALAYA RICE

Gulf Coast Jambalaya Rice

As the stew of the South, jambalaya is a definite staple. For ages, home cooks have been making their own versions of the traditional recipe. This slow-cooked rendition is my favorite.

—**JUDY BATSON** TAMPA, FL

PREP: 20 MIN. • **COOK:** 3¼ HOURS
MAKES: 8 SERVINGS

- 1 **pound boneless skinless chicken breasts, cut into 1-inch cubes**
- 1 **pound smoked kielbasa, cut into ¼-inch slices**
- 2 **cups chicken stock**
- 1 **large green pepper, chopped**
- 1 **cup chopped sweet onion**
- 2 **celery ribs, chopped**
- 2 **garlic cloves, minced**
- 2 **teaspoons Creole seasoning**
- 1 **teaspoon seafood seasoning**
- 1 **teaspoon pepper**
- 1 **pound uncooked medium shrimp, peeled and deveined**
- 2 **cups uncooked instant rice**

1. Place the first 10 ingredients in a 5-qt. slow cooker. Cook, covered, on low 3-4 hours or until the chicken is tender.

2. Stir in shrimp and rice. Cook, covered, 15-20 minutes longer or until shrimp turn pink and rice is tender.

NOTE *The following spices may be substituted for 1 teaspoon Creole seasoning: ¼ teaspoon each salt, garlic powder and paprika, and a pinch each of dried thyme, ground cumin and cayenne pepper.*

HOW TO

PEEL AND DEVEIN SHRIMP

❶ Peel the shrimp, then remove the black vein running down the back with a small sharp knife.
❷ Rinse shrimp under cold water to remove all traces of the vein.

WARM APPLE-CRANBERRY DESSERT

Served with ice cream, this heartwarming dessert promises to become a favorite in your house! I love that on nights when we have this, dessert practically makes itself.

—**MARY JONES** WILLIAMSTOWN, WV

Warm Apple-Cranberry Dessert

PREP: 20 MIN. • **COOK:** 2 HOURS
MAKES: 10 SERVINGS

- 5 **large apples, peeled and sliced**
- 1 **cup fresh or frozen cranberries, thawed**
- ¾ **cup packed brown sugar, divided**
- 2 **tablespoons lemon juice**
- ½ **cup all-purpose flour**
  Dash salt
- ⅓ **cup cold butter**
  Vanilla ice cream
  Toasted chopped pecans

1. In a greased 5-qt. slow cooker, combine apples, cranberries, ¼ cup brown sugar and lemon juice. In a small bowl, mix flour, salt and the remaining brown sugar; cut in butter until crumbly. Sprinkle over the fruit mixture.

2. Cook, covered, on high for 2 to 2½ hours or until apples are tender. Serve with ice cream and pecans.

Hot Wing Dip

Since I usually have all the ingredients on hand, this is a great go-to snack for entertaining friends and family.

—**COLEEN CORNER** GROVE CITY, PA

PREP: 10 MIN. • **COOK:** 1 HOUR
MAKES: 18 SERVINGS (¼ CUP EACH)

- 2 **cups shredded cooked chicken**
- 1 **package (8 ounces) cream cheese, cubed**
- 2 **cups (8 ounces) shredded cheddar cheese**
- 1 **cup ranch salad dressing**
- ½ **cup Louisiana-style hot sauce**
  Tortilla chips and celery sticks
  Minced fresh parsley, optional

In a 3-qt. slow cooker, mix the first five ingredients. Cook, covered, on low for 1-2 hours or until cheese is melted. Serve with chips and celery. If desired, sprinkle with parsley.

Sunday Chicken Supper

Here's a hearty dish for two that satisfies the biggest appetites. It's loaded with good old-fashioned flavor.

—**RUTHANN MARTIN** LOUISVILLE, OH

PREP: 15 MIN. • **COOK:** 6 HOURS
MAKES: 2 SERVINGS

- 2 small carrots, cut into 2-inch pieces
- ½ medium onion, chopped
- ½ celery rib, cut into 2-inch pieces
- 1 cup cut fresh green beans (2-inch pieces)
- 2 small red potatoes, halved
- 2 bone-in chicken breast halves (7 ounces each), skin removed
- 2 bacon strips, cooked and crumbled
- ¾ cup hot water
- 1 teaspoon chicken bouillon granules
- ¼ teaspoon salt
- ¼ teaspoon dried thyme
- ¼ teaspoon dried basil
  Pinch pepper

1. In a 3-qt. slow cooker, layer the first seven ingredients in the order listed. Combine the water, bouillon, salt, thyme, basil and pepper; pour over the top. Do not stir.

2. Cover and cook on low for 6-8 hours or until vegetables are tender and a thermometer reads 170°. Remove chicken and vegetables. Thicken cooking juices for gravy if desired.

SLOW-SIMMERING PASTA SAUCE

Slow-Simmering Pasta Sauce

Spaghetti with sauce is my kids' favorite dinner, so through trial and error, I came up with this winning result. I love that my version is made in a slow cooker.

—**SAMANTHA VICARS** KENOSHA, WI

PREP: 20 MIN. • **COOK:** 6 HOURS
MAKES: 6 SERVINGS

- 1 pound bulk Italian sausage
- 1 medium onion, chopped
- 3 garlic cloves, minced
- 2 cans (14½ ounces each) diced tomatoes, undrained
- 1 can (8 ounces) tomato sauce
- 1 can (6 ounces) tomato paste
- 1 tablespoon brown sugar
- 2 bay leaves
- 2 teaspoons dried oregano
- 2 teaspoons dried basil
- 1 teaspoon salt
- ½ teaspoon dried thyme
- ¼ cup minced fresh basil, divided
  Hot cooked pasta

1. In a large skillet, cook sausage and onion over medium heat for 7-8 minutes or until sausage is no longer pink and onion is tender. Add garlic; cook 1 minute longer. Drain. Transfer to a 3-qt. slow cooker.

2. Stir in the tomatoes, tomato sauce, tomato paste, brown sugar, bay leaves, oregano, dried basil, salt and thyme. Cover and cook on low for 6-8 hours.

3. Discard bay leaves; stir in half of the fresh basil. Serve with pasta. Top with remaining basil.

DID YOU KNOW?

You can purchase fresh bay leaves in the herb section of large supermarkets. Fresh leaves are more aromatic than dried, and you can finely mince them to season kabobs and Mediterranean dishes. To preserve leftover bay leaves, rinse and pat them dry, freeze quickly in a single layer, then store in a freezer container to use for soups.

SUNDAY CHICKEN SUPPER

Warm Rocky Road Cake

When this dessert is warm, it reminds me of super-moist lava cake. And until I made it, I didn't think a slow-cooker cake could be so attractive. It's a real winner.

—**SCARLETT ELROD** NEWNAN, GA

PREP: 20 MIN. • **COOK:** 3 HOURS
MAKES: 16 SERVINGS

- 1 **package German chocolate cake mix (regular size)**
- 1 **package (3.9 ounces) instant chocolate pudding mix**
- 1 **cup (8 ounces) sour cream**
- ⅓ **cup butter, melted**
- 3 **eggs**
- 1 **teaspoon vanilla extract**
- 3¾ **cups 2% milk, divided**
- 1 **package (3.4 ounces) cook-and-serve chocolate pudding mix**
- 1½ **cups miniature marshmallows**
- 1 **cup (6 ounces) semisweet chocolate chips**
- ½ **cup chopped pecans, toasted**
  Vanilla ice cream, optional

1. In a large bowl, combine the first six ingredients; add 1¼ cups milk. Beat on low speed 30 seconds. Beat on medium 2 minutes. Transfer to a greased 4- or 5-qt. slow cooker. Sprinkle cook-and-serve pudding mix over batter.

2. In a small saucepan, heat remaining milk until bubbles form around the sides of pan; gradually pour over dry pudding mix.

3. Cook, covered, on high 3-4 hours or until a toothpick inserted into cake portion comes out with moist crumbs.

4. Turn off slow cooker. Sprinkle marshmallows, chocolate chips and pecans over cake; let stand, covered, 5 minutes or until marshmallows begin to melt. Serve warm. If desired, top with ice cream.

NOTE *To toast nuts, spread in a 15x10x1-in. baking pan. Bake at 350° for 5-10 minutes or until lightly browned, stirring occasionally. Or, spread in a dry nonstick skillet and heat over low heat until lightly browned, stirring occasionally.*

WARM ROCKY ROAD CAKE

SLOW-COOKED BOSTON BEANS

Chocolate Peanut Clusters

I turn to my slow cooker to prepare these convenient chocolate treats. Making candies couldn't be any easier!

—**PAM POSEY** WATERLOO, SC

PREP: 25 MIN.
COOK: 2 HOURS + STANDING
MAKES: 4 POUNDS

- 1 jar (16 ounces) salted dry roasted peanuts
- 1 jar (16 ounces) unsalted dry roasted peanuts
- 1 package (11½ ounces) milk chocolate chips
- 1 package (10 ounces) peanut butter chips
- 3 packages (10 to 12 ounces each) white baking chips
- 2 packages (10 ounces each) 60% cacao bittersweet chocolate baking chips

1. In a 5-qt. slow cooker, combine peanuts. Layer with the remaining ingredients in order given (do not stir). Cover and cook on low for 2 to 2½ hours or until chips are melted.
2. Stir to combine. Drop by tablespoonfuls onto waxed paper. Let stand until set. Store in an airtight container at room temperature.

These slow-cooked beans have a little more zip than the usual Boston baked beans, and rum is my secret ingredient. My grandfather would add extra black pepper to his serving, so I now add extra pepper to the entire recipe.

—**ANN SHEEHY** LAWRENCE, MA

FREEZE IT
Slow-Cooked Boston Beans

PREP: 10 MIN. + SOAKING • **COOK:** 9 HOURS
MAKES: 8 SERVINGS

- 1 pound dried navy beans
- ¼ pound sliced salt pork belly or bacon strips, chopped
- 1½ cups water
- 1 medium onion, chopped
- ½ cup molasses
- ⅓ cup packed brown sugar
- ⅓ cup rum or unsweetened apple juice
- 2 teaspoons ground mustard
- ½ teaspoon salt
- ½ teaspoon pepper

1. Sort beans and rinse in cold water. Place beans in a large bowl; add water to cover by 2 in. Let stand, covered, overnight.

2. Drain and rinse beans, discarding liquid. Transfer beans to a greased 3-qt. slow cooker; add salt pork. In a small bowl, combine remaining ingredients. Stir into slow cooker.
3. Cook, covered, on low 9-11 hours or until beans are tender.
FREEZE OPTION *Freeze cooled beans in freezer containers. To use, partially thaw in refrigerator overnight. Heat through in a saucepan, stirring occasionally and adding a little water or broth if necessary.*

DID YOU KNOW?

Boston baked beans originated with the Puritans. The dish includes small beans, such as navy or pea beans; salt pork or bacon; and molasses or maple syrup.

CHOCOLATE PEANUT CLUSTERS

TEX-MEX SHREDDED
BEEF SANDWICHES

Pork with Peach Picante Sauce

When fresh peaches are in season, I cook up these pork ribs for family and friends. I love the recipe because I only need six ingredients. The slow cooker does the work for me and the ribs turn out tender and tasty.

—**CONNIE JENISTA** VALRICO, FL

PREP: 20 MIN. + CHILLING
COOK: 5½ HOURS
MAKES: 4 SERVINGS

- 2 **pounds boneless country-style pork ribs**
- 2 **tablespoons taco seasoning**
- ½ **cup mild salsa**
- ¼ **cup peach preserves**
- ¼ **cup barbecue sauce**
- 2 **cups chopped fresh peeled peaches or frozen unsweetened sliced peaches, thawed and chopped**

1. In a large bowl, toss ribs with the taco seasoning. Cover and refrigerate overnight.
2. Place pork in a 3-qt. slow cooker. In a small bowl, combine the salsa, preserves and barbecue sauce. Pour over ribs. Cover and cook on low for 5-6 hours or until meat is tender.
3. Add the peaches; cover and cook 30 minutes longer or until peaches are tender.

Tex-Mex Shredded Beef Sandwiches

Slow cooker meals, like this shredded beef sandwich, are my favorite kind because after I combine a few ingredients and let them cook, there is time for me to do my own thing. Plus, I have a hearty, satisfying and enticing meal when I come home!

—**KATHERINE WHITE** CLEMMONS, NC

PREP: 5 MIN. • **COOK:** 8 HOURS
MAKES: 8 SERVINGS

- 1 **boneless beef chuck roast (3 pounds)**
- 1 **envelope chili seasoning**
- ½ **cup barbecue sauce**
- 8 **onion rolls, split**
- 8 **slices cheddar cheese**

1. Cut roast in half; place in a 3-qt. slow cooker. Sprinkle with chili seasoning. Pour barbecue sauce over top. Cover and cook on low for 8-10 hours or until meat is tender.
2. Remove roast; cool slightly. Shred meat with two forks. Skim fat from cooking juices. Return meat to slow cooker; heat through. Using a slotted spoon, place ½ cup meat mixture on each roll bottom; top with cheese. Replace tops.

Hot Spiced Cherry Cider

This hot cider is great to have in the slow cooker after you've been out in the cold.

—**MARLENE WICZEK** LITTLE FALLS, MN

PREP: 5 MIN. • **COOK:** 4 HOURS
MAKES: 4 QUARTS

- 1 **gallon apple cider or juice**
- 2 **cinnamon sticks (3 inches)**
- 2 **packages (3 ounces each) cherry gelatin**

Place cider in a 6-qt. slow cooker; add cinnamon sticks. Cover and cook on high for 3 hours. Stir in gelatin; cook 1 hour longer. Discard cinnamon sticks before serving.

PORK WITH PEACH
PICANTE SAUCE

HEARTY VEGETABLE
SPLIT PEA SOUP

FREEZE IT **EAT SMART**

Hearty Vegetable Split Pea Soup

This slow-cooked soup is my secret weapon on busy days. It's delicious served with oyster crackers tossed in a bit of melted butter and herbs, and then lightly toasted in the oven.
—**WHITNEY JENSEN** SPRING LAKE, MI

PREP: 10 MIN. • **COOK:** 7 HOURS
MAKES: 8 SERVINGS (2 QUARTS)

- 1 **package (16 ounces) dried green split peas, rinsed**
- 1 **large carrot, chopped**
- 1 **celery rib, chopped**
- 1 **small onion, chopped**
- 1 **bay leaf**
- 1½ **teaspoons salt**
- ½ **teaspoon dried thyme**
- ½ **teaspoon pepper**
- 6 **cups water**

In a 3- or 4-qt. slow cooker, combine all ingredients. Cook, covered, on low 7-9 hours or until peas are tender. Stir before serving. Discard bay leaf.

FREEZE OPTION *Freeze cooled soup in freezer containers. To use, partially thaw in refrigerator overnight. Heat through in a saucepan, stirring occasionally and adding a little water if necessary.*

PER SERVING *202 cal., 1 g fat (trace sat. fat), 0 chol., 462 mg sodium, 36 g carb., 15 g fiber, 14 g pro.* **Diabetic Exchanges:** *2 starch, 1 lean meat.*

Slow Cooker Sweet & Spicy Pulled Pork

PREP: 20 MIN. • **COOK:** 6 HOURS
MAKES: 8 SERVINGS

- 1 **boneless pork shoulder butt roast (3 to 4 pounds)**
- 1 **can (15 ounces) tomato sauce**
- 1 **bottle (12 ounces) beer or 1½ cups beef broth**
- 1 **cup packed brown sugar**
- ½ **cup honey**
- ¼ **cup tomato paste**
- 3 **tablespoons paprika**
- 4 **teaspoons garlic powder**
- 1½ **teaspoons crushed red pepper flakes**
- 1 **teaspoon salt**
- 1 **teaspoon cayenne pepper**
- 1 **tablespoon hickory liquid smoke, optional**
- 8 **Hawaiian sweet hamburger buns, split**

1. Place roast in a greased 4- or 5-qt. slow cooker. In a large bowl, combine tomato sauce, beer, brown sugar, honey, tomato paste, seasonings and, if desired, liquid smoke; pour over meat. Cook, covered, on low 6-8 hours or until meat is tender.

2. Remove roast. When cool enough to handle, shred meat with two forks. Skim fat from cooking juices. Return meat to slow cooker; heat through.

3. Using tongs, place meat mixture on bun bottoms. Replace tops.

While I don't enjoy drinking beer, I love cooking with it. This quick recipe also goes great on plain burger buns with a side of slaw.
—**RENEE HERRINGTON** PLANO, TX

SLOW COOKER SWEET &
SPICY PULLED PORK

Maple Creme Brulee

The slow cooker is a handy way to cook the classic dessert creme brulee. This version has a kiss of maple flavor. The crispy burned sugar on top is what always makes the dish.

—TASTE OF HOME TEST KITCHEN

PREP: 20 MIN. • **COOK:** 2 HOURS + CHILLING
MAKES: 3 SERVINGS

- 1⅓ cups heavy whipping cream
- 3 egg yolks
- ½ cup packed brown sugar
- ¼ teaspoon ground cinnamon
- ½ teaspoon maple flavoring

TOPPING
- 1½ teaspoons sugar
- 1½ teaspoons brown sugar

1. In a small saucepan, heat cream until bubbles form around sides of pan. In a small bowl, whisk the egg yolks, brown sugar and cinnamon. Remove cream from the heat; stir a small amount of hot cream into egg mixture. Return all to the pan, stirring constantly. Stir in maple flavoring.

2. Transfer to three 6-oz. ramekins or custard cups. Place in a 6-qt. slow cooker; add 1 in. of boiling water to slow cooker. Cover and cook on high for 2 to 2½ hours or until centers are just set (mixture will jiggle). Carefully remove ramekins from slow cooker; cool for 10 minutes. Cover and refrigerate for at least 4 hours.

3. For topping, combine sugar and brown sugar. If using a creme brulee torch, sprinkle custards with sugar mixture. Heat sugar with the torch until caramelized. Serve immediately.

4. If broiling the custards, place ramekins on a baking sheet; let stand at room temperature for 15 minutes. Sprinkle with sugar mixture. Broil 8 in. from the heat for 3-5 minutes or until sugar is caramelized. Refrigerate for 1-2 hours or until firm.

TOP TIP

If you don't want to make the brulee sugar topping, you can skip it and simply call these creamy desserts maple custard.

HASH BROWN EGG BRUNCH

Hash Brown Egg Brunch

Slow cookers aren't just for preparing dinner. I make this often when we're having company overnight. I can prep it the night before and when we all get up in the morning, breakfast is waiting.

—BARB KEITH EAU CLAIRE, WI

PREP: 20 MIN. • **COOK:** 4 HOURS
MAKES: 10 SERVINGS

- 1 package (32 ounces) frozen shredded hash brown potatoes, thawed
- 1 pound bacon strips, cooked and crumbled
- 1 medium onion, chopped
- 1 medium green pepper, chopped
- 1½ cups (6 ounces) shredded cheddar cheese
- 12 eggs
- 1 cup 2% milk
- ½ teaspoon salt
- ½ teaspoon pepper

1. In a greased 5-qt. slow cooker, layer a third of each of the following: potatoes, bacon, onion, green pepper and cheese. Repeat layers twice. In a large bowl, whisk eggs, milk, salt and pepper; pour over layers.

2. Cook, covered, on high 30 minutes. Reduce heat to low; cook, covered, for 3½ to 4 hours or until a thermometer reads 160°.

Pepperoni Pizza Dip

This dip is so easy to make and transport. You won't have to keep it warm long, because it'll be gone in a flash. It's a great appetizer for any party.

—LISA FRANCIS ELBA, AL

PREP: 20 MIN. • **COOK:** 2½ HOURS
MAKES: 5 CUPS

- 4 cups (16 ounces) shredded cheddar cheese
- 4 cups (16 ounces) shredded part-skim mozzarella cheese
- 1 cup mayonnaise
- 1 jar (6 ounces) sliced mushrooms, drained
- 2 cans (2¼ ounces each) sliced ripe olives, drained
- 1 package (3½ ounces) pepperoni slices, quartered
- 1 tablespoon dried minced onion
  Assorted crackers

1. In a 3-qt. slow cooker, combine the cheeses, mayonnaise, mushrooms, olives, pepperoni and onion.

2. Cover and cook on low for 1½ hours; stir. Cover and cook 1 hour longer or until heated through. Serve with crackers.

FREEZE IT
Best Italian Sausage Sandwiches

Need a different type of sandwich for a party? Everyone will be complimenting these great-tasting sausages smothered in rich tomato sauce.

—TASTE OF HOME TEST KITCHEN

PREP: 10 MIN. • **COOK:** 4 HOURS
MAKES: 10 SERVINGS

- 2 jars (24 ounces each) meatless spaghetti sauce
- 2 medium green peppers, cut into strips
- 2 medium onions, thinly sliced
- ½ teaspoon garlic powder
- ½ teaspoon fennel seed, crushed
- 2 packages (20 ounces each) Italian turkey sausage links
- 10 hoagie buns, split

1. In a 3-qt. slow cooker, combine the first five ingredients. Cook, covered, on low 4 hours or until vegetables are tender.

2. Grill sausages according to package directions. Serve on buns with sauce.

FREEZE OPTION *Freeze cooled sauce in freezer containers. To use, partially thaw in refrigerator overnight. Heat through in a saucepan, stirring occasionally and adding a little water if necessary.*

BEST ITALIAN SAUSAGE SANDWICHES

SPICY SHREDDED CHICKEN

FREEZE IT EAT SMART
Spicy Shredded Chicken

I love Mexican food, but not the calories that often come with it. This dish is easy to prepare, healthy, delicious and a definite crowd-pleaser! I like to serve the chicken with warm tortillas, rice, beans and salsa.

—HEATHER WALKER SCOTTSDALE, AZ

PREP: 40 MIN. • **COOK:** 4¼ HOURS
MAKES: 8 SERVINGS

- 2 tablespoons olive oil
- 1 pound boneless skinless chicken thighs
- 1 pound boneless skinless chicken breasts
- 3 cups reduced-sodium chicken broth, divided
- 6 green onions, chopped
- 1 medium green pepper, chopped
- 2 tablespoons ground cumin
- 1 tablespoon garlic powder
- 1 tablespoon chili powder
- 1 tablespoon paprika
- 1 teaspoon cayenne pepper
- ½ teaspoon salt
- ¼ teaspoon pepper
- 1 plum tomato, chopped

1. In a large skillet, heat oil over medium-high heat. Brown chicken in batches. Transfer to a 3- or 4-qt. slow cooker. Add 1 cup broth to pan. Cook, stirring to loosen browned bits from the pan.

2. Stir in onions and green pepper; cook and stir 3-5 minutes or until vegetables are tender. Stir in seasonings; cook 1-2 minutes. Add tomato and remaining broth; pour over chicken. Cook, covered, on low 4-5 hours or until chicken is tender.

3. When cool enough to handle, shred meat with two forks; return to slow cooker. Cook, covered, on low 15-20 minutes or until heated through. Serve with a slotted spoon.

FREEZE OPTION *Freeze cooled chicken mixture in freezer containers. To use, partially thaw in refrigerator overnight. Heat through in a saucepan, stirring occasionally and adding a little reduced-sodium broth or water if necessary.*

PER (¾-CUP) SERVING *202 cal., 10 g fat (2 g sat. fat), 69 mg chol., 436 mg sodium, 5 g carb., 2 g fiber, 24 g pro.* **Diabetic Exchanges:** *3 lean meat, 1 fat.*

Cranberry-Apricot Pork Roast with Potatoes

Here's a delightful meal that's perfect for the chilly fall and winter months. The apricots, whole-berry cranberry sauce and hint of cayenne blend beautifully in this heartwarming dish. I got the recipe from one of my dearest friends.

—**PAT BARNES** PANAMA CITY, FL

PREP: 15 MIN. • **COOK:** 5 HOURS
MAKES: 8 SERVINGS

- 4 medium potatoes, peeled and quartered
- 1 boneless pork loin roast (3 pounds)
- 1 can (14 ounces) whole-berry cranberry sauce
- 1 can (15 ounces) apricot halves, drained
- 1 medium onion, quartered
- ½ cup chopped dried apricots
- 1 tablespoon sugar
- ½ teaspoon ground mustard
- ¼ teaspoon cayenne pepper

1. Place the potatoes in a 5-qt. slow cooker. Add pork.
2. In a blender, combine the cranberry sauce, apricots, onion, dried apricots, sugar, mustard and cayenne. Cover and process for 30 seconds or until almost smooth. Pour over pork.
3. Cover and cook on low for 5-6 hours or until meat is tender. Serve meat and potatoes with cooking juices.
PER SERVING *433 cal., 8 g fat (3 g sat. fat), 85 mg chol., 71 mg sodium, 56 g carb., 4 g fiber, 35 g pro.*

(5) INGREDIENTS
Cheddar Creamed Corn

PREP: 10 MIN. • **COOK:** 3 HOURS
MAKES: 9 SERVINGS

- 2 packages (one 16 ounces, one 12 ounces) frozen corn, thawed
- 1 package (8 ounces) cream cheese, cubed
- ¾ cup shredded cheddar cheese
- ¼ cup butter, melted
- ¼ cup heavy whipping cream
- ½ teaspoon salt
- ¼ teaspoon pepper

In a 3- or 4-qt. slow cooker, combine all ingredients. Cook, covered, on low 3 to 3½ hours or until cheese is melted and corn is tender. Stir before serving.

I brought this super-easy recipe to a school potluck once and it was gone in no time. I've been asked to bring it to every function since.
—**JESSICA MAXWELL** ENGLEWOOD, NJ

CHEDDAR CREAMED CORN

**Apple-Marinated
Chicken & Vegetables**
PAGE 212

Hot Off the Grill

Take your grill game to a sizzling new level with scrumptious steaks, chops, shrimp and kabobs. Savor smoky veggie packs, hot buttered corn and thrilling new takes on burgers and dogs. Celebrate summer with these tempting grilled greats.

Shrimp & Tomato Linguine
PAGE 205

Meat 'n' Potato Kabobs
PAGE 203

Garlic-Herb Salmon Sliders
PAGE 215

HASH BROWN-TOPPED STEAK

My husband and I enjoy cooking together, even on busy days. One night, we were craving grilled steak and cheese-stuffed baked potatoes, but didn't want to wait for the baking. Here's what we invented.

—JUDY ARMSTRONG PRAIRIEVILLE, LA

FAST FIX

Hash Brown-Topped Steak

START TO FINISH: 30 MIN.
MAKES: 4 SERVINGS

- 2 **tablespoons butter**
- 1 **small onion, chopped**
- 3 **garlic cloves, minced**
- 2 **cups frozen shredded hash brown potatoes, thawed**
- ¾ **teaspoon salt, divided**
- 1 **cup (4 ounces) shredded Jarlsberg cheese**
- 1 **beef top sirloin steak (1 inch thick and 1½ pounds), cut into 4 portions**
- ½ **teaspoon pepper**
- 2 **tablespoons minced fresh chives**

1. In a large skillet, heat butter over medium-high heat. Add onion; cook and stir 2-3 minutes or until tender. Add garlic; cook 2 minutes longer.
2. Stir in the hash browns and ¼ teaspoon salt; spread in an even layer. Reduce heat to medium; cook 5 minutes. Turn hash browns over; cook, covered, 5-6 minutes longer or until heated through and bottom is lightly browned. Sprinkle with cheese; cover and remove from heat. Keep warm.
3. Sprinkle beef with pepper and remaining salt. Grill, covered, over medium heat 5-7 minutes on each side or until the meat reaches desired doneness (for medium-rare, a thermometer should read 145°; medium, 160°; well-done, 170°).
4. Remove steaks from heat; top each with a fourth of the potato mixture. Sprinkle with chives.

⑤ INGREDIENTS FAST FIX

Honey Mustard Grilled Chicken

At my house, honey mustard chicken plus a baked potato plus roasted veggies equals one happy family. Just ask my three active teenage girls and hungry husband.

—JACKIE DEIBERT KLINGERSTOWN, PA

START TO FINISH: 15 MIN.
MAKES: 4 SERVINGS

- 1 **cup mayonnaise**
- 1 **tablespoon honey**
- 1 **tablespoon prepared mustard**
- 4 **boneless skinless chicken breast halves (4 ounces each)**

1. In a small bowl, mix mayonnaise, honey and mustard. Reserve ½ cup mixture for sauce. Spread remaining mixture over chicken.
2. Moisten a paper towel with cooking oil; using long-handled tongs, rub on grill rack to coat lightly. Grill chicken, covered, over medium heat or broil 4 in. from heat 4-6 minutes on each side or until a thermometer reads 165°. Serve with reserved sauce.

Chicago-Style Hot Dogs

I decided to give a Chicago-style dog a healthy twist for my family. Our kids love it. You can use other fresh toppings to please just about anyone.
—**GREGG MAY** COLUMBUS, OH

START TO FINISH: 20 MIN.
MAKES: 4 SERVINGS

- 4 turkey hot dogs
- 4 thin sandwich pickle slices
- ½ medium cucumber, peeled and thinly sliced
- 2 plum tomatoes, cut into thin wedges
- ½ cup chopped sweet onion
- 4 whole wheat tortillas (8 inches), warmed
  Optional toppings: prepared mustard, shredded reduced-fat cheddar cheese, and sport peppers or other pickled hot peppers

Prepare hot dogs according to package directions. To serve, place pickle, cucumber, tomatoes and onion on center of tortillas. Add hot dogs and toppings as desired. Fold up tortillas over filling.

⑤ INGREDIENTS **EAT SMART** FAST FIX
Banana Boats

This recipe, given to me years ago by a good friend, is a favorite with my family when we go camping. It's quick, fun to make and scrumptious!
—**BRENDA LOVELESS** GARLAND, TX

START TO FINISH: 20 MIN.
MAKES: 4 SERVINGS

- 4 medium unpeeled ripe bananas
- 4 teaspoons miniature chocolate chips
- 4 tablespoons miniature marshmallows

1. Cut banana peel lengthwise about ½ in. deep, leaving ½ in. at both ends. Open peel wider to form a pocket. Fill each with 1 teaspoon chocolate chips and 1 tablespoon marshmallows. Crimp and shape four pieces of heavy-duty foil (about 12 in. square) around bananas, forming boats.

2. Grill bananas, covered, over medium heat for 5-10 minutes or until the marshmallows melt and are golden brown.
PER SERVING *136 cal., 2 g fat (1 g sat. fat), 0 chol., 3 mg sodium, 32 g carb., 3 g fiber, 1 g pro.*

⑤ INGREDIENTS **EAT SMART** FAST FIX
Salmon Salad with Glazed Walnuts

This main-dish salad was inspired by a dinner I ate while on a trip. The glazed walnuts give it a little something special. I've also served it with grilled chicken or portobello mushrooms when I have them on hand instead of salmon.
—**JOANNA KOBERNIK** BERKLEY, MI

START TO FINISH: 15 MIN.
MAKES: 2 SERVINGS

- 2 salmon fillets (4 ounces each)
- 6 tablespoons reduced-fat balsamic vinaigrette, divided
- ⅛ teaspoon pepper
- 4 cups spring mix salad greens
- ¼ cup glazed walnuts
- 2 tablespoons crumbled blue cheese

1. Brush salmon with 2 tablespoons vinaigrette; sprinkle with pepper. Moisten a paper towel with cooking oil; using long-handled tongs, lightly coat the grill rack. Grill salmon, covered, over medium heat or broil 4 in. from heat 3-4 minutes on each side or just until fish begins to flake easily with a fork.
2. In a bowl, toss salad greens with remaining vinaigrette. Divide between two plates; sprinkle with walnuts and cheese. Top with salmon.
PER SERVING *374 cal., 25 g fat (5 g sat. fat), 64 mg chol., 607 mg sodium, 13 g carb., 4 g fiber, 24 g pro.* **Diabetic Exchanges:** *3 lean meat, 3 fat, ½ starch.*

SALMON SALAD WITH GLAZED WALNUTS

GRILLED SHRIMP &
TOMATO SALAD

Cola BBQ Chicken

My dad has been making a basic version of this family favorite for years. I recently spiced it up with hoisin sauce and red pepper flakes. Sometimes I let the chicken and sauce simmer in my slow cooker.

—BRIGETTE SCHROEDER YORKVILLE, IL

START TO FINISH: 30 MIN.
MAKES: 6 SERVINGS

- 1 cup cola
- ⅓ cup finely chopped onion
- ⅓ cup barbecue sauce
- 2 teaspoons hoisin sauce
- 1 garlic clove, minced
- ⅛ teaspoon salt
- ⅛ teaspoon pepper
- ⅛ teaspoon crushed red pepper flakes
- 6 boneless skinless chicken thighs (about 1½ pounds)
  Hot cooked rice

1. In a small saucepan, combine the first eight ingredients; bring to a boil. Reduce heat; simmer, uncovered, 10-15 minutes or until slightly thickened, stirring occasionally. Reserve ¾ cup for serving.
2. Grill chicken, covered, over medium heat or broil 4 in. from heat 5-7 minutes on each side or until a thermometer reads 170°, basting occasionally with remaining sauce during the last 5 minutes of cooking. Serve chicken with rice and the reserved sauce.

COLA BBQ CHICKEN

Grilled Shrimp & Tomato Salad

Make this a main-dish salad, or put it in an appetizer buffet for extra-good grazing. I always serve it with little bowls of chili sauce for dipping.

—MARUJA HUGHES TORONTO, ON

PREP: 25 MIN. + MARINATING
GRILL: 10 MIN.
MAKES: 12 SERVINGS

- ½ cup lemon juice
- ½ cup lime juice
- 3 pounds uncooked jumbo shrimp, peeled and deveined
- 24 cherry tomatoes
- ½ cup chili sauce
- 2 teaspoons canola oil
- 1 teaspoon red wine vinegar
- 3 medium ripe avocados, peeled and sliced
  Minced fresh parsley, optional

1. In a large resealable plastic bag, combine lemon and lime juices. Add shrimp; seal bag and turn to coat. Refrigerate 30 minutes.

2. Drain shrimp, discarding marinade. On 12 metal or soaked wooden skewers, alternately thread shrimp and tomatoes. Moisten a paper towel with cooking oil; using long-handled tongs, rub on grill rack to coat lightly. Grill kabobs, covered, over medium heat 8-10 minutes or until shrimp turn pink, turning occasionally and basting frequently with chili sauce.
3. In a small bowl, combine oil and vinegar. Arrange avocados on a large platter; top with shrimp and tomatoes. If desired, sprinkle with parsley. Drizzle with oil mixture.
PER SERVING *177 cal., 8 g fat (1 g sat. fat), 138 mg chol., 293 mg sodium, 8 g carb., 3 g fiber, 19 g pro.* **Diabetic Exchanges:** *3 lean meat, 1½ fat.*

DID YOU KNOW?

Avocado is high in monounsaturated fat, a so-called "good fat" that can lower your blood cholesterol along with the risk of stroke and heart disease. Each fruit also contains about 9 grams of healthy fiber.

Meat 'n' Potato Kabobs

They're summery, but these kabobs really stick to your ribs. A microwave makes quick work of cooking the potatoes, so grilling is done in a flash.
—TASTE OF HOME TEST KITCHEN

START TO FINISH: 30 MIN.
MAKES: 4 SERVINGS

- 1 **pound beef top sirloin steak, cut into 1-inch cubes**
- 1½ **teaspoons steak seasoning, divided**
- 1 **garlic clove, minced**
- 1 **cup cola**
- 3 **small red potatoes (about 8 ounces), cubed**
- 1 **tablespoon water**
- 1 **cup cherry tomatoes**
- 1 **medium sweet orange pepper, cut into 1-inch pieces**
- 1 **teaspoon canola oil**
- 1 **cup pineapple chunks**

1. Sprinkle beef with 1 teaspoon steak seasoning and the garlic. Place cola in a large bowl. Add beef and toss to coat. Set aside.
2. Place potatoes and water in a microwave-safe bowl. Microwave, covered, on high for 4-5 minutes or just until tender; drain. Return to bowl. Add tomatoes, pepper, oil and the remaining steak seasoning, then gently toss to coat.
3. Drain beef, discarding marinade. On eight metal or soaked wooden skewers, alternately thread beef, vegetables and pineapple.
4. Grill, covered, over medium heat or broil 4 in. from heat 6-8 minutes or until beef reaches desired doneness and pepper is crisp-tender, turning occasionally.
NOTE *This recipe was tested in a 1,100-watt microwave. This recipe was tested with McCormick's Montreal Steak Seasoning. Look for it in the spice aisle.*
PER SERVING *279 cal., 6 g fat (2 g sat. fat), 46 mg chol., 321 mg sodium, 30 g carb., 3 g fiber, 26 g pro.* **Diabetic Exchanges:** *3 lean meat, 2 starch.*

Spice-Rubbed Salmon

We eat this salmon a lot, along with couscous and fresh veggies. Even my two-year-old happily devours it.
—LYNDSAY RENSING KATY, TX

START TO FINISH: 20 MIN.
MAKES: 4 SERVINGS

- 1 **teaspoon brown sugar**
- 1 **teaspoon ground cumin**
- ½ **teaspoon salt**
- ½ **teaspoon dried parsley flakes**
- ½ **teaspoon chili powder**
- ¼ **teaspoon garlic powder**
- ¼ **teaspoon ground mustard**
- ¼ **teaspoon paprika**
- ¼ **teaspoon pepper**
- ⅛ **teaspoon ground cinnamon**
- 4 **salmon fillets (6 ounces each)**
- 2 **teaspoons olive oil**

1. In a small bowl, mix the first 10 ingredients. Rub fillets with seasoning mixture; drizzle with oil.
2. Moisten a paper towel with cooking oil; using long-handled tongs, rub on grill rack to coat lightly. Place salmon on grill rack, skin side up. Grill, covered, over high heat or broil 3-4 in. from heat 5 minutes. Turn; grill 4-6 minutes longer or until fish just begins to flake easily with a fork.
PER SERVING *295 cal., 18 g fat (3 g sat. fat), 85 mg chol., 385 mg sodium, 2 g carb., trace fiber, 29 g pro.* **Diabetic Exchanges:** *5 lean meat, ½ fat.*

Grilled Curry Pork Chops with Apricot Sauce

A little curry powder and a pinch of cilantro take this best-loved flavor combo—pork chops with apricots—in a whole new direction. The recipe is so easy and so fantastic, frequent requests are a sure bet.
—JULIE HANSON CHARLESTON, ME

START TO FINISH: 25 MIN.
MAKES: 4 SERVINGS

- ¼ **cup apricot preserves**
- 2 **teaspoons curry powder**
- 4 **bone-in pork loin chops (¾ inch thick and 7 ounces each)**

SAUCE
- 1 **cup canned apricot halves, chopped**
- 2 **tablespoons apricot preserves**
- 2 **teaspoons minced fresh cilantro**

1. In a small bowl, mix preserves and curry powder; brush over pork chops. Moisten a paper towel with cooking oil; using long-handled tongs, rub on grill rack to coat lightly.
2. Grill chops, covered, over medium heat or broil 4 in. from heat 8-10 minutes or until a thermometer reads 145°, turning occasionally. Let rest 5 minutes before serving.
3. Meanwhile, in a small bowl, mix sauce ingredients. Serve pork chops with sauce.
PER SERVING *334 cal., 9 g fat (3 g sat. fat), 86 mg chol., 78 mg sodium, 34 g carb., 1 g fiber, 31 g pro.*

FAST FIX ▶

Seasoned Steaks with Horseradish Cream

My buttery tenderloin is summer comfort at its best. It's simple, but it's a big treat anytime. Pull dinner together fast with a few simple sides.

—JENNA EWALD OCONOMOWOC, WI

START TO FINISH: 30 MIN.
MAKES: 4 SERVINGS

- ½ teaspoon salt
- ½ teaspoon garlic powder
- ¼ teaspoon dried parsley flakes
- ¼ teaspoon chili powder
- ¼ teaspoon pepper
- 4 beef tenderloin steaks (6 ounces each)

HORSERADISH CREAM

- 2 tablespoons butter, softened
- 1 tablespoon prepared horseradish
- 1 garlic clove, minced
- 2 tablespoons heavy whipping cream

1. Moisten a paper towel with cooking oil; using long-handled tongs, rub on grill rack to coat lightly. Mix salt, garlic powder, parsley flakes, chili powder and pepper. Rub mixture over both sides of steaks.

2. Grill steaks, covered, over medium heat or broil 4 in. from heat 6-8 minutes on each side or until meat reaches desired doneness (for medium-rare, a thermometer should read 145°; medium, 160°; well-done, 170°).

3. Meanwhile, in a small bowl, mix butter, horseradish and garlic until blended; gradually whisk in cream. Serve with steaks.

SEASONED STEAKS WITH
HORSERADISH CREAM

GRILLED SAUSAGE-BASIL PIZZAS

FAST FIX ▶

Grilled Sausage-Basil Pizzas

These easy little pizzas are a wonderful change of pace from the classic cookout menu. Let your guests top their own.

—LISA SPEER PALM BEACH, FL

START TO FINISH: 30 MIN.
MAKES: 4 SERVINGS

- 4 Italian sausage links (4 ounces each)
- 4 naan flatbreads or whole pita breads
- ¼ cup olive oil
- 1 cup tomato basil pasta sauce
- 2 cups (8 ounces) shredded part-skim mozzarella cheese
- ½ cup grated Parmesan cheese
- ½ cup thinly sliced fresh basil

1. Grill sausages, covered, over medium heat 10-12 minutes or until a thermometer reads 160°, turning occasionally. Cut into ¼-in. slices.

2. Brush both sides of flatbreads with oil. Grill, covered, over medium heat 2-3 minutes or until bottoms are lightly browned.

3. Remove from grill. Layer grilled sides with sauce, sausage, cheeses and basil. Return to grill; cook, covered, 2-3 minutes or until cheese is melted.

TOP TIP

For a three-ingredient dessert, grill sliced pound cake and serve with whipped cream and your favorite fruit curd or berry sauce. Or sandwich mini marshmallows and chocolate chips between frozen waffles; wrap in foil and grill.

This pasta came about one night when I started making up dinner as I went along, using what was on hand. We knew it turned out great with the very first bite.

—LISA BYNUM BRANDON, MS

Shrimp & Tomato Linguine

START TO FINISH: 30 MIN.
MAKES: 4 SERVINGS

- 8 ounces uncooked linguine
- 16 cherry tomatoes
- 2 tablespoons olive oil
- 1 pound uncooked large shrimp, peeled and deveined
- ½ teaspoon pepper
- ¼ teaspoon salt
- ¼ teaspoon garlic powder
- ¼ teaspoon Italian seasoning
- 2 tablespoons butter
- ¼ cup grated Parmesan cheese
- 2 tablespoons torn fresh basil

1. In a large saucepan, cook linguine according to package directions. Meanwhile, thread tomatoes onto metal or soaked wooden skewers; brush with 1 tablespoon oil. Thread shrimp onto skewers; brush with remaining oil. Mix seasonings; sprinkle over shrimp.

2. Grill shrimp, covered, over medium heat 3-4 minutes on each side or until shrimp turn pink. Grill tomatoes, covered, over medium heat 2-3 minutes or until slightly softened, turning occasionally.

3. Drain linguine, reserving ¼ cup pasta water. In same saucepan, melt butter over medium heat. Add linguine, cheese and reserved pasta water, tossing to combine. Remove shrimp and tomatoes from skewers; serve with pasta. Sprinkle with basil.

PER SERVING *445 cal., 17 g fat (6 g sat. fat), 158 mg chol., 416 mg sodium, 45 g carb., 3 g fiber, 29 g pro.* **Diabetic Exchanges:** *3 starch, 3 lean meat, 3 fat.*

Grilled Garlic Bread

Until several years ago, I'd never thought of making garlic bread outdoors. But this quick recipe makes it easy. The results are always delicious, whether we're having steak or chicken.

—**PRISCILLA WEAVER** HAGERSTOWN, MD

START TO FINISH: 10 MIN.
MAKES: 8 SERVINGS

- 1 loaf (16 ounces) French bread
- ¼ cup butter, softened
- 1 teaspoon garlic powder

Cut the bread into eight slices. In a small bowl, combine the butter and garlic powder. Spread on one side of each slice of bread. Place bread, buttered side up, on a grill over medium heat for 2 minutes or until browned. Turn and grill 2 minutes longer or until browned.

SHRIMP & TOMATO LINGUINE

BASIL CHICKEN

FREEZE IT **EAT SMART**

Basil Chicken

This cinch of a marinade gives the chicken lots of Italian flavor. Serve with a tossed green salad and garlic breadsticks, or put slices on a ciabatta roll along with lettuce, tomato and mozzarella cheese for a zesty sandwich.

—LISA MORIARTY WILTON, NH

PREP: 10 MIN. + MARINATING
GRILL: 10 MIN.
MAKES: 4 SERVINGS

- 3 tablespoons red wine vinegar
- 3 tablespoons olive oil
- 2 tablespoons chopped red onion
- 2 tablespoons minced fresh basil
- 1 garlic clove, minced
- ¼ teaspoon salt
- ¼ teaspoon pepper
- 4 boneless skinless chicken breast halves (6 ounces each)
  Grilled romaine, optional

1. In a large resealable plastic bag, combine the first seven ingredients. Add chicken; seal bag and turn to coat. Refrigerate 8 hours or overnight.
2. Drain chicken, discarding marinade. Grill chicken, covered, over medium heat or broil 4 in. from heat 5-7 minutes on each side or until a thermometer reads 165°. If desired, serve over grilled romaine.
FREEZE OPTION *Freeze chicken with marinade in a resealable plastic freezer bag. To use, thaw in refrigerator overnight. Drain chicken, discarding marinade. Grill as directed.*
PER SERVING *231 cal., 9 g fat (2 g sat. fat), 94 mg chol., 156 mg sodium, 1 g carb., trace fiber, 34 g pro.* **Diabetic Exchanges:** *5 lean meat, 1 fat.*

FAST FIX
Berried Treasure Angel Food Cake

START TO FINISH: 25 MIN.
MAKES: 4 SERVINGS

- 8 slices angel food cake (1½ inches thick)
- ¼ cup butter, softened
- ½ cup heavy whipping cream
- ¼ teaspoon almond extract
- ¼ cup almond cake and pastry filling
- ½ cup fresh blueberries
- ½ cup fresh raspberries
- ½ cup sliced fresh strawberries
- ¼ cup mixed nuts, coarsely chopped
  Confectioners' sugar

1. Using a 1½-in. round cookie cutter, cut out the centers of half of the cake slices (discard removed cake or save for another use). Spread butter over both sides of cake slices. Grill cake, covered, over medium heat or broil 4 in. from heat 1-2 minutes on each side or until toasted.
2. In a small bowl, beat cream until it begins to thicken. Add extract; beat until soft peaks form.
3. To serve, stack one solid and one cutout slice of cake on each dessert plate, placing the outer edges on opposite sides for a more even thickness. Spoon almond filling into the holes; top with whipped cream, berries and nuts. Sprinkle with confectioners' sugar.

My husband grills anything and everything—even dessert! With his encouragement, I came up with this easy and colorful recipe that takes just a few minutes to prepare, yet always impresses dinner guests. **—ANITA ARCHIBALD** RICHMOND HILL, ON

BERRIED TREASURE ANGEL FOOD CAKE

SHRIMP KABOBS WITH
SPICY-SWEET SAUCE

(5)INGREDIENTS EAT SMART FAST FIX
Shrimp Kabobs with Spicy-Sweet Sauce

Just the right amount of spice adds a zip to the plump and juicy shrimp in this 5-ingredient appetizer.

—**SUSAN HARRISON** LAUREL, MD

START TO FINISH: 30 MIN.
MAKES: 15 SERVINGS (⅓ CUP SAUCE)

- 3 **tablespoons reduced-fat mayonnaise**
- 2 **tablespoons sweet chili sauce**
- 1 **green onion, thinly sliced**
- ¾ **teaspoon Sriracha Asian hot chili sauce or ½ teaspoon hot pepper sauce**
- 45 **uncooked large shrimp (about 1½ pounds), peeled and deveined**
- ¼ **teaspoon salt**
- ¼ **teaspoon pepper**

1. In a small bowl, mix mayonnaise, chili sauce, green onion and Sriracha. Sprinkle shrimp with salt and pepper. Thread three shrimp onto each of 15 metal or soaked wooden skewers.
2. Moisten a paper towel with cooking oil; using long-handled tongs, rub on grill rack to coat lightly. Grill shrimp, covered, over medium heat or broil 4 in. from heat 3-4 minutes on each side or until shrimp turn pink. Serve with sauce.

PER SERVING *56 cal., 2 g fat (trace sat. fat), 61 mg chol., 156 mg sodium, 2 g carb., trace fiber, 8 g pro.* **Diabetic Exchange:** *½ lean meat.*

FAST FIX
Grilled Chicken with Arugula Salad

When my husband found out he had diabetes, I was challenged to start cooking our old favorites in new, healthy ways that he would love just as much. This was the first one that made him say, "I can eat like this all the time!"

—**LYNNE KEAST** MONTE SERENO, CA

START TO FINISH: 30 MIN.
MAKES: 4 SERVINGS

- ⅔ **cup plus 2 tablespoons olive oil, divided**
- ¼ **cup finely chopped shallots**
- ¼ **cup champagne vinegar or white wine vinegar**
- 1 **teaspoon salt, divided**
- ½ **teaspoon pepper, divided**
- ½ **pound sliced baby portobello mushrooms**
- ½ **pound sliced fresh mushrooms**
- 4 **boneless skinless chicken breast halves (6 ounces each)**
- 6 **cups fresh baby arugula or baby spinach**
- ½ **cup shredded Parmesan cheese**

1. In a small bowl, whisk ⅔ cup oil, shallots, vinegar, ½ teaspoon salt and ¼ teaspoon pepper until blended. Reserve 3 tablespoons for dressing. Pour remaining vinaigrette into a large bowl; add mushrooms and toss to coat. Let stand 5 minutes.
2. Using a slotted spoon, remove mushrooms from vinaigrette. Transfer to a grill wok or basket; place on grill rack. Grill, covered, over medium heat 8-10 minutes or until tender, stirring occasionally.
3. Brush chicken with remaining oil; sprinkle with remaining salt and pepper. Grill, covered, over medium heat 6-8 minutes on each side or until a thermometer reads 165°.
4. Place arugula, grilled mushrooms and cheese in a large bowl. Add reserved vinaigrette; toss to coat. Serve with chicken.
NOTE *If you do not have a grill wok or basket, use a disposable foil pan. Poke holes in the bottom of the pan with a meat fork to allow liquid to drain.*

GRILLED
CHICKEN WITH
ARUGULA SALAD

GRILLED LEMON-
GARLIC SALMON

A lot of people fish for salmon here on the shore of Lake Michigan, so I've developed quite a few recipes for it. I love this recipe, and so do my friends and family. When we don't have local salmon, I look for wild-caught Alaskan salmon at the grocery store.
—**DIANE NEMITZ** LUDINGTON, MI

(5) INGREDIENTS FAST FIX
Grilled Lemon-Garlic Salmon

START TO FINISH: 30 MIN.
MAKES: 4 SERVINGS

- 2 garlic cloves, minced
- 2 teaspoons grated lemon peel
- ½ teaspoon salt
- ½ teaspoon minced fresh rosemary
- ½ teaspoon pepper
- 4 salmon fillets (6 ounces each)

1. In a small bowl, mix the first five ingredients; rub over fillets. Let stand 15 minutes. Moisten a paper towel with cooking oil; using long-handled tongs, rub on grill rack to coat lightly.

2. Place salmon on grill rack, skin side up. Grill, covered, over medium heat or broil 4 in. from heat 4 minutes. Turn; grill 3-6 minutes longer or until fish just begins to flake easily with a fork.

EAT SMART
Vegetable Steak Kabobs
The marinade for this steak and vegetable skewer is the best one I've ever found. I use it on chicken and pork, too.
—**NORMA HARDER** WEYAKWIN, , SK

PREP: 20 MIN. + MARINATING
GRILL: 10 MIN.
MAKES: 6 SERVINGS

- ½ cup olive oil
- ⅓ cup red wine vinegar
- 2 tablespoons ketchup
- 2 to 3 garlic cloves, minced
- 1 teaspoon Worcestershire sauce
- ½ teaspoon each dried marjoram, basil and oregano
- ½ teaspoon dried rosemary, crushed
- 1 beef top sirloin steak (1½ pounds), cut into 1-inch cubes
- ½ pound whole fresh mushrooms
- 2 medium onions, cut into wedges
- 1½ cups cherry tomatoes
- 2 small green peppers, cut into 1-inch pieces

1. In a small bowl, whisk oil, vinegar, ketchup, garlic, Worcestershire sauce and seasonings. Pour ½ cup marinade into a large resealable plastic bag. Add beef; seal bag and turn to coat. Pour remaining marinade into another large resealable plastic bag. Add mushrooms, onions, tomatoes and peppers; seal bag and turn to coat. Refrigerate beef and vegetables 8 hours or overnight.

2. Drain beef, discarding marinade. Drain vegetables, reserving marinade for basting. On six metal or soaked wooden skewers, alternately thread beef and vegetables.

3. Grill, covered, over medium heat or broil 4 in. from heat for 10-15 minutes or until beef reaches desired doneness and vegetables are crisp-tender, turning occasionally. Baste with reserved marinade during the last 5 minutes.

PER SERVING *234 cal., 10 g fat (2 g sat. fat), 69 mg chol., 99 mg sodium, 10 g carb., 2 g fiber, 26 g pro.* **Diabetic Exchanges:** *3 lean meat, 2 vegetable.*

VEGETABLE
STEAK KABOBS

Bruschetta Chicken Wraps

As an Italian-American, I love the garlic, tomatoes and basil that traditionally go into bruschetta. This recipe was created in celebration of the first tomatoes to come out of the garden.

—GINA RINE CANFIELD, OH

START TO FINISH: 30 MIN.
MAKES: 4 SERVINGS

- 2 **plum tomatoes, finely chopped (about 1 cup)**
- 1 **cup fresh baby spinach, coarsely chopped**
- ¼ **cup finely chopped red onion**
- 1 **tablespoon shredded Parmesan or Romano cheese**
- 1 **tablespoon minced fresh basil**
- 1 **teaspoon olive oil**
- 1 **teaspoon balsamic vinegar**
- ⅛ **teaspoon plus ¼ teaspoon pepper, divided**
  Dash garlic powder
- 4 **boneless skinless chicken breast halves (4 ounces each)**
- ½ **teaspoon salt**
- 2 **ounces fresh mozzarella cheese, cut into 4 slices**
- 4 **whole wheat tortillas (8 inches)**

1. In a small bowl, mix tomatoes, spinach, onion, Parmesan cheese, basil, oil, vinegar, ⅛ teaspoon pepper and garlic powder.

2. Moisten a paper towel with cooking oil; using long-handled tongs, rub on grill rack to coat lightly. Sprinkle chicken with salt and remaining pepper; place on grill rack. Grill, covered, over medium heat 4-6 minutes on each side or until a thermometer reads 165°.

3. Top each chicken breast with one cheese slice; cover and grill 1-2 minutes longer or until cheese is melted. Grill tortillas over medium heat 20-30 seconds or until heated through.

4. Place chicken on center of each tortilla; top with about ¼ cup tomato mixture. Fold bottom of tortilla over filling; fold both sides to close.

PER SERVING *330 cal., 10 g fat (3 g sat. fat), 75 mg chol., 569 mg sodium, 25 g carb., 3 g fiber, 31 g pro.* **Diabetic Exchanges:** *3 lean meat, 2 starch, 1 fat.*

BBQ Yumburgers

My husband absolutely can't resist these. I freeze patties ahead of time so I'm ready whenever a craving hits.

—ALAN HOYE WHITMORE LAKE, MI

START TO FINISH: 30 MIN.
MAKES: 4 SERVINGS

- 2 **teaspoons canola oil**
- 1 **large onion, halved and sliced**
- 1 **pound lean ground beef (90% lean)**
- 2 **tablespoons finely chopped onion**
- 2 **tablespoons barbecue sauce**
- 2 **garlic cloves, minced**
- 1 **teaspoon onion powder**
- ½ **teaspoon salt**
- ¼ **teaspoon pepper**
- 4 **whole wheat hamburger buns, split**
  Optional toppings: tomato slices, lettuce leaves and additional barbecue sauce

1. In a small skillet, heat oil over medium-high heat. Add sliced onion; cook and stir 4-6 minutes or until tender.

2. In a large bowl, combine beef, chopped onion, barbecue sauce, garlic, onion powder, salt and pepper, mixing lightly but thoroughly. Shape into four ½-in.-thick patties.

3. Grill burgers, covered, over medium heat or broil 4 in. from heat 4-6 minutes on each side or until a thermometer reads 160°. Serve on buns with cooked onions and, if desired, optional toppings.

FREEZE OPTION *Place patties on a plastic wrap-lined baking sheet; wrap and freeze until firm. Remove from pan and transfer to a resealable plastic freezer bag; return to freezer. To use, prepare sliced onions. Grill frozen patties as directed, increasing time as necessary for a thermometer to read 160°. Serve on buns with toppings.*

PER SERVING *341 cal., 14 g fat (4 g sat. fat), 71 mg chol., 634 mg sodium, 28 g carb., 4 g fiber, 26 g pro.* **Diabetic Exchanges:** *3 lean meat, 2 starch, ½ fat.*

BBQ YUMBURGERS

PEPPERED TUNA KABOBS

Peppered Tuna Kabobs

We like to wow our guests when we barbecue, so hot dogs and burgers are out! We make tuna skewers topped with salsa—the perfect easy recipe. My five kids like to help me put them together.

—JENNIFER INGERSOLL HERNDON, VA

START TO FINISH: 30 MIN.
MAKES: 4 SERVINGS

- ½ cup frozen corn, thawed
- 4 green onions, chopped
- 1 jalapeno pepper, seeded and chopped
- 2 tablespoons coarsely chopped fresh parsley
- 2 tablespoons lime juice
- 1 pound tuna steaks, cut into 1-inch cubes
- 1 teaspoon coarsely ground pepper
- 2 large sweet red peppers, cut into 2x1-inch pieces
- 1 medium mango, peeled and cut into 1-inch cubes

1. For salsa, in a small bowl, combine the first five ingredients; set aside.

2. Moisten a paper towel with cooking oil; using long-handled tongs, rub on grill rack to coat lightly. Rub tuna with pepper. On four metal or soaked wooden skewers, alternately thread red peppers, tuna and mango.

3. Grill, covered, over medium heat 10-12 minutes for medium-rare or until slightly pink in the center and peppers are tender, turning occasionally. Serve with salsa.

NOTE *Wear disposable gloves when cutting hot peppers; the oils can burn skin. Avoid touching your face.*

PER SERVING *205 cal., 2 g fat (trace sat. fat), 51 mg chol., 50 mg sodium, 20 g carb., 4 g fiber, 29 g pro.* **Diabetic Exchanges:** *3 lean meat, 1 starch.*

TOP TIP

To substitute fresh corn when it's in season, just cut the kernels from one ear of corn instead of using frozen. If desired, microwave corn, covered, with 1 tablespoon of water for 1 minute or until crisp-tender; cool.

Strawberry-Chicken Pasta Salad

PREP: 25 MIN. • **GRILL:** 15 MIN.
MAKES: 4 SERVINGS

- ½ cup sliced fresh strawberries
- 1 tablespoon sugar
- 1 tablespoon balsamic vinegar
- ½ teaspoon salt, divided
- ¼ teaspoon pepper, divided
- 3 tablespoons olive oil
- 4 boneless skinless chicken breast halves (6 ounces each)

ASSEMBLY
- 1 package (10 ounces) hearts of romaine salad mix
- 1 cup cooked gemelli or spiral pasta
- 1 small red onion, halved and thinly sliced
- 1 cup sliced fresh strawberries
- ½ cup glazed pecans

1. Place strawberries, sugar, vinegar, ¼ teaspoon salt and ⅛ teaspoon pepper in a blender; cover and process until smooth. While processing, gradually add oil in a steady stream. Refrigerate until serving.

2. Moisten a paper towel with cooking oil; using long-handled tongs, rub on grill rack to coat lightly. Sprinkle chicken with remaining salt and pepper; grill, covered, over medium heat 6-8 minutes on each side or until a thermometer reads 165°.

3. Cut chicken into slices. Divide salad mix among four plates; top with pasta, onion, chicken and strawberries. Drizzle with vinaigrette; sprinkle with pecans.

When I figured out how to re-create this restaurant dish at home, my family was so excited. For a different spin, use raspberries or peaches instead of strawberries.
—JANE OZMENT PURCELL, OK

STRAWBERRY-CHICKEN PASTA SALAD

I actually created this at a campground, so you know it's easy. Using the same marinade for the chicken and veggies keeps it simple so we can spend more time outside and less making dinner.

—**JAYME SCHERTZ** CLINTONVILLE, WI

APPLE-MARINATED CHICKEN & VEGETABLES

Apple-Marinated Chicken & Vegetables

PREP: 20 MIN. + MARINATING
GRILL: 25 MIN.
MAKES: 6 SERVINGS

- 1 **cup apple juice**
- ½ **cup canola oil**
- ¼ **cup packed brown sugar**
- ¼ **cup reduced-sodium soy sauce**
- 3 **tablespoons lemon juice**
- 2 **tablespoons minced fresh parsley**
- 3 **garlic cloves, minced**
- 6 **boneless skinless chicken breast halves (6 ounces each)**
- 4 **large carrots**
- 2 **medium zucchini**
- 2 **medium yellow summer squash**

1. In a small bowl, whisk the first seven ingredients until blended. Place 1 cup marinade and chicken in a large resealable plastic bag; seal bag and turn to coat. Refrigerate 6 hours or overnight. Cover and refrigerate remaining marinade.
2. Cut carrots, zucchini and squash lengthwise into quarters; cut crosswise into 2-in. pieces. Toss with ½ cup reserved marinade.
3. Drain chicken, discarding marinade in bag. Grill chicken, covered, over medium heat or broil 4 in. from heat 6-8 minutes on each side or until a thermometer reads 165°, basting frequently with remaining marinade during the last 5 minutes. Keep warm.
4. Transfer vegetables to a grill wok or basket; place on grill rack. Grill, covered, over medium heat 10-12 minutes or until crisp-tender, stirring frequently. Serve chicken with vegetables.
NOTE *If you do not have a grill wok or basket, use a disposable foil pan. Poke holes in the bottom of the pan with a meat fork to allow liquid to drain.*
PER SERVING *367 cal., 16 g fat (2 g sat. fat), 94 mg chol., 378 mg sodium, 19 g carb., 3 g fiber, 37 g pro.*

⑤ INGREDIENTS FAST FIX ▶

Loaded Flank Steak

I wanted to do something a little different with flank steak, so I stuffed it with bacon, green onions and ranch dressing. The recipe is fast, but it's a little bit fancy, too.

—**TAMMY THOMAS** MUSTANG, OK

START TO FINISH: 25 MIN.
MAKES: 6 SERVINGS

- ½ **cup butter, softened**
- 6 **bacon strips, cooked and crumbled**
- 3 **green onions, chopped**
- 2 **tablespoons ranch salad dressing mix**
- ½ **teaspoon pepper**
- 1 **beef flank steak (1½ to 2 pounds)**

1. In a small bowl, beat the first five ingredients. Cut a pocket horizontally in steak; fill with butter mixture.
2. Grill the steak, covered, over medium heat or broil 4 in. from heat 5-7 minutes on each side or until the meat reaches desired doneness (for medium-rare, a thermometer should read 145°; medium, 160°; well-done, 170°). Let stand for 5 minutes before serving. To serve, slice meat across the grain.

LOADED FLANK STEAK

HEARTY PORK CHOPS

Hearty Pork Chops

Just a few quick ingredients turn these pork chops into something fantastic. The marinade works its magic overnight so you can have dinner on the table in no time tomorrow.

—TASTE OF HOME TEST KITCHEN

PREP: 15 MIN. + MARINATING
GRILL: 10 MIN.
MAKES: 6 SERVINGS

- ⅔ cup diet lemon-lime soda
- ½ cup reduced-sodium soy sauce
- ¼ cup honey
- 1 teaspoon dried thyme
- ¾ teaspoon dried rosemary, crushed
- ¼ teaspoon pepper
- 6 bone-in pork loin chops (¾ inch thick and 7 ounces each)

1. In a large resealable plastic bag, combine the first six ingredients. Add pork chops; seal bag and turn to coat. Refrigerate 4 hours or overnight.

2. Drain pork, discarding marinade. Moisten a paper towel with cooking oil; using long-handled tongs, rub on grill rack to coat lightly.

3. Grill pork, covered, over medium heat or broil 4 in. from heat 4-5 minutes on each side or until a thermometer reads 145°. Let stand 5 minutes.

FREEZE OPTION *Freeze pork with marinade in a resealable plastic freezer bag. To use, thaw in refrigerator overnight. Drain pork, discarding marinade. Grill as directed.*

PER SERVING *227 cal., 8 g fat (3 g sat. fat), 86 mg chol., 387 mg sodium, 5 g carb., trace fiber, 31 g pro.* **Diabetic Exchange:** *4 lean meat.*

Whiskey Cheddar Burgers

This juicy burger has big flavors to satisfy even the heartiest appetites. It always impresses at our cookouts.

—AMBER NICHOLSON WINOOSKI, VT

START TO FINISH: 30 MIN.
MAKES: 8 SERVINGS

- ¼ cup whiskey
- 1 tablespoon reduced-sodium soy sauce
- 1 tablespoon Worcestershire sauce
- 1 cup (4 ounces) shredded sharp cheddar cheese
- ¼ cup finely chopped onion
- 2 tablespoons seasoned bread crumbs
- 3 garlic cloves, minced
- ½ teaspoon salt
- ½ teaspoon paprika
- ½ teaspoon dried basil
- ½ teaspoon pepper
- 1½ pounds lean ground beef (90% lean)
- 8 onion rolls or hamburger buns, split
  Optional toppings: lettuce leaves, sliced tomato, cheddar cheese slices and barbecue sauce

1. In a large bowl, combine the first 11 ingredients. Add beef; mix lightly but thoroughly. Shape into eight ½-in.-thick patties.

2. Moisten a paper towel with cooking oil; using long-handled tongs, rub on grill rack to coat lightly. Grill burgers, covered, over medium heat or broil 4 in. from heat 4-5 minutes on each side or until a thermometer reads 160°. Serve burgers on rolls with toppings as desired.

FREEZE OPTION *Place patties on a plastic wrap-lined baking sheet; wrap and freeze until firm. Remove from pan and transfer to a resealable plastic freezer bag; return to freezer. To use, grill frozen patties as directed, increasing time as necessary for a thermometer to read 160°.*

WHISKEY CHEDDAR BURGERS

FAST FIX ▶
Marinated Pork Mixed Grill

My whole family gets so happy when they see me prepping this simple meal. When we have leftovers, it's sandwich heaven.

—MARIA BARAL BOZRAH, CT

START TO FINISH: 30 MIN.
MAKES: 4 SERVINGS

- 2 **medium onions, cut into ½-inch-thick slices**
- 2 **medium sweet red peppers, cut into 1½-inch strips**
- 2 **medium green peppers, cut into 1½-inch strips**
- 2 **medium zucchini, cut lengthwise into ½-inch-thick slices**
- ½ **cup balsamic vinaigrette**
- 1 **peppercorn pork tenderloin (1 pound), halved lengthwise**
- 1 **loaf (10 ounces) frozen garlic bread**
   Additional balsamic vinaigrette, optional

1. In a large bowl, combine vegetables and vinaigrette. Grill pork, covered, over medium heat 4 minutes. Turn; add vegetables. Grill 4-5 minutes longer or until a thermometer inserted in pork reads 145°. Remove pork from grill; tent with foil.

2. Place garlic bread on grill rack, cut side up. Turn vegetables; grill, covered, over medium heat 4-6 minutes longer or until the vegetables are tender, garlic bread is heated through and bottom is toasted.

3. Cut tenderloin and garlic bread into serving-size pieces. Serve with vegetables and, if desired, additional vinaigrette.

FAST FIX ▶
Loaded Grilled Chicken Sandwich

I threw these ingredients together on a whim and the sandwich turned out so well, I surprised myself! If you're in a rush, try microwaving the bacon. Just cover it with some paper towel to keep it from splattering too much.

—DANA YORK KENNEWICK, WA

START TO FINISH: 30 MIN.
MAKES: 4 SERVINGS

- 4 **boneless skinless chicken breast halves (4 ounces each)**
- 2 **teaspoons Italian salad dressing mix**
- 4 **slices pepper jack cheese**

LOADED GRILLED CHICKEN SANDWICH

- 4 **ciabatta or kaiser rolls, split**
- 2 **tablespoons mayonnaise**
- ¾ **teaspoon Dijon mustard**
- 4 **cooked bacon strips, halved**
- 4 **slices tomato**
- ½ **medium ripe avocado, peeled and thinly sliced**
- ½ **pound deli coleslaw (about 1 cup)**

1. Pound chicken with a meat mallet to flatten slightly; sprinkle both sides with dressing mix. Moisten a paper towel with cooking oil; using long-handled tongs, rub on the grill rack to coat lightly.

2. Grill chicken, covered, over medium heat or broil 4 in. from heat 4-6 minutes on each side or until a thermometer reads 165°. Place cheese on chicken; grill, covered, 1-2 minutes longer or until cheese is melted. Meanwhile, grill rolls, cut side down, 1-2 minutes or until toasted.

3. Mix mayonnaise and mustard; spread on roll tops. Layer roll bottoms with chicken, bacon, tomato, avocado and coleslaw. Replace tops.

TOP TIP

The best part of this dish, in my opinion, was the sauce. I doubled the amount of mayo and mustard, then added about a teaspoon of crushed rosemary. Delicious! My mind immediately began thinking of all the possible ways this sauce could be used.
—AMYGRANTFAN TASTEOFHOME.COM

MARINATED PORK MIXED GRILL

SPICED GRILLED CORN

1 tablespoon prepared horseradish
1 egg, beaten
¼ teaspoon salt
⅛ teaspoon pepper
1 pound salmon fillet, skin removed and cut into 1-inch cubes
8 whole wheat dinner rolls, split and toasted
¼ cup reduced-fat garlic-herb spreadable cheese
8 small lettuce leaves

1. In a large bowl, combine the first seven ingredients. Place salmon in food processor; pulse until coarsely chopped and add to bread crumb mixture. Mix lightly but thoroughly. Shape into eight ½-in.-thick patties.

2. Moisten a paper towel with cooking oil; using long-handled tongs, rub on grill rack to coat lightly. Grill burgers, covered, over medium heat or broil 4 in. from heat 3-4 minutes on each side or until a thermometer reads 160°. Serve on rolls with spreadable cheese and lettuce.

PER SERVING *442 cal., 17 g fat (5 g sat. fat), 119 mg chol., 676 mg sodium, 42 g carb., 6 g fiber, 30 g pro.* **Diabetic Exchanges:** *3 starch, 3 lean meat, 1 fat.*

Spiced Grilled Corn

The wonderful spice mixture doesn't add heat...only great flavor. This just may be the best corn you've ever had!
—*TASTE OF HOME* TEST KITCHEN

START TO FINISH: 20 MIN.
MAKES: 8 SERVINGS

2 teaspoons ground cumin
2 teaspoons ground coriander
1 teaspoon salt
1 teaspoon dried oregano
½ teaspoon ground ginger
¼ teaspoon ground cinnamon
¼ teaspoon pepper
⅛ teaspoon ground cloves
2 tablespoons olive oil
8 medium ears sweet corn, husks removed

1. In a small bowl, combine the first eight ingredients. Brush oil over corn; sprinkle with spice mixture. Place each on a piece of heavy-duty foil (about 14x12-in. rectangle). Fold foil over corn, sealing tightly.

2. Grill corn, covered, over medium heat 10-12 minutes or until tender, turning occasionally. Open foil carefully to allow steam to escape.

PER SERVING *113 cal., 5 g fat (1 g sat. fat), 0 chol., 310 mg sodium, 18 g carb., 3 g fiber, 3 g pro.* **Diabetic Exchanges:** *1 starch, ½ fat.*

Garlic-Herb Salmon Sliders

I serve these as full-size burgers on kaiser rolls, too. The fresh flavors of salmon and herbs are just unbeatable.
—**MARGEE BERRY** WHITE SALMON, WA

PREP: 25 MIN. • **GRILL:** 10 MIN.
MAKES: 4 SERVINGS

⅓ cup panko (Japanese) bread crumbs
4 teaspoons finely chopped shallot
2 teaspoons snipped fresh dill

GARLIC-HERB SALMON SLIDERS

FREEZE IT (5) INGREDIENTS

Chili Sauce Chicken

Chili sauce, with plenty of garlic and basil, makes this meal pop. In my family, grilled chicken is on the menu all year long—not just in summer.

—MARILYN WALTZ IDYLLWILD, CA

PREP: 15 MIN. + MARINATING
GRILL: 25 MIN.
MAKES: 8 SERVINGS

- 1 bottle (12 ounces) chili sauce
- ⅓ cup white wine or chicken broth
- ¼ cup olive oil
- 10 to 12 garlic cloves, minced
- 4½ teaspoons dried basil
- ½ teaspoon salt
- ⅛ teaspoon pepper
- 8 bone-in chicken thighs (about 3 pounds)

1. In a large bowl, whisk the first seven ingredients until blended. Pour 1½ cups marinade into a large resealable plastic bag. Add chicken; seal bag and turn to coat. Refrigerate 8 hours or overnight. Cover and refrigerate remaining marinade.
2. Drain chicken, discarding marinade in bag. Moisten a paper towel with cooking oil; using long-handled tongs, rub on grill rack to coat lightly.
3. Place chicken on grill rack, skin side down. Grill, covered, over medium heat or broil 4 in. from heat for 15 minutes. Turn chicken; grill 10-15 minutes longer or until a thermometer reads 170°-175°, basting occasionally with reserved marinade.

FREEZE OPTION *Freeze chicken with 1½ cups marinade in a resealable plastic freezer bag. Freeze reserved marinade in a freezer container. To use, thaw chicken with marinade and reserved marinade in refrigerator overnight. Drain chicken, discarding marinade in bag. Grill as directed, basting with reserved marinade.*

GRILLED PORTOBELLO BURGERS

EAT SMART FAST FIX

Grilled Portobello Burgers

You won't miss the meat on this hearty burger. The savory veggies and creamy mozzarella will satisfy you with plenty of flavor.

—MARY HAAS HEWITT, NJ

START TO FINISH: 25 MIN.
MAKES: 4 SERVINGS

- 4 large portobello mushrooms (4 to 4½ inches), stems removed
- 6 tablespoons reduced-fat balsamic vinaigrette, divided
- 4 slices red onion
- 1 cup roasted sweet red peppers, drained
- 3 ounces fresh mozzarella cheese, cut into 4 slices
- 4 kaiser rolls, split
- ¼ cup fat-free mayonnaise

1. Brush mushrooms with 4 tablespoons vinaigrette. Grill mushrooms and onion, covered, over medium heat 3-4 minutes on each side or until tender. Top mushrooms with red peppers, onion and cheese. Grill, covered, 2-3 minutes longer or until cheese is melted. Grill rolls, cut side down, 1-2 minutes or until toasted.
2. Spread kaiser roll bottoms with mayonnaise and drizzle with the remaining vinaigrette. Top with mushrooms; replace roll tops.

PER SERVING *329 cal., 11 g fat (4 g sat. fat), 19 mg chol., 860 mg sodium, 42 g carb., 3 g fiber, 12 g pro.*

CHILI SAUCE CHICKEN

Every year, my father and I plant a garden together. We like to use fresh herbs from our garden, but you could use 1/3 teaspoon of each dried herb that you don't have available fresh.

—BERNADETTE BENNETT WACO, TX

Herbed Potato Packet

PREP: 10 MIN. • **GRILL:** 25 MIN.
MAKES: 4 SERVINGS

- 1 **pound baby red potatoes (about 16), halved**
- ¼ **cup cranberry juice**
- 2 **tablespoons butter, cubed**
- 1 **teaspoon each minced fresh dill, oregano, rosemary and thyme**
- ½ **teaspoon salt**
- ⅛ **teaspoon pepper**

1. In a large bowl, combine all ingredients; place on a piece of heavy-duty foil (about 18x12-in. rectangle). Fold foil around mixture, sealing tightly.

2. Grill, covered, over medium heat 25-30 minutes or until potatoes are tender. Open foil carefully to allow steam to escape.

PER SERVING *117 cal., 6 g fat (4 g sat. fat), 15 mg chol., 351 mg sodium, 15 g carb., 1 g fiber, 2 g pro.* **Diabetic Exchanges:** *1 starch, 1 fat*

FREEZE IT EAT SMART
Easy Marinated Flank Steak

I got this recipe from a friend 15 years ago. Even now, when my family makes steak on the grill, this is the recipe we use. It's a must when we're having company.

—DEBBIE BONCZEK TARIFFVILLE, CT

PREP: 10 MIN. + MARINATING
GRILL: 15 MIN.
MAKES: 8 SERVINGS

- 3 **tablespoons ketchup**
- 1 **tablespoon chopped onion**
- 1 **tablespoon canola oil**
- 1 **teaspoon brown sugar**
- 1 **teaspoon Worcestershire sauce**
- 1 **garlic clove, minced**
- ⅛ **teaspoon pepper**
- 1 **beef flank steak (about 2 pounds)**

1. In a large resealable plastic bag, combine the first seven ingredients. Add beef; seal bag and turn to coat. Refrigerate 8 hours or overnight.

2. Drain beef, discarding marinade. Moisten a paper towel with cooking oil; using long-handled tongs, rub on grill rack to coat lightly.

3. Grill beef, covered, over medium heat or broil 4 in. from heat 6-8 minutes on each side or until meat reaches desired doneness (for medium-rare, a thermometer should read 145°; medium, 160°; well-done, 170°). To serve, thinly slice beef across the grain.

FREEZE OPTION *Freeze beef with marinade in a resealable plastic freezer bag. To use, thaw in refrigerator overnight. Drain beef, discarding marinade. Grill as directed.*

PER SERVING *192 cal., 10 g fat (4 g sat. fat), 54 mg chol., 145 mg sodium, 2 g carb., trace fiber, 22 g pro.* **Diabetic Exchange:** *3 lean meat.*

HERBED POTATO PACKET

CHICKEN PARMESAN BURGERS

We love chicken Parmesan and thought, "Why not make it a burger?" I like to use fresh mozzarella on these. I've also made the burgers with ground turkey. —CHARLOTTE GEHLE BROWNSTOWN, MI

FREEZE IT EAT SMART FAST FIX

Chicken Parmesan Burgers

START TO FINISH: 30 MIN.
MAKES: 4 SERVINGS

- ½ **cup dry bread crumbs**
- ¼ **cup grated Parmesan cheese**
- 3 **garlic cloves, minced**
- 1 **tablespoon minced fresh basil or 1 teaspoon dried basil**
- ½ **teaspoon dried oregano**
- 1 **pound lean ground chicken**
- 1 **cup meatless spaghetti sauce, divided**
- 2 **slices part-skim mozzarella cheese, cut in half**
- 4 **slices Italian bread (¾ inch thick)**

1. In a large bowl, combine the first five ingredients. Add chicken; mix lightly but thoroughly. Shape into four ½-in.-thick oval patties.
2. Grill burgers, covered, over medium heat or broil 4 in. from heat 4-7 minutes on each side or until a thermometer reads 165°. Top burgers with ½ cup spaghetti sauce and cheese. Cover and grill 30-60 seconds longer or until cheese is melted.
3. Grill bread, uncovered, over medium heat or broil 4 in. from heat 30-60 seconds on each side or until toasted. Top with remaining spaghetti sauce. Serve burgers on toasted bread.

FREEZE OPTION *Place patties on a plastic wrap-lined baking sheet; wrap and freeze until firm. Remove from pan and transfer to a resealable plastic freezer bag; return to freezer. To use, grill frozen patties as directed, increasing time as necessary for a thermometer to read 165°.*

PER SERVING *381 cal., 12 g fat (5 g sat. fat), 93 mg chol., 784 mg sodium, 32 g carb., 3 g fiber, 35 g pro.* **Diabetic Exchanges:** *3 lean meat, 2 starch, 1 fat.*

⑤INGREDIENTS **EAT SMART** **FAST FIX**

Teriyaki Salmon

For this delectable glaze, I blend maple syrup from our neck of the woods with teriyaki sauce from the other side of the world. It makes the salmon moist and absolutely delicious.
—LENITA SCHAFER PRINCETON, MA

START TO FINISH: 30 MIN.
MAKES: 4 SERVINGS

- ¾ **cup reduced-sodium teriyaki sauce**
- ½ **cup maple syrup**
- 4 **salmon fillets (6 ounces each)**
  Mixed salad greens, optional

1. In a small bowl, whisk teriyaki sauce and syrup. Pour 1 cup marinade into a large resealable plastic bag. Add salmon; seal bag and turn to coat. Refrigerate 15 minutes. Cover and refrigerate remaining marinade.
2. Drain salmon, discarding marinade in bag. Moisten a paper towel with cooking oil; using long-handled tongs, rub on grill rack to coat lightly.
3. Place salmon on grill rack, skin side down. Grill, covered, over medium heat or broil 4 in. from heat 8-12 minutes or until fish just begins to flake easily with a fork, basting frequently with reserved marinade. If desired, serve over lettuce salad.

PER SERVING *362 cal., 18 g fat (4 g sat. fat), 100 mg chol., 422 mg sodium, 12 g carb., 0 fiber, 35 g pro.* **Diabetic Exchanges:** *5 lean meat, 1 starch.*

TERIYAKI SALMON

BOURBON CHOPS

1. In a small bowl, mix mayonnaise, cheese and ketchup. In a large bowl, mix tomato paste, salt and pepper. Add beef; mix lightly but thoroughly. Shape into eight ¾-in.-thick patties.
2. Grill burgers, covered, over medium heat or broil 4 in. from the heat 5-8 minutes on each side or until a thermometer reads 160°. Serve burgers on buns with sauce, lettuce, bacon and, if desired, tomato.

FREEZE OPTION *Place patties on a plastic wrap-lined baking sheet; wrap and freeze until firm. Remove from pan and transfer to a resealable plastic freezer bag; return to freezer. To use, grill frozen patties as directed, increasing time as necessary for a thermometer to read 160°.*

FAST FIX
Grilled Romaine with Chive-Buttermilk Dressing

I was grilling steak one night and wanted to make a special side dish. I'd recently seen a grilled Caesar salad recipe, and decided to create my own version. This goes well with chicken, too, and it couldn't be easier.
—**CRYSTAL SCHLUETER** NORTHGLENN, CO

START TO FINISH: 25 MIN.
MAKES: 4 SERVINGS

- 2 **romaine hearts, halved lengthwise**
- 3 **tablespoons olive oil**
- 3 **tablespoons buttermilk**
- 3 **tablespoons reduced-fat plain Greek yogurt**
- 4 **teaspoons minced fresh chives**
- 2 **teaspoons lemon juice**
- ½ **teaspoon minced garlic**
  Dash salt
  Dash pepper
- ¼ **cup shredded Parmesan cheese**
- 4 **bacon strips, cooked and crumbled**

1. Brush romaine halves with oil. Grill romaine, uncovered, over medium-high heat 6-8 minutes or until leaves begin to wilt and color, turning once.
2. Meanwhile, in a small bowl, whisk buttermilk, yogurt, chives, lemon juice, garlic, salt and pepper until blended; drizzle over cut sides of romaine. Top with cheese and bacon.

FAST FIX
Bourbon Chops

My husband is a grill master and loves a good bourbon, making this recipe perfect for us! Sometimes we use thicker chops. If you do, too, remember to cook them long enough to reach 145°.
—**DONNA BRYAN** COLUMBIA FALLS, MT

START TO FINISH: 25 MIN.
MAKES: 4 SERVINGS

- ¼ **cup bourbon or unsweetened apple juice**
- 2 **tablespoons brown sugar**
- 2 **tablespoons Dijon mustard**
- 3 **garlic cloves, minced**
- 1 **teaspoon onion powder**
- ½ **teaspoon salt**
- ¼ **teaspoon pepper**
- 4 **bone-in pork loin chops (½ inch thick and 8 ounces each)**

1. In a small saucepan, mix bourbon, brown sugar, mustard and garlic cloves; bring to a boil. Reduce heat; simmer, uncovered, 2-3 minutes or until slightly thickened.
2. Mix onion powder, salt and pepper; sprinkle over pork chops. Grill, covered, over medium heat or broil 4 in. from heat 3-5 minutes on each side or until a thermometer reads 145°. Let stand 5 minutes before serving. Serve with sauce.

FREEZE IT **FAST FIX**
BLT Burgers

My husband loves a good BLT, but sometimes he wants something a little more substantial. That's where these burgers come in. He can't get enough of them.
—**DEBORAH BIGGS** OMAHA, NE

START TO FINISH: 30 MIN.
MAKES: 8 SERVINGS

- 1 **cup mayonnaise**
- ½ **cup crumbled blue cheese**
- ¼ **cup ketchup**
- 3 **tablespoons tomato paste**
- 1 **teaspoon salt**
- 1 **teaspoon pepper**
- 3 **pounds ground beef**
- 8 **hamburger buns, split**
- 8 **lettuce leaves**
- 24 **cooked bacon strips**
- 8 **slices tomato, optional**

Pesto Pasta & Potatoes
PAGE 244

Speedy Sides & Salads

The fresh-picked salads and hot veggie sides in this chapter will effortlessly complement your entree for weeknight dinners, picnics and even holidays. You'll also find satisfying potato dishes, flavorful grains and smart main-dish salads perfect for the summer months.

Honey-Lime Berry Salad
PAGE 233

Chive & Onion Hash Brown Potatoes
PAGE 227

Thymed Zucchini Saute
PAGE 230

APPLE SALAD WITH MAPLE-MUSTARD VINAIGRETTE

Christmas Cauliflower Casserole

Filled with tender cauliflower and topped with a sprinkling of crispy herb stuffing, this holiday classic appeals to both kids and adults alike.

—**CAROL REX** OCALA, FL

PREP: 20 MIN. • **BAKE:** 20 MIN.
MAKES: 12 SERVINGS (¾ CUP EACH)

- 3 packages (16 ounces each) frozen cauliflower
- 2 cups (16 ounces) sour cream
- 2 cups (8 ounces) shredded cheddar cheese
- 3 teaspoons chicken bouillon granules
- 1½ teaspoons ground mustard
- ¼ cup butter, cubed
- 1 cup stuffing mix
- ¾ cup chopped walnuts

1. Preheat oven to 375°. Cook cauliflower according to package directions; drain.
2. In a large bowl, mix sour cream, cheese, bouillon and mustard until blended. Stir in cauliflower; transfer to a greased 13x9-in. baking dish.
3. In a large skillet, heat butter over medium heat. Add stuffing mix and walnuts; cook and stir until lightly toasted. Sprinkle over casserole. Bake, uncovered, 17-20 minutes or until heated through and topping is browned.

CHRISTMAS CAULIFLOWER CASSEROLE

EAT SMART | **FAST FIX**

Apple Salad with Maple-Mustard Vinaigrette

Take this seasonal salad to any get-together. Making it for a smaller group? No problem! Just halve the recipe.

—**BETH DAUENHAUER** PUEBLO, CO

START TO FINISH: 15 MIN.
MAKES: 12 SERVINGS (1 CUP EACH)

- ¼ cup thawed frozen apple juice concentrate
- 2 tablespoons cider vinegar
- 2 tablespoons canola oil
- 2 tablespoons spicy brown mustard
- 2 tablespoons maple syrup
- ¼ teaspoon salt
- ⅛ teaspoon pepper
- **SALAD**
- 9 cups torn mixed salad greens
- 2 large tart apples, chopped
- 1 small red onion, thinly sliced
- ⅓ cup chopped walnuts, toasted

In a small bowl, whisk the first seven ingredients. In a large bowl, combine salad greens, apples, onion and walnuts. Drizzle with vinaigrette; toss to coat.

NOTE *To toast nuts, spread in a 15x10x1-in. baking pan. Bake at 350° for 5-10 minutes or until lightly browned, stirring occasionally. Or, spread in a dry nonstick skillet and heat over low heat until lightly browned, stirring occasionally.*
PER SERVING *87 cal., 5 g fat (trace sat. fat), 0 chol., 103 mg sodium, 11 g carb., 2 g fiber, 1 g pro.* **Diabetic Exchanges:** *1 vegetable, 1 fat, ½ starch.*

VERMICELLI PASTA SALAD

I started making this salad because it's loaded with peppers, my husband's favorite. Don't be surprised when there are no leftovers to take home after the family reunion, picnic or church potluck.

—JANIE COLLE HUTCHINSON, KS

Vermicelli Pasta Salad

PREP: 20 MIN. + CHILLING
MAKES: 10 SERVINGS

- 12 ounces uncooked vermicelli
- 1 bottle (16 ounces) creamy Italian salad dressing
- 1 small green pepper, chopped
- 1 small sweet red pepper, chopped
- 6 green onions, chopped
- 1 teaspoon dill seed
- 1 teaspoon caraway seeds
- 1 teaspoon poppy seeds

Cook vermicelli according to package directions. Drain; transfer to a large bowl. Add remaining ingredients; toss to coat. Refrigerate until cold.

TOP TIP

When I accidentally chop too many green onions, I store the leftovers in a covered glass jar in the refrigerator. That way, I'm all set for my next recipe that calls for green onions.

—ZELMA K. BONITA, CA

Creamy Roasted Garlic & Spinach Orzo

This side dish brings instant comfort. I first made it without spinach so my husband and daughter would like it. The next time I made it, I added spinach and they still devoured it. In my book, that's a win-win.

—**DAWN MOORE** WARREN, PA

PREP: 35 MIN. • **COOK:** 20 MIN.
MAKES: 6 SERVINGS

- 1 whole garlic bulb
- 1 teaspoon plus 1 tablespoon olive oil, divided
- 1¾ cups uncooked whole wheat orzo pasta
- 2½ cups chicken stock
- 3 ounces reduced-fat cream cheese, cubed
- 1 package (9 ounces) fresh spinach, trimmed and chopped
- ¼ cup shredded Asiago cheese
- ¼ cup fat-free milk
- 1 teaspoon salt-free garlic pepper seasoning blend
- ¼ teaspoon salt
- 2 tablespoons minced fresh parsley

1. Preheat oven to 425°. Remove papery outer skin from garlic bulb, but do not peel or separate the cloves. Cut off top of garlic bulb, exposing the individual cloves. Drizzle cut cloves with 1 teaspoon oil. Wrap in foil. Bake 30-35 minutes or until cloves are soft. Unwrap. When cool enough to handle, squeeze garlic from skins.
2. In a Dutch oven, heat remaining oil over medium-high heat. Add pasta; cook and stir over medium-high heat 2-3 minutes or until lightly browned. Add stock; bring to a boil. Reduce heat; simmer, covered, 10-12 minutes or until pasta is tender and liquid is absorbed.
3. Stir in cream cheese until melted. Add spinach, Asiago cheese, milk, seasoning blend, salt and roasted garlic; cook and stir until spinach is wilted. Sprinkle with parsley.
PER SERVING *271 cal., 8 g fat (3 g sat. fat), 14 mg chol., 422 mg sodium, 37 g carb., 9 g fiber, 12 g pro.* **Diabetic Exchanges:** *2 starch, 1½ fat, 1 vegetable.*

Crispy Shrimp Caesar Salad

My friend Jane and I have a favorite lunch spot that serves a fantastic salad on Wednesdays. I made my own version at home, so I can enjoy it whenever I want. Save a lot of prep time and buy peeled, deveined shrimp and pre-washed lettuce.

—MARLA CLARK ALBUQUERQUE, NM

START TO FINISH: 30 MIN.
MAKES: 4 SERVINGS

- 2 romaine hearts, coarsely chopped
- 1 cup cherry tomatoes, halved
- ¼ cup shredded Parmesan cheese
- ½ cup all-purpose flour
- ¾ teaspoon salt
- ½ teaspoon pepper
- 1 pound uncooked large shrimp, peeled and deveined
  Oil for frying
- ½ cup creamy Caesar salad dressing
  Additional shredded Parmesan cheese and pepper, optional

1. In a large bowl, combine romaine, tomatoes and cheese; refrigerate until serving. In a shallow bowl, mix flour, salt and pepper. Add shrimp, a few pieces at a time, and toss to coat; shake off excess.

2. In a deep skillet, heat ¼ in. oil to 375°. Fry shrimp, a few at a time, 1-2 minutes on each side or until golden brown. Drain on paper towels.

3. Drizzle dressing over romaine mixture and toss to coat. Top with shrimp. If desired, sprinkle with additional cheese and pepper; serve immediately.

TOP TIP

This salad has just the right balance between tender and crispy, though I did add extra ingredients, like cucumber, red onion and radish in order to make it a meal. I cut down on the prep by using popcorn shrimp.

—ANNRMS TASTEOFHOME.COM

APRICOT GELATIN MOLD

⑤ INGREDIENTS EAT SMART
Apricot Gelatin Mold

After my husband and I got married, he asked me to get this special holiday recipe from my mother. Mom prepared it for every family celebration, and now I make it just as often. You can substitute peach or orange gelatin if you prefer.

—SUZANNE HOLCOMB ST. JOHNSVILLE, NY

PREP: 25 MIN. + CHILLING
MAKES: 12 SERVINGS (½ CUP EACH)

- 1 can (8 ounces) unsweetened crushed pineapple
- 2 packages (3 ounces each) apricot or peach gelatin
- 1 package (8 ounces) reduced-fat cream cheese
- ¾ cup grated carrots
- 1 carton (8 ounces) frozen fat-free whipped topping, thawed

1. Drain pineapple, reserving juice in a 2-cup measuring cup; add enough water to measure 2 cups. Set pineapple aside. Pour juice mixture into a small saucepan. Bring to a boil; remove from heat. Dissolve gelatin in juice mixture. Cool for 10 minutes.

2. In a large bowl, beat cream cheese until creamy. Gradually add gelatin mixture, beating until smooth. Refrigerate for 30-40 minutes or until slightly thickened.

3. Fold in pineapple and carrots, then whipped topping. Transfer to an 8-cup ring mold coated with cooking spray. Refrigerate until set. Unmold onto a serving platter.

PER SERVING *144 cal., 4 g fat (3 g sat. fat), 13 mg chol., 128 mg sodium, 23 g carb., trace fiber, 3 g pro.* **Diabetic Exchanges:** *1½ starch, 1 fat.*

CRISPY SHRIMP CAESAR SALAD

My husband and I fell hard for the curried chicken salad from our local grocery store deli, and I knew I could find a way to make something similar. My special version has now become a tasty staple for our trips to the beach. —JANINE COOPER-MOREN PORTLAND, OR

EAT SMART FAST FIX
Cashew-Curry Chicken Salad

START TO FINISH: 20 MIN.
MAKES: 6 SERVINGS

- 3 cups cubed cooked chicken breast
- 4 celery ribs, chopped
- 2 medium carrots, chopped
- ⅔ cup golden raisins
- ½ cup chopped cashews

DRESSING
- ⅔ cup honey Greek yogurt
- 4 teaspoons lemon juice
- 4 teaspoons honey
- 1 teaspoon curry powder
- ¼ teaspoon salt
- ¼ teaspoon garlic powder
- ¼ teaspoon pepper
- ⅛ teaspoon ground ginger

1. In a large bowl, combine chicken, celery, carrots, raisins and cashews.
2. In a small bowl, mix yogurt, lemon juice, honey and spices. Pour over chicken mixture; toss to coat.
PER SERVING *287 cal., 10 g fat (3 g sat. fat), 60 mg chol., 267 mg sodium, 27 g carb., 2 g fiber, 24 g pro.* **Diabetic Exchanges:** *3 lean meat, 1½ starch, 1 vegetable, ½ fruit.*

⑤ INGREDIENTS FAST FIX
Garlic Potato Balls

I've used this recipe since I was married, 47 years ago. Both my husband and I worked, and we liked to have a hearty meal together when we came home at night. This was easy and quick to make on busy days. Sized just right for two, there were never any leftovers.

—ALPHA WILSON ROSWELL, NM

START TO FINISH: 20 MIN.
MAKES: 2 SERVINGS

- 1 tablespoon butter
- 1 can (15 ounces) small white potatoes, drained
- ¼ teaspoon garlic salt
- ½ teaspoon minced fresh parsley

In a skillet, melt butter over medium heat. Add potatoes; sprinkle with garlic salt. Cook and stir for 15-18 minutes or until golden brown. Sprinkle with parsley.

CASHEW-CURRY CHICKEN SALAD

(5) INGREDIENTS EAT SMART
Red Potato Salad Dijon

PREP: 25 MIN. • **COOK:** 15 MIN.
MAKES: 12 SERVINGS (¾ CUP EACH)

- 3½ **pounds red potatoes (about 12 medium), cubed**
- ¼ **cup Dijon-mayonnaise blend**
- 3 **tablespoons seasoned rice vinegar**
- 3 **tablespoons olive oil**
- 4 **teaspoons minced fresh tarragon**
- 1½ **teaspoons salt**
- ¾ **teaspoon pepper**
- 6 **green onions, thinly sliced**

1. Place potatoes in a Dutch oven; add water to cover. Bring to a boil. Reduce heat; cook, uncovered, 10-15 minutes or until tender. Drain; transfer to a large bowl.

2. In a small bowl, mix mayonnaise blend, vinegar, oil, tarragon, salt and pepper. Drizzle over potatoes; toss to coat. Gently stir in green onions. Serve warm. Refrigerate leftovers.

PER SERVING *139 cal., 4 g fat (1 g sat. fat), 0 chol., 557 mg sodium, 24 g carb., 2 g fiber, 3 g pro.* **Diabetic Exchanges:** *1½ starch, 1 fat.*

> My mother made the best warm potato salad, and now it's a tradition at all of our tables. Sometimes I use Yukon Gold potatoes to make it even prettier.
>
> —PATRICIA SWART GALLOWAY, NJ

LEMONY ALMOND-FETA GREEN BEANS

FAST FIX
Lemony Almond-Feta Green Beans

When you find a vegetable recipe that demands second helpings, it's definitely worth sharing. I made these green beans for a dinner party, and they were the fastest to disappear. I like to use haricots verts, the skinny type of green bean.

—SAMANTHA BOWMAN HOUSTON, TX

START TO FINISH: 30 MIN.
MAKES: 6 SERVINGS

- 1 **pound fresh green beans, trimmed**
- 2 **tablespoons butter**
- 1 **small onion, halved and sliced**
- 3 **garlic cloves, sliced**
- ½ **cup sliced almonds**
- 1 **teaspoon grated lemon peel**
- 3 **tablespoons lemon juice**
- ¼ **teaspoon salt**
- ⅛ **teaspoon pepper**
- ½ **cup crumbled feta cheese**

1. In a large saucepan, bring 4 cups water to a boil. Add green beans; cook, uncovered, 4-5 minutes or until beans turn bright green. Remove beans and immediately drop into ice water. Drain and pat dry.

2. In a large skillet, heat butter over medium heat. Add onion; cook and stir 6-8 minutes or until tender. Add garlic; cook 1 minute longer.

3. Add green beans and almonds; cook and stir 3-4 minutes or until beans are crisp-tender. Sprinkle with lemon peel, lemon juice, salt and pepper; toss to combine. Top with cheese.

RED POTATO SALAD DIJON

Coleslaw with Poppy Seed Dressing

I love this salad because I can keep it in the fridge for a couple of days and it just gets better. It packs lots of crunch and flavor for very little effort. If you prefer raisins or dried cranberries, feel free to toss some in.

—**TRISHA KRUSE** EAGLE, ID

PREP: 20 MIN. + CHILLING
MAKES: 12 SERVINGS (¾ CUP EACH)

- ½ **medium head cabbage, shredded (about 4½ cups)**
- 6 **large carrots, shredded (about 4½ cups)**
- 8 **green onions, chopped (about 1 cup)**
- 1 **cup fat-free poppy seed salad dressing**
- ⅓ **cup sunflower kernels**

In a large bowl, combine cabbage, carrots and green onions. Drizzle with dressing; toss to coat. Refrigerate, covered, at least 1 hour. Top with sunflower kernels just before serving.

PER SERVING *83 cal., 2 g fat (trace sat. fat), 3 mg chol., 102 mg sodium, 15 g carb., 3 g fiber, 2 g pro.* **Diabetic Exchanges:** *1 vegetable, ½ starch, ½ fat.*

Chive & Onion Hash Brown Potatoes

A friend told me about a potato dish her mother used to make. I decided to re-create it and my friend actually liked it better than her mom's version, which I was totally thrilled about!

—**BARB TEMPLIN** NORWOOD, MN

PREP: 15 MIN. • **BAKE:** 45 MIN. + STANDING
MAKES: 12 SERVINGS (¾ CUP EACH)

- 1½ **cups half-and-half cream**
- 1 **container (8 ounces) spreadable chive and onion cream cheese**
- 2 **tablespoons dried minced onion**
- 1 **teaspoon salt**
- ½ **teaspoon pepper**
- 2 **packages (20 ounces each) refrigerated shredded hash brown potatoes**
- 2 **cups shredded Swiss cheese**
- 3 **tablespoons minced fresh chives, divided**
- 2 **tablespoons butter, cubed**

1. Preheat oven to 375°. In a Dutch oven, combine the first five ingredients; cook and stir over medium heat until blended. Stir in the potatoes.

2. In a greased 13x9-in. or 3-qt. baking dish, layer a third of the hash brown mixture and ⅔ cup Swiss cheese; sprinkle with 1 tablespoon chives. Repeat layers. Top with remaining hash brown mixture and cheese; dot with butter.

3. Bake, covered, 35 minutes. Bake, uncovered, 10-20 minutes longer or until edges begin to brown and the potatoes are heated through. Let stand 10 minutes before serving. Sprinkle with remaining chives.

CHIVE & ONION HASH BROWN POTATOES

TOP TIP

If you forget to defrost frozen hash browns beforehand, put them in a colander and rinse with cold water until thawed. Then give them a whirl in a salad spinner to remove excess water. —**JANET S.** OVIEDO, FL

COLESLAW WITH POPPY SEED DRESSING

My youngest daughter recently learned she has to avoid gluten, dairy and eggs, which gave me a new challenge in the kitchen. I put this satisfying side dish together as one we could all share. We love the leftovers, too. —CATHERINE TURNBULL BURLINGTON, ON

COLORFUL QUINOA SALAD

EAT SMART
Colorful Quinoa Salad

PREP: 30 MIN. + COOLING
MAKES: 8 SERVINGS

- 2 **cups water**
- 1 **cup quinoa, rinsed**
- 2 **cups fresh baby spinach, thinly sliced**
- 1 **cup grape tomatoes, halved**
- 1 **medium cucumber, seeded and chopped**
- 1 **medium sweet orange pepper, chopped**
- 1 **medium sweet yellow pepper, chopped**
- 2 **green onions, chopped**

DRESSING
- 3 **tablespoons lime juice**
- 2 **tablespoons olive oil**
- 4 **teaspoons honey**
- 1 **tablespoon grated lime peel**
- 2 **teaspoons minced fresh gingerroot**
- ¼ **teaspoon salt**

1. In a large saucepan, bring water to a boil. Add quinoa. Reduce heat; simmer, covered, 12-15 minutes or until liquid is absorbed. Remove from heat; fluff with a fork. Transfer to a large bowl; cool completely.

2. Stir spinach, tomatoes, cucumber, peppers and green onions into quinoa. In a small bowl, whisk the dressing ingredients until blended. Drizzle over quinoa mixture; toss to coat. Then, refrigerate until serving.

PER SERVING *143 cal., 5 g fat (1 g sat. fat), 0 chol., 88 mg sodium, 23 g carb., 3 g fiber, 4 g pro.* ***Diabetic Exchanges:** 1 starch, 1 vegetable, 1 fat.*

Mexican Roasted Potato Salad

My husband usually doesn't like potato salad, but he loves this one! It makes a fabulous side dish for grilled chicken or burgers. I usually serve it warm, but the leftovers are also great straight from the refrigerator.
—**ELISABETH LARSEN** PLEASANT GROVE, UT

PREP: 20 MIN. • **BAKE:** 25 MIN.
MAKES: 10 SERVINGS

- 4 **pounds potatoes, peeled and cut into ½-inch cubes (about 8 cups)**
- 1 **tablespoon canola oil**
- 1½ **teaspoons salt, divided**
- ½ **teaspoon pepper**
- 1 **can (15 ounces) black beans, rinsed and drained**
- 1 **can (4 ounces) chopped green chilies**
- 2 **tablespoons minced fresh cilantro**
- ¾ **cup sour cream**
- ¾ **cup mayonnaise**
- 2 **teaspoons lime juice**
- 1 **teaspoon ground chipotle pepper or 2 teaspoons chili powder**
- ½ **teaspoon ground cumin**
- ¼ **teaspoon garlic powder**

1. Preheat oven to 425°. Place potatoes in a greased 15x10x1-in. baking pan. Drizzle with oil; sprinkle with 1 teaspoon salt and pepper. Toss to coat. Roast 25-30 minutes or until tender, stirring occasionally.

2. In a large bowl, mix potatoes, beans, chilies and cilantro. In a small bowl, combine sour cream, mayonnaise, lime juice, chipotle pepper, cumin, garlic powder and remaining salt. Pour dressing over potato mixture; toss to coat. Serve warm.

TOMATO-ONION GREEN BEANS

EAT SMART
Cherry Tomato Salad

This recipe evolved from a need to use the bumper crops of cherry tomatoes we grow. It's become a beloved summer favorite, especially at cookouts.

—**SALLY SIBLEY** ST. AUGUSTINE, FL

PREP: 15 MIN. + MARINATING
MAKES: 6 SERVINGS

- 1 quart cherry tomatoes, halved
- ¼ cup canola oil
- 3 tablespoons white vinegar
- ½ teaspoon salt
- ½ teaspoon sugar
- ¼ cup minced fresh parsley
- 1 to 2 teaspoons minced fresh basil
- 1 to 2 teaspoons minced fresh oregano

Place tomatoes in a shallow bowl. In a small bowl, whisk oil, vinegar, salt and sugar until blended; stir in herbs. Pour over tomatoes; gently toss to coat. Refrigerate, covered, overnight.

PER SERVING *103 cal., 10 g fat (1 g sat. fat), 0 chol., 203 mg sodium, 4 g carb., 1 g fiber, 1 g pro.* **Diabetic Exchanges:** *2 fat, 1 vegetable.*

EAT SMART **FAST FIX**
Southwestern Sauteed Corn

My mother-in-law came up with this dish one night for dinner. Everyone who tries it absolutely loves it.

—**CHANDY WARD** AUMSVILLE, OR

START TO FINISH: 20 MIN.
MAKES: 5 SERVINGS

- 1 package (16 ounces) frozen corn, thawed or 3⅓ cups fresh corn
- 1 tablespoon butter
- 1 plum tomato, chopped
- 1 tablespoon lime juice
- ½ teaspoon salt
- ½ teaspoon ground cumin
- ⅓ cup minced fresh cilantro

In a large nonstick skillet, saute corn in butter until tender. Reduce heat to medium-low; add the tomato, lime juice, salt and cumin. Cook and stir for 3-4 minutes or until heated through. Remove from the heat; stir in cilantro.

PER SERVING *104 cal., 3 g fat (2 g sat. fat), 6 mg chol., 256 mg sodium, 20 g carb., 2 g fiber, 3 g pro.* **Diabetic Exchanges:** *1 starch, ½ fat.*

⑤ INGREDIENTS **EAT SMART** **FAST FIX**
Tomato-Onion Green Beans

Fresh green beans are the star of this healthy side. Serve with a hearty main dish for a delicious end to a busy day.

—**DAVID FEDER** BUFFALO GROVE, IL

START TO FINISH: 30 MIN.
MAKES: 6 SERVINGS

- 2 tablespoons olive oil
- 1 large onion, finely chopped
- 1 pound fresh green beans, trimmed
- 3 tablespoons tomato paste
- ½ teaspoon salt
- 2 tablespoons minced fresh parsley

1. In a large skillet, heat oil over medium-high heat. Add onion; cook until tender and lightly browned, stirring occasionally.

2. Meanwhile, place green beans in a large saucepan; add water to cover. Bring to a boil. Cook, covered, 5-7 minutes or until crisp-tender. Drain; add to onion. Stir in the tomato paste and salt; heat through. Sprinkle with parsley.

PER SERVING *81 cal., 5 g fat (1 g sat. fat), 0 chol., 208 mg sodium, 9 g carb., 3 g fiber, 2 g pro.* **Diabetic Exchanges:** *1 vegetable, 1 fat.*

CHERRY TOMATO SALAD

THYMED ZUCCHINI SAUTE

EAT SMART FAST FIX
Thymed Zucchini Saute
Simple and flavorful, this recipe is a tasty, good-for-you way to use up all those zucchini taking over your garden. Plus, it's ready in no time!

—**BOBBY TAYLOR** ULSTER PARK, NY

START TO FINISH: 15 MIN.
MAKES: 4 SERVINGS

- 1 tablespoon olive oil
- 1 pound medium zucchini, quartered lengthwise and halved
- ¼ cup finely chopped onion
- ½ vegetable bouillon cube, crushed
- 2 tablespoons minced fresh parsley
- 1 teaspoon minced fresh thyme or ¼ teaspoon dried thyme

In a large skillet, heat oil over medium-high heat. Add zucchini, onion and bouillon; cook and stir 4-5 minutes or until zucchini is crisp-tender. Sprinkle with herbs.
NOTE *This recipe was prepared with Knorr vegetable bouillon.*
PER SERVING *53 cal., 4 g fat (1 g sat. fat), 0 chol., 135 mg sodium, 5 g carb., 2 g fiber, 2 g pro.* **Diabetic Exchanges:** *1 vegetable, ½ fat.*

BLT Twice-Baked Potatoes
Two favorites come together in this side dish: BLTs and twice-baked potatoes. I like to serve these potatoes with either grilled steaks or barbecued chicken.

—**MARY SHENK** DEKALB, IL

PREP: 25 MIN. • **BAKE:** 15 MIN.
MAKES: 8 SERVINGS

- 4 medium potatoes (about 8 ounces each)
- ½ cup mayonnaise
- 1 cup (4 ounces) shredded cheddar cheese
- 8 bacon strips, cooked and crumbled
- ⅓ cup oil-packed sun-dried tomatoes, patted dry and chopped
- 1 green onion, thinly sliced
- ½ teaspoon salt
- ¼ teaspoon pepper
- 1 cup shredded lettuce

1. Preheat oven to 400°. Scrub potatoes; pierce several times with a fork. Place on a microwave-safe plate. Microwave, uncovered, on high 12-15 minutes or until tender, turning once.
2. When cool enough to handle, cut each potato lengthwise in half. Scoop out pulp, leaving ¼-in.-thick shells. In a small bowl, mash the pulp with mayonnaise, adding cheese, bacon, tomatoes, green onion, salt and pepper.
3. Spoon into potato shells. Place on a baking sheet. Bake 12-15 minutes or until heated through. Sprinkle with lettuce.

FAST FIX
Taco Salad
I found this recipe in an old cookbook, and I've taken it to many potlucks since then. The layers look so pretty in a glass bowl.

—**SANDY FYNAARDT** NEW SHARON, IA

START TO FINISH: 25 MIN.
MAKES: 8 SERVINGS (1 CUP DRESSING)

- 1 pound ground beef
- 1 envelope taco seasoning, divided
- 1 medium head iceberg lettuce, torn
- 1 can (16 ounces) kidney beans, rinsed and drained
- 1 large red onion, chopped
- 4 medium tomatoes, seeded and finely chopped
- 2 cups (8 ounces) shredded cheddar cheese
- 4 cups crushed tortilla chips (about 8 ounces)
- 1 bottle (8 ounces) Thousand Island salad dressing
- 2 tablespoons taco sauce

1. In a large skillet, cook beef over medium heat 6-8 minutes or until no longer pink, breaking into crumbles; drain. Stir in 3 tablespoons taco seasoning.
2. In a large bowl, layer the beef mixture, lettuce, beans, onion, tomatoes, cheese and crushed chips. In a small bowl, mix salad dressing, taco sauce and remaining taco seasoning; serve with salad.

TOP TIP
To remove the core from a head of iceberg lettuce, hold the head with both hands and firmly hit it, core side down, against a countertop. The core should then come right out by twisting it.

TACO SALAD

Balsamic Three-Bean Salad

PREP: 15 MIN. • **COOK:** 10 MIN. + CHILLING
MAKES: 12 SERVINGS (¾ CUP EACH)

- 2 **pounds fresh green beans, trimmed and cut into 2-inch pieces**
- ½ **cup balsamic vinaigrette**
- ¼ **cup sugar**
- 1 **garlic clove, minced**
- ¾ **teaspoon salt**
- 2 **cans (16 ounces each) kidney beans, rinsed and drained**
- 2 **cans (15 ounces each) white kidney or cannellini beans, rinsed and drained**
- 4 **fresh basil leaves, torn**

1. Fill a Dutch oven three-fourths full with water; bring to a boil. Add green beans; cook, uncovered, 3-6 minutes or until crisp-tender. Drain and immediately drop into ice water. Drain and pat dry.

2. In a large bowl, whisk vinaigrette, sugar, garlic and salt until sugar is dissolved. Add canned beans and green beans; toss to coat. Refrigerate, covered, at least 4 hours. Stir in basil just before serving.

Here's my little girl's favorite salad. She eats it just about as fast as I can make it. Prepare it ahead of time so the flavors have plenty of opportunity to meld.
—STACEY FEATHER JAY, OK

LEMON ROASTED FINGERLINGS AND BRUSSELS SPROUTS

BALSAMIC THREE-BEAN SALAD

GRAND PRIZE

Lemon Roasted Fingerlings and Brussels Sprouts

My trick to roasting veggies is to choose ones that cook in the same amount of time. Try pairing up cauliflower florets with baby carrots or okra with cherry tomatoes for best results.
—**COURTNEY GAYLORD** COLUMBUS, IN

PREP: 15 MIN. • **BAKE:** 20 MIN.
MAKES: 8 SERVINGS

- 1 **pound fingerling potatoes, halved**
- 1 **pound Brussels sprouts, trimmed and halved**
- 6 **tablespoons olive oil, divided**
- ¾ **teaspoon salt, divided**
- ¼ **teaspoon pepper**
- 3 **tablespoons lemon juice**
- 1 **garlic clove, minced**
- 1 **teaspoon Dijon mustard**
- 1 **teaspoon honey**

1. Preheat oven to 425°. Place potatoes and Brussels sprouts in a greased 15x10x1-in. baking pan. Drizzle with 2 tablespoons oil; sprinkle with ½ teaspoon salt and pepper. Toss to coat. Roast 20-25 minutes or until tender, stirring once.

2. In a small bowl, whisk the lemon juice, garlic, mustard, honey and remaining oil and salt until blended. Transfer vegetables to a large bowl; drizzle with vinaigrette and toss to coat. Serve warm.

HONEY-LIME BERRY SALAD

FAST FIX ▶
Marmalade Candied Carrots

Crisp-tender carrots have a citrusy sweet flavor that's perfect for special occasions. It's my favorite carrot recipe.
—**HEATHER CLEMMONS** SUPPLY, NC

START TO FINISH: 30 MIN.
MAKES: 8 SERVINGS

- 2 **pounds fresh baby carrots**
- ⅔ **cup orange marmalade**
- 3 **tablespoons brown sugar**
- 2 **tablespoons butter**
- ½ **cup chopped pecans, toasted**
- 1 **teaspoon rum extract**

1. In a large saucepan, place steamer basket over 1 in. of water. Place carrots in basket. Bring water to a boil. Reduce heat to maintain a low boil; steam, covered, 12-15 minutes or until carrots are crisp-tender.
2. Meanwhile, in a small saucepan, combine marmalade, brown sugar and butter; cook and stir over medium heat until mixture is thickened and reduced to about ½ cup. Stir in pecans and extract.

3. Place the carrots in a large bowl. Add marmalade mixture and toss gently to coat.

⑤ INGREDIENTS **EAT SMART** **FAST FIX**
Lemon Parmesan Orzo

Fresh lemon peel and minced parsley make this orzo one of my family's most-requested springtime sides. It's fantastic with chicken, pork and fish.
—**LESLIE PALMER** SWAMPSCOTT, MA

START TO FINISH: 20 MIN.
MAKES: 4 SERVINGS

- 1 **cup uncooked whole wheat orzo pasta**
- 1 **tablespoon olive oil**
- ¼ **cup grated Parmesan cheese**
- 2 **tablespoons minced fresh parsley**
- ½ **teaspoon grated lemon peel**
- ¼ **teaspoon salt**
- ¼ **teaspoon pepper**

Cook orzo according to package directions; drain. Transfer to a small bowl; drizzle with oil. Stir in remaining ingredients.
PER SERVING *191 cal., 6 g fat (1 g sat. fat), 4 mg chol., 225 mg sodium, 28 g*

carb., 7 g fiber, 7 g pro. **Diabetic Exchanges:** *2 starch, ½ fat.*

EAT SMART **FAST FIX** ▶
Honey-Lime Berry Salad

I picked up this dish a couple of years ago, and really like the mint and fruit combo. Cilantro is one of my summer favorites, so sometimes I use it instead of the mint.
—**KAYLA SPENCE** WILBER, NE

START TO FINISH: 15 MIN.
MAKES: 10 SERVINGS

- 4 **cups fresh strawberries, halved**
- 3 **cups fresh blueberries**
- 3 **medium Granny Smith apples, cubed**
- ⅓ **cup lime juice**
- ¼ **to ⅓ cup honey**
- 2 **tablespoons minced fresh mint**

In a large bowl, combine strawberries, blueberries and apples. In a small bowl, whisk lime juice, honey and mint. Pour over fruit; toss to coat.
PER SERVING *93 cal., trace fat (trace sat. fat), 0 chol., 2 mg sodium, 24 g carb., 3 g fiber, 1 g pro.* **Diabetic Exchanges:** *1 fruit, ½ starch.*

Tzatziki Potato Salad

My son has an egg allergy, so this potato salad is perfect for him. For great color, add radishes, apple and garlic dill pickles.

—CINDY ROMBERG MISSISSAUGA, ON

PREP: 25 MIN. + CHILLING
MAKES: 12 SERVINGS (¾ CUP EACH)

- 3 pounds small red potatoes, halved
- 1 carton (12 ounces) refrigerated tzatziki sauce
- 2 celery ribs, thinly sliced
- ½ cup plain Greek yogurt
- 2 green onions, chopped
- 2 tablespoons snipped fresh dill
- 2 tablespoons minced fresh parsley
- ½ teaspoon salt
- ¼ teaspoon celery salt
- ¼ teaspoon pepper
- 1 tablespoon minced fresh mint, optional

1. Place potatoes in a Dutch oven; add water to cover. Bring to a boil. Reduce heat; cook, uncovered, 10-15 minutes or until tender. Drain and place in a large bowl. Refrigerate, covered, until chilled.

2. In a small bowl, mix tzatziki sauce, celery, yogurt, green onions, dill, parsley, salt, celery salt, pepper and mint, if desired. Spoon over potatoes; toss to coat.

TZATZIKI POTATO SALAD

MARINA'S GOLDEN
CORN FRITTERS

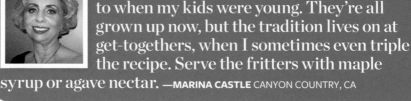

Just one bite of these fritters takes me back to when my kids were young. They're all grown up now, but the tradition lives on at get-togethers, when I sometimes even triple the recipe. Serve the fritters with maple syrup or agave nectar. —MARINA CASTLE CANYON COUNTRY, CA

FAST FIX
Marina's Golden Corn Fritters

START TO FINISH: 30 MIN.
MAKES: 32 FRITTERS

- 2½ cups all-purpose flour
- 3 teaspoons baking powder
- 2 teaspoons dried parsley flakes
- 1 teaspoon salt
- 2 eggs
- ¾ cup 2% milk
- 2 tablespoons butter, melted
- 2 teaspoons grated onion
- 1 can (15¼ ounces) whole kernel corn, drained
  Oil for deep-fat frying

1. In a large bowl, whisk flour, baking powder, parsley and salt. In another bowl, whisk eggs, milk, melted butter and onion until blended. Add to dry ingredients, stirring just until moistened. Fold in corn.

2. In an electric skillet or deep fryer, heat oil to 375°. Drop batter by tablespoonfuls, several at a time, into hot oil. Fry 2-3 minutes on each side or until golden brown. Drain on paper towels.

DID YOU KNOW?

When melted butter is called for in a recipe, you should measure the butter first, then melt. The markings on the wrappers make it easy to slice off the exact amount you need.

Easy Pasta Salad for a Crowd

Spinach, peppers and onions mingle with tangy feta cheese in this simple pasta salad. Feel free to make it ahead of time, so it's ready when you are.

—**JACQUELYN SAINT JOHN** CAMBRIDGE, MA

START TO FINISH: 30 MIN.
MAKES: 13 SERVINGS (¾ CUP EACH)

- 1 package (14½ ounces) multigrain penne pasta
- 1 jar (12 ounces) roasted sweet red peppers, drained and chopped
- 1 package (10 ounces) frozen chopped spinach, thawed and squeezed dry
- 1 bottle (8 ounces) Italian salad dressing
- 1 bottle (8 ounces) ranch salad dressing
- 6 green onions, chopped
- 1 small red onion, chopped
- 1 cup (4 ounces) crumbled feta cheese

1. Cook pasta according to package directions. In a large bowl, combine the remaining ingredients.
2. Drain pasta and rinse in cold water; add to the spinach mixture. Toss to coat. Refrigerate until serving.

Spinach Beef Salad

Here's a main-dish salad that's just plain fun to eat. It's crunchy, beefy and has a little kick. Best of all, it's good for you.

—**JANET DINGLER** CEDARTOWN, GA

START TO FINISH: 25 MIN.
MAKES: 4 SERVINGS

- 1 pound beef top sirloin steak, cut into thin strips
- 1 jalapeno pepper, seeded and chopped
- 1 garlic clove, minced
- ¼ cup lime juice
- 2 tablespoons brown sugar
- 2 tablespoons reduced-sodium soy sauce
- 1 teaspoon dried basil
- 1 teaspoon minced fresh mint or ½ teaspoon dried mint
- 1 teaspoon minced fresh gingerroot
- 6 cups torn fresh spinach
- 1 large sweet red pepper, julienned
- ½ medium cucumber, peeled and julienned

1. In a large nonstick skillet coated with cooking spray, cook beef and jalapeno over medium heat until beef is no longer pink. Add garlic; cook 1 minute longer.
2. In a small bowl, whisk lime juice, brown sugar, soy sauce, basil, mint and ginger. Place spinach, red pepper and cucumber in a large bowl; add beef mixture. Drizzle dressing over salad; toss to coat.
NOTE *Wear disposable gloves when cutting hot peppers; the oils can burn skin. Avoid touching your face.*
PER SERVING *207 cal., 5 g fat (2 g sat. fat), 46 mg chol., 383 mg sodium, 14 g carb., 2 g fiber, 27 g pro.* **Diabetic Exchanges:** *3 lean meat, 2 vegetable.*

EASY PASTA SALAD FOR A CROWD

GORGONZOLA-PEAR
MESCLUN SALAD

FAST FIX ▶
Gorgonzola-Pear Mesclun Salad

This salad is a tasty way to get your daily greens. To change it up, swap apples for the pears and pecans for the walnuts.
—**JOYLYN TRICKEL** HELENDALE, CA

START TO FINISH: 10 MIN.
MAKES: 8 SERVINGS

- 2 **large pears, sliced**
- 1 **tablespoon lemon juice**
- 6 **cups spring mix salad greens**
- 1 **cup (4 ounces) crumbled Gorgonzola cheese**
- 1 **cup chopped walnuts, toasted**
- ½ **cup raspberry vinaigrette**

Toss pears with lemon juice. In a large bowl, combine greens, cheese, walnuts and pears. Drizzle with vinaigrette and toss to coat. Serve immediately.
NOTE *To toast nuts, spread in a 15x10x1-in. baking pan. Bake at 350° for 5-10 minutes or until lightly browned, stirring occasionally. Or, spread in a dry nonstick skillet and heat over low heat until lightly browned, stirring occasionally.*

⑤INGREDIENTS
Baked Three-Bean Casserole

Hosting a gathering? You'll want to bake up these crowd-pleasing beans. Best of all, this dish is a snap to double for block parties, reunions, church picnics or other large gatherings.
—**DARLENE BRENDEN** SALEM, OR

PREP: 10 MIN. • **BAKE:** 1¼ HOURS
MAKES: 8 SERVINGS

- 1 **can (16 ounces) maple-cured bacon baked beans**
- 1 **can (16 ounces) hot chili beans, undrained**
- 1 **can (15 ounces) black beans, rinsed and drained**
- 1 **can (10 ounces) diced tomatoes and green chilies, undrained**
- 1½ **teaspoons minced chipotle peppers in adobo sauce**

1. In a large bowl, combine all ingredients. Transfer to a greased 11x7-in. baking dish.
2. Cover and bake at 350° for 1 hour. Uncover; bake 15-20 minutes longer or until bubbly.

FAST FIX ▶
Turkey Salad with Grapes & Cashews

I used to get turkey salad from a local deli until I experimented and came up with this recipe myself. It's even better than the kind I used to buy.
—**CONNIE LAUX** ENGLEWOOD, OH

START TO FINISH: 20 MIN.
MAKES: 4 SERVINGS

- ¼ **cup mayonnaise**
- ¼ **cup plain yogurt**
- 1 **tablespoon honey Dijon mustard**
- 3 **cups cubed cooked turkey**
- 1 **cup halved green grapes**
- 2 **celery ribs, chopped**
- ½ **cup chopped cashews**
- 2 **green onions, thinly sliced Lettuce leaves**

In a bowl, mix mayonnaise, yogurt and mustard. Add turkey, grapes, celery, cashews and green onions; toss to coat. Serve on lettuce.

BACON-TOMATO SALAD

Spring Green Risotto

PREP: 15 MIN. • **COOK:** 30 MIN.
MAKES: 8 SERVINGS

- 1 carton (32 ounces) vegetable stock
- 1 to 1½ cups water
- 1 tablespoon olive oil
- 2 cups sliced fresh mushrooms
- 1 medium onion, chopped
- 1½ cups uncooked arborio rice
- 2 garlic cloves, minced
- ½ cup white wine or additional vegetable stock
- 1 teaspoon dried thyme
- 3 cups fresh baby spinach
- 1 cup frozen peas
- 3 tablespoons grated Parmesan cheese
- 1 tablespoon red wine vinegar
- ½ teaspoon salt
- ¼ teaspoon pepper

1. In a large saucepan, bring stock and water to a simmer; keep hot. In a Dutch oven, heat oil over medium-high heat. Add mushrooms and onion; cook and stir 5-7 minutes or until tender. Add rice and garlic; cook and stir 1-2 minutes or until rice is coated.
2. Stir in wine and thyme. Reduce heat to maintain a simmer; cook and stir until wine is absorbed. Add hot stock mixture, ½ cup at a time, cooking and stirring until stock has been absorbed after each addition, until rice is tender but firm to the bite and risotto is creamy. Stir in spinach, peas, cheese, vinegar, salt and pepper; heat through. Serve immediately.
PER SERVING *198 cal., 3 g fat (1 g sat. fat), 2 mg chol., 477 mg sodium, 37 g carb., 2 g fiber, 5 g pro.*

(5)**INGREDIENTS** **FAST FIX**
Bacon-Tomato Salad

We love this wonderful salad that tastes like a piled-high BLT without the time or effort. Plus, you can make it hours ahead and keep it in the fridge until serving time.
—**DENISE THURMAN** COLUMBIA, MO

START TO FINISH: 15 MIN.
MAKES: 6 SERVINGS

- 1 package (9 ounces) iceberg lettuce blend
- 2 cups grape tomatoes, halved
- ¾ cup coleslaw salad dressing
- ¾ cup shredded cheddar cheese
- 12 bacon strips, cooked and crumbled

In a large bowl, combine lettuce blend and tomatoes. Drizzle with dressing; sprinkle with cheese and bacon.

TOP TIP

Always check the date stamp on packages of bacon to make sure it's fresh before you buy it. The date stamp reflects the last possible date of sale. Once the package is opened, use the bacon within a week, or freeze it up to a month for even longer storage.

Once a week, I create a new recipe for my blog, An Officer and a Vegan. I first made this risotto when I needed something cheerful and satisfying. It would be fantastic with asparagus, zucchini or summer squash, but you can use whatever veggies are in season. —**DEANNA MCDONALD** KALAMAZOO, MI

SPRING GREEN RISOTTO

Potato Wedges with Sweet & Spicy Sauce

PREP: 20 MIN. • **BAKE:** 45 MIN.
MAKES: 12 SERVINGS (1½ CUPS SAUCE)

- 6 **medium potatoes (about 3 pounds)**
- ¼ **cup olive oil**
- 1½ **teaspoons chili powder**
- ½ **teaspoon salt**
- ½ **teaspoon onion powder**
- ½ **teaspoon Greek seasoning**
- ¼ **teaspoon garlic salt**
- ¼ **teaspoon smoked paprika**
- ¼ **teaspoon pepper**
- ⅛ **teaspoon cayenne pepper**

SAUCE

- 1 **cup Miracle Whip**
- ½ **cup barbecue sauce**
- ¼ **cup honey**
- ½ **teaspoon chili powder**
- ¼ **teaspoon smoked paprika**
- ⅛ **teaspoon cayenne pepper**

1. Preheat oven to 425°. Cut each potato lengthwise into six wedges; place in a large bowl. Add oil and seasonings; toss to coat. Transfer to two foil-lined 15x10x1-in. baking pans. Bake 45-50 minutes or until tender, turning once.
2. In a small bowl, mix the sauce ingredients. Serve with potato wedges.

Loaded Stuffed Potato Pancakes

When I prepare mashed potatoes, I always cook extra so I can make these over-the-top pancakes. Fill them with sour cream, ranch dressing, melted cheese—or all three.
—**JANE MCMILLAN** DANIA BEACH, FL

PREP: 25 MIN. • **COOK:** 5 MIN./BATCH
MAKES: 8 POTATO PANCAKES

- 2 **cups mashed potatoes (with added milk and butter)**
- ⅔ **cup shredded cheddar cheese**

LOADED STUFFED POTATO PANCAKES

- ⅓ **cup all-purpose flour**
- 1 **egg, lightly beaten**
- 1 **tablespoon minced chives**
- ½ **teaspoon salt**
- ½ **teaspoon pepper**
- ⅔ **cup seasoned bread crumbs**
- 1 **teaspoon garlic powder**
- 1 **teaspoon onion powder**
- ½ **teaspoon cayenne pepper**
- ⅓ **cup cream cheese, softened**
  Oil for deep-fat frying

1. In a large bowl, combine the first seven ingredients. In a shallow bowl, mix bread crumbs, garlic powder, onion powder and cayenne.
2. Shape 2 teaspoons cream cheese into a ball. Wrap ¼ cup of potato mixture around cream cheese to cover completely. Drop into the crumb mixture. Gently coat and shape into a ½-in.-thick patty. Repeat with the remaining cream cheese and the potato mixture.
3. In an electric skillet or deep-fat fryer, heat oil to 375°. Fry stuffed pancakes, a few at a time, 1-2 minutes on each side or until golden brown. Drain on paper towels.

Many of my recipes are the result of not having time to run to the store and having to use what is on hand. This recipe is a perfect example. My family likes everything dipped in something, so the sweet and spicy sauce is a nice alternative to ketchup! —**DANA ALEXANDER** LEBANON, MO

POTATO WEDGES WITH SWEET & SPICY SAUCE

CRUNCHY TUNA SALAD
WITH TOMATOES

⑤ INGREDIENTS **EAT SMART** FAST FIX
Balsamic Cucumber Salad

This fast, fresh salad is a winner. It's an easygoing side dish for kabobs, chicken or anything hot off the grill.

—BLAIR LONERGAN ROCHELLE, VA

START TO FINISH: 15 MIN.
MAKES: 6 SERVINGS

- 1 **large English cucumber, halved and sliced**
- 2 **cups grape tomatoes, halved**
- 1 **medium red onion, halved and thinly sliced**
- ½ **cup balsamic vinaigrette**
- ¾ **cup crumbled reduced-fat feta cheese**

In a large bowl, combine cucumber, tomatoes and onion. Add vinaigrette; toss to coat. Refrigerate, covered, until serving. Just before serving, stir in cheese. Serve with a slotted spoon.
PER SERVING *90 cal., 5 g fat (1 g sat. fat), 5 mg chol., 356 mg sodium, 9 g carb., 1 g fiber, 4 g pro.* **Diabetic Exchanges:** *1 vegetable, 1 fat.*

🔖 TOP TIP

When setting up a potluck, mark the table with sticky notes labeled for main dishes, sides, salads, drinks and desserts. That way, attendees will know where to place items and not have to ask.

EAT SMART FAST FIX
Crunchy Tuna Salad with Tomatoes

On a hot summer day, there's nothing more refreshing than this recipe. I grow a few tomato plants in my garden and the fresh-picked taste makes it even more of a treat.

—DIANE SELICH VASSAR, MI

START TO FINISH: 20 MIN.
MAKES: 4 SERVINGS

- ⅔ **cup reduced-fat mayonnaise**
- ½ **cup chopped sweet onion**
- 1 **celery rib, chopped**
- 1 **teaspoon minced fresh parsley or ¼ teaspoon dried parsley flakes**
- ¾ **teaspoon pepper**
- 1 **can (12 ounces) albacore white tuna in water, drained and flaked**
- 4 **medium tomatoes, cut into wedges**

In a small bowl, combine mayonnaise, onion, celery, parsley and pepper. Stir in tuna. Serve with tomato wedges.
PER SERVING *280 cal., 16 g fat (3 g sat. fat), 50 mg chol., 656 mg sodium, 12 g carb., 2 g fiber, 22 g pro.* **Diabetic Exchanges:** *3 lean meat, 2 fat, 1 vegetable.*

BALSAMIC
CUCUMBER SALAD

SKILLET POTATO MEDLEY

¾ teaspoon salt
½ teaspoon ground mustard
½ teaspoon white pepper
2 cups half-and-half cream
1½ cups (6 ounces) shredded sharp white cheddar cheese
1½ cups (6 ounces) shredded sharp cheddar cheese
6 cups thinly sliced peeled Yukon Gold potatoes (about 2 pounds)
2 small onions, finely chopped

1. Preheat oven to 350°. In a large saucepan, heat butter over medium heat. Stir in flour, salt, mustard and pepper until blended; cook and stir 2-3 minutes or until lightly browned. Gradually whisk in cream. Bring to a boil, stirring constantly; cook and stir 1-2 minutes or until thickened. Remove from heat.

2. In a small bowl, combine cheeses. Layer a third of the potatoes, a third of the onions and ¾ cup cheese mixture in a greased 3-qt. baking dish. Repeat layers twice. Pour sauce over top; sprinkle with remaining cheese.

3. Bake, covered, 45 minutes. Uncover; bake 25-30 minutes longer or until potatoes are tender and top is lightly browned.

Skillet Potato Medley

The pretty potatoes I had just harvested inspired me to mix them up for dinner. The results: a wonderful side dish.

—LORI MERRICK DANVERS, IL

PREP: 25 MIN. • **COOK:** 15 MIN.
MAKES: 8 SERVINGS

2 medium Yukon Gold potatoes (about ¾ pound)
2 medium red potatoes (about ¾ pound)
2 small purple potatoes (about ½ pound)
5 tablespoons butter
1 tablespoon olive oil
1 large sweet potato (about 1 pound)
1 cup chopped sweet onion
1 teaspoon garlic salt
¼ teaspoon dried rosemary, crushed
¼ teaspoon dried thyme
¼ teaspoon pepper

1. Cut Yukon Gold, red and purple potatoes into ¼-in. cubes. In a large skillet, heat butter and oil over medium heat. Add cubed potatoes; cook and stir 5 minutes.

2. Peel and cut the sweet potato into ¼-in. cubes; add to skillet. Add remaining ingredients; cook and stir 10-12 minutes or until potatoes are tender.

Sharp Cheddar Scalloped Potatoes

Try as I might, I can never follow a recipe exactly, so here's what I came up with when I made a family friend's scalloped potatoes in my own kitchen. They're so good, you'll keep going back for more.

—SUSAN SIMONS EATONVILLE, WA

PREP: 30 MIN. • **BAKE:** 70 MIN.
MAKES: 8 SERVINGS

¼ cup butter, cubed
⅓ cup all-purpose flour

SHARP CHEDDAR SCALLOPED POTATOES

TORTELLINI & CHICKEN
CAESAR SALAD

My family loved this pasta salad right from the start, so these days I serve it a lot. When warm weather hits, grilled chicken is a special treat here. —**LEE REESE** ROLLA, MO

Tortellini & Chicken Caesar Salad

START TO FINISH: 25 MIN.
MAKES: 6 SERVINGS

- 1 package (20 ounces) refrigerated cheese tortellini
- 1 pound boneless skinless chicken breasts, cut into 1½-inch pieces
- ⅓ cup finely chopped onion
- 1 tablespoon olive oil
- 2 garlic cloves, minced
- ¾ teaspoon salt
- ¼ teaspoon pepper
- 1 package (10 ounces) hearts of romaine salad mix
- 1½ cups grape tomatoes
- 1 can (6½ ounces) sliced ripe olives, drained
- ¾ cup creamy Caesar salad dressing
- ¾ cup shredded Parmesan cheese
- 6 bacon strips, cooked and crumbled

1. Cook tortellini according to package directions. Drain; rinse with cold water.

2. Meanwhile, in a small bowl, combine chicken, onion, oil, garlic, salt and pepper; toss to coat. Heat a large skillet over medium-high heat. Add chicken mixture; cook and stir 4-6 minutes or until chicken is no longer pink. Remove from heat.

3. In a large bowl, combine salad mix, tomatoes, olives, tortellini and chicken mixture. Drizzle with dressing; toss to coat. Sprinkle with cheese and bacon. Serve immediately.

GARDEN-FRESH CHEF SALAD

Garden-Fresh Chef Salad

For much of the year, I can use my garden's produce when I make this cool salad. In spring, it's salad mix and radishes, and in summer, we have tomatoes, cabbage and carrots. What a good feeling!

—**EVELYN GUBERNATH** BUCYRUS, OH

START TO FINISH: 25 MIN.
MAKES: 6 SERVINGS

- 6 cups spring mix salad greens
- 2 medium tomatoes, coarsely chopped
- 6 hard-cooked eggs, coarsely chopped
- 3 slices deli turkey, cut into thin strips
- 3 slices deli ham, cut into thin strips
- ½ cup shredded cabbage
- 4 green onions, sliced
- 4 fresh baby carrots, sliced
- 4 radishes, thinly sliced
- ¼ teaspoon garlic powder
- ¼ teaspoon pepper
- ½ cup reduced-fat Thousand Island salad dressing or dressing of your choice

In a large bowl, combine the first nine ingredients. Sprinkle with garlic powder and pepper; toss to coat. Serve with salad dressing.
PER SERVING *171 cal., 9 g fat (2 g sat. fat), 227 mg chol., 508 mg sodium, 11 g carb., 2 g fiber, 12 g pro.* **Diabetic Exchanges:** *2 lean meat, 2 vegetable, 1 fat.*

TOP TIP

Here's how I easily peel hard-cooked eggs: After cooling them off under cold running water, I put all the eggs in a saucepan large enough for them to move around in. I shake the pan vigorously from side to side until all the eggshells are cracked. The shells should peel right off!
—**JERRY S.** CHARLOTTE, NC

Holiday Brussels Sprouts

Make Brussels sprouts special with peas, celery and, of course, bacon. The recipe can be doubled if needed.

—**JODIE BECKMAN** COUNCIL BLUFFS, IA

START TO FINISH: 25 MIN.
MAKES: 6 SERVINGS

- 1 package (16 ounces) frozen Brussels sprouts
- 1 package (10 ounces) frozen peas
- 2 tablespoons butter
- 2 celery ribs, chopped
- 2 bacon strips, cooked and crumbled
- 2 tablespoons minced fresh chives

1. Cook Brussels sprouts and peas according to package directions; drain.
2. In a large skillet, heat butter over medium-high heat. Add celery; cook and stir until crisp-tender. Add Brussels sprouts, peas, bacon and chives; toss to combine.
PER SERVING *115 cal., 5 g fat (3 g sat. fat), 12 mg chol., 147 mg sodium, 13 g carb., 5 g fiber, 6 g pro.* **Diabetic Exchanges:** *2 vegetable, 1 fat.*

Peasant Peppers

My mother-in-law, who lives in Italy, taught me to make this simple side dish. It's considered wholesome peasant fare, but you'll feel like royalty eating these peppers.

—**ROBYN SCOLLO** FAIRPORT, NY

PREP: 15 MIN. • **BAKE:** 45 MIN.
MAKES: 5 SERVINGS

- 3 large green peppers, thinly sliced
- 3 large sweet red peppers, thinly sliced
- 2 tablespoons olive oil
- 1½ teaspoons salt
- 1 teaspoon pepper
- ½ cup soft bread crumbs

1. Preheat oven to 400°. Place peppers in two 15x10x1-in. baking pans. Drizzle with oil and sprinkle with salt and pepper; toss to coat.
2. Bake until tender and skins are slightly blackened, about 30-35 minutes. Stir pepper mixture; sprinkle with bread crumbs. Bake 15-20 minutes longer or until lightly browned.

HOLIDAY BRUSSELS SPROUTS

(5) INGREDIENTS EAT SMART FAST FIX
Pesto Pasta & Potatoes

Although this healthy pasta dish is pretty simple to begin with, it's made even simpler because you can throw the green beans and pasta into one big pot to cook.
—LAURA FLOWERS MOSCOW, ID

START TO FINISH: 30 MIN.
MAKES: 12 SERVINGS

- 1½ **pounds small red potatoes, halved**
- 12 **ounces uncooked whole grain spiral pasta**
- 3 **cups cut fresh or frozen green beans**
- 1 **jar (6½ ounces) prepared pesto**
- 1 **cup grated Parmigiano-Reggiano cheese**

1. Place potatoes in a large saucepan; add water to cover. Bring to a boil. Reduce heat; cook, uncovered, 9-11 minutes or until tender. Drain; transfer to a large bowl.
2. Meanwhile, cook pasta according to package directions, adding green beans during the last 5 minutes of cooking; drain, reserving ¾ cup pasta water.
3. Add pasta and green beans to potatoes. Stir in pesto, cheese and enough reserved pasta water to coat.
PER SERVING *261 cal., 10 g fat (3 g sat. fat), 11 mg chol., 233 mg sodium, 34 g carb., 5 g fiber, 11 g pro.* **Diabetic Exchanges:** *2 starch, 2 fat.*

PESTO PASTA & POTATOES

SKILLET SCALLOPED POTATOES

FAST FIX
Skillet Scalloped Potatoes

Our garden is a big inspiration when I'm cooking. This recipe turns produce from my husband's potato patch into a side dish we want to eat at every meal.
—LORI LEE DANIELS BEVERLY, WV

START TO FINISH: 30 MIN.
MAKES: 4 SERVINGS

- 1 **tablespoon butter**
- 1 **pound small red potatoes, thinly sliced (about 3 cups)**
- 1 **tablespoon dried minced onion**
- ¾ **cup chicken broth**
- ½ **cup half-and-half cream**
- ¾ **teaspoon salt**
- ¼ **teaspoon pepper**
- 1 **cup (4 ounces) shredded cheddar cheese**

1. In a large nonstick skillet, heat butter over medium heat. Add potatoes and onion; cook and stir 5 minutes.
2. Stir in broth, cream, salt and pepper. Bring to a boil. Reduce heat; simmer, covered, 10-12 minutes or until potatoes are tender. Sprinkle with cheese; cook, covered, 2-3 minutes longer or until cheese is melted.

(5) INGREDIENTS
Dilly Sweet Onions

As soon as Vidalia or other sweet onions are available each year, I make this salad. Everyone loves it, and I've received many recipe requests over the years.
—PEGGY POTTS LIMA, OH

PREP: 15 MIN. + CHILLING
MAKES: 4 SERVINGS

- 1 **pound sweet onions, thinly sliced**
- ½ **cup sugar**
- ½ **cup cider vinegar**
- ¼ **cup canola oil**
- 2 **teaspoons dill weed**
- 1 **teaspoon salt**

Place the onions in a large bowl. In a small saucepan, combine the sugar, vinegar, oil, dill and salt; bring to a boil, stirring constantly. Pour over the onions and toss to coat. Cover and refrigerate for at least 5 hours. Serve with a slotted spoon.

Tropical Fusion Salad with Spicy Tortilla Ribbons

START TO FINISH: 30 MIN.
MAKES: 4 SERVINGS

- 2 cups cubed peeled papaya
- 1 can (15 ounces) black beans, rinsed and drained
- 1 medium ripe avocado, peeled and cubed
- 1 cup frozen corn, thawed
- ½ cup golden raisins
- ¼ cup minced fresh cilantro
- ¼ cup orange juice
- 2 serrano peppers, seeded and chopped
- 2 tablespoons lime juice
- 1 tablespoon cider vinegar
- 2 garlic cloves, minced
- 2 teaspoons ground ancho chili pepper, divided
- ¼ teaspoon sugar
- ¼ teaspoon salt
- 2 corn tortillas (6 inches), cut into ¼-inch strips
  Cooking spray

1. Preheat oven to 350°. In a large bowl, combine the papaya, beans, avocado, corn, raisins, cilantro, orange juice, peppers, lime juice, vinegar, garlic, ½ teaspoon chili pepper, sugar and salt.

2. Place tortilla strips on a greased baking sheet; spritz with cooking spray. Sprinkle with remaining chili pepper. Bake 8-10 minutes or until crisp. Top salad with tortilla strips.

NOTE *Wear disposable gloves when cutting hot peppers; the oils can burn skin. Avoid touching your face.*
PER SERVING *321 cal., 8 g fat (1 g sat. fat), 0 chol., 380 mg sodium, 58 g carb., 11 g fiber, 9 g pro.*

TOP TIP

This salad was easy to make, and tasted excellent. I didn't buy enough fresh papaya, so I used some from a can in light syrup, which actually worked out really well. And any leftover tortilla strips make a good snack anytime!
—ASHLEYVA90 TASTEOFHOME.COM

The fresh taste of this colorful salad makes it an ideal choice for a spring or summer meal. Served with spicy tortilla strips, it's a unique, delicious offering.
—JENNIFER FISHER AUSTIN, TX

TROPICAL FUSION SALAD WITH SPICY TORTILLA RIBBONS

**Chocolate Chip–
Cranberry Scones**
PAGE 252

Breads in a Jiffy

It's easy to turn your kitchen into an aromatic bakery with the smart and simple recipes in this chapter! Whether you're looking for a special brunch sweet, a quick accompaniment to soup or a hearty loaf that rounds out dinner, you're sure to find it here.

Garlic Loaf
PAGE 248

Honey Spice Bread
PAGE 251

Crab Crescent Loaf
PAGE 254

ARTICHOKE BREAD

Artichoke Bread

A creamy, rich artichoke topping is spread over fresh-baked bread for a flavor that folks love. You won't find a quicker or more delicious way to round out your menu. It's especially good with Italian food.
—**SHERRY CAMPBELL** ST. AMANT, LA

PREP: 30 MIN. + COOLING • **BAKE:** 15 MIN.
MAKES: 1 LOAF (12 SLICES)

- 1 **tube (11 ounces) refrigerated crusty French loaf**
- 1 **can (14 ounces) water-packed artichoke hearts, rinsed, drained and chopped**
- ½ **cup seasoned bread crumbs**
- ⅓ **cup grated Parmesan cheese**
- ⅓ **cup reduced-fat mayonnaise**
- 2 **garlic cloves, minced**
- 1 **cup (4 ounces) shredded part-skim mozzarella cheese**

1. Bake loaf according to package directions; cool. Cut bread in half lengthwise; place on an ungreased baking sheet.
2. In a small bowl, combine the artichokes, bread crumbs, Parmesan cheese, mayonnaise and garlic; spread evenly over cut sides of bread. Sprinkle with mozzarella cheese.
3. Bake at 350° for 15-20 minutes or until cheese is melted. Serve warm.
PER SERVING *151 cal., 5 g fat (2 g sat. fat), 10 mg chol., 456 mg sodium, 18 g carb., 1 g fiber, 7 g pro.* **Diabetic Exchanges:** *1 starch, 1 fat.*

⑤ INGREDIENTS **FAST FIX**
Easy Parmesan Biscuits

It doesn't get any easier than these simple, but good, biscuits. The kids will enjoy lending a hand with them, dipping the biscuits into butter and cheese.
—**LINDA BECKER** OLYMPIA, WA

START TO FINISH: 15 MIN.
MAKES: 5 BISCUITS

- 1 **tube (6 ounces) refrigerated buttermilk biscuits**
- 3 **tablespoons butter, melted**
- ½ **cup grated Parmesan cheese**

1. Dip both sides of each biscuit into melted butter, then into cheese. Place 1 in. apart in a well-greased 9-in. round baking pan.
2. Bake at 400° for 8-11 minutes or until golden brown. Serve warm.

⑤ INGREDIENTS
Garlic Loaf

This golden loaf has garlic goodness in every bite. People go wild over its savory flavor. Try serving it with an herb-infused or lightly salted olive oil for dunking.
—*TASTE OF HOME* COOKING SCHOOL

PREP: 15 MIN. + RISING • **BAKE:** 20 MIN.
MAKES: 1 LOAF (24 PIECES)

- 2 **loaves (1 pound each) frozen bread dough or 24 frozen unbaked white dinner rolls, thawed**
- ½ **cup finely chopped sweet onion**
- ½ **cup butter, melted**
- 2 **garlic cloves, minced**
- 1 **teaspoon dried parsley flakes**
- ¼ **teaspoon salt**
  Herb-seasoned olive oil, optional

1. Divide dough into 24 pieces. In a small bowl, combine the onion, butter, garlic, parsley and salt. Dip each piece of dough into butter mixture; place in a 10-in. fluted tube pan coated with cooking spray. Cover and let rise in a warm place until doubled, about 1 hour.
2. Bake at 375° for 20-25 minutes or until golden brown. Serve warm with olive oil if desired.

GARLIC LOAF

ONION SWISS LOAF

English Marmalade Pecan Bread

FREEZE IT

PREP: 20 MIN. • **BAKE:** 50 MIN. + COOLING
MAKES: 1 LOAF (16 SLICES)

½ cup butter, softened
½ cup packed brown sugar
2 eggs
1 jar (10 ounces) orange marmalade spreadable fruit
2⅔ cups all-purpose flour
3 teaspoons baking powder
2 teaspoons ground cinnamon
1 teaspoon salt
⅓ cup orange juice
½ cup chopped pecans

1. Preheat oven to 350°. Grease and flour a 9x5-in. loaf pan. In a large bowl, beat butter and brown sugar until blended. Add eggs, one at a time, beating well after each addition. Gradually beat in marmalade. In another bowl, whisk flour, baking powder, cinnamon and salt; add to butter mixture alternately with orange juice, beating well after each addition. Fold in pecans.

2. Transfer to prepared pan. Bake 50-60 minutes or until a toothpick inserted in center comes out clean. Cool in pan 10 minutes before removing to a wire rack to cool.

FREEZE OPTION *Securely wrap the cooled loaf in plastic wrap and foil. To use, thaw the wrapped loaf at room temperature. If desired, warm slices in toaster or microwave.*

Onion Swiss Loaf

This oniony bread is one of our favorites. I hope you enjoy it just as much as our family and friends do. Try it with French onion or lentil soup for a heartwarming meal. It's simply delicious!

—**PAT BREMSON** KANSAS CITY, MO

PREP: 20 MIN. • **BAKE:** 15 MIN.
MAKES: 8 SERVINGS

½ cup butter, cubed
1 large sweet or yellow onion, halved and thinly sliced
½ teaspoon prepared mustard
¼ teaspoon lemon juice
1 loaf (1 pound) French bread, halved lengthwise
12 slices Swiss cheese

1. Melt butter in a large skillet over medium heat. Add the onion, mustard and lemon juice; cook and stir for 10-12 minutes or until tender. Remove from the heat.

2. Brush cut sides of bread with some of the butter from the pan. Spoon onion mixture onto bread bottom; top with cheese. Replace bread top.

3. Wrap loaf in foil; place on a baking sheet. Bake at 350° for 15 minutes or until cheese is melted. Serve warm.

My dad was Canadian but had a very British upbringing. And boy, did he ever love his marmalade! I know it's an acquired taste for some, but when I baked the jam into this nutty bread, everyone adored it– even my kids. —**NANCY HEISHMAN** LAS VEGAS, NV

ENGLISH MARMALADE PECAN BREAD

Swiss Beer Bread

This recipe is a favorite because it isn't greasy like other cheese breads I have tried in the past. It won't last long!

—DEBI WALLACE CHESTERTOWN, NY

PREP: 15 MIN. • **BAKE:** 50 MIN. + COOLING
MAKES: 1 LOAF (12 SLICES)

- 4 ounces Jarlsberg or Swiss cheese
- 3 cups all-purpose flour
- 3 tablespoons sugar
- 3 teaspoons baking powder
- 1½ teaspoons salt
- ½ teaspoon pepper
- 1 bottle (12 ounces) beer or nonalcoholic beer
- 2 tablespoons butter, melted

1. Divide cheese in half. Cut half of cheese into ¼-in. cubes; shred remaining cheese. In a large bowl, combine the flour, sugar, baking powder, salt and pepper. Stir beer into dry ingredients just until moistened. Fold in cheese.

2. Transfer to a greased 8-in. x 4-in. loaf pan. Drizzle with butter. Bake at 375° for 50-60 minutes or until a toothpick inserted near the center of the pan comes out clean. Cool bread for 10 minutes before removing from pan to a wire rack.

CHEESE-FILLED GARLIC ROLLS

SWISS BEER BREAD

To change up plain old dinner rolls, I added mozzarella. Now my family wants them at every gathering, but they're so easy to make, I don't mind, even in a time crunch.

—ROSALIE FITTERY PHILADELPHIA, PA

Cheese-Filled Garlic Rolls

PREP: 20 MIN. + RISING • **BAKE:** 15 MIN.
MAKES: 2 DOZEN

- 1 loaf (1 pound) frozen bread dough, thawed
- 24 cubes part-skim mozzarella cheese (¾ inch each), about 10 ounces
- 3 tablespoons butter, melted
- 2 teaspoons minced fresh parsley
- 1 garlic clove, minced
- ½ teaspoon Italian seasoning
- ½ teaspoon crushed red pepper flakes
- 2 tablespoons grated Parmigiano-Reggiano cheese

1. Divide dough into 24 portions. Shape each portion around a cheese cube to cover completely; pinch to seal. Place each roll in a greased muffin cup, seam side down. Cover with kitchen towels; let rise in a warm place until doubled, about 30 minutes. Preheat oven to 350°.

2. In a small bowl, mix butter, parsley, garlic, Italian seasoning and pepper flakes. Brush over rolls; sprinkle with cheese. Bake 15-18 minutes or until golden brown.

3. Cool 5 minutes before removing from pans. Serve warm.

Honey Spice Bread

The texture of this bread is almost like a cake, so I usually serve slices of it for dessert. Plus, the loaf looks so festive with the glaze drizzled on top.

—GAYE O'DELL BINGHAMTON, NY

PREP: 20 MIN. • **BAKE:** 55 MIN. + COOLING
MAKES: 1 LOAF (12 SLICES)

- ⅔ cup packed brown sugar
- ⅓ cup 2% milk
- 2 cups all-purpose flour
- 1½ teaspoons baking powder
- ½ teaspoon ground cinnamon
- ½ teaspoon ground nutmeg
- ⅛ teaspoon ground cloves
- 2 eggs
- ½ cup honey
- ⅓ cup canola oil

GLAZE

- ⅓ cup confectioners' sugar
- 2 teaspoons 2% milk

1. Preheat oven to 350°. In a small saucepan, combine brown sugar and milk. Cook and stir over low heat until sugar is dissolved. Remove from heat.
2. In a large bowl, whisk flour, baking powder and spices. In another bowl, whisk eggs, honey, oil and brown sugar mixture until blended. Add to flour mixture; stir just until moistened.
3. Transfer to a greased 8x4-in. loaf pan. Bake 55-60 minutes or until a toothpick inserted in center comes out clean (cover top loosely with foil if needed to prevent overbrowning).
4. Cool in pan 10 minutes before removing to a wire rack to cool completely. In a small bowl, stir glaze ingredients until smooth; drizzle over bread.

FREEZE OPTION *Securely wrap and freeze cooled loaf in plastic wrap and foil. To use, thaw at room temperature. Glaze bread as directed.*

PER SERVING *187 cal., 6 g fat (1 g sat. fat), 27 mg chol., 53 mg sodium, 33 g carb., 1 g fiber, 3 g pro.* **Diabetic Exchanges:** *2 starch, 1 fat.*

Peachy Cheese Danish

I've prepared these pretty sweet rolls for late-night snacks and for breakfast when we have guests. It can be your secret how quickly these gorgeous little pastries come together.

—CAROLYN KYZER ALEXANDER, AR

PREP: 20 MIN. • **BAKE:** 15 MIN.
MAKES: 4 SERVINGS

- 1 tube (8 ounces) refrigerated crescent rolls
- 4 ounces cream cheese, softened
- ¼ cup sugar
- 2 tablespoons lemon juice
- 8 teaspoons peach preserves or flavor of your choice

GLAZE

- ¼ cup confectioners' sugar
- ½ teaspoon vanilla extract
- 1 to 2 teaspoons milk

1. Separate dough into four rectangles; seal perforations. On a lightly floured surface, roll each into a 7-in. x 3½-in. rectangle. In a small bowl, combine cream cheese, sugar and lemon juice until smooth; spread over rectangles. Roll up from a long side; pinch edges to seal. Holding one end, loosely coil each.
2. Place on an ungreased baking sheet. Top each coil with 2 teaspoons preserves. Bake at 350° for 15-20 minutes or until golden brown. Remove from pan to wire rack.
3. For glaze, in a small bowl, combine confectioners' sugar, vanilla and enough milk to achieve desired consistency. Drizzle over the tops.

TOP TIP

I've made these Danish three times already, and they are soooo good! Mine didn't look quite perfect, but nevertheless, they were enjoyed immensely by my family. I have also used apricot and raspberry preserves with excellent results.
—XICOTA TASTEOFHOME.COM

HONEY SPICE BREAD

Chocolate Chip-Cranberry Scones

FREEZE IT   EAT SMART   FAST FIX

START TO FINISH: 30 MIN.
MAKES: 1 DOZEN

- 2 **cups all-purpose flour**
- 3 **tablespoons brown sugar**
- 2 **teaspoons baking powder**
- 1 **teaspoon grated orange peel**
- ½ **teaspoon salt**
- ½ **teaspoon baking soda**
- ¼ **cup cold butter**
- 1 **cup (8 ounces) plain yogurt**
- 1 **egg yolk**
- ½ **cup dried cranberries**
- ½ **cup semisweet chocolate chips**

1. Preheat oven to 400°. In a large bowl, whisk the first six ingredients. Cut in butter until mixture resembles coarse crumbs. In another bowl, whisk yogurt and egg yolk; stir into crumb mixture just until moistened. Stir in cranberries and chocolate chips.

2. Turn onto a floured surface; knead gently 10 times. Pat dough into an 8-in. circle. Cut into 12 wedges. Place wedges on a baking sheet coated with cooking spray. Bake 10-12 minutes or until golden brown. Serve warm.

FREEZE OPTION *Freeze the cooled scones in resealable plastic freezer bags. To use, thaw scones at room temperature or, if desired, microwave each scone on high for 20-30 seconds or until heated through.*

PER SERVING *189 cal., 7 g fat (4 g sat. fat), 28 mg chol., 264 mg sodium, 29 g carb., 1 g fiber, 3 g pro.* **Diabetic Exchanges:** *2 starch, 1 fat.*

CHOCOLATE CHIP-CRANBERRY SCONES

> My daughter started making these as a healthier alternative to cookies, since we seem to like cookies of any kind. For a more citrusy flavor, use orange-flavored cranberries. —**NICHOLE JONES** IDAHO FALLS, ID

Granola Blueberry Muffins

FREEZE IT   EAT SMART

I wanted to put a new spin on muffins, so I mixed in some granola. I brought a batch to work the next morning—success. The granola I used contained lots of nuts, pumpkin seeds and shredded coconut.
—**MEGAN WEISS** MENOMONIE, WI

PREP: 20 MIN. • **BAKE:** 15 MIN.
MAKES: 1 DOZEN

- 1½ **cups whole wheat flour**
- ½ **cup all-purpose flour**
- ¼ **cup packed brown sugar**
- 2 **teaspoons baking powder**
- ½ **teaspoon salt**
- ½ **teaspoon baking soda**
- 1 **cup granola without raisins, divided**
- 1 **egg**
- 1 **cup buttermilk**
- ¼ **cup canola oil**
- 2 **tablespoons orange juice**
- 1 **tablespoon lemon juice**
- 1 **cup fresh or frozen unsweetened blueberries**

1. Preheat oven to 400°. In a small bowl, whisk flours, brown sugar, baking powder, salt and baking soda. Stir in ½ cup granola. In another bowl, whisk the egg, buttermilk, oil and juices until blended. Add to flour mixture; stir just until moistened. Fold in blueberries.

2. Fill greased muffin cups three-fourths full; sprinkle remaining granola over batter. Bake 12-15 minutes or until a toothpick inserted in center comes out clean. Cool 5 minutes before removing from pan to a wire rack.

NOTE *If using frozen blueberries, use without thawing to avoid discoloring the batter.*

FREEZE OPTION *Freeze cooled muffins in resealable plastic freezer bags. To use, thaw muffins at room temperature or, if desired, microwave each muffin on high for 20-30 seconds or until heated through.*

PER SERVING *188 cal., 7 g fat (1 g sat. fat), 18 mg chol., 251 mg sodium, 28 g carb., 4 g fiber, 6 g pro.* **Diabetic Exchanges:** *2 starch, 1 fat.*

GRANOLA BLUEBERRY MUFFINS

Crab Crescent Loaf

Golden crescent dough is scrumptious filled with cream cheese, dill and tender crab. You're sure to appreciate the rich flavor and easy preparation.

—**MAUREEN DONGOSKI** PETERSBURG, WV

PREP: 20 MIN. • **BAKE:** 20 MIN.
MAKES: 1 LOAF (12 SLICES)

- 1 **tube (8 ounces) refrigerated crescent rolls**
- 6 **ounces cream cheese, softened**
- ⅓ **cup chopped onion**
- ½ **teaspoon dill weed**
- 1 **cup chopped imitation crabmeat or 1 can (6 ounces) lump crabmeat, drained**
- 1 **egg yolk, lightly beaten**

1. On a greased baking sheet, unroll crescent dough into one long rectangle; seal seams and perforations. In a small bowl, beat the cream cheese, onion and dill until blended. Spread mixture lengthwise over half of the dough to within ½ in. of edges. Top with crab.

2. Fold dough over filling; pinch seam to seal. Brush the top with egg yolk. Bake at 375° for 18-22 minutes or until golden brown. Cut into slices.

⑤ INGREDIENTS FAST FIX

Tomato Rosemary Focaccia

My super quick version of Italian flatbread makes a great snack, but it's also good with hot soup or a main-dish salad.

—**DOROTHY SMITH** EL DORADO, AR

START TO FINISH: 30 MIN.
MAKES: 6 SERVINGS

- 1 **tube (13.8 ounces) refrigerated pizza crust**
- 2 **tablespoons olive oil**
- 2 **garlic cloves, minced**
- ¼ **teaspoon salt**
- 1 **tablespoon minced fresh rosemary or 1 teaspoon dried rosemary, crushed, divided**
- 2 **to 3 plum tomatoes, thinly sliced**
- 1 **small red onion, thinly sliced**

Unroll pizza crust onto a greased baking sheet. Combine the oil, garlic, salt and half of the rosemary; spread over crust. Top with tomatoes and onion; sprinkle with remaining rosemary. Bake at 425° for 12-15 minutes or until golden. Cut into rectangles.

DID YOU KNOW?

You can use a less expensive olive oil than virgin or extra-virgin for cooking and baking. The higher grades have a more delicate flavor that shines in salads and uncooked foods, but is generally lost in recipes that require cooking. Pure olive oil works fine– and sometimes even better–for cooked recipes.

CRAB CRESCENT LOAF

EASY MOLASSES STICKY BUNS

> Your family will jump right out of bed when they smell these ooey-gooey caramel rolls baking in the oven. And, these tender treats taste just as delicious as they look!
>
> —**NANCY FOUST** STONEBORO, PA

Easy Molasses Sticky Buns

PREP: 20 MIN. + RISING • **BAKE:** 25 MIN.
MAKES: 1 DOZEN

- 2 loaves (16 ounces each) frozen bread dough, thawed
- ⅓ cup butter, softened
- ½ cup sugar
- 1½ teaspoons ground cinnamon

MOLASSES SAUCE
- 1 cup packed brown sugar
- ½ cup butter, cubed
- ½ cup water
- ¼ cup molasses

1. Roll out each loaf of bread dough into a 10-in. square. Spread with butter to within ½ in. of edges. Combine sugar and cinnamon;

sprinkle over butter. Roll up jelly-roll style; pinch seams to seal. Cut each loaf into six slices.

2. For sauce, in a small saucepan, bring the brown sugar, butter, water and molasses to a boil. Pour mixture into a greased 13x9-in. baking dish. Place rolls, cut side down, in the molasses sauce.

3. Cover and let rise in a warm place until doubled, about 30 minutes. Bake at 350° for 25-30 minutes or until golden brown. Cool rolls in dish for 5 minutes; invert onto a serving platter. Serve warm.

⑤ INGREDIENTS EAT SMART
Oatmeal Bread
This bread has a lightly sweet flavor with good texture and crust.

—**RUTH ANDREWSON** LEAVENWORTH, WA

PREP: 10 MIN • **BAKE:** 3 HOURS
MAKES: 1 LOAF (2 POUNDS, 20 SLICES)

- 1 cup warm water (70° to 80°)
- ½ cup molasses
- 1 tablespoon canola oil
- 1 teaspoon salt
- 3 cups bread flour
- 1 cup quick-cooking oats
- 1 package (¼ ounce) active dry yeast

1. In bread machine pan, place all ingredients in order suggested by manufacturer. Select basic bread

setting. Choose crust color and loaf size if available.

2. Bake according to bread machine directions (check the dough after 5 minutes of mixing; add 1 to 2 tablespoons of water or flour if needed).

PER SERVING *105 cal., 1 g fat (trace sat. fat), 0 chol., 121 mg sodium, 22 g carb., 1 g fiber, 3 g pro.* **Diabetic Exchange:** *1½ starch.*

⑤ INGREDIENTS FAST FIX ▸
Cheesy Pesto Bread
I topped a ready-made pizza crust with pesto and cheese one night when I was in a rush. Now it's expected whenever I make pasta and salad. This bread is great heated up for lunch the next day, too.

—**KAREN GRANT** TULARE, CA

START TO FINISH: 20 MIN.
MAKES: 6-8 SERVINGS

- 1 prebaked 12-inch pizza crust
- 3 tablespoons prepared pesto
- ⅛ teaspoon garlic salt
- 1 cup (4 ounces) shredded mozzarella cheese
- ½ cup shredded Parmesan cheese

Place crust on a pizza pan or baking sheet. Spread with pesto; sprinkle with garlic salt and cheeses. Bake at 325° for 12-15 minutes or until cheese is melted. Cut into wedges.

OATMEAL BREAD

Chocolate-Peppermint Sandwich Cookies
PAGE 283

Holiday & Seasonal Pleasers

Discover more than 70 mouthwatering reasons to celebrate in this giant chapter. Prepare a dazzling Easter brunch where every dish comes together with five or fewer ingredients! Whip up simple Fourth of July stunners sure to steal the show. Serve amazing—yet easy—Christmas feasts and give home-baked gifts to delight everyone on your list.

Rainbow Sherbet
Angel Food Cake
PAGE 260

Ghostly Hot Cocoa
PAGE 269

Marshmallow Pumpkin Pie
PAGE 274

MY BEST EVER JAMBALAYA

I tried to mimic jambalaya from my favorite restaurant and it turned out so well that my daughter and husband now prefer my recipe. They won't order the jambalaya when we go to the restaurant!

—ALEXIS VAN VULPEN ST. ALBERT, ALBERTA

My Best-Ever Jambalaya

PREP: 20 MIN. • **COOK:** 40 MIN.
MAKES: 10 SERVINGS

- 2 **tablespoons canola oil**
- ½ **pound fully cooked Spanish chorizo links, sliced**
- 2 **cups cubed fully cooked ham**
- ¾ **pound boneless skinless chicken breasts, cubed**
- 1 **can (28 ounces) diced tomatoes, undrained**
- 3 **cups chicken broth**
- 2 **large green peppers, chopped**
- 1 **large onion, chopped**
- 1 **tablespoon Cajun seasoning**
- 2 **teaspoons hot pepper sauce**
- 3 **cups instant brown rice**
- ½ **pound uncooked medium shrimp, peeled and deveined**

1. In a Dutch oven, heat oil over medium-high heat. Add chorizo and ham; cook and stir 3-4 minutes or until browned.
2. Add chicken to pan; cook 5-7 minutes or until no longer pink. Stir in tomatoes, broth, peppers, onion, Cajun seasoning and pepper sauce. Bring to a boil. Reduce heat; simmer, uncovered, 8-10 minutes or until peppers are crisp-tender.
3. Return to a boil; stir in rice and shrimp. Reduce heat; simmer, covered, 7-9 minutes or until shrimp turn pink. Remove from heat; let stand, covered, 5 minutes or until rice is tender.

⑤ INGREDIENTS FAST FIX

Quick Gumbo

This gumbo recipe could not be any easier to make. Try it on a busy weeknight with a side of crusty bread for dipping!

—AMY FLACK HOMER CITY, PA

START TO FINISH: 20 MIN.
MAKES: 6 SERVINGS

- 3 **Italian turkey sausage links, sliced**
- 1 **can (14½ ounces) diced tomatoes with green peppers and onions, undrained**
- 1 **can (14½ ounces) reduced-sodium chicken broth**
- ½ **cup water**
- 1 **cup uncooked instant rice**
- 1 **can (7 ounces) whole kernel corn, drained**

In a large saucepan, cook sausage until no longer pink; drain. Stir in the tomatoes, broth and water; bring to a boil. Stir in rice and corn; cover and remove from the heat. Let stand for 5 minutes.

Bourbon Slush

We experiment with different teas whenever we make these slushes for parties. We like black tea, green tea and orange spice. Try your own favorite tea to personalize this great drink.

—**DARCENE SIGLER** LOUISVILLE, OH

PREP: 10 MIN. + FREEZING
MAKES: 24 SERVINGS (1 CUP EACH)

- 7 **cups water**
- 1½ **cups sugar**
- 1 **can (12 ounces) frozen orange juice concentrate**
- 1 **can (12 ounces) frozen lemonade concentrate**
- 2 **cups strong brewed tea, cooled**
- 2 **cups bourbon**
- 3 **liters lemon-lime soda, chilled**

1. In a Dutch oven, combine water and sugar; bring to a boil, stirring to dissolve sugar. Remove from heat.

2. Stir in orange juice and lemonade concentrates, tea and bourbon. Transfer to freezer containers; freeze 12 hours or overnight.

3. To serve, place about ½ cup bourbon mixture in each glass; top with ½ cup soda.

EAT SMART

King Cake with Cream Cheese Filling

Round out your Mardi Gras celebration with a king cake—a colorful ring-shaped pastry drizzled with green, gold and purple icing. This stunning treat has become the holiday's signature dessert.

—**ALICE LEJEUNE** VILLE PLATTE, LA

PREP: 25 MIN. • **BAKE:** 20 MIN.
MAKES: 16 SERVINGS

- 2 **tubes (8 ounces each) refrigerated reduced-fat crescent rolls**
- 4 **ounces reduced-fat cream cheese**

KING CAKE WITH CREAM CHEESE FILLING

- 2 **tablespoons confectioners' sugar**
- 1 **teaspoon vanilla extract**
- ⅓ **cup light brown sugar**
- 2 **tablespoons butter, softened**
- 3 **teaspoons ground cinnamon**

ICING

- 1 **cup confectioners' sugar**
- 1 **to 2 tablespoons 2% milk**
- ½ **teaspoon vanilla extract**
  Red, blue, yellow and green food coloring

1. Unroll both tubes of crescent dough and separate into triangles. Place triangles on a greased 12-in. pizza pan, forming a ring with pointed ends facing toward the center and wide ends overlapping. Lightly press wide ends together.

2. In a small bowl, beat the cream cheese, confectioners' sugar and vanilla until smooth. Spoon over wide ends of ring. In another bowl, stir the brown sugar, butter and cinnamon until crumbly. Sprinkle over cream cheese mixture.

3. Fold points over filling and fold wide ends over points to seal. Bake at 350° for 20-25 minutes or until golden brown. Cool for 5 minutes.

4. Meanwhile, combine the confectioners' sugar, vanilla and enough milk to achieve desired consistency. Divide icing among three bowls. Using red and blue food coloring, tint one portion purple. Tint another portion yellow and the remaining portion green. Drizzle over cake. Serve warm.

PER SERVING *184 cal., 8 g fat (3 g sat. fat), 9 mg chol., 275 mg sodium, 26 g carb., trace fiber, 3 g pro.* **Diabetic Exchanges:** *1½ starch, 1½ fat.*

BOURBON SLUSH

(5) INGREDIENTS
Rainbow Sherbet Angel Food Cake

Talk about a dessert that pops! Sometimes, I make this easy cake even more eye-catching by coloring the whipped cream, too. Use whatever sherbet flavor combination you like.
—**BONNIE HAWKINS** ELKHORN, WI

PREP: 25 MIN. + FREEZING
MAKES: 12 SERVINGS

- 1 prepared angel food cake (8 to 10 ounces)
- 3 cups rainbow sherbet, softened if necessary

WHIPPED CREAM
- 2 cups heavy whipping cream
- ⅓ cup confectioners' sugar
- 1 teaspoon vanilla extract

1. Using a long serrated knife, cut cake horizontally into four layers. Place bottom layer on a freezer-safe serving plate; spread with 1 cup sherbet. Repeat twice. Top with remaining cake layer. Freeze, covered, until sherbet is firm, about 1 hour.

2. In a large bowl, beat cream until it begins to thicken. Add confectioners' sugar and vanilla; beat until soft peaks form. Frost top and sides of cake. Freeze until firm.

3. Thaw in refrigerator 30 minutes before serving. Cut cake with a serrated knife.

CHIVE BUTTERED CARROTS

(5) INGREDIENTS FAST FIX
Chive Buttered Carrots

It's nice to have a reliable side dish like this that pairs well with any entree. A friend shared the recipe with me years ago.
—**OPAL SNELL** JAMESTOWN, OH

START TO FINISH: 25 MIN.
MAKES: 8 SERVINGS

- 2½ pounds carrots, diagonally sliced ½ inch thick
- 6 tablespoons butter, cubed
- ¼ to ½ teaspoon seasoned salt
- ¼ teaspoon pepper
- 1 to 2 tablespoons minced fresh chives

1. Place 1 in. of water and carrots in a large saucepan; bring to a boil. Cook, covered, 3-4 minutes or until crisp-tender. Drain well.

2. In a large skillet, heat butter over medium-high heat. Add carrots, seasoned salt and pepper; cook and stir 1-2 minutes or until carrots are tender. Sprinkle with chives.

HOW TO

FREEZE FLAVORED BUTTER

You can freeze scoops or rosettes of flavored butter on a parchment paper-lined baking sheet. Once frozen, arrange the butter portions on layers of paper in a freezer container. Remove the desired number of butter portions from the freezer when needed.

RAINBOW SHERBET ANGEL FOOD CAKE

(5) INGREDIENTS FAST FIX

Hurry-Up Biscuits

When I was young, my mom would make these biscuits with fresh cream she got from a local farmer. I don't go to those lengths anymore, but this family recipe is still a real treat.

—**BEVERLY SPRAGUE** BALTIMORE, MD

START TO FINISH: 30 MIN.
MAKES: 1 DOZEN

- **3 cups all-purpose flour**
- **4 teaspoons baking powder**
- **4 teaspoons sugar**
- **1 teaspoon salt**
- **2 cups heavy whipping cream**

1. Preheat oven to 375°. In a large bowl, whisk flour, baking powder, sugar and salt. Add cream; stir just until moistened.
2. Drop by 1/4 cupfuls 1 in. apart onto greased baking sheets. Bake 17-20 minutes or until bottoms are golden brown. Serve warm.

(5) INGREDIENTS

Fresh Herb Butter

My dinner guests are impressed when they see these decorative butter pats on the table. I cut them in different shapes for variety and then freeze them so they're always ready to go. They're so easy to have on hand, and they make a flavorful complement to bread, rolls or fish.

—**PAM DUNCAN** SUMMERS, AR

PREP: 25 MIN. + FREEZING
MAKES: ABOUT 2 DOZEN

- **1 cup butter, softened**
- **2 tablespoons minced fresh chives**
- **2 tablespoons minced fresh parsley**
- **1 tablespoon minced fresh tarragon**
- **1 tablespoon lemon juice**
- **¼ teaspoon pepper**

1. In a small bowl, beat all ingredients until blended. Spread onto a baking sheet to 1/2-in. thickness. Freeze, covered, until firm.
2. Cut butter with a 1-in. cookie cutter. Store, layered between waxed paper, in an airtight container in the refrigerator up to 1 week or in the freezer up to 3 months.

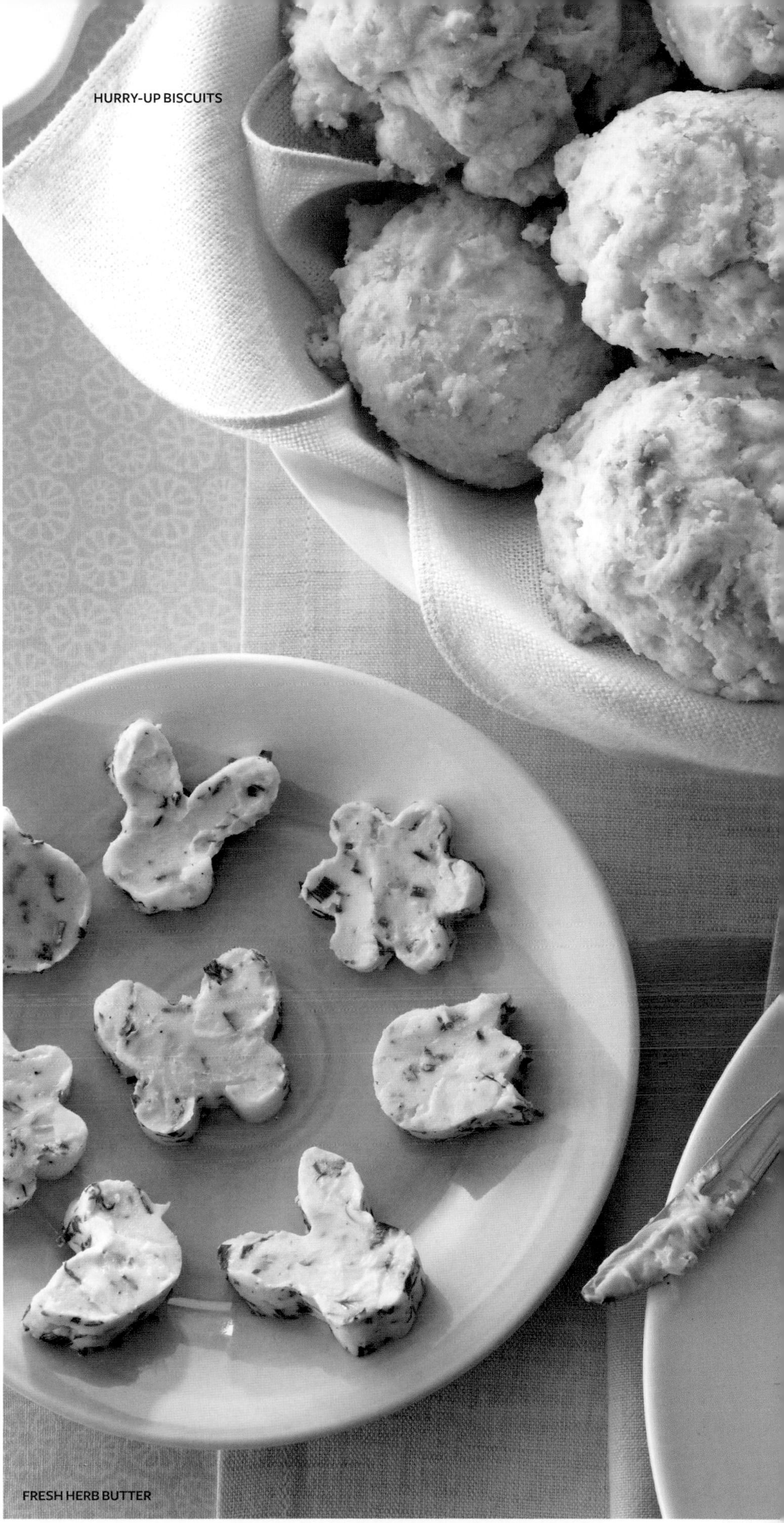

HURRY-UP BISCUITS

FRESH HERB BUTTER

⑤ INGREDIENTS EAT SMART
Dilled New Potatoes

I try to grow as much of our own food as possible, and our big potato patch means easy and affordable meals for much of the year. For this dish, I use homegrown dill.

—**JENNIFER FERRIS** BRONSON, MI

START TO FINISH: 25 MIN.
MAKES: 8 SERVINGS

- 2 **pounds baby red potatoes (1¾ inches wide, about 24)**
- ¼ **cup butter, melted**
- 2 **tablespoons snipped fresh dill**
- 1 **tablespoon lemon juice**
- 1 **teaspoon salt**
- ½ **teaspoon pepper**

1. Place potatoes in a Dutch oven; add water to cover. Bring to a boil. Reduce heat; cook, uncovered, 15-20 minutes or until tender.

2. Drain; return to pan. Mix the remaining ingredients; drizzle over potatoes and toss to coat.

PER SERVING *180 cal., 8 g fat (5 g sat. fat), 20 mg chol., 447 mg sodium, 27 g carb., 2 g fiber, 3 g pro.* **Diabetic Exchanges:** *2 starch, 1½ fat.*

TOP TIP

I had already cut several potatoes into quarters when I came across this recipe, and decided to add the dill flavorings even though the instructions said to use whole potatoes. The results were fantastic. Maybe even better was that the flavoring wasn't just on the outer skins, but all over the potatoes.

—**BEEMA** TASTEOFHOME.COM

DILLED NEW POTATOES

LEMON-ROASTED ASPARAGUS

When it comes to fixing asparagus, I think it's hard to go wrong. The springy and citrusy flavors in this easy recipe burst with every single bite.

—**JENNIFER TIDWELL** FAIR OAKS, CA

⑤ INGREDIENTS EAT SMART
Lemon-Roasted Asparagus

START TO FINISH: 20 MIN.
MAKES: 8 SERVINGS

- 2 **pounds fresh asparagus, trimmed**
- ¼ **cup olive oil**
- 4 **teaspoons grated lemon peel**
- 2 **garlic cloves, minced**
- ½ **teaspoon salt**
- ½ **teaspoon pepper**

Preheat oven to 425°. Place asparagus in a greased 15x10x1-in. baking pan. Mix remaining ingredients; drizzle over asparagus. Toss to coat. Roast 8-12 minutes or until crisp-tender.

PER SERVING *75 cal., 7 g fat (1 g sat. fat), 0 chol., 154 mg sodium, 3 g carb., 1 g fiber, 2 g pro.* **Diabetic Exchanges:** *1½ fat, 1 vegetable.*

Shrimp Salad Appetizers

This refreshing hors d'oeuvre has gained a big following since a friend shared her family recipe with me. My 7-year-old son says it best: The celery and shrimp are so good together.
—**SOLIE KIMBLE** KANATA, ON

START TO FINISH: 15 MIN.
MAKES: 2 DOZEN

- 1 **pound peeled and deveined cooked shrimp, chopped**
- 1 **can (6 ounces) lump crabmeat, drained**
- 2 **celery ribs, finely chopped**
- ¼ **cup Dijon-mayonnaise blend**
- 24 **Belgian endive leaves (3-4 heads) or small butterhead lettuce leaves**

In a large bowl, combine shrimp, crab and celery. Add mayonnaise blend; toss to coat. To serve, top each leaf with about 2 tablespoons shrimp mixture.

PER SERVING *31 cal., trace fat (trace sat. fat), 35 mg chol., 115 mg sodium, 1 g carb., trace fiber, 5 g pro.*

SHRIMP SALAD APPETIZERS

CHUTNEY-TOPPED CREAM CHEESE SPREAD

Chutney-Topped Cream Cheese Spread

I've had the pleasure of introducing many of my friends and family to chutney, a sweet and savory fruit sauce. Make the spread even faster by using chive-flavored whipped cream cheese.
—**MICHELLE TORKELSON** HAM LAKE, MN

START TO FINISH: 10 MIN.
MAKES: 1¾ CUPS

- 1 **package (8 ounces) cream cheese, softened**
- 3 **green onions, chopped**
- ¾ **cup chutney**
- ¼ **cup chopped salted peanuts Assorted crackers**

1. In a small bowl, beat cream cheese until smooth; stir in green onions. Spread into a shallow serving dish.
2. Top with chutney; sprinkle with peanuts. Serve with crackers.

Glazed Spiral-Sliced Ham

In my mind, few foods in a holiday spread are as tempting as a big baked ham. I always hope for leftovers so we can have ham sandwiches in the following days.
—**EDIE DESPAIN** LOGAN, UT

PREP: 10 MIN. • **BAKE:** 1 HOUR 35 MIN.
MAKES: 12 SERVINGS

- 1 **spiral-sliced fully cooked bone-in ham (7 to 9 pounds)**
- ½ **cup pineapple preserves**
- ½ **cup seedless raspberry jam**
- ¼ **cup packed brown sugar**
- ¼ **teaspoon ground cloves**

1. Preheat oven to 300°. Place ham directly on roasting pan, cut side down. Bake, covered, 1¼ to 1¾ hours.
2. In a bowl, mix remaining ingredients. Spread over ham. Bake, uncovered, 20-30 minutes longer or until a thermometer reads 140° (do not overcook).

STRAWBERRY SALSA

Salami & Provolone Pasta Salad

Everyone needs a perfect pasta salad that's easy to make, especially on busy nights when your family wants a dish that's fast, light and cool. This is just the thing.

—JILL DONLEY WARSAW, IN

PREP: 25 MIN. + CHILLING
MAKES: 8 SERVINGS

- 3 cups uncooked cellentani pasta or elbow macaroni
- 1 medium sweet red pepper, chopped
- 4 ounces provolone cheese, cubed (about 1 cup)
- 4 ounces hard salami, cubed (about 1 cup)
- ⅓ cup prepared Italian salad dressing
  Additional Italian salad dressing and minced fresh basil, optional

1. Cook pasta according to package directions. Meanwhile, in a large bowl, combine pepper, cheese and salami.
2. Drain pasta and rinse in cold water. Add to pepper mixture. Drizzle with ⅓ cup dressing and toss to coat. Refrigerate, covered, at least 1 hour. If desired, stir in additional salad dressing to moisten and sprinkle with basil before serving.

SALAMI & PROVOLONE PASTA SALAD

Here's a sweet and tangy salsa that's miles away from the spicy version people expect. Serve it as an appetizer with tortilla chips for scooping, or make it part of the main event and spoon it over white meat.

—AMY HINKLE TOPEKA, KS

Strawberry Salsa

START TO FINISH: 25 MIN.
MAKES: 6 CUPS

- 2 pints cherry tomatoes, quartered
- 1 pint fresh strawberries, chopped
- 8 green onions, chopped
- ½ cup minced fresh cilantro
- 6 tablespoons olive oil
- 2 tablespoons balsamic vinegar
- ½ teaspoon salt

In a large bowl, combine tomatoes, strawberries, green onions and cilantro. In a small bowl, whisk oil, vinegar and salt; gently stir into tomato mixture. Refrigerate until serving.
PER SERVING *41 cal., 4 g fat (trace sat. fat), 0 chol., 53 mg sodium, 3 g carb., 1 g fiber, trace pro.*

Marinated Chicken & Zucchini Kabobs

These tasty (and healthy!) kabobs are a family favorite. You can change them up with turkey tenderloins and other veggies, like summer squash or sweet bell peppers.

—**TAMMY SLADE** STANSBURY PARK, UT

PREP: 25 MIN. + MARINATING
GRILL: 10 MIN.
MAKES: 8 SERVINGS

- ¾ **cup lemon-lime soda**
- ½ **cup reduced-sodium soy sauce**
- ½ **cup canola oil, divided**
- 2 **pounds boneless skinless chicken breasts or turkey breast tenderloins, cut into 1-inch cubes**
- 3 **medium zucchini, cut into 1-inch pieces**
- 2 **medium red onions, cut into 1-inch pieces**
- ½ **teaspoon salt**
- ¼ **teaspoon pepper**

1. In a large resealable plastic bag, combine soda, soy sauce and ¼ cup oil. Add chicken; seal bag and turn to coat. Refrigerate 8 hours or overnight.
2. Drain chicken, discarding marinade. On eight metal or soaked wooden skewers, alternately thread chicken and vegetables. Brush vegetables with remaining oil; sprinkle with salt and pepper.
3. Moisten a paper towel with cooking oil; using long-handled tongs, rub on grill rack to coat lightly. Grill kabobs, covered, over medium heat 8-10 minutes or until chicken is no longer pink and vegetables are tender, turning occasionally.
PER SERVING *224 cal., 11 g fat (1 g sat. fat), 63 mg chol., 344 mg sodium, 6 g carb., 1 g fiber, 24 g pro.* **Diabetic Exchanges:** *3 lean meat, 2 fat, 1 vegetable.*

DID YOU KNOW?

Marinade is a seasoned liquid used to flavor the food that is added to it. If it contains an acid, such as citrus juice, vinegar or wine, it will also tenderize meat by breaking down its fibers.

Southwest Steak

For grilling, my husband and I make an easy marinade that bumps up steak to a new level. Chili powder and pepper flakes really add some sizzle.

—**CAROLINE SHIVELY** NEW YORK, NY

PREP: 15 MIN. + MARINATING
GRILL: 15 MIN.
MAKES: 8 SERVINGS

- ¼ **cup lime juice**
- 6 **garlic cloves, minced**
- 4 **teaspoons chili powder**
- 4 **teaspoons canola oil**
- 1 **teaspoon salt**
- 1 **teaspoon crushed red pepper flakes**
- 1 **teaspoon pepper**
- 2 **beef flank steaks (1 pound each)**

1. In a small bowl, mix the first seven ingredients; spread over both sides of steaks. Place in a large resealable plastic bag; refrigerate 6 hours or overnight, turning occasionally.
2. Moisten a paper towel with cooking oil; using long-handled tongs, rub on grill rack to coat lightly. Grill steaks, covered, over medium heat or broil 4 in. from heat 6-9 minutes on each side or until meat reaches desired doneness (for medium-rare, a thermometer should read 145°; medium, 160°; well-done, 170°).
3. Let steaks stand 5 minutes. Thinly slice across the grain.
PER SERVING *187 cal., 10 g fat (4 g sat. fat), 54 mg chol., 259 mg sodium, 2 g carb., trace fiber, 22 g pro.* **Diabetic Exchanges:** *3 lean meat, 1 fat.*

SOUTHWEST STEAK

MARINATED CHICKEN & ZUCCHINI KABOBS

Grilling is a huge summer highlight for my family, which is one reason we're such fans of this recipe. Whenever I put out a plate of these cute little appetizers, people come flocking.

—**TARA CRUZ** KERSEY, CO

BLUE CHEESE & BACON STUFFED PEPPERS

(5)INGREDIENTS FAST FIX

Blue Cheese & Bacon Stuffed Peppers

START TO FINISH: 20 MIN.
MAKES: 1 DOZEN

- 3 **medium sweet yellow, orange or red peppers**
- 4 **ounces cream cheese, softened**
- ½ **cup crumbled blue cheese**
- 3 **bacon strips, cooked and crumbled**
- 1 **green onion, thinly sliced**

1. Cut peppers into quarters. Remove and discard stems and seeds. In a small bowl, mix cream cheese, blue cheese, bacon and green onion until blended.
2. Grill peppers, covered, over medium-high heat or broil 4 in. from heat 2-3 minutes on each side or until slightly charred.

3. Remove peppers from grill; fill each with about 1 tablespoon cheese mixture. Grill 2-3 minutes longer or until cheese is melted.

(5)INGREDIENTS EAT SMART FAST FIX

Minty Watermelon-Cucumber Salad

Capturing fantastic flavors of summer, this refreshing, beautiful salad will be the talk of any picnic or potluck.
—**ROBLYNN HUNNISETT** GUELPH, ON

START TO FINISH: 20 MIN.
MAKES: 16 SERVINGS (¾ CUP EACH)

- 8 **cups cubed seedless watermelon**
- 2 **medium English cucumbers, halved lengthwise and sliced**
- 6 **green onions, chopped**
- ¼ **cup minced fresh mint**
- ¼ **cup balsamic vinegar**
- ¼ **cup olive oil**
- ½ **teaspoon salt**
- ½ **teaspoon pepper**

In a large bowl, combine watermelon, cucumbers, green onions and mint. In a small bowl, whisk remaining ingredients. Pour over salad and toss to coat. Serve immediately or refrigerate, covered, up to 2 hours before serving.
PER SERVING *60 cal., 3 g fat (trace sat. fat), 0 chol., 78 mg sodium, 9 g carb., 1 g fiber, 1 g pro.* **Diabetic Exchanges:** *½ fruit, ½ fat.*

(5)INGREDIENTS EAT SMART FAST FIX

No-Fuss Avocado Onion Salad

My mother, Nena, grew up in Cuba and learned many styles of cooking. She had a knack for making something incredibly simple taste incredibly amazing. This salad is proof. By itself, the dressing is really tart, but add the avocados and onions and it's the perfect complement.
—**MARINA CASTLE** CANYON COUNTRY, CA

START TO FINISH: 15 MIN.
MAKES: 12 SERVINGS

- 3 **medium ripe avocados, peeled and thinly sliced**
- 1 **large sweet onion, halved and thinly sliced**
- ⅓ **cup olive oil**
- ¼ **cup stone-ground mustard**

- 2 **tablespoons lemon juice**
- 1 **tablespoon honey**

Arrange avocado and onion slices on a large platter. In a small bowl, whisk remaining ingredients; drizzle over salad. Serve immediately.
PER SERVING *147 cal., 13 g fat (2 g sat. fat), 0 chol., 108 mg sodium, 8 g carb., 3 g fiber, 1 g pro.* **Diabetic Exchanges:** *2 fat, ½ starch.*

(5)INGREDIENTS EAT SMART

Chocolaty S'mores Bars

One night, my husband had some friends over to play poker and he requested these s'mores bars. They polished off the pan and asked for more! I shared the recipe, and now his friends can enjoy them at home, too.
—**REBECCA SHIPP** BEEBE, AR

PREP: 15 MIN. + COOLING
MAKES: 1½ DOZEN

- ¼ **cup butter, cubed**
- 1 **package (10 ounces) large marshmallows**
- 1 **package (12 ounces) Golden Grahams**
- ⅓ **cup milk chocolate chips, melted**

1. In a large saucepan, melt butter over low heat. Add marshmallows; cook and stir until blended. Remove from heat. Stir in cereal until coated.
2. Using a buttered spatula, press evenly into a greased 13x9-in. pan. Drizzle with melted chocolate chips. Cool completely. Cut into bars. Store in an airtight container.
PER SERVING *159 cal., 4 g fat (2 g sat. fat), 7 mg chol., 197 mg sodium, 30 g carb., 1 g fiber, 1 g pro.*

TOP TIP

We like the smoky flavor of bacon in our burgers and meat loaf. To save time, I sometimes mix packaged bacon bits into the meat instead of cooking the bacon beforehand. Use 2 tablespoons of bacon bits for each bacon strip that is called for in the recipe.
—**CHARLENE F.** COALDALE, AB

MINTY WATERMELON-CUCUMBER SALAD

NO-FUSS AVOCADO ONION SALAD

CHOCOLATY S'MORES BARS

FREEZE IT FAST FIX
Bewitched Chili

One pot and 30 minutes—yes, please!
Kids and grown-ups love this warm-you-up
chili for Halloween.

—JANICE WESTMORELAND BROOKSVILLE, FL

START TO FINISH: 30 MIN.
MAKES: 12 SERVINGS (3 QUARTS)

- 1 pound bulk pork sausage
- 1 large onion, chopped
- 2 cans (16 ounces each) chili beans, undrained
- 1 can (28 ounces) crushed tomatoes
- 3 cups water
- 1 can (4 ounces) chopped green chilies
- 1 envelope chili seasoning mix
- 2 tablespoons sugar
- 12 round blue tortilla chips, halved
- 12 triangular blue tortilla chips

1. In a Dutch oven, cook sausage and onion over medium heat 5-7 minutes or until meat is no longer pink, breaking up sausage into crumbles; drain. Add beans, tomatoes, water, chilies, seasoning mix and sugar; bring to a boil. Reduce heat; simmer, covered, 20 minutes to allow flavors to blend, stirring frequently.

2. Top each serving with two halved round tortilla chips and one triangular tortilla chip inserted vertically into the chili between the round halves to resemble a witch's hat.

FREEZE OPTION *Freeze cooled chili in freezer containers. To use, partially thaw in refrigerator overnight. Heat through in a saucepan, stirring occasionally and adding a little water if necessary.*

JACK SKELLINGTON POPS

Jack Skellington Pops

Cake mix makes quick work of these cake pops decorated to look like Jack the Pumpkin King from *The Nightmare Before Christmas.*

—*TASTE OF HOME* TEST KITCHEN

PREP: 1 HOUR + CHILLING
BAKE: 25 MIN. + COOLING
MAKES: 1½ DOZEN

- 1 package white cake mix (regular size)
- ½ cup white baking chips
- 1 cup vanilla frosting
- 18 lollipop sticks
- ½ pound white candy coating, coarsely chopped
  Styrofoam block, optional
  Black decorating gel

1. Prepare and bake cake mix batter according to package directions. Cool completely.

2. Crumble cake into a large bowl. In a microwave, melt baking chips; stir until smooth. Stir in frosting until blended. Add to cake crumbs; mix well. Shape into 1½-in. balls. Place on waxed paper-lined baking sheets. Freeze for 2 hours or until firm.

3. In a microwave, melt candy coating; stir until smooth. Dip one tip of the lollipop sticks in coating; insert into balls. Dip balls in coating; allow excess to drip off. If desired, insert pops into Styrofoam to keep upright. Refrigerate until set. Decorate as desired with decorating gel.

BEWITCHED CHILI

SUPERNATURAL SPAGHETTI

FAST FIX ▶
Ghostly Hot Cocoa

Chocolate milk mix and pudding mix give this homemade cocoa a quick start. Kids of all ages get a kick out of the marshmallow ghosts floating on top.

—**RUBY GIBSON** NEWTON, NC

START TO FINISH: 15 MIN.
MAKES: 30 SERVINGS (10 CUPS MIX)

- 6⅔ **cups nonfat dry milk powder**
- 1 **cup instant chocolate drink mix**
- 1 **package (5 ounces) cook-and-serve chocolate pudding mix**
- ½ **cup confectioners' sugar**
- ½ **cup powdered nondairy creamer**
- ½ **cup baking cocoa**

ADDITIONAL INGREDIENTS
- 30 **cups boiling water**
- 30 **Peeps ghost candy**

In a very large bowl, combine the first six ingredients. Store in an airtight container in a cool dry place for up to 3 months.

TO PREPARE HOT COCOA *Dissolve ⅓ cup cocoa mix in 1 cup boiling water. Float a Peeps ghost in each cup of hot cocoa.*

FREEZE IT EAT SMART
Supernatural Spaghetti

I got the idea for my pizza-flavored spaghetti when I saw someone dip a slice of pizza into a pasta dish. My wife and kids love it and so do my friends!

—**ROBERT SMITH** LAS VEGAS, NV

PREP: 20 MIN. • **COOK:** 30 MIN.
MAKES: 6 SERVINGS

- ½ **pound lean ground beef (90% lean)**
- ½ **pound Italian turkey sausage links, casings removed**
- ½ **cup chopped sweet onion**
- 4 **cans (8 ounces each) no-salt-added tomato sauce**
- 3 **ounces sliced turkey pepperoni**
- 1 **tablespoon sugar**
- ½ **teaspoon dried parsley flakes**
- ½ **teaspoon dried basil**
- 9 **ounces uncooked whole wheat spaghetti**
- 3 **tablespoons grated Parmesan cheese**
- 12 **fresh mozzarella cheese pearls**
- 12 **slices pimiento-stuffed olives**

1. In a large nonstick skillet, cook beef, sausage and onion over medium heat 6-8 minutes or until meat is no longer pink, breaking up meat into crumbles; drain.

2. Stir in tomato sauce, pepperoni, sugar, parsley and basil. Bring to a boil. Reduce heat; simmer, uncovered, 20-25 minutes or until thickened. Meanwhile, cook spaghetti according to package directions.

3. Drain spaghetti; toss with sauce. Sprinkle with Parmesan cheese. Top each serving with two cheese pearls and two olive slices to resemble eyes.

FREEZE OPTION *Do not cook or add spaghetti. Freeze cooled beef mixture in freezer containers. To use, partially thaw in refrigerator overnight. Cook spaghetti according to package directions. Place beef mixture in a large skillet; heat through, stirring occasionally and adding a little water if necessary. Proceed as directed.*

PER SERVING *400 cal., 12 g fat (4 g sat. fat), 65 mg chol., 764 mg sodium, 47 g carb., 7 g fiber, 25 g pro.* ***Diabetic Exchanges:*** *3 starch, 3 lean meat, ½ fat.*

GHOSTLY HOT COCOA

I based this recipe on one that my mother gave me. Ready-to-go veggies and gravy make it so simple and quick.
—**PAULA ZSIRAY** LOGAN, UT

SPOOKY SHEPHERD'S PIE

Spooky Shepherd's Pie

PREP: 10 MIN. • **BAKE:** 30 MIN.
MAKES: 8 SERVINGS

- 2 **pounds ground beef**
- 2 **cups frozen peas and carrots**
- 2 **cans (12 ounces each) home-style beef gravy**
- 2 **cups frozen corn**
- 2 **teaspoons dried minced onion**
- 6 **cups mashed potatoes**

1. Preheat oven to 350°. In a Dutch oven, cook beef over medium heat 10-12 minutes or until no longer pink, breaking into crumbles; drain.
2. Set aside 16 carrot pieces for eyes; add remaining frozen peas and carrots to pan. Stir in gravy, corn and onion. Spoon into two greased 2-qt. baking dishes or eight greased ovenproof 2-cup baking dishes.
3. Place mashed potatoes in a large resealable plastic bag; cut a 2-in. hole

in corner of bag. Pipe ghost-shaped potatoes onto beef mixture; add carrot pieces for eyes. Bake, uncovered, 30-35 minutes or until heated through.

FREEZE IT FAST FIX
Party Time Mini Cheeseburgers
Favorite toppings like pickle relish, mustard and ketchup are cooked right into the meat in these fun sliders.
—**TASTE OF HOME** TEST KITCHEN

START TO FINISH: 30 MIN.
MAKES: 5 SERVINGS

- 1 **egg, lightly beaten**
- ¼ **cup quick-cooking oats**
- 2 **tablespoons dill pickle relish**
- 2 **tablespoons ketchup**
- 2 **teaspoons prepared mustard**
- 2 **teaspoons Worcestershire sauce**
- ¼ **teaspoon pepper**
- ⅛ **teaspoon garlic powder**

- 1 **pound ground beef**
- 3 **to 4 slices process American cheese**
- 10 **dinner rolls, split**

1. Preheat broiler. In a large bowl, combine the first eight ingredients. Add beef; mix lightly but thoroughly. Shape into 10 patties. Transfer to a 15x10x1-in. baking pan. Broil 3-4 in. from heat 4-6 minutes on each side or until a meat thermometer reads 160°.
2. Meanwhile, using a 1-in. pumpkin-shaped cookie cutter, cut out 10 pumpkin shapes from cheese slices or cut slices into thirds. Immediately place on burgers; serve on rolls.
FREEZE OPTION *Place patties on a plastic wrap-lined baking sheet; wrap and freeze until firm. Remove from pan and transfer to a large resealable plastic bag; return to freezer. To use, broil frozen patties as directed, increasing time as necessary.*

Frankenstein Boo-ritos

The kids will get a charge out of these monster burritos. The mild-tasting filling will appeal to even the pickiest eater.

—CLARA COULSON MINNEY
WASHINGTON COURT HOUSE, OH

START TO FINISH: 25 MIN.
MAKES: 4 SERVINGS

- 1 envelope (5.6 ounces) Spanish rice and pasta mix
- 2 cups cubed cooked chicken
- 1 can (15¼ ounces) whole kernel corn, drained
- 1 can (14½ ounces) diced tomatoes, drained
- 8 spinach tortillas (10 inches)
  Toppings: sour cream, blue corn tortilla chips, cubed and shredded cheese, ripe olives and sweet red pepper

1. In a large saucepan, prepare rice mix according to package directions. Stir in chicken, corn and tomatoes; heat through.

2. Spoon about ⅔ cup rice mixture across center of each tortilla. Fold bottom and sides of tortilla over filling and roll up. Using toppings, create a face on each burrito.

Witches' Brew

Stir up some Halloween beverages that are as bewitching as the rest of your menu. For a nonalcoholic version, just omit the vodka. Then the kids can have some, too!

—TASTE OF HOME TEST KITCHEN

PREP: 20 MIN. + CHILLING
MAKES: 6 SERVINGS

- 1 cup sugar
- 1 cup water

WITCHES' BREW

- 8 medium kiwifruit, peeled and quartered
- ½ cup fresh mint leaves
  Green food coloring, optional
- 1 cup vodka, optional
- 1 liter ginger ale, chilled
  Ice cubes

1. In a small saucepan, bring sugar and water to a boil. Cook and stir until sugar is dissolved; set aside to cool.

2. Place the kiwi, mint and sugar syrup in a blender; cover and process until blended. Tint green if desired. Pour into a large pitcher; stir in vodka if desired. Refrigerate until chilled.

3. Just before serving, stir in ginger ale. Serve over ice.

NOTE *To make each broom, cut 1 green shoestring licorice into 1-in. lengths. Arrange around end of 1 pretzel rod to form broom bristles; tightly wrap bristles with 1 piece black shoestring licorice, tucking in ends to secure.*

TOP TIP

Hosting a Halloween party? You can make a tasty black punch by mixing grape and orange Kool-Aid. I like to use the unsweetened kind.

—MERRILL POWERS SPEARVILLE, KANSAS

FRANKENSTEIN BOO-RITOS

NO-FUSS
HERB-ROASTED
TURKEY & STUFFING

No-Fuss Herb-Roasted Turkey & Stuffing

I learned to bake turkey in a brown paper bag, but now I use an oven roasting bag for perfect results that keep the white meat tender and juicy.
—**MARLA HYATT** ST. PAUL, MN

PREP: 20 MIN.
BAKE: 2¼ HOURS + STANDING
MAKES: 12 SERVINGS (8 CUPS STUFFING)

- 1 turkey (12 to 14 pounds)
- ½ cup butter, softened
- 2 tablespoons salt
- 1 teaspoon ground sage
- ½ teaspoon dried rosemary, crushed
- ½ teaspoon pepper
- 1 tablespoon all-purpose flour
- 1 turkey-size oven roasting bag

STUFFING
- ½ cup butter, cubed
- 1 small onion, chopped
- 1 celery rib, thinly sliced
- 1 package (14 ounces) seasoned stuffing cubes
- 1 can (10¾ ounces) condensed cream of chicken soup, undiluted
- 1 cup chicken broth
- 1 egg, lightly beaten

1. Preheat oven to 350°. With fingers, carefully loosen skin from turkey breast; rub butter under the skin. In a small bowl, mix salt, sage, rosemary and pepper; rub over outside and inside of turkey. Tuck wings under turkey; tie drumsticks together.
2. Sprinkle flour into oven bag; shake to coat. Place in a shallow roasting pan; add turkey to bag, breast side up. Cut six ½-in. slits in top of bag; close with tie provided. Bake 2¼ to 2¾ hours or until a thermometer inserted in thickest part of thigh reads 170°-175°.
3. Meanwhile, for stuffing, in a large skillet, heat butter over medium-high heat. Add onion and celery; cook and stir until tender. Transfer to a large bowl. Stir in stuffing cubes, soup, broth and egg. Transfer to a greased 11x7-in. baking dish.
4. Bake, covered, 30 minutes. Uncover; bake 10-15 minutes longer or until lightly browned. Remove turkey from bag to serving platter; tent with foil. Let stand 20 minutes before carving. Serve with stuffing.

⑤ INGREDIENTS
Pineapple-Strawberry Cranberry Relish

I'll always remember the look on my son's face the first time he tried this relish. It was love! Now the holiday wouldn't be the same without the sweet-tart condiment.
—**KAREN WILKES** LAKEWOOD, CA

PREP: 5 MIN. + CHILLING
MAKES: 22 SERVINGS (¼ CUP EACH)

- 2 cans (14 ounces each) whole-berry cranberry sauce
- 1 can (20 ounces) crushed pineapple, drained
- 1 package (14 ounces) frozen unsweetened sliced strawberries, thawed and drained
- ½ cup chopped walnuts

In a large bowl, gently mix cranberry sauce, pineapple and strawberries until blended. Refrigerate, covered, 1-2 hours or until cold. Just before serving, stir in walnuts.

TOP TIP

Use these pointers for leftovers:
- Stock up on storage containers and bags to store leftovers or send them home with guests.
- Promptly refrigerate leftovers; don't allow foods to stand at room temperature for over 2 hours.
- Use up leftovers with recipes such as Turkey Gnocchi Soup (p. 130) or Turkey Cordon Bleu Casserole (p. 162).

PINEAPPLE-STRAWBERRY CRANBERRY RELISH

Marshmallow Pumpkin Pie

This was one of my mother's all-time favorite pies. She was a great cook and was always generous with her recipes. It also tastes great in baked pastry crust or gingersnap crust.

—RUTH FERRIS BILLINGS, MT

PREP: 20 MIN. + CHILLING
MAKES: 8 SERVINGS

- 1 **package (10 ounces) large marshmallows**
- 1 **cup canned pumpkin**
- 1 **teaspoon ground cinnamon**
- ½ **teaspoon salt**
- ½ **teaspoon ground ginger**
- ½ **teaspoon ground nutmeg**
- 2 **cups whipped topping**
- 1 **graham cracker crust (9 inches)**
  Additional whipped topping, optional

1. In a large saucepan, combine the first six ingredients; cook and stir over medium heat 8-10 minutes or until marshmallows are melted. Remove from heat; cool to room temperature.
2. Fold in whipped topping. Spoon into crust. Refrigerate 3 hours or until set. If desired, serve with additional whipped topping.

SAGE & PROSCIUTTO PINWHEELS

I love appetizers for entertaining. I came up with this recipe because I can make them ahead and keep the rolls in the freezer, then slice and bake as needed.

—KATE DAMPIER QUAIL VALLEY, CA

FREEZE IT ⑤**INGREDIENTS** **FAST FIX**

Sage & Prosciutto Pinwheels

START TO FINISH: 30 MIN.
MAKES: 3 DOZEN

- 1 **package (17.3 ounces) frozen puff pastry, thawed**
- ¼ **cup honey mustard**
- 1 **cup (4 ounces) shredded Gruyere or Swiss cheese**
- 8 **thin slices prosciutto or deli ham, chopped**
- 2 **tablespoons chopped fresh sage**

1. Preheat oven to 400°. Unfold puff pastry. Spread mustard over each sheet to within ½ in. of edges. Sprinkle with cheese; top with prosciutto and sage. Roll up jelly-roll style. Using a serrated knife, cut each crosswise into 18 slices.
2. Place cut side down on greased baking sheets. Bake 12-15 minutes or until golden brown. Serve warm.
FREEZE OPTION *Cover and freeze unbaked rolls on a waxed paper-lined baking sheet until firm. Transfer to resealable plastic freezer bags; return to freezer. To use, let rolls stand at room temperature 10 minutes. Cut and bake pinwheels as directed, increasing time as necessary.*

MARSHMALLOW PUMPKIN PIE

BACON BLUE CHEESE APPETIZER

Green Beans with Peppers

We created this festive side that's simple to make for a holiday dinner.

—*TASTE OF HOME* TEST KITCHEN

START TO FINISH: 20 MIN.
MAKES: 12 SERVINGS (¾ CUP EACH)

- 2 **pounds fresh green beans, trimmed**
- 2 **tablespoons olive oil**
- 2 **medium sweet red peppers, finely chopped (about 2 cups)**
- 1 **small onion, finely chopped**
- 3 **tablespoons chopped fresh basil or 1 tablespoon dried basil**
- ¾ **teaspoon salt**
- ¼ **teaspoon pepper**

1. In a large saucepan, place steamer basket over 1 in. of water. Place beans in batches in basket. Bring water to a boil. Reduce heat to maintain a simmer; steam, covered, 6-8 minutes or until crisp-tender.

2. In a nonstick skillet, heat oil over medium-high heat. Add red peppers and onion; cook and stir until tender. Add beans, basil, salt and pepper; toss to coat.

PER SERVING *53 cal., 2 g fat (trace sat. fat), 0 chol., 152 mg sodium, 8 g carb., 1 g fiber, 2 g pro.* **Diabetic Exchanges::** *1 vegetable, ½ fat.*

---

(5) INGREDIENTS FAST FIX

Bacon Blue Cheese Appetizer

Nothing is easier than this three-ingredient starter. Salty, sweet and rich, it's a surefire people pleaser.

—**JAKE HAEN** OCALA, FL

START TO FINISH: 5 MIN.
MAKES: 8 SERVINGS

- 1 **wedge (8 ounces) blue cheese**
- 1 **tablespoon honey**
- 3 **bacon strips, cooked and crumbled Assorted crackers**

Place cheese on a serving dish. Drizzle with honey. Sprinkle with bacon. Serve with crackers.

TOP TIP

I buy several pounds of bacon when it's on sale. I put the strips in a single layer on jelly-roll pans and pop them in the oven to bake at 350° until crisp. I then place the strips on paper towels to drain before storing them in single layers in a freezer container. It's easy to remove only the number of strips I need for a quick breakfast, sandwich or salad. A short time in the microwave reheats the bacon.

—**DALE H.** HOLLAND, MI

GREEN BEANS WITH PEPPERS

COCONUT-PECAN
SWEET POTATOES

These sweet potatoes cook effortlessly in the slow cooker so you can tend to other things. Coconut gives the classic dish new flavor. —RAQUEL HAGGARD EDMOND, OK

EAT SMART
Coconut-Pecan Sweet Potatoes

PREP: 15 MIN. • **COOK:** 4 HOURS
MAKES: 12 SERVINGS (¾ CUP EACH)

- 4 **pounds sweet potatoes (about 6 medium), peeled and cubed**
- ½ **cup chopped pecans**
- ½ **cup flaked coconut**
- ⅓ **cup sugar**
- ⅓ **cup packed brown sugar**
- ¼ **cup reduced-fat butter, melted**
- ½ **teaspoon ground cinnamon**
- ¼ **teaspoon salt**
- ½ **teaspoon coconut extract**
- ½ **teaspoon vanilla extract**

1. Place sweet potatoes in a 5-qt. slow cooker coated with cooking spray. In a small bowl, combine pecans, coconut, sugars, butter, cinnamon and salt; sprinkle over potatoes.
2. Cook, covered, on low 4 to 4½ hours or until potatoes are tender. Stir in extracts.
NOTE *This recipe was tested with Land O'Lakes light stick butter.*
PER SERVING *211 cal., 7 g fat (3 g sat. fat), 5 mg chol., 103 mg sodium, 37 g carb., 3 g fiber, 2 g pro.*

Mom's Vegetable Dip

This is one dip my mother brought along to potluck dinners and made when guests came over. Every time I prepare it, I am reminded of her and her love of cooking.
—JILL OLOFSON WOODBURY, MN

START TO FINISH: 10 MIN.
MAKES: 3 CUPS

- 2 **packages (8 ounces each) cream cheese, softened**
- ⅓ **cup 2% milk**
- ¼ **cup ketchup**
- ¼ **cup grated onion**
- 1 **teaspoon garlic salt**
- 1 **teaspoon ground mustard**
- ⅛ **teaspoon pepper**
- ⅛ **teaspoon Worcestershire sauce**
  Assorted fresh vegetables and/or crackers

In a large bowl, beat cream cheese, milk and ketchup until smooth. Beat in onion, garlic salt, mustard, pepper and Worcestershire sauce until blended. Refrigerate until serving. Serve with vegetables and crackers.

TOP TIP

Ketchup lends complexity to dip and sauce recipes because it contributes sweet, sour and salty flavors. Be sure to use a good-quality ketchup with flavors you like.

MOM'S VEGETABLE DIP

FREEZE IT

Cranberry Layer Cake

I adapted a Bundt cake recipe to create this layer cake. Cranberries, walnuts and homemade frosting make it so good that you'd never guess it starts with a cake mix.
—**SANDY BURKETT** GALENA, OH

PREP: 20 MIN. • **BAKE:** 30 MIN. + COOLING
MAKES: 12 SERVINGS

- 1 **package white cake mix (regular size)**
- 1⅓ **cups water**
- 3 **eggs**
- ⅓ **cup canola oil**
- 1 **tablespoon grated orange peel**
- 1 **cup fresh or frozen cranberries, thawed and coarsely chopped**
- 1 **cup finely chopped walnuts**

CREAM CHEESE FROSTING

- 1 **package (8 ounces) cream cheese, softened**
- ½ **cup butter, softened**
- 1 **teaspoon vanilla extract**
- 3½ **cups confectioners' sugar**
- ½ **teaspoon grated orange peel**
- ¼ **cup finely chopped walnuts**

1. Preheat oven to 350°. Line bottoms of two greased 9-in. round baking pans with parchment paper; grease paper. In a large bowl, combine the first five ingredients; beat on low speed 30 seconds. Beat on medium 2 minutes. Stir in cranberries and walnuts. Transfer the batter to prepared pans.

2. Bake 30-35 minutes or until a toothpick inserted in center comes out clean. Cool in pans 10 minutes before removing to wire racks; remove paper. Cool completely.

3. In a large bowl, beat cream cheese, butter and vanilla until blended. Gradually beat in confectioners' sugar and orange peel until smooth. Spread frosting between layers and over top and sides of cake. Sprinkle with walnuts. Refrigerate leftovers.

FREEZE OPTION *Wrap cooled cake layers in plastic wrap, then cover securely in foil; freeze. To use, thaw cakes before unwrapping. Assemble as directed.*

SPINACH 'N' SAUSAGE
PORK LOIN

Beef Tips & Caramelized Onion Casserole

The inviting flavor of beef sweetened with rich caramelized onions makes this a recipe you'll want to repeat. Mashed potatoes make the perfect partner.

—**LINDA STEMEN** MONROEVILLE, IN

PREP: 40 MIN. • **BAKE:** 1½ HOURS
MAKES: 8 SERVINGS

- 4 **pounds beef sirloin tip roast, cut into 1-inch cubes**
- ½ **teaspoon salt**
- ½ **teaspoon pepper**
- 2 **tablespoons olive oil**
- 4 **large sweet onions, halved and thinly sliced**
- 3 **tablespoons butter**
- 4 **garlic cloves, minced**
- ⅔ **cup all-purpose flour**
- 2 **cans (10½ ounces each) condensed beef consomme, undiluted**
- 1 **can (14½ ounces) reduced-sodium beef broth**
- 2 **tablespoons Worcestershire sauce**
- 2 **bay leaves**
- ½ **cup heavy whipping cream**
- 8 **slices French bread (½ inch thick), toasted**
- 1 **cup (4 ounces) shredded part-skim mozzarella cheese**

1. Sprinkle beef with salt and pepper. In a large skillet, brown meat in oil in batches; drain. Transfer to a greased 13x9-in. baking dish.

2. In the same skillet, cook onions in butter over medium-low heat for 25-30 minutes or until golden brown, stirring occasionally. Add garlic; cook 1 minute longer.

3. Preheat oven to 325°. Stir flour into onion mixture until blended; gradually add consomme and broth. Stir in Worcestershire sauce and bay leaves. Bring to a boil; cook and stir for 1 minute or until thickened. Pour over beef.

4. Cover and bake 1 hour. Carefully stir in cream; discard bay leaves. Bake, uncovered, 25-35 minutes or until meat is tender. Place toast over beef mixture; sprinkle with cheese. Bake 5 minutes or until cheese is melted.

Spinach 'n' Sausage Pork Loin

Two of our grown children often have dinner with us. They seem to enjoy the fact that Dad has done the cooking. This special roast is one of our favorites.

—**ED LELAND** VAN WERT, OH

PREP: 20 MIN. • **BAKE:** 2 HOURS + STANDING
MAKES: 8 SERVINGS

- 1 **egg, lightly beaten**
- ½ **cup slivered almonds, toasted**
- ¼ **cup dry bread crumbs**
- 2 **tablespoons minced fresh parsley**
- 1 **tablespoon onion soup mix**
- 4 **garlic cloves, minced**
- 1 **teaspoon pepper**
- 5 **ounces frozen chopped spinach, thawed and squeezed dry (about ½ cup)**
- 1 **teaspoon dried thyme, divided**
- ½ **pound bulk Italian sausage**
- 1 **boneless pork loin roast (about 3 pounds)**
- 1 **tablespoon olive oil**

1. Preheat oven to 350°. In a large bowl, combine the first seven ingredients; stir in spinach and ½ teaspoon thyme. Add sausage; mix lightly but thoroughly.

2. Cut lengthwise through center of pork roast to within ½ in. of bottom. Open roast flat; cover with plastic wrap. Pound with a meat mallet to flatten slightly. Remove plastic; spread sausage mixture over roast. Starting at a long side, roll up jelly-roll style; tie at 2-in. intervals with kitchen string. Secure ends with toothpicks.

3. Place roast on a rack in a shallow roasting pan, seam side down. Brush with oil; sprinkle with remaining thyme. Roast 2 to 2½ hours or until a thermometer reads 160°. Remove roast from oven; tent with foil. Let stand 10 minutes before slicing.

NOTE *To toast nuts, spread in a 15x10x1-in. baking pan. Bake at 350° for 5-10 minutes or until lightly browned, stirring occasionally. Or, spread in a dry nonstick skillet and heat over low heat until lightly browned, stirring occasionally.*

Lemon-Shrimp Fettuccine

PREP: 20 MIN. • COOK: 20 MIN.
MAKES: 6 SERVINGS

- 1 package (12 ounces) fettuccine
- 3 tablespoons butter
- 1 tablespoon olive oil
- 1 pound uncooked medium shrimp, peeled and deveined
- 1 small onion, chopped
- 2 garlic cloves, minced
- 1 can (15 ounces) white kidney or cannellini beans, rinsed and drained
- ½ cup soft sun-dried tomato halves (not packed in oil), julienned
- 1 tablespoon grated lemon peel
- 2 tablespoons lemon juice
- ½ teaspoon salt
- ¼ teaspoon crushed red pepper flakes
- ½ cup shredded Parmesan cheese

1. In a Dutch oven, cook fettuccine according to package directions. Drain pasta, reserving 1 cup pasta water. Return pan to heat; heat butter and oil over medium heat. Add shrimp and onion; cook and stir 3-4 minutes or until shrimp turn pink. Add garlic; cook 1 minute longer.

2. Stir in beans, tomatoes, lemon peel, lemon juice, salt and pepper flakes. Add fettuccine and cheese; toss to combine, adding enough reserved pasta water to moisten pasta.

This pasta is one-pot easy and doesn't make a mess out of the kitchen. You could also make it with shredded rotisserie chicken instead of shrimp. Fresh lemon gives it a nice light touch. **—MIKE McCORMICK** MOORE, SC

LEMON-SHRIMP FETTUCCINE

Cornish Hens with Rice Stuffing

I came across this recipe a few years ago around Thanksgiving. The golden, juicy hens and festive rice stuffing make a memorable feast for two. Best of all, we're not eating leftovers for days on end.
—KATHY MEYER KENOSHA, WI

PREP: 50 MIN. • BAKE: 1 HOUR
MAKES: 2 SERVINGS

- 1 package (6 ounces) long grain and wild rice mix
- 2 tablespoons butter, divided
- ½ cup chopped pecans
- 1⅓ cups orange juice
- 1 cup water
- ¼ cup raisins
- 2 Cornish game hens (20 to 24 ounces each)
- ½ teaspoon salt
- ¼ teaspoon pepper

1. Set the seasoning packet from rice mix aside. In a saucepan, melt 1 tablespoon butter. Add rice and pecans; cook and stir over low heat for 10 minutes or until rice is golden brown. Stir in the orange juice, water, raisins and contents of seasoning packet; bring to a boil over medium heat. Reduce heat; cover and simmer for 25 minutes or until the liquid is absorbed.

2. Spoon about ½ cup rice mixture into each hen; refrigerate remaining rice mixture. Tie legs of each hen together; turn wing tips under backs. Place on a greased rack in a roasting pan. Melt remaining butter; brush over hens. Sprinkle with salt and pepper.

3. Bake at 350° for 1 to 1¼ hours or until a thermometer reads 165° when inserted in center of stuffing and thigh reaches at least 170°. Baste hens occasionally with pan drippings. Heat reserved rice mixture; serve with hens.

TOP TIP

Delish! This was quite tasty, especially the slightly orange-flavored rice. We substituted dried cranberries for the raisins.
—WILLIAMSEGRAVES
TASTEOFHOME.COM

Seafood en Croute

When I got married, I received this cherished recipe from family overseas. It looks difficult, but it's really quite easy. Now that I have children, I don't have time to spend all day in the kitchen, so I choose my "recipes to impress" carefully. This one's always a winner!

—ALEXANDRA ARMITAGE NOTTINGHAM, NH

PREP: 25 MIN. • **BAKE:** 20 MIN.
MAKES: 4 SERVINGS

- 1 package (17.3 ounces) frozen puff pastry, thawed
- 4 salmon fillets (6 ounces each)
- ½ pound fresh sea or bay scallops, finely chopped
- ⅓ cup heavy whipping cream
- 2 green onions, chopped
- 1 tablespoon minced fresh parsley
- ½ teaspoon minced fresh dill
- ¼ teaspoon salt
- ⅛ teaspoon pepper
- 1 egg white
- 1 egg, beaten

1. On a lightly floured surface, roll each pastry sheet into a 12x10-in. rectangle. Cut each sheet into four 6x5-in. rectangles. Place a salmon fillet in the center of four rectangles.

2. In a small bowl, combine the scallops, cream, onions, parsley, dill, salt and pepper. In another bowl, beat egg white on medium speed until soft peaks form; fold into scallop mixture. Spoon about ½ cup mixture over each salmon fillet.

3. Top each with a pastry rectangle and crimp to seal. With a small sharp knife, cut several slits in the top. Place in a greased 15x10x1-in. baking pan; brush with egg. Bake at 400° for 20-25 minutes or until a thermometer reads 160°.

EASY & ELEGANT TENDERLOIN ROAST

SEAFOOD EN CROUTE

⑤ INGREDIENTS

Easy & Elegant Tenderloin Roast

A friend of mine served this tenderloin several years ago and passed along the recipe to me. The trick is not to skimp on the seasonings. You'll get predictably delicious results every time.

—MARY KANDELL HURON, OH

PREP: 10 MIN. • **BAKE:** 50 MIN. + STANDING
MAKES: 12 SERVINGS

- 1 beef tenderloin (5 pounds)
- 2 tablespoons olive oil
- 4 garlic cloves, minced
- 2 teaspoons sea salt
- 1½ teaspoons coarsely ground pepper

1. Preheat oven to 425°. Place roast on a rack in a shallow roasting pan. In a small bowl, mix the oil, garlic, salt and pepper; rub over roast.

2. Roast 50-70 minutes or until the meat reaches desired doneness (for medium-rare, a thermometer should read 145°; medium, 160°; well-done, 170°). Remove from oven and tent with foil. Let stand for 15 minutes before slicing.

Artichoke Spinach Lasagna

Friends of ours served this homey dish when we visited them in Maryland. We just had to get the recipe and since then have added a few items to make it even tastier.

—**CAROLE RAGO** ALTOONA, PA

PREP: 25 MIN. • **BAKE:** 55 MIN. + STANDING
MAKES: 12 SERVINGS

- 1 tablespoon olive oil
- 1 small onion, chopped
- ½ cup sliced fresh mushrooms
- 4 garlic cloves, minced
- 1 can (14½ ounces) vegetable or chicken broth
- 1 can (14 ounces) water-packed artichoke hearts, drained and coarsely chopped
- 1 package (10 ounces) frozen chopped spinach, thawed and squeezed dry
- 1 teaspoon dried rosemary, crushed
- ¼ teaspoon ground nutmeg
- ¼ teaspoon pepper
- 1 jar (16 ounces) roasted garlic Parmesan or roasted garlic Alfredo sauce

ASSEMBLY
- 12 no-cook lasagna noodles
- 3 cups (12 ounces) shredded part-skim mozzarella cheese
- 1 cup crumbled tomato and basil feta cheese or feta cheese
- ⅛ teaspoon garlic powder
- ⅛ teaspoon each dried oregano, parsley flakes and basil

1. Preheat oven to 350°. In a large saucepan, heat oil over medium-high heat. Add onion and mushrooms; cook and stir until tender. Add garlic; cook 1 minute longer. Stir in broth, artichokes, spinach and seasonings; bring just to a boil. Reduce heat and simmer for 5 minutes, stirring occasionally. Stir in Alfredo sauce; remove from heat.

2. Spread 1 cup sauce into a greased 13x9-in. baking dish. Layer with three noodles and ⅔ cup mozzarella cheese. Repeat layers three times. Top with remaining sauce and mozzarella cheese. Sprinkle with feta cheese, garlic powder and herbs.

3. Bake, covered, 40 minutes. Bake, uncovered, 15 minutes longer or until noodles are tender. Let stand 10 minutes before serving.

ARTICHOKE SPINACH LASAGNA

CRANBERRY PECAN TASSIES

A traditional pecan tassie is a small tart with nuts. This holiday version adds cranberries. How festive!

—**PEGGY WEST** GEORGETOWN, DE

Cranberry Pecan Tassies

PREP: 25 MIN. + CHILLING
BAKE: 20 MIN. + COOLING
MAKES: 2 DOZEN

- ½ **cup butter, softened**
- 3 **ounces cream cheese, softened**
- 1 **cup all-purpose flour**
- 1 **egg**
- ⅔ **cup packed brown sugar**
- 1 **tablespoon butter, melted**
- 1 **teaspoon grated orange peel**
- ½ **cup chopped pecans**
- ½ **cup fresh or frozen cranberries, thawed**

1. In a small bowl, beat butter and cream cheese until smooth; gradually beat in flour. Refrigerate dough, covered, 30 minutes or until firm enough to shape.

2. Preheat oven to 325°. Shape dough into 1-in. balls; place in greased mini-muffin cups. Press evenly onto bottoms and up sides of cups.

3. In a small bowl, beat egg, brown sugar, melted butter and orange peel until blended. Stir in pecans. Spoon 1½ teaspoons filling into each cup; top with cranberries.

4. Bake 20-25 minutes or until crust is golden and filling is set. Cool in pans 2 minutes before removing to wire racks to cool.

FREEZE OPTION *Freeze cookies, layered between waxed paper, in freezer containers. To use, thaw before serving.*

⑤ INGREDIENTS
Apple Brandy

I spend a lot of time developing recipes for the many fruits and vegetables we grow on our farm. In this creation, brandy is enhanced with apples and spices for a delightful drink.

—**DEANNA SEIPPEL** LANCASTER, WI

PREP: 35 MIN. + STANDING
MAKES: 2 QUARTS

- 4 **cups sugar**
- 2 **cups water**
- 4 **pounds apples, sliced**
- 1 **liter brandy**
- 3 **whole cloves**
- 1 **cinnamon stick (3 inches)**
  Additional whole cloves and cinnamon sticks

1. Combine sugar and water in a large saucepan. Bring to a boil; cook and stir until sugar is dissolved. Remove from the heat.

2. Place apples in a large glass or plastic container; add the sugar mixture, brandy, cloves and cinnamon stick. Cover and let stand at room temperature for at least two weeks, stirring once a week.

3. Strain brandy mixture; discard the apples and spices. Pour into glass bottles. Place an additional three cloves and one cinnamon stick in each bottle.

APPLE BRANDY

temperature 5-10 minutes to soften. Add flour to cookie dough; beat until blended.

2. On a lightly floured surface, roll dough to ¼-in. thickness. Cut with a floured 2-in. round cookie cutter. Place 2 in. apart on ungreased baking sheets.

3. Bake 8-10 minutes or until edges are light brown. Remove from pans to wire racks to cool completely.

4. Meanwhile, place ⅔ cup chocolate chips in a small bowl. In a small saucepan, bring cream just to a boil. Pour over chocolate; stir with a whisk until smooth. Stir in extract. Refrigerate until mixture reaches a spreading consistency, about 30 minutes. Spread filling on bottoms of half of the cookies; cover with remaining cookies.

5. In a microwave, melt remaining chocolate chips with oil; stir until smooth. Dip tops of cookies in chocolate mixture, allowing excess to drip off. Immediately sprinkle with crushed candies; let stand until set. Refrigerate leftovers.

FREEZE OPTION *Freeze cookies in freezer containers. To use, thaw cookies in covered containers. Fill and decorate as directed.*

Crunchy Party Mix

Here's a bold party mix you can make anytime. It's hot, spicy and packed with flavor—just the way we like things in Texas!
—**NANCY ELLIOTT** HOUSTON, TX

PREP: 10 MIN.
COOK: 5 MIN./BATCH + COOLING
MAKES: 3 QUARTS

- 3 **cups Corn Chex**
- 3 **cups Rice Chex**
- 3 **cups Wheat Chex**
- 1 **package (4 ounces) corn nuts**
- 1 **cup salted peanuts**
- 1 **cup miniature pretzels**
- ⅓ **cup butter, melted**
- 2 **teaspoons crushed red pepper flakes**
- ½ **teaspoon salt**
- ½ **teaspoon garlic powder**
- ½ **teaspoon chili powder**
- ½ **teaspoon lemon-pepper seasoning**

1. In a large bowl, combine the first six ingredients; toss to combine. In a small bowl, mix the remaining ingredients; drizzle over cereal mixture and toss to coat.

2. Working in batches, microwave mixture on high in a microwave-safe bowl for 4-5 minutes, stirring twice. Spread on baking sheets; cool completely. Store in airtight containers.

NOTE *This recipe was tested in a 1,100-watt microwave.*

FREEZE IT
Chocolate-Peppermint Sandwich Cookies

Chocolate and mint make a great holiday pair. Try them in this sandwich cookie with crushed candy canes on top.
—**EVANGELINE BRADFORD** ERLANGER, KY

PREP: 30 MIN. + CHILLING
BAKE: 10 MIN./BATCH + STANDING
MAKES: ABOUT 1½ DOZEN

- 1 **tube (16½ ounces) refrigerated sugar cookie dough**
- ½ **cup all-purpose flour**
- ⅔ **cup plus ½ cup semisweet chocolate chips, divided**
- ¼ **cup heavy whipping cream**
- ⅛ **teaspoon peppermint extract**
- ½ **teaspoon canola oil**
- 8 **candy canes, crushed**

1. Preheat oven to 350°. Place cookie dough in a large bowl; let stand at room

CHOCOLATE-PEPPERMINT SANDWICH COOKIES

⑤ INGREDIENTS
Brazil Nut & Coconut Bark

I usually make these treats around Christmastime, but also take them to special events at our church. I love that they only use four ingredients.

—PHYL BROICH-WESSLING GARNER, IA

PREP: 25 MIN. + CHILLING
MAKES: 2½ POUNDS

- 1½ **pounds white candy coating, chopped**
- 1½ **cups Brazil nuts, coarsely chopped and toasted**
- ¾ **cup flaked coconut**
- 2 **cups (12 ounces) semisweet chocolate chips**

1. In a large microwave-safe bowl, melt candy coating; stir until smooth. Stir in Brazil nuts and coconut.

2. Spread onto a waxed paper-lined baking sheet. In a microwave, melt chocolate chips; stir until smooth. Drizzle over top. Refrigerate 30 minutes or until firm. Break into pieces. Store in an airtight container.

NOTE *To toast nuts, spread in a 15x10x1-in. baking pan. Bake at 350° for 5-10 minutes or until lightly browned, stirring occasionally. Or, spread in a dry nonstick skillet and heat over low heat until lightly browned, stirring occasionally.*

BRAZIL NUT & COCONUT BARK

POPPY SEED THUMBPRINTS

My oldest son is a huge fan of these thumbprints, so I make sure they're on my baking list every Christmas. Lemon peel and poppy seeds help give this crisp cookie fantastic flavor. —**KELLY PEMBER** WHEELER, WI

FREEZE IT
Poppy Seed Thumbprints

PREP: 15 MIN.
BAKE: 10 MIN./BATCH + COOLING
MAKES: 5 DOZEN

- ½ **cup butter, softened**
- 1 **cup confectioners' sugar**
- 1 **egg**
- ½ **cup canola oil**
- 1 **teaspoon grated lemon peel**
- 1 **teaspoon vanilla extract**
- 2⅔ **cups all-purpose flour**
- 2 **tablespoons poppy seeds**
- ½ **teaspoon salt**
- ⅓ **cup seedless raspberry preserves**

1. Preheat oven to 325°. In a large bowl, beat butter and confectioners' sugar until smooth. Beat in egg, oil, lemon peel and vanilla. In another bowl, whisk the flour, poppy seeds and salt; gradually beat into the butter mixture.

2. Shape dough into 1-in. balls. Place 1 in. apart on ungreased baking sheets. Press a deep indentation in center of each with the end of a wooden spoon handle. Fill with preserves.

3. Bake 10-12 minutes or until bottoms are light brown. Remove from pans to wire racks to cool.

FREEZE OPTION *Freeze cookies, layered between waxed paper, in freezer containers. To use, thaw before serving.*

Christmas Mice Cookies

These whimsical little cuties taste like truffles. Every Christmas, we make sure to have enough for friends and neighbors.

—**DEBORAH ZABOR** FORT ERIE, ON

PREP: 30 MIN. + CHILLING
MAKES: 1½ DOZEN

- ⅔ **cup semisweet chocolate chips**
- 2 **cups chocolate wafer crumbs, divided**
- ⅓ **cup sour cream**
- 36 **red nonpareils**
- ¼ **cup sliced almonds**
- 18 **pieces black shoestring licorice (2 inches each)**

1. In a microwave, melt chocolate chips; stir until smooth. Stir in 1 cup wafer crumbs and sour cream. Refrigerate, covered, 1 hour or until firm enough to shape.
2. Place remaining wafer crumbs in a shallow bowl. For each mouse, roll about 1 tablespoon crumb mixture into a ball; taper one end to resemble a mouse. Roll in wafer crumbs to coat.

Attach nonpareils for eyes, sliced almonds for ears and licorice pieces for tails. Store in an airtight container in the refrigerator.

FREEZE IT
Calypso Cups

My tropical-flavored cookies go over great at any occasion. I like to tint the frosting to coordinate with the event.

—**LORRAINE KACZMAREK** STEUBENVILLE, OH

PREP: 30 MIN. + CHILLING
BAKE: 15 MIN./BATCH + COOLING
MAKES: 4 DOZEN

- 1 **cup butter, softened**
- 6 **ounces cream cheese, softened**
- 2 **cups all-purpose flour**

FILLING
- 1 **egg, lightly beaten**
- 1 **can (8 ounces) crushed pineapple, undrained**
- ½ **cup flaked coconut**
- ½ **cup sugar**
- 1½ **teaspoons cornstarch**

FROSTING
- 2 **cups confectioners' sugar**

- ½ **cup shortening**
- 1 **teaspoon vanilla extract**
- 3 **to 5 tablespoons 2% milk**
  Finely chopped walnuts and/or additional flaked coconut, optional

1. In a large bowl, beat butter and cream cheese until smooth. Gradually beat in flour. Refrigerate, covered, 1 hour or until firm enough to shape.
2. Preheat oven to 350°. Shape dough into 1-in. balls; place in greased mini-muffin cups. Press evenly onto bottoms and up the sides of cups.
3. In a small bowl, mix filling ingredients; spoon into cups. Bake 15-20 minutes or until edges are light brown. Cool completely in pans on wire racks.
4. For frosting, beat confectioners' sugar, shortening, vanilla and enough milk to reach desired consistency. Remove cups from pans. Top with frosting. If desired, sprinkle with walnuts and/or coconut.

CHRISTMAS MICE COOKIES

FREEZE IT

Lemony Coconut Macaroons

These chewy gems have wonderfully refreshing lemon flavor. They freeze well and thaw quickly in the fridge, so you can cure a craving anytime.

—**KARLA JOHNSON** EAST HELENA, MT

PREP: 15 MIN.
BAKE: 15 MIN./BATCH + COOLING
MAKES: 2½ DOZEN

- 1 **egg white**
  Dash salt
  Dash cream of tartar
- 1 **can (14 ounces) sweetened condensed milk**
- 1 **teaspoon lemon extract**
- 1 **package (14 ounces) flaked coconut**
- ½ **teaspoon baking powder**

1. Preheat oven to 350°. In a small bowl, beat egg white, salt and cream of tartar on high speed until stiff peaks form. In a large bowl, mix milk and extract until blended. Stir in coconut and baking powder. Fold in the beaten egg white.

2. Drop coconut mixture by rounded tablespoonfuls 2 in. apart onto greased baking sheets. Bake 11-13 minutes or just until golden brown. Remove from pans to wire racks to cool.

FREEZE OPTION *Freeze cookies, layered between waxed paper, in freezer containers. To use, thaw before serving.*

FREEZE IT

Cream Cheese Turtle Cups

Sometimes the best thing about a cookie is the memories made. My little girl and I love to make and eat these "turtles."

—**LESA RENNER** KINGSPORT, TN

PREP: 25 MIN. • **BAKE:** 15 MIN. + COOLING
MAKES: 3 DOZEN

- 1 **tube (16½ ounces) refrigerated sugar cookie dough**
- 2 **tablespoons all-purpose flour**

CREAM CHEESE TURTLE CUPS

- 1 **package (8 ounces) cream cheese, softened**
- ⅓ **cup hot caramel ice cream topping**
- ⅓ **cup chopped pecans**
- ⅓ **cup hot fudge ice cream topping, warmed**
- 36 **pecan halves**

1. Preheat oven to 350°. Place cookie dough in a large bowl; let stand at room temperature 5-10 minutes to soften. Add flour; beat until blended. Shape dough into 1-in. balls; place in greased mini-muffin cups. Press evenly onto bottoms and up the sides of cups.

2. Bake 6-8 minutes or until edges are light golden brown. Press a deep indentation in center of each with the end of a wooden spoon handle. Bake 8-10 minutes longer or until golden brown. Cool in pans 5 minutes. Remove to wire racks to cool completely.

3. In a small bowl, beat cream cheese until fluffy; gradually beat in caramel topping. Fold in chopped pecans. Spoon 2 teaspoons filling into each cup. Drizzle with fudge topping; top with pecan halves. Refrigerate until serving.

FREEZE OPTION *Freeze undecorated cookies, layered between waxed paper, in freezer containers. To use, thaw in covered containers and decorate as directed.*

LEMONY COCONUT MACAROONS

Caramel Heavenlies

PREP: 20 MIN. • **BAKE:** 15 MIN. + COOLING
MAKES: ABOUT 6 DOZEN

- 12 whole graham crackers
- 2 cups miniature marshmallows
- ¾ cup butter, cubed
- ¾ cup packed brown sugar
- 1 teaspoon ground cinnamon
- 1 teaspoon vanilla extract
- 1 cup sliced almonds
- 1 cup flaked coconut

1. Preheat oven to 350°. Line a 15x10x1-in. baking pan with foil, letting foil extend over sides by 1 in.; lightly coat foil with cooking spray. Arrange graham crackers in prepared pan; sprinkle with marshmallows.
2. In a small saucepan, combine butter, brown sugar and cinnamon; cook and stir over medium heat until butter is melted and sugar is dissolved. Remove from heat; stir in vanilla.

3. Spoon butter mixture over marshmallows. Sprinkle with almonds and coconut. Bake 14-16 minutes or until browned. Cool completely in pan on a wire rack.
4. Using foil, lift cookies out of pan. Cut into triangles; discard foil.

My mom made these treats for cookie exchanges when I was little, letting me sprinkle on the almonds and coconut. They're so easy to fix, making them perfect when you're crunched for time during the holiday season. —**DAWN BURNS** LAKE ST. LOUIS, MO

CARAMEL HEAVENLIES

CHERRY MOCHA BALLS

FREEZE IT
Cherry Mocha Balls

My mother-in-law gave me this recipe before my wedding, and I've made mocha balls nearly every Christmas since. Because they freeze so well, I'll frequently bake some early and put them away to call on as last-minute holiday treats.
—**JEANA CROWELL** WHITEWATER, KS

PREP: 15 MIN. + CHILLING
BAKE: 15 MIN./BATCH + COOLING
MAKES: ABOUT 6 DOZEN

- 1 cup butter, softened
- ½ cup sugar
- 4 teaspoons vanilla extract
- 2 cups all-purpose flour
- ¼ cup baking cocoa
- 1 tablespoon instant coffee granules
- ½ teaspoon salt
- 1 cup finely chopped pecans
- ⅔ cup chopped red candied cherries
  Confectioners' sugar

1. In a large bowl, cream butter and sugar until light and fluffy. Beat in vanilla. In another bowl, whisk flour, cocoa, coffee granules and salt; gradually beat into creamed mixture. Stir in pecans and cherries. If necessary, cover and refrigerate dough until firm enough to shape.
2. Preheat oven to 350°. Shape dough into 1-in. balls; place 2 in. apart on ungreased baking sheets. Bake for 15 minutes or until cookies are set. Cool completely on wire racks. Dust with confectioners' sugar.
FREEZE OPTION *Freeze cookies, layered between waxed paper, in freezer containers. To use, thaw before serving.*

TOP TIP

Easily dress up a holiday gift tin by including a recipe card for the sweet treats the recipient will find inside. Secure the recipe to the lid with a festive magnet.

CINNAMON PRALINE NUTS

½ cup baking cocoa
⅛ teaspoon salt
1¼ cups semisweet chocolate chips, melted
1 to 2 tablespoons confectioners' sugar
Flaked coconut, optional

1. In a large bowl, cream butter and sugar until light and fluffy. Beat in almonds and vanilla. In another bowl, whisk flour, cocoa and salt; gradually beat into the creamed mixture. Refrigerate, covered, 2 hours or until firm enough to shape.

2. Preheat oven to 350°. Shape 2 teaspoons of dough into 2-in.-long logs. Form each into a crescent. Place 2 in. apart on ungreased baking sheets. Bake 10-12 minutes or until set. Remove from pans to wire racks to cool completely.

3. Dip cookies halfway into melted chocolate, allowing excess to drip off. Place on waxed paper. If desired, sprinkle with coconut. Let stand until set. Cover dipped sides of cookies with waxed paper; dust undipped sides with confectioners' sugar. Store between pieces of waxed paper in airtight containers.

Cinnamon Praline Nuts

Take these crunchy bites anywhere! Serve them at your holiday party, wrap up a batch for your favorite hostess, or sneak some for a midnight snack.

—AMY MILLER HOLSTEIN, IA

PREP: 10 MIN. • **BAKE:** 20 MIN. + COOLING
MAKES: 3 CUPS

½ cup packed brown sugar
⅓ cup heavy whipping cream
1 teaspoon ground cinnamon
½ teaspoon grated orange peel
¼ teaspoon ground nutmeg
2 cups pecan halves
1 cup walnut halves

1. Preheat oven to 350°. In a large bowl, mix the first five ingredients until blended. Add pecans and walnuts; toss to coat.

2. Transfer to a greased baking sheet. Bake 20-25 minutes or until toasted, stirring twice. Cool completely. Store in an airtight container.

Chocolate Almond Crescents

If you like chocolate-covered almonds, you're in for a treat. These buttery, crumbly cookies make a thoughtful gift for the holidays.

—VICKI RAATZ WATERLOO, WI

PREP: 20 MIN. + CHILLING
BAKE: 10 MIN./BATCH + COOLING
MAKES: 6 DOZEN

1¼ cups butter, softened
⅔ cup sugar
2 cups finely chopped almonds
1½ teaspoons vanilla extract
2 cups all-purpose flour

CHOCOLATE ALMOND CRESCENTS

POLKA-DOT MACAROONS

Beat in egg and extracts. In another bowl, whisk flour, baking powder and salt; gradually beat into creamed mixture. Refrigerate, covered, at least 30 minutes or until dough is firm enough to shape.

2. Preheat oven to 325°. Place remaining sugar in a shallow bowl. For each cookie, shape dough to make one 1-in. ball, one ¾-in. ball and one ½-in. ball; press together to form a snowman. Gently coat with sugar. Repeat with remaining dough. Place snowmen 2 in. apart on ungreased baking sheets.

3. Break pretzel sticks in half; press into snowmen for arms. Bake 15-18 minutes or until bottoms of cookies are light brown.

4. Cool on pans 1 minute. Remove to wire racks to cool completely. Pipe icing on snowmen to form scarves, eyes, buttons and mouths. Use icing to attach gumdrops for noses.

TOP TIP

Each year, my mom hides small framed pictures of each grandchild on her Christmas tree. On Christmas Day, the kids have such a good time searching for their picture-perfect gift. And we all get a kick out of seeing how much they've grown over the past year!
—**BRYAN C.** WAUKESHA, WI

SNOWMAN CHRISTMAS COOKIES

FREEZE IT **5 INGREDIENTS**

Polka-Dot Macaroons

Macaroons studded with M&M's are easy to mix up in a hurry. That's good, because believe me, they never last long.
— **JANICE LASS** DORR, MI

PREP: 15 MIN.
BAKE: 10 MIN./BATCH + COOLING
MAKES: ABOUT 4½ DOZEN

- 5 cups flaked coconut
- 1 can (14 ounces) sweetened condensed milk
- ½ cup all-purpose flour
- 1½ cups M&M's Minis

1. Preheat oven to 350°. In a large bowl, combine coconut, milk and flour. Stir in M&M's.
2. Drop by rounded tablespoonfuls 2 in. apart onto greased baking sheets. Bake 8-10 minutes or until edges are lightly browned. Remove from pans to wire racks to cool.
FREEZE OPTION *Freeze cookies, layered between waxed paper, in freezer containers. To use, thaw before serving.*

Snowman Christmas Cookies

While my family loves the subtle cheesecake flavor of these cookies, I like the fact that I don't need to use a cookie cutter to shape them. The scrumptious snowmen look so cute on a cookie tray.
— **CATHY MEDLEY** CLYDE, OH

PREP: 45 MIN. + CHILLING
BAKE: 15 MIN./BATCH + COOLING
MAKES: ABOUT 4 DOZEN

- 1 cup butter, softened
- 1 package (8 ounces) cream cheese, softened
- 2¼ cups sugar, divided
- 1 egg
- 1 teaspoon vanilla extract
- ¼ teaspoon almond extract
- 3¾ cups all-purpose flour
- 1 teaspoon baking powder
- 1 teaspoon salt
- 50 pretzel sticks
  Decorating icing of your choice
  Orange gumdrops

1. In a large bowl, cream butter, cream cheese and 2 cups sugar until blended.

Maple-Spice Cashew Brittle

Crunchy cashews dot this tasty golden brittle, and a hint of spice bumps it up to just plain festive.

—*TASTE OF HOME* TEST KITCHEN

PREP: 10 MIN. • **COOK:** 10 MIN. + COOLING
MAKES: ABOUT ¾ POUND

- 2 **teaspoons butter, divided**
- 1 **cup sugar**
- ½ **cup light corn syrup**
- 1 **cup chopped cashews**
- ½ **teaspoon ground cinnamon**
- ¼ **teaspoon cayenne pepper**
- ⅛ **teaspoon salt**
- 1 **teaspoon baking soda**
- 1 **teaspoon maple flavoring**

1. Grease a 15x10x1-in. pan with 1 teaspoon butter.

2. In a microwave-safe 8-cup glass measuring bowl, mix sugar and corn syrup until blended. Microwave, uncovered, on high for 3 minutes; stir. Microwave, uncovered, on high 2½ minutes longer. Stir in cashews, cinnamon, cayenne, salt and remaining butter.

3. Microwave, uncovered, on high for 2 to 2½ minutes or until mixture turns a light amber color (mixture will be very hot). Quickly stir in baking soda and maple flavoring (mixture will foam). Immediately pour into the prepared pan, spreading with a metal spatula. Cool completely.

4. Break brittle into pieces. Store between layers of waxed paper in an airtight container.

NOTE *This recipe was tested in a 1,100-watt microwave.*

MAPLE-SPICE CASHEW BRITTLE

LEMON SNOWDROPS

FREEZE IT

Lemon Snowdrops

I save my snowdrop cookies for special occasions. The crunchy, buttery sandwich cookie has a puckery lemon filling.

—**BERNICE MARTINONI** PETALUMA, CA

PREP: 40 MIN. + CHILLING
BAKE: 10 MIN./BATCH + COOLING
MAKES: 2 DOZEN

- 1 **cup butter, softened**
- ½ **cup confectioners' sugar**
- ¼ **teaspoon salt**
- 1 **teaspoon lemon extract**
- 2 **cups all-purpose flour**
  Granulated sugar

FILLING

- 1 **egg, lightly beaten**
- ⅔ **cup granulated sugar**
- 3 **tablespoons lemon juice**
- 2 **teaspoons grated lemon peel**
- 4 **teaspoons butter**
  Additional confectioners' sugar

1. Preheat oven to 350°. In a small bowl, cream butter, confectioners' sugar and salt until light and fluffy. Beat in extract. Gradually beat in flour. If necessary, cover and refrigerate dough until firm enough to shape.

2. Shape teaspoonfuls of dough into balls. Place 1 in. apart on ungreased baking sheets; flatten slightly with bottom of a glass dipped in granulated sugar. Bake 10-12 minutes or until light brown. Remove from pans to wire racks to cool completely.

3. For filling, in a small heavy saucepan, whisk egg, granulated sugar, lemon juice and lemon peel until blended. Add butter; cook over medium heat, whisking constantly, until thickened and a thermometer reads at least 170°, about 20 minutes. Do not allow to boil. Remove from heat immediately. Transfer to a small bowl; cool. Press plastic wrap onto surface of filling. Refrigerate until cold, about 1 hour.

4. To serve, spread lemon filling on bottoms of half of the cookies; cover with remaining cookies. Dust with confectioners' sugar. Store leftovers in refrigerator.

FREEZE OPTION *Freeze cookies in freezer containers. To use, thaw cookies in covered containers. Fill and decorate as directed.*

Cherry Kiss Cookies

Chocolate-covered-cherry lovers, get ready for these. This playful variation on thumbprint cookies will be your new favorite holiday treat.

—**JOY YURK** GRAFTON, WI

PREP: 20 MIN.
BAKE: 10 MIN./BATCH + COOLING
MAKES: 4½ DOZEN

- 1 **cup butter, softened**
- 1 **cup confectioners' sugar**
- ½ **teaspoon salt**
- 2 **teaspoons maraschino cherry juice**
- ½ **teaspoon almond extract**
- 6 **drops red food coloring, optional**
- 2¼ **cups all-purpose flour**
- ½ **cup chopped maraschino cherries**
- 54 **milk chocolate kisses, unwrapped**

1. Preheat oven to 350°. In a large bowl, beat butter, confectioners' sugar and salt until blended. Beat in cherry juice, extract and, if desired, food coloring. Gradually beat in flour. Stir in cherries.

2. Shape dough into 1-in. balls. Place 1 in. apart on greased baking sheets.

3. Bake 8-10 minutes or until bottoms are light brown. Immediately press a chocolate kiss into center of each cookie (cookie will crack around edges). Cool on pans 2 minutes. Remove to wire racks to cool.

⑤ INGREDIENTS FAST FIX

Chocolate Peppermint Bark

These treats are such a snap to make, I almost feel guilty serving them. But nobody seems to mind that I didn't put in much effort—they just keep coming back for more.

—**KESLIE HOUSER** PASCO, WA

PREP: 15 MIN. + CHILLING
MAKES: ABOUT 1 POUND

- 6 **ounces white baking chocolate, chopped**
- 1 **cup crushed peppermint or spearmint candies, divided**
- 1 **cup (6 ounces) semisweet chocolate chips**

1. In a microwave, melt white chocolate at 70% power; stir until smooth. Stir in ⅓ cup crushed candies. Repeat with chocolate chips and an additional ⅓ cup candies. Alternately drop spoonfuls of chocolate and white chocolate mixtures onto a waxed paper-lined baking sheet.

2. Using a metal spatula, cut through candy to swirl and spread to ¼-in. thickness. Sprinkle with remaining crushed candies.

3. Refrigerate until firm. Break into pieces. Store between layers of waxed paper in an airtight container.

NOTE *This recipe was tested in a 1,100-watt microwave.*

DID YOU KNOW?

Because it contains no cocoa solids, white chocolate technically isn't a chocolate at all. It does contain cocoa butter, which gives white chocolate its rich, buttery texture. Higher-quality white chocolate has a greater percentage of cocoa butter, while imitation chocolate doesn't have any.

CHERRY KISS COOKIES

RED VELVET WHOOPIE PIES

Hazelnut Bonbon Cookies

Take hazelnuts to a whole new level. Wrap them up in cookie dough, dip in chocolate and finish with sprinkles or colored sugar.
—**NANCY MUELLER** MENOMONEE FALLS, WI

PREP: 30 MIN.
BAKE: 10 MIN./BATCH + COOLING
MAKES: 3½ DOZEN

- 2 **teaspoons instant espresso powder**
- 2 **teaspoons hot water**
- ½ **cup butter, softened**
- ¾ **cup confectioners' sugar**
- ⅛ **teaspoon salt**
- 3 **teaspoons vanilla extract**
- 1½ **cups all-purpose flour**
- 42 **whole hazelnuts**

GLAZE
- 3 **ounces semisweet chocolate, chopped**
- 2 **tablespoons plus 1½ teaspoons butter**
- 1 **tablespoon confectioners' sugar**
  Chocolate and gold jimmies

1. In a small bowl, dissolve espresso powder in hot water; cool. Preheat oven to 350°. In a large bowl, cream butter, confectioners' sugar and salt until light and fluffy. Beat in vanilla and espresso mixture. Gradually beat in flour.
2. Wrap 1 heaping teaspoon dough around each hazelnut to cover completely. Place 2 in. apart on ungreased baking sheets. Bake for 8-10 minutes or until bottoms are golden brown. Remove to wire racks to cool completely.
3. For glaze, in a microwave, melt chocolate and butter; stir until smooth. Whisk in confectioners' sugar until blended. Dip tops of cookies in glaze; allow excess to drip off. Place on waxed paper; sprinkle with jimmies and let stand until set.
FREEZE OPTION *Freeze unglazed cookies, layered between waxed paper, in freezer containers. To use, thaw cookies in covered containers. Dip in glaze as directed.*

Red Velvet Whoopie Pies

Everyone gets a kick out of this fun take on the trendy cake. Take a simple shortcut and use packaged cream cheese frosting for the filling.
—**JUDI DEXHEIMER** STURGEON BAY, WI

PREP: 40 MIN.
BAKE: 10 MIN./BATCH + COOLING
MAKES: 2 DOZEN

- ¾ **cup butter, softened**
- 1 **cup sugar**
- 2 **eggs**
- ½ **cup sour cream**
- 1 **tablespoon red food coloring**
- 1½ **teaspoons white vinegar**
- 1 **teaspoon clear vanilla extract**
- 2¼ **cups all-purpose flour**
- ¼ **cup baking cocoa**
- 2 **teaspoons baking powder**
- ½ **teaspoon salt**
- ¼ **teaspoon baking soda**
- 2 **ounces semisweet chocolate, melted and cooled**

FILLING
- 1 **package (8 ounces) cream cheese, softened**
- ½ **cup butter, softened**
- 2½ **cups confectioners' sugar**
- 2 **teaspoons clear vanilla extract**

TOPPINGS
  White baking chips, melted
  Finely chopped pecans

1. Preheat oven to 375°. In a large bowl, cream butter and sugar until light and fluffy. Beat in eggs, sour cream, food coloring, vinegar and vanilla. In another bowl, whisk flour, cocoa, baking powder, salt and baking soda; gradually beat into creamed mixture. Stir in cooled chocolate.
2. Drop dough by tablespoonfuls 2 in. apart onto parchment paper-lined baking sheets. Bake 8-10 minutes or until edges are set. Cool on pans for 2 minutes. Remove to wire racks to cool completely.
3. For filling, in a large bowl, beat cream cheese and butter until fluffy. Beat in confectioners' sugar and vanilla until smooth. Spread filling on bottom of half of the cookies; cover with remaining cookies.
4. Drizzle with melted baking chips; sprinkle with pecans. Refrigerate until serving.
FREEZE OPTION *Freeze cookies in freezer containers. To use, thaw cookies in covered containers. Fill and decorate as directed.*

Pine Nut Snowballs

PREP: 30 MIN.
BAKE: 10 MIN./BATCH + COOLING
MAKES: 4 DOZEN

- 1 **cup pine nuts, toasted and cooled**
- 2¼ **cups all-purpose flour, divided**
- 1 **cup butter, softened**
- 2 **cups confectioners' sugar, divided**
- ¼ **teaspoon salt**
- 1 **tablespoon amaretto**

1. Preheat oven to 400°. Place pine nuts and ¼ cup flour in a food processor. Pulse until pine nuts are finely chopped. In a large bowl, cream butter, ½ cup confectioners' sugar and salt until light and fluffy. Beat in amaretto. Gradually beat in remaining flour and the pine nut mixture.
2. Shape dough into 1-in. balls; place 2 in. apart on ungreased baking sheets. Bake 6-8 minutes or until set. Cool on pans 2 minutes.
3. Roll warm cookies in remaining confectioners' sugar. Cool on wire racks. When cooled, reroll cookies in confectioners' sugar.

FREEZE OPTION *Freeze undecorated cookies, layered between waxed paper, in freezer containers. To use, thaw before serving. Roll cookies in confectioners' sugar.*

Cranberry-Pistachio Thumbprint Cookies

For years, I made Swedish thumbprint cookies with raspberry jam and walnuts. Now at Christmas, I use pistachios and cranberries for holiday color.
—**DION FRISCHER** ANN ARBOR, MI

PREP: 40 MIN.+ CHILLING
BAKE: 10 MIN./BATCH + COOLING
MAKES: 3 DOZEN

- ½ **cup butter, softened**
- ¼ **cup sugar**
- ¼ **cup packed brown sugar**
- 1 **egg yolk**
- 1 **teaspoon grated orange peel**
- 1 **cup all-purpose flour**
- 1 **cup dried cranberries**
- ¾ **cup plus 2 tablespoons finely chopped pistachios, divided**
- ⅔ **cup white baking chips**

CRANBERRY-PISTACHIO THUMBPRINT COOKIES

- ¼ **cup heavy whipping cream**
- 36 **dried cranberries**

1. Preheat oven to 350°. In a small bowl, cream butter and sugars until light and fluffy. Beat in egg yolk and orange peel. Gradually beat in flour. Stir in the cranberries and ¾ cup of pistachios.
2. Shape dough into 1-in. balls. Place 2 in. apart on ungreased baking sheets. Press a deep indentation in center of each with the end of a wooden spoon handle.
3. Bake 9-11 minutes or until edges are light brown. Remove from pans to wire racks to cool completely.
4. Meanwhile, place baking chips in a small bowl. In a small saucepan, bring cream just to a boil. Pour over baking chips; stir with a whisk until smooth. Cool to room temperature, stirring occasionally. Refrigerate, covered, until thickened.
5. Spoon ganache onto cookies; sprinkle with remaining pistachios. Top each with a cranberry. Refrigerate any leftovers.
FREEZE OPTION *Freeze undecorated cookies in freezer containers. To use, thaw cookies in covered containers and decorate as directed.*

My great-aunt's Russian tea cakes inspired this recipe. I added pine nuts and amaretto, and wrote about it on my blog, cookiechronicles.com.
—**CHRISTIANNA GOZZI** ASTORIA, NY

PINE NUT SNOWBALLS

This perfect macaroon has dark chocolate, chewy coconut and macadamia nuts—and it's dipped in chocolate—sinful and delicious!
—**DARLENE BRENDEN** SALEM, OR

CHOCOLATE MACADAMIA MACAROONS

FREEZE IT
Chocolate Macadamia Macaroons

PREP: 20 MIN. • **BAKE:** 15 MIN. + COOLING
MAKES: 1½ DOZEN

- 2 **cups flaked coconut**
- ½ **cup finely chopped macadamia nuts**
- ⅓ **cup sugar**
- 3 **tablespoons baking cocoa**
- 2 **tablespoons all-purpose flour**
  Pinch salt
- 2 **egg whites, lightly beaten**
- 1 **tablespoon light corn syrup**
- 1 **teaspoon vanilla extract**
- 4 **ounces semisweet chocolate, melted**

1. Preheat oven to 325°. In a large bowl, mix the first six ingredients. Stir in egg whites, corn syrup and vanilla until blended.
2. Drop by rounded tablespoonfuls 2 in. apart onto greased baking sheets. Bake 15-20 minutes or until set and dry to the touch. Cool on pans for 5 minutes. Remove to wire racks to cool completely.
3. Dip bottom of each cookie in melted chocolate, allowing excess to drip off. Place on waxed paper; let stand until set.
FREEZE OPTION *Freeze cookies, layered between waxed paper, in freezer containers. To use, thaw before serving.*

Favorite Pecan Pie Bars

Send your favorite holiday travelers on their way with a package of these nutty little bars to eat when they get home.
—**SYLVIA FORD** KENNETT, MO

PREP: 10 MIN. • **BAKE:** 45 MIN. + COOLING
MAKES: 4 DOZEN

- 2 **cups all-purpose flour**
- ⅓ **cup sugar**
- ¼ **teaspoon salt**
- ¾ **cup cold butter, cubed**
- **FILLING**
- 4 **eggs**
- 1½ **cups corn syrup**
- 1½ **cups sugar**
- 3 **tablespoons butter, melted**
- 1½ **teaspoons vanilla extract**
- 2½ **cups chopped pecans**

1. Preheat oven to 350°. In a large bowl, mix flour, sugar and salt; cut in cold butter until mixture resembles coarse crumbs. Press into a greased 15x10x1-in. baking pan. Bake for 20 minutes.
2. For filling, in a large bowl, whisk eggs, corn syrup, sugar, melted butter and vanilla. Stir in pecans. Spread over hot crust.
3. Bake 25-30 minutes longer or until filling is set. Cool completely in pan on a wire rack. Cut into bars.

DID YOU KNOW?

Pecans have a higher fat content than other nuts, so be careful that they don't go rancid. They'll stay fresh for twice as long in the freezer as they would at room temperature.

Glazed Bonbon Cookies

The chocolate in the middle of these cookies is such a fun surprise. And the dough is so simple to make, with just the right amount of sweetness.

—**APRIL SHUTTLEWORTH** FORT WAYNE, IN

PREP: 40 MIN.
BAKE: 15 MIN./BATCH + STANDING
MAKES: 1½ DOZEN

- ½ cup butter, softened
- ¾ cup confectioners' sugar
- ⅛ teaspoon salt
- 1 tablespoon vanilla extract
- 1½ cups all-purpose flour
- ⅓ cup semisweet chocolate chips
- ½ cup vanilla frosting
  Sprinkles

1. Preheat oven to 350°. In a large bowl, beat butter, confectioners' sugar and salt until blended. Beat in vanilla. Gradually beat in flour. (Dough will be crumbly.)

2. Press a tablespoon of dough around five chocolate chips, covering completely. Repeat with remaining dough and chocolate chips. Place 2 in. apart on ungreased baking sheets. Bake 12-15 minutes or until bottoms are light brown. Remove from pans to wire racks to cool completely.

3. For glaze, place frosting in a microwave-safe bowl. Microwave on high 10-15 seconds or until melted; stir until blended. (Frosting may separate slightly when warmed but will become smooth after stirring.) Dip tops of cookies in glaze or spoon glaze over cookies; top with sprinkles. Let stand until set.

FREEZE OPTION *Freeze unglazed cookies in freezer containers. To use, thaw cookies in covered containers and decorate as directed.*

GLAZED BONBON COOKIES

Kahlua Truffles

I discovered this recipe tucked away in a box of my mother's things. It's such a sweet way to remember her during the Christmas season.

—**BETSY KING** DULUTH, MN

PREP: 20 MIN. + CHILLING
MAKES: 1½ DOZEN

- 1 cup (6 ounces) semisweet chocolate chips
- ¼ cup butter, cubed
- 1 egg yolk, lightly beaten
- 3 tablespoons Kahlua (coffee liqueur)
- 2 tablespoons cream cheese, softened
- ⅔ cup salted roasted almonds or pistachios, chopped

1. In top of a double boiler or a metal bowl over simmering water, melt chocolate chips and butter; stir mixture until smooth.

2. In a small bowl, whisk a small amount of hot mixture into the egg yolk; return all to double boiler, whisking constantly. Cook over low heat until mixture reaches 160°, whisking constantly.

3. Remove from heat; stir in Kahlua and cream cheese until blended. Cool to room temperature, stirring occasionally. Refrigerate, covered, 1 hour or until easy to shape.

4. Place almonds in a small bowl. Shape mixture into 1-in. balls; roll in almonds. Refrigerate, covered, until firm, about 2 hours. Store in an airtight container in the refrigerator.

KAHLUA TRUFFLES

Peaches 'n' Cream Bars
PAGE 298

Delectable Desserts

Sweeten up every day with dozens of pretty pies, fun freezer pops, impressive cakes, cookie-jar favorites and much, much more. And because these treats are a snap to prepare, you can surprise the people you love anytime you like!

Cherry Berry Pie
PAGE 305

Cafe Mocha Cookies
PAGE 306

Simple Turtle Cheesecake
PAGE 302

WHITE CHOCOLATE-
STRAWBERRY TIRAMISU

Here's a twist on a classic dessert that highlights another flavor combo my husband and I love: strawberries and white chocolate. Lighten it up if you'd like—I've had good luck with light non-dairy whipped topping and reduced-fat cream cheese. **—ANNA GINSBERG** AUSTIN, TX

FAST FIX
White Chocolate-Strawberry Tiramisu

START TO FINISH: 30 MIN.
MAKES: 15 SERVINGS

- 2 **cups heavy whipping cream**
- 1 **package (8 ounces) cream cheese, softened**
- ½ **cup (4 ounces) mascarpone cheese**
- 9 **ounces white baking chocolate, melted and cooled**
- 1 **cup confectioners' sugar, divided**
- 1 **teaspoon vanilla extract**
- 2 **packages (3 ounces each) ladyfingers, split**
- ⅔ **cup orange juice**
- 4 **cups sliced fresh strawberries**
  Chocolate syrup, optional

1. In a large bowl, beat cream until soft peaks form. In another bowl, beat cheeses until light and fluffy. Beat in cooled chocolate, ½ cup confectioners' sugar and vanilla. Fold in 2 cups of the whipped cream.
2. Brush half of the ladyfingers with half of the orange juice; arrange in a 13x9-in. dish. Spread with 2 cups cream cheese mixture; top with half of the strawberries. Brush remaining ladyfingers with remaining orange juice; arrange over berries.
3. Gently stir the remaining confectioners' sugar into remaining cream cheese mixture; fold in remaining whipped cream. Spread over ladyfingers. Top with remaining strawberries. Refrigerate until serving. If desired, drizzle with chocolate syrup before serving.

Peaches 'n' Cream Bars

For a new spin on peach pie, try these easy-to-love bars. The mellow fruit flavor really comes through.
—HUBERT SCOTT COCKEYSVILLE, MD

PREP: 20 MIN. • **BAKE:** 25 MIN. + COOLING
MAKES: 2 DOZEN

- 1 **tube (8 ounces) refrigerated seamless crescent dough sheet**
- 1 **package (8 ounces) cream cheese, softened**
- ½ **cup sugar**
- ¼ **teaspoon almond extract**
- 1 **can (21 ounces) peach pie filling**
- ½ **cup all-purpose flour**
- ¼ **cup packed brown sugar**
- 3 **tablespoons cold butter**
- ½ **cup sliced almonds**

1. Preheat oven to 375°. Unroll crescent dough sheet into a rectangle. Press onto bottom and slightly up sides of a greased 13x9-in. baking pan. Bake 5 minutes. Cool completely on a wire rack.
2. In a large bowl, beat cream cheese, sugar and extract until smooth. Spread over crust. Spoon pie filling over cream cheese layer.
3. In a small bowl, whisk flour and brown sugar. Cut in butter until mixture resembles coarse crumbs. Stir in almonds; sprinkle over peach filling.
4. Bake 25-28 minutes or until edges are golden brown. Cool in pan on a wire rack. Cut into bars. Store in an airtight container in the refrigerator.

PEACHES 'N' CREAM BARS

COCONUT PECAN PIE

TOPPING
- ⅓ cup old-fashioned oats
- ¼ cup all-purpose flour
- 2 tablespoons flaked coconut, toasted
- 2 tablespoons brown sugar
- ¼ teaspoon ground nutmeg
- ¼ cup cold butter, cubed

1. Preheat oven to 350°. In a large bowl, combine pineapple and bananas. Sprinkle with brown sugar and flour; toss to coat. Transfer to an 11x7-in. baking dish coated with cooking spray.
2. In a small bowl, mix the first five topping ingredients; cut in butter until crumbly. Sprinkle over the pineapple mixture.
3. Bake 30-35 minutes or until filling is bubbly and topping is golden brown. Serve warm or at room temperature.
NOTE *To toast coconut, spread in a 15x10x1-in. baking pan. Bake at 350° for 5-10 minutes or until golden brown, stirring frequently.*
PER SERVING *188 cal., 6 g fat (4 g sat. fat), 13 mg chol., 44 mg sodium, 34 g carb., 3 g fiber, 2 g pro.* **Diabetic Exchanges:** *1 starch, 1 fruit, 1 fat.*

Coconut Pecan Pie

We top this with sliced bananas, whipped cream and more sliced bananas. It's based on a recipe my mom got from a pot holder she bought at Patti's 1880s Settlement in Grand Rivers, Kentucky.

—**JENNIFER CHOISSER** PADUCAH, KY

PREP: 15 MIN. • **BAKE:** 25 MIN. + COOLING
MAKES: 8 SERVINGS

- **Pastry for single-crust pie (9 inches)**
- 7 egg whites
- 1½ cups sugar
- 1½ cups flaked coconut
- 1½ cups graham cracker crumbs
- 1½ cups chopped pecans
- **Whipped cream**

1. Preheat oven to 325°. On a lightly floured surface, roll dough to a ⅛-in.-thick circle; transfer to a 9-in. pic plate. Trim pastry to ½ in. beyond rim of plate; flute edge.
2. In a large bowl, combine egg whites, sugar, coconut, cracker crumbs and pecans. Pour into pastry shell. Bake 25-30 minutes or until set. Cool on a wire rack. Serve with whipped cream.

EAT SMART
Tropical Crisp

One bite of this sweet, juicy, crunchy fruit crisp, and you just might hear the crash of ocean waves and feel the warm sand under your toes!

—*TASTE OF HOME* TEST KITCHEN

PREP: 20 MIN. • **BAKE:** 30 MIN.
MAKES: 9 SERVINGS

- 1 fresh pineapple, peeled and cubed
- 4 medium bananas, sliced
- ¼ cup packed brown sugar
- 2 tablespoons all-purpose flour

TROPICAL CRISP

Rum-Glazed Pumpkin Cake

For years, my co-workers were taste testers as I perfected my recipe for pumpkin cake. This luscious version wins, hands down.

—GILDA SMITH SANTEE, CA

PREP: 20 MIN. • **BAKE:** 55 MIN. + COOLING
MAKES: 12 SERVINGS

- ½ cup chopped pecans
- 1 can (15 ounces) solid-pack pumpkin
- ½ cup sugar
- ½ cup canola oil
- 4 eggs
- ¼ cup water
- 1 package yellow cake mix (regular size)
- 1½ teaspoons ground cinnamon
- ½ teaspoon ground nutmeg
- ⅛ teaspoon ground cloves

GLAZE
- 1 cup sugar
- ½ cup butter, cubed
- ¼ teaspoon ground cinnamon
  Dash ground cloves
- ½ cup rum

1. Preheat oven to 350°. Grease and flour a 10-in. fluted tube pan; sprinkle pecans onto bottom of pan.

2. In a large bowl, beat pumpkin, sugar, oil, eggs and water until well blended. In another bowl, whisk cake mix and spices; gradually beat into pumpkin mixture. Transfer to prepared pan.

3. Bake 55-60 minutes or until a toothpick inserted in center comes out clean. Cool in pan 10 minutes before removing to a wire rack.

4. In a small saucepan, combine sugar, butter, cinnamon and cloves; cook and stir over medium heat until butter is melted. Remove from heat. Stir in rum; cook and stir 2-3 minutes longer or until sugar is dissolved.

5. Gradually brush glaze onto warm cake, about ¼ cup at a time, allowing glaze to soak into cake before adding more. Cool completely.

NOTE *To remove cakes easily, use solid shortening to grease plain and fluted tube pans.*

RUM-GLAZED PUMPKIN CAKE

Fresh blackberries, sugar and brandy make a rich-tasting sauce to serve over ice cream, cheesecake, pancakes, angel food cake...the possibilities are endless, and it makes everything look gorgeous.

—CRYSTAL JO BRUNS ILIFF, CO

BLACKBERRY BRANDY SAUCE

⑤INGREDIENTS FAST FIX

Blackberry Brandy Sauce

START TO FINISH: 25 MIN.
MAKES: 12 SERVINGS (¼ CUP EACH)

- 1 cup sugar
- 2 tablespoons cornstarch
- ¼ cup cold water
- 4 cups fresh or frozen blackberries, thawed
- 1 tablespoon brandy or ½ teaspoon vanilla extract
  Vanilla ice cream, optional

In a large saucepan, mix sugar and cornstarch; stir in water. Add blackberries; bring to a boil. Reduce heat; simmer, uncovered, 10-12 minutes or until sauce is thickened, stirring occasionally. Remove from heat; stir in brandy. Cool slightly. If desired, serve with ice cream.

Juicy Peach & Strawberry Crumb Pie

You've had peach pie and strawberry pie, and maybe even peach-strawberry pie. But throw in some garden-fresh basil and you're in for a real treat. Trust me.

—LINDSAY SPRUNK NOBLESVILLE, IN

PREP: 25 MIN. • **BAKE:** 45 MIN. + COOLING
MAKES: 8 SERVINGS

- 1 sheet refrigerated pie pastry
- 3½ cups sliced peeled peaches (about 4 medium)
- 2½ cups sliced fresh strawberries
- 2 tablespoons lemon juice
- ¾ cup sugar
- ¼ cup cornstarch
- 2 tablespoons minced fresh basil
- ¾ cup all-purpose flour
- ½ cup packed brown sugar
- 6 tablespoons cold butter

1. Preheat oven to 375°. Unroll pastry sheet into a 9-in. pie plate; flute edge. In a large bowl, combine peaches, strawberries and lemon juice. In a small bowl, mix sugar, cornstarch and basil. Add to fruit and toss gently to coat. Transfer to crust.

2. In a small bowl, mix flour and brown sugar; cut in butter until crumbly. Sprinkle over filling. Place pie on a foil-lined baking pan.

3. Bake on a lower oven rack 45-55 minutes or until topping is golden brown and filling is bubbly. Cool on a wire rack.

Date Nut Torte

I always get compliments on this sweet and nutty torte. It's wonderful after a meal or as a little snack with coffee. My husband, three children and five grandchildren all enjoy this dessert, too!

—JUNE HOVLAND ROCHESTER, MN

PREP: 15 MIN. • **BAKE:** 30 MIN. + COOLING
MAKES: 9 SERVINGS

- 2 eggs
- ½ cup sugar
- ½ cup packed brown sugar
- ⅔ cup all-purpose flour
- 1 teaspoon baking powder
- ¼ teaspoon salt
- 1 cup chopped walnuts
- 1 cup chopped dates
  Whipped cream

1. In a bowl, beat eggs. Gradually add sugars and beat until well mixed. Combine the flour, baking powder and salt; add to egg mixture and stir until moistened. Stir in nuts and dates. Pour into a greased 8-in.-square baking pan.

2. Bake at 350° for 30 minutes. Torte top will be crusty and the inside chewy. Cool. Serve with whipped cream.

TOP TIP

Peaches and basil make an exciting flavor duo. Try them in a hot fruit sundae with blackberries, plums, brown sugar and a little peach schnapps. Or make crostini with goat cheese, grilled peaches, toasted pecans, a vinegar glaze and basil.

JUICY PEACH & STRAWBERRY CRUMB PIE

Simple Turtle Cheesecake

For an almost instant dessert, I spread homemade ganache and caramel sauce over premade cheesecake. It makes the holidays feel slightly less hectic.

—LAURA MCDOWELL LAKE VILLA, IL

START TO FINISH: 25 MIN.
MAKES: 8 SERVINGS

- 1 frozen New York-style cheesecake (30 ounces), thawed
- ½ cup semisweet chocolate chips
- ½ cup heavy whipping cream, divided
- 3 tablespoons chopped pecans, toasted
- ¼ cup butter, cubed
- ½ cup plus 2 tablespoons packed brown sugar
- 1 tablespoon light corn syrup

1. Place cheesecake on a serving plate. Place chocolate chips in a small bowl. In a small saucepan, bring ¼ cup cream just to a boil. Pour over chocolate; stir with a whisk until smooth. Cool slightly, stirring occasionally. Pour over cheesecake; sprinkle with pecans. Refrigerate until set.

2. In a small saucepan, melt butter; stir in brown sugar and corn syrup.

Bring to a boil. Reduce heat; cook and stir until sugar is dissolved. Stir in remaining cream and return to a boil. Remove from heat. Serve sauce warm with cheesecake or, if desired, cool completely and drizzle over cheesecake.

NOTE *To toast nuts, spread in a 15x10x1-in. baking pan. Bake at 350° for 5-10 minutes or until lightly browned, stirring occasionally. Or, spread in a dry nonstick skillet and heat over low heat until lightly browned, stirring occasionally.*

Mini Peanut Butter Sandwich Cookies

Peanut butter lovers are guaranteed to go nuts for these rich little sandwich cookies. On a hot day, sandwich ice cream between the cookies instead of frosting. It cools you right down.

—KERI WOLFE NAPPANEE, IN

PREP: 25 MIN.
BAKE: 15 MIN./BATCH + COOLING
MAKES: ABOUT 3½ DOZEN

- 1 cup shortening
- 1 cup creamy peanut butter
- 1 cup sugar
- 1 cup packed brown sugar
- 3 eggs
- 1 teaspoon vanilla extract
- 3½ cups all-purpose flour
- 2 teaspoons baking soda
- ½ teaspoon salt

FILLING

- ¾ cup creamy peanut butter
- ½ cup 2% milk
- 1½ teaspoons vanilla extract
- 4 cups confectioners' sugar

1. Preheat oven to 350°. In a large bowl, cream shortening, peanut butter and sugars until blended. Beat in eggs and vanilla. In another bowl, whisk flour, baking soda and salt; gradually beat into creamed mixture.

2. Shape into 1-in. balls; place 2 in. apart on ungreased baking sheets. Bake 11-13 minutes or until set. Remove from pans to wire racks to cool completely.

3. In a small bowl, beat peanut butter, milk and vanilla until blended. Beat in confectioners' sugar until smooth. Spread filling on bottoms of half of the cookies; cover with remaining cookies.

FREEZE OPTION *Freeze unfilled cookies in freezer containers. To use, thaw cookies and fill as directed.*

NOTE *Reduced-fat peanut butter is not recommended for this recipe.*

DID YOU KNOW?

Because shortening melts at a higher temperature than butter, it's useful for baking cookies that you want to have a nice uniform shape.

MINI PEANUT BUTTER SANDWICH COOKIES

SIMPLE TURTLE CHEESECAKE

Coconut-Pineapple Sherbet Torte

PREP: 25 MIN. + FREEZING
MAKES: 10 SERVINGS

- 1 package (10 to 12 ounces) white baking chips
- 1 cup flaked coconut
- 1 cup cream of coconut
- 2 cups crushed crisp oatmeal cookies (about 20)
- ⅓ cup butter, melted
- 4 cups pineapple or other tropical-flavored sherbet, slightly softened if necessary

1. In a small saucepan, combine baking chips, coconut and cream of coconut; cook and stir over medium heat until chips are melted. Cool completely.

2. Line a 9x5-in. loaf pan with plastic wrap, letting edges extend over sides. In a small bowl, mix crushed cookies and butter.

3. To assemble, spoon 2 cups sherbet into prepared pan, spreading evenly.

Sprinkle with half of the cookie mixture; press to make a firm layer. Spread with half of the coconut mixture. Repeat layers. Wrap securely and freeze overnight.

4. Lifting with plastic wrap, unmold torte onto a serving plate. Cut torte lengthwise in half; cut each half crosswise into slices. Serve immediately.

FREEZE IT
Almond Chocolate Biscotti

My neighbors look forward to getting my gifts of these chocolate-drizzled cookies. They're such a cinch to make.

—GINGER CHATFIELD MUSCATINE, IA

PREP: 20 MIN. • **BAKE:** 40 MIN. + COOLING
MAKES: ABOUT 3½ DOZEN

- 1 package chocolate cake mix (regular size)
- 1 cup all-purpose flour
- ½ cup butter, melted
- 2 eggs
- ¼ cup chocolate syrup
- 1 teaspoon vanilla extract
- ½ teaspoon almond extract
- ½ cup slivered almonds
- ½ cup miniature semisweet chocolate chips
- 1 cup white baking chips
- 1 tablespoon shortening

ALMOND CHOCOLATE BISCOTTI

1. Preheat oven to 350°. In a large bowl, beat cake mix, flour, butter, eggs, chocolate syrup and extracts until well blended. Stir in almonds and chocolate chips. Divide dough in half. On ungreased baking sheets, shape each portion into a 12x2-in. log.

2. Bake 30-35 minutes or until firm to the touch. Carefully remove to wire racks; cool 20 minutes.

3. Transfer baked logs to a cutting board. Using a serrated knife, cut diagonally into ½-in. slices. Place on ungreased baking sheets, cut side down. Bake 10-15 minutes or until firm. Remove from pans to wire racks to cool completely.

4. In a microwave, melt baking chips and shortening; stir until smooth. Drizzle over biscotti; let stand until set. Store between pieces of waxed paper in airtight containers.

FREEZE OPTION *Freeze undrizzled cookies in freezer containers. To use, thaw in covered containers. Drizzle with baking chips as directed.*

I made up this torte one afternoon, and when I served it that night, it vanished within minutes. That's when I knew I'd struck gold. **—JONI HILTON** ROCKLIN, CA

COCONUT-PINEAPPLE SHERBET TORTE

Every time someone drops in for coffee, I bake up a batch of these fruit and nut pastries—I always keep the ingredients in my pantry. The recipe's a cinch to double, too, so it's good for parties and potlucks.

—**LORI MCLAIN** DENTON, TX

DATE-WALNUT PINWHEELS

FAST FIX
Date-Walnut Pinwheels

START TO FINISH: 25 MIN.
MAKES: 1 DOZEN

- 3 **tablespoons sugar**
- ½ **teaspoon ground cinnamon**
- 1 **refrigerated pie pastry**
- 1 **tablespoon apricot preserves**
- ⅔ **cup finely chopped pitted dates**
- ½ **cup finely chopped walnuts**

1. Preheat oven to 350°. Mix sugar and cinnamon. On a lightly floured surface, unroll pastry sheet; roll pastry into a 12-in. square. Spread preserves over top; sprinkle with dates, walnuts and cinnamon-sugar.
2. Roll up jelly-roll style; pinch seam to seal. Cut crosswise into 12 slices, about 1 in. thick. Place 1 in. apart on an ungreased baking sheet. Bake 12-14 minutes or until golden brown. Remove pastries from pan to a wire rack to cool.

FAST FIX
Microwave Apple Cobbler

I make this quick cobbler often, and sometimes use blackberries in addition to apples. It's so tasty served warm with ice cream or whipped cream.

—**MIRIAM CHRISTOPHEL** GOSHEN, IN

START TO FINISH: 20 MIN.
MAKES: 6 SERVINGS

- 5 **cups sliced peeled tart apples**
- ½ **cup sugar**
- 2 **tablespoons all-purpose flour**
- ½ **teaspoon ground cinnamon or cloves**

TOPPING
- ¾ **cup biscuit/baking mix**
- 3 **tablespoons sugar, divided**
- ⅓ **cup milk**
- ½ **teaspoon ground cinnamon or cloves**

1. Place apples in a 1½-qt. microwave-safe dish. Combine the sugar, flour and cinnamon; sprinkle over apples. Toss to coat. Cover and microwave on high 3-4 minutes or until apples are tender.
2. Meanwhile, in a bowl, combine the biscuit mix, 2 tablespoons sugar and milk. Drop by tablespoonfuls over hot apple mixture. Combine cinnamon and remaining sugar; sprinkle over topping. Microwave, uncovered, for 4-6 minutes or until a toothpick comes out clean. Serve warm.
NOTE *This recipe was tested in a 1,100-watt microwave.*

TOP TIP

I use a lot of nuts in my cooking and baking. To keep from running out, I buy large bags of nuts from wholesale stores, pour them into freezer bags, and label and freeze them. When preparing a recipe, I just pour what I need.
—**DORIS R.** FALLSTON, MD

One-Bowl Chocolate Cake

This cake mixes up quickly and bakes while we enjoy our dinner. My son, David, loves to help decorate it.

—**COLEEN MARTIN** BROOKFIELD, WI

PREP: 15 MIN. • **BAKE:** 35 MIN. + COOLING
MAKES: 15 SERVINGS

- 2 **cups all-purpose flour**
- 2 **cups sugar**
- ½ **cup baking cocoa**
- 2 **teaspoons baking soda**
- 1 **teaspoon baking powder**
- ½ **teaspoon salt**
- 2 **eggs, lightly beaten**
- 1 **cup canola oil**
- 1 **cup buttermilk**
- 1 **cup hot water**
   Frosting of your choice
   Colored sprinkles, optional

1. Preheat oven to 350°. Grease a 13x9-in. baking pan. In a large bowl, whisk the first six ingredients. Stir in eggs, oil and buttermilk. Add water; stir until combined.
2. Transfer batter to the prepared pan. Bake 35-40 minutes or until a toothpick inserted in center comes out clean. Cool completely in pan on a wire rack. Frost cake. If desired, decorate with sprinkles.

CHOCOLATE BUTTERCREAM FROSTING *In a large bowl, beat ½ cup softened butter until creamy. Beat in 2 cups confectioners' sugar, ¼ cup baking cocoa, 1½ teaspoons vanilla and 3-4 tablespoons 2% milk to achieve desired consistency.*

FREEZE IT

Cherry Berry Pie

A neighbor shared this pie with me years ago, and now it has a big fan club. I'm always looking for new treats to bake for my family, but this is one I turn to again and again, especially in summer.

—**WANDA VAN VOORHIS** PLAIN CITY, OH

PREP: 25 MIN. + STANDING
BAKE: 35 MIN. + COOLING
MAKES: 8 SERVINGS

- 2½ **cups fresh or frozen pitted tart cherries, thawed**
- 1½ **cups fresh or frozen raspberries, thawed**
- 1 **teaspoon lemon juice**

CHERRY BERRY PIE

- 1½ **cups sugar**
- ¼ **cup plus 2 teaspoons quick-cooking tapioca**
- ⅛ **teaspoon salt**
- 1 **package (14.1 ounces) refrigerated pie pastry**
- 1 **tablespoon butter**
- 1 **egg**
- 1 **tablespoon 2% milk**
   Coarse sugar

1. Preheat oven to 400°. Combine cherries, raspberries and lemon juice in a large bowl. In a small bowl, mix sugar, tapioca and salt; add to fruit and toss gently to coat. Let stand for 15 minutes.
2. Unroll one pastry sheet into a 9-in. pie plate; trim pastry to ¾ in. beyond rim of plate. Add fruit filling; dot with butter.
3. Unroll remaining pastry; cut into 2½-in.-wide strips. Arrange over filling in a lattice pattern. Trim and seal strips to edge of bottom pastry; flute edge. In a small bowl, whisk egg and milk; brush over lattice top. Sprinkle with sugar.
4. Cover edge loosely with foil. Bake 30 minutes. Remove foil; bake 5-10 minutes longer or until crust is golden brown and filling is bubbly. Cool on a wire rack.

FREEZE OPTION *Cover and freeze unbaked pie. To use, remove from freezer 30 minutes before baking (do not thaw). Preheat oven to 400°. Bake as directed, increasing time as necessary.*

ONE-BOWL CHOCOLATE CAKE

CAFE MOCHA COOKIES

- 1 envelope unflavored gelatin
- 1 teaspoon vanilla extract
- 1 teaspoon almond extract
- 2 cups (16 ounces) sour cream
- 1 cup fresh or frozen raspberries

1. In a large saucepan, combine cream and 1 cup sugar; cook and stir over low heat until a thermometer reads 160° (do not allow to boil). Stir in gelatin until dissolved.
2. Remove from heat; stir in extracts. Cool 10 minutes. Whisk in sour cream. Pour into eight dessert dishes. Refrigerate at least 1 hour.
3. Just before serving, lightly crush raspberries; gently stir in remaining sugar. Spoon over tops.

FAST FIX
Blueberry Crumble Tarts

Pop one into a lunch box, share a batch at work or wait until after dinner—these are sweet anytime, anywhere. Sometimes I refrigerate prepared tarts overnight and bake them while making dinner the next day. Foolproof.
—**CAROLE FRASER** NORTH YORK, ON

START TO FINISH: 30 MIN.
MAKES: 6 SERVINGS

- 2 cups fresh blueberries
- ¼ cup sugar
- 1 tablespoon cornstarch
- 1 package (6 count) individual graham cracker tart shells
- ¼ cup all-purpose flour
- ¼ cup quick-cooking oats
- ¼ cup packed brown sugar
- 2 tablespoons cold butter
    Ice cream or whipped cream, optional

1. Preheat oven to 375°. In a bowl, toss blueberries with sugar and cornstarch; spoon into tart shells. In a small bowl, mix flour, oats and brown sugar; cut in butter until crumbly. Sprinkle over the blueberries.
2. Place tarts on a baking sheet. Bake 20-25 minutes or until topping is golden brown and filling is bubbly. Serve warm or at room temperature. If desired, top with ice cream.

These taste like my favorite coffeehouse drink in cookie form. They're crispy outside, but soft in the middle.
—**ANGELA SPENGLER** MECHANICSBURG, PA

FREEZE IT
Cafe Mocha Cookies

PREP: 20 MIN. • **BAKE:** 10 MIN./BATCH
MAKES: ABOUT 3 DOZEN

- 6 tablespoons butter, softened
- ⅓ cup shortening
- ½ cup packed brown sugar
- ⅓ cup sugar
- 1 egg
- 2 tablespoons hot caramel ice cream topping
- 1 teaspoon vanilla extract
- 1½ cups all-purpose flour
- 4 teaspoons dark roast instant coffee granules
- ½ teaspoon baking soda
- ½ teaspoon salt
- 1½ cups (9 ounces) dark chocolate chips

1. Preheat oven to 350°. In a large bowl, cream butter, shortening and sugars until light and fluffy. Beat in egg, ice cream topping and vanilla. In another bowl, whisk flour, coffee granules, baking soda and salt; gradually beat into creamed mixture. Fold in chocolate chips.
2. Drop dough by rounded tablespoonfuls 2 in. apart onto ungreased baking sheets. Bake 8-10 minutes or until set. Cool on pans 2 minutes. Remove to wire racks to cool.
FREEZE OPTION *Drop dough by rounded tablespoonfuls onto waxed paper-lined baking sheets; freeze until firm. Transfer to resealable plastic freezer bags; return to freezer. To use, bake frozen cookies as directed, increasing time by 1-2 minutes.*

Swedish Creme

This thick and creamy dessert with just a hint of almond flavor is my interpretation of my mother's traditional Swedish Krem. It looks spectacular with the bright red berries on top. Serve it in glasses to match the occasion.
—**LINDA NILSEN** ANOKA, MN

PREP: 20 MIN. + CHILLING
MAKES: 8 SERVINGS

- 2 cups heavy whipping cream
- 1 cup plus 2 teaspoons sugar, divided

BLUEBERRY CRUMBLE TARTS

PEACH MELBA TRIFLE

Raspberry Coconut Cream Pie

I like coconut pies and my husband likes raspberries. Here's a little stroke of genius I had when I wanted to make the ultimate dessert for both of us.

—**SUSAN JOLLY** WILMINGTON, DE

PREP: 20 MIN. + CHILLING
MAKES: 8 SERVINGS

- ⅓ **cup white baking chips, melted**
- 1 **graham cracker crust (9 inches)**
- 2 **cups cold whole milk**
- 2 **packages (3.4 ounces each) instant vanilla pudding mix**
- ½ **cup flaked coconut**
- 1 **carton (8 ounces) frozen whipped topping, thawed, divided**
- 1 **cup fresh raspberries**
  Toasted coconut

1. Spread melted baking chips onto bottom of crust. In a large bowl, whisk milk and pudding mixes 2 minutes. (Mixture will be thick.) Stir in ½ cup coconut. Fold in 2 cups whipped topping.
2. Spread half of the mixture into crust. Sprinkle with raspberries. Spread remaining pudding mixture over raspberries; top with remaining whipped topping. Sprinkle with toasted coconut. Refrigerate 3 hours or until set.
NOTE *To toast coconut, spread in a 15x10x1-in. baking pan. Bake at 350° for 5-10 minutes or until golden brown, stirring frequently.*

RASPBERRY COCONUT CREAM PIE

EAT SMART
Peach Melba Trifle

This dream of a dessert tastes extra good on a busy day because you can make it ahead of time. If you don't have fresh peaches handy, use canned ones.

—**CHRISTINA MOORE** CASAR, NC

PREP: 20 MIN. + CHILLING
MAKES: 12 SERVINGS

- 2 **packages (12 ounces each) frozen unsweetened raspberries, thawed**
- 1 **tablespoon cornstarch**
- 1½ **cups (12 ounces) fat-free peach yogurt**
- ⅛ **teaspoon almond extract**
- 1 **carton (8 ounces) frozen reduced-fat whipped topping, thawed**
- 2 **prepared angel food cakes (8 to 10 ounces each), cut into 1-inch cubes (about 8 cups)**
- 4 **small peaches, peeled and sliced (about 2 cups)**

1. In a large saucepan, combine raspberries and cornstarch. Bring to a boil; cook and stir 1-2 minutes or until thickened. Strain seeds from sauce; cover and chill.
2. In a large bowl, mix yogurt and extract; fold in whipped topping. In a 4-qt. bowl, layer half of the cake cubes, yogurt mixture and peaches. Repeat layers. Refrigerate, covered, at least 3 hours before serving. Serve with raspberry sauce.
PER SERVING *201 cal., 3 g fat (2 g sat. fat), 1 mg chol., 298 mg sodium, 41 g carb., 3 g fiber, 4 g pro.*

TOP TIP

When a recipe calls for frozen raspberries to be drained, I always save the juice. It makes a refreshing drink when stirred into orange juice!
—**LILLIAN K.** GAINESVILLE, FL

GINGERSNAP PUMPKIN CAKE

until smooth. Frost cake; sprinkle with crushed cookies.

NOTE *To remove cake easily, use solid shortening to grease plain and fluted tube pans.*

FREEZE OPTION *Wrap cooled cake in plastic wrap, then cover securely with foil; freeze. To use, thaw cake before unwrapping. Frost and decorate as directed.*

FAST FIX ▶

Baklava Tartlets

Want a quick treat that's delicious and easy to do? These tartlets will do the trick. You can serve them right away, but they're better after chilling for about an hour in the refrigerator.

—ASHLEY EAGON KETTERING, OH

START TO FINISH: 25 MIN.
MAKES: 45 TARTLETS

- ¾ cup honey
- ½ cup butter, melted
- 1 teaspoon ground cinnamon
- 1 teaspoon lemon juice
- ¼ teaspoon ground cloves
- 2 cups finely chopped walnuts
- 3 packages (1.9 ounces each) frozen miniature phyllo tart shells

In a small bowl, mix the first five ingredients until blended; stir in walnuts. Spoon 2 teaspoons mixture into each tart shell. Refrigerate until serving.

BAKLAVA TARTLETS

On the first day we had cool weather following all of the summer heat, we were getting together with friends. I baked this pumpkin cake because I could feel fall in the air. **—KONI BREWER** FORT WORTH, TX

FREEZE IT

Gingersnap Pumpkin Cake

PREP: 20 MIN. • **BAKE:** 50 MIN. + COOLING
MAKES: 12 SERVINGS

- 1 can (15 ounces) solid-pack pumpkin
- 2 cups sugar
- 4 eggs
- 1 cup canola oil
- 2 cups all-purpose flour
- 2 teaspoons baking soda
- 2 teaspoons pumpkin pie spice
- ½ teaspoon salt

ICING

- 4 ounces cream cheese, softened
- ¼ cup butter, softened
- ½ teaspoon vanilla extract
- 1¾ cups confectioners' sugar
- 5 gingersnap cookies, crushed

1. Preheat oven to 350°. Grease and flour a 10-in. fluted tube pan.

2. In a large bowl, beat pumpkin, sugar, eggs and oil until well blended. In another bowl, whisk flour, baking soda, pie spice and salt; gradually beat into pumpkin mixture.

3. Transfer batter to prepared pan. Bake 50-55 minutes or until a toothpick inserted in center comes out clean. Cool in pan 10 minutes before removing cake to a wire rack to cool completely.

4. In a small bowl, beat cream cheese, butter and vanilla until blended. Gradually beat in confectioners' sugar

Bake-Sale Lemon Bars

The recipe for these tangy lemon bars comes from my cousin Bernice, a farmer's wife famous for cooking up feasts.

—**MILDRED KELLER** ROCKFORD, IL

PREP: 25 MIN. • **BAKE:** 20 MIN. + COOLING
MAKES: 4 DOZEN

- ¾ **cup butter, softened**
- ⅔ **cup confectioners' sugar**
- 1½ **cups plus 3 tablespoons all-purpose flour, divided**
- 3 **eggs**
- 1½ **cups sugar**
- ¼ **cup lemon juice**
  Additional confectioners' sugar

1. Preheat oven to 350°. In a large bowl, beat butter and confectioners' sugar until blended. Gradually beat in 1½ cups flour. Press onto bottom of a greased 13x9-in. baking pan. Bake 18-20 minutes or until golden brown.
2. Meanwhile, in a small bowl, whisk eggs, sugar, lemon juice and remaining flour until frothy; pour over hot crust.
3. Bake 20-25 minutes or until lemon mixture is set and lightly browned. Cool completely on a wire rack. Dust with additional confectioners' sugar. Cut into bars. Refrigerate leftovers.

BAKE-SALE LEMON BARS

FROZEN FRUIT YOGURT POPS

My grandson, Patrick, who's now in high school, was "Grammy's Helper" for years. We made these frozen pops for company and everyone, including the adults, loved them. They're delicious and good for you!

—**JUNE DICKENSON** PHILIPPI, WV

⑤ INGREDIENTS EAT SMART

Frozen Fruit Yogurt Pops

PREP: 15 MIN. + FREEZING
MAKES: 1 DOZEN

- 2¼ **cups (18 ounces) raspberry yogurt**
- 2 **tablespoons lemon juice**
- 2 **medium ripe bananas, cut into chunks**
- 12 **freezer pop molds or 12 paper cups (3 ounces each) and wooden pop sticks**

1. Place yogurt, lemon juice and bananas in a blender; cover and process until smooth, stopping to stir if necessary.
2. Pour mixture into molds or paper cups. Top molds with holders. If using cups, top with foil and insert sticks through foil. Freeze until firm.
PER SERVING *60 cal., 1 g fat (trace sat. fat), 2 mg chol., 23 mg sodium, 13 g carb., 1 g fiber, 2 g pro.* **Diabetic Exchange:** *1 starch.*

Chocolate Cheesecake Pie

Guests always go for this rich but simple pie. I like topping it with fresh raspberries or cherry pie filling.

—**SANDY SCHWARTZ** BROOKLYN, NY

START TO FINISH: 30 MIN.
MAKES: 8 SERVINGS

- 1 package (8 ounces) cream cheese, softened
- ¼ cup butter, softened
- ⅓ cup sugar
- 1½ teaspoons vanilla extract
- 1½ cups milk chocolate chips, melted and cooled
- 1 carton (8 ounces) frozen whipped topping, thawed
- 1 graham cracker crust (9 inches)
  Chocolate curls, optional

In a large bowl, beat cream cheese, butter, sugar and vanilla until smooth. Beat in cooled chocolate. Fold in whipped topping. Spoon into crust. Refrigerate until serving. Decorate with chocolate curls as desired.

Caramel Apple-Pear Crisp

This crisp is packed with a combination of healthy pears and apples, and just the right amount of walnuts in the topping.

—**AMANDA PETTIT** LOGAN, OH

PREP: 20 MIN. • **BAKE:** 40 MIN.
MAKES: 6 SERVINGS

- 3 medium pears, peeled and sliced (about 3 cups)
- 2 medium tart apples, peeled and sliced (about 2 cups)
- 2 tablespoons sugar
- ¼ teaspoon ground allspice
- ⅓ cup sugar-free caramel topping

TOPPING
- ¼ cup quick-cooking oats
- ¼ cup packed brown sugar
- 2 tablespoons all-purpose flour
- 3 tablespoons cold reduced-fat butter
- ¼ cup chopped walnuts
  Reduced-fat vanilla ice cream, optional

1. Preheat oven to 375°. In a large bowl, combine pears, apples, sugar and allspice. Transfer to an 8-in.-square baking dish coated with cooking spray. Drizzle with caramel topping.
2. For topping, in a small bowl, combine oats, brown sugar and flour. Cut in butter until crumbly. Stir in walnuts. Sprinkle over fruit mixture.
3. Bake 40-45 minutes or until topping is golden brown and fruit is tender. Serve warm with ice cream if desired.
NOTE *This recipe was tested with Land O'Lakes light stick butter.*
PER SERVING *260 cal., 8 g fat (3 g sat. fat), 10 mg chol., 65 mg sodium, 49 g carb., 3 g fiber, 3 g pro.*

CHOCOLATE CHEESECAKE PIE

Ginger Plum Tart

Sweet cravings, begone: This free-form plum tart is done in only 35 minutes. Plus, it's super-delicious when served warm.

—TASTE OF HOME TEST KITCHEN

PREP: 15 MIN. • **BAKE:** 20 MIN. + COOLING
MAKES: 8 SERVINGS

- 1 **sheet refrigerated pie pastry**
- 3½ **cups sliced fresh plums (about 10 medium)**
- 3 **tablespoons plus 1 teaspoon coarse sugar, divided**
- 1 **tablespoon cornstarch**
- 2 **teaspoons finely chopped crystallized ginger**
- 1 **egg white**
- 1 **tablespoon water**

1. Preheat oven to 400°. On a work surface, unroll pastry sheet. Roll to a 12-in. circle. Transfer to a parchment paper-lined baking sheet.
2. Toss plums with 3 tablespoons sugar and cornstarch. Arrange plums on pastry to within 2 in. of edges; sprinkle with ginger. Fold pastry edge over plums, pleating as you go.
3. In a small bowl, whisk egg white and water; brush over folded pastry. Sprinkle with remaining sugar.
4. Bake 20-25 minutes or until crust is golden brown. Cool on pan on a wire rack. Serve warm or at room temperature.

PER SERVING *190 cal., 7 g fat (3 g sat. fat), 5 mg chol., 108 mg sodium, 30 g carb., 1 g fiber, 2 g pro.* **Diabetic Exchanges:** *1½ starch, 1 fat, ½ fruit.*

Molten Peppermint-Chocolate Cakes

I doctored up a recipe I found in the newspaper years ago. Top yours with crushed candy canes or chopped mint chocolates for a little extra wow.

—GENISE KRAUSE STURGEON BAY, WI

START TO FINISH: 30 MIN.
MAKES: 4 SERVINGS

- ½ **cup butter, cubed**
- 4 **ounces bittersweet chocolate, chopped**
- 2 **eggs**
- 2 **egg yolks**
- ⅓ **cup sugar**
- ½ **teaspoon peppermint extract**
- ⅛ **teaspoon salt**
- ¼ **cup all-purpose flour**
  Confectioners' sugar

1. Preheat oven to 425°. In a small heavy saucepan, heat butter and chocolate over low heat until blended, stirring constantly; transfer mixture to a large bowl.
2. Add eggs, egg yolks, sugar, extract and salt to chocolate mixture; mix well. Stir in flour. Pour mixture into four greased 6-oz. custard cups or ramekins.
3. Place custard cups on a baking sheet. Bake 10-12 minutes or until a thermometer reads 160° and edges of cakes are set.
4. Remove from oven; let stand 1 minute. Run a knife around sides of cakes; remove to dessert plates. Sprinkle with confectioners' sugar. Serve immediately.

MOLTEN PEPPERMINT-CHOCOLATE CAKES

TOP TIP

Well, that hit the chocolate craving spot like no other. I did a few things differently. I left out the peppermint extract because I didn't want to mess with pure chocolate. I added vanilla instead. I didn't have bittersweet chocolate so I used ⅔ cup of semisweet chocolate chips.

—KARYNP6 TASTEOFHOME.COM

GINGER PLUM TART

PEANUT BUTTER
BROWNIE BITES

Spice Cake Bars with Salted Caramel Icing

As a busy mom, I was always looking for baking shortcuts. When I found these cake mix bars, I knew I'd hit the jackpot. I still make them for my kids and grandkids.
—**ELLEN HARTMAN** CHICO, CA

PREP: 20 MIN. • **BAKE:** 15 MIN. + COOLING
MAKES: 2 DOZEN

- 1 **package spice cake mix (regular size)**
- ¾ **cup butter, melted**
- ⅓ **cup evaporated milk**
- 1 **egg**

FROSTING

- ⅓ **cup packed brown sugar**
- ⅓ **cup evaporated milk**
- ¼ **cup butter, cubed**
- 2 **cups confectioners' sugar**
- 1 **teaspoon vanilla extract**
- ½ **teaspoon sea salt**

1. Preheat oven to 350°. Grease a 13x9-in. baking pan. In a large bowl, combine cake mix, butter, milk and egg; beat on low speed 30 seconds. Beat on medium 2 minutes (batter will be thick).
2. Transfer to prepared pan. Bake 15-20 minutes or until a toothpick inserted into center comes out clean. Cool in pan on a wire rack.
3. For frosting, in a large saucepan, combine brown sugar, milk and butter over medium heat; bring to a boil, stirring occasionally. Reduce heat; simmer, uncovered, 3 minutes.
4. Remove from heat. Stir in confectioners' sugar and vanilla. Immediately spread icing over cake; sprinkle with salt. Cool completely. Cut into bars. Store in airtight containers.

SPICE CAKE BARS WITH
SALTED CARAMEL ICING

I used to make these brownie bites with a cherry in the center. Then I discovered that my granddaughter Lily is big on peanut butter, so I switched it up. Now she loves to help me make them. —**DONNA MCGINNIS** TAYLOR RIDGE, IL

Peanut Butter Brownie Bites

PREP: 20 MIN. • **BAKE:** 20 MIN. + COOLING
MAKES: 3½ DOZEN

- 1 **package fudge brownie mix (13x9-inch pan size)**

FROSTING

- ½ **cup creamy peanut butter**
- 3 **ounces cream cheese, softened**
- 2 **cups confectioners' sugar**
- 4 **teaspoons 2% milk**
- 1 **teaspoon vanilla extract**
  Chopped salted peanuts, optional

1. Preheat the oven to 350°. Line 42 mini-muffin cups with paper or foil liners.
2. Prepare brownie mix according to package directions. Fill prepared cups two-thirds full. Bake 18-22 minutes or until a toothpick inserted into center comes out clean (do not overbake).
3. Place pans on wire racks. Using the end of a wooden spoon handle, make a ½-in.-deep indentation in the center of each brownie. Cool 10 minutes before removing from pans.
4. For frosting, in a large bowl, beat peanut butter and cream cheese until blended. Gradually beat in the confectioners' sugar, milk and vanilla until smooth. Spoon or pipe frosting into the indentations. If desired, sprinkle with chopped peanuts. Refrigerate leftovers.

As soon as strawberries and rhubarb come into season, I pull out this recipe so I'm ready to make it when the fruit is at its peak. The sweet-tart flavor simply can't be beat. This cheesecake truly tastes like springtime! —LEEANN MCCUE CHARLOTTE, NC

RHUBARB BERRY CHEESECAKE PIE

Rhubarb Berry Cheesecake Pie

PREP: 35 MIN. + CHILLING
MAKES: 8 SERVINGS

- 1 **package (8 ounces) cream cheese, softened**
- 1 **can (14 ounces) sweetened condensed milk**
- 6 **tablespoons lemon juice**
- 1 **teaspoon grated lemon peel**
- 1 **teaspoon vanilla extract**
  Dash salt
- 1 **graham cracker crust (9 inches)**
TOPPING
- 2 **cups sliced fresh or frozen rhubarb**
- ½ **cup sugar**
- ¼ **cup water**
- 1 **pint fresh strawberries, hulled and halved lengthwise**
- 2 **teaspoons lemon juice**

1. In a large bowl, beat cream cheese and milk until smooth. Beat in lemon juice, lemon peel, vanilla and salt; pour into crust. Refrigerate, covered, for 2 hours.

2. Meanwhile, in a large saucepan, bring rhubarb, sugar and water to a boil. Reduce heat; simmer, uncovered, 6-8 minutes or until rhubarb is tender. Drain.

3. Stir in strawberries and lemon juice. Refrigerate until cold. Serve pie with topping.

Sugar Cookie Tarts

Whenever my husband and I visit family in Maryland, we all cook dinner together. Everybody offers up ways to improve recipes, and that's how this dessert came to be. Sugar cookies from the bakery make a speedy "crust."
—**BARB WHITE** LIGONIER, PA

PREP: 20 MIN. + CHILLING
MAKES: 4 SERVINGS

- 1 **teaspoon cornstarch**
- 3 **tablespoons water**
- 2 **tablespoons orange juice**
- 1 **tablespoon lemon juice**
  Dash salt
- 5 **tablespoons sugar, divided**
- 3 **ounces cream cheese, softened**
- 4 **large sugar cookies (3 inches)**
  Assorted fresh fruit

1. For glaze, in a small saucepan, whisk the first five ingredients until smooth; stir in 3 tablespoons sugar. Bring to a boil over medium heat; cook and stir 2 minutes or until thickened. Cool slightly.

2. In a small bowl, mix cream cheese and remaining sugar until smooth. Spread over cookies. Arrange fruit over top; brush or drizzle with glaze. Refrigerate 1-2 hours or until cold.

SUGAR COOKIE TARTS

RAINBOW LAYER CAKE

Rainbow Layer Cake

Fruity gelatin helps create the rainbow effect for this pretty cake. Lemon frosting is a nice and springy finishing touch.

—**DAWN SHACKELFORD** FORT WORTH, TX

PREP: 20 MIN. • **BAKE:** 20 MIN. + COOLING
MAKES: 12 SERVINGS

- 1 **package white cake mix (regular size)**
- 3 **eggs**
- 3 **tablespoons each lemon, strawberry and orange gelatin powder**
- 2 **cans (16 ounces each) lemon frosting**

1. Preheat oven to 350°. Line bottoms of three greased 9-in. round baking pans with parchment paper; grease the paper.

2. Prepare cake mix batter according to package directions, substituting three whole eggs for egg whites. Divide evenly among three bowls. Stir one flavor of gelatin into each bowl until blended. Pour each into a prepared pan. Bake 20-25 minutes or until a toothpick inserted in center comes out clean.

3. Cool in pans 10 minutes before removing to wire racks; remove paper. Cool completely. Spread frosting between layers and over top and sides of cake.

NOTE *This recipe was tested with a Betty Crocker white cake mix.*

FREEZE OPTION *Wrap cooled cake layers in plastic wrap, then cover securely in foil; freeze. To use, thaw cakes before unwrapping. Assemble as directed.*

White Chocolate Macadamia Cookies

White baking chips and macadamia nuts are a fantastic duo in these buttery cookies. They are a nice change from the classic chocolate chip ones.

—**CATHY LENNON** NEWPORT, TN

PREP: 15 MIN. • **BAKE:** 10 MIN./BATCH
MAKES: 4½ DOZEN

- ½ **cup butter, softened**
- ⅔ **cup sugar**
- 1 **egg**
- 1 **teaspoon vanilla extract**
- 1 **cup plus 2 tablespoons all-purpose flour**
- ½ **teaspoon baking soda**
- 1 **cup macadamia nuts, chopped**
- 1 **cup white baking chips**

1. Preheat oven to 350°. In a large bowl, cream butter and sugar until light and fluffy. Beat in egg and vanilla. In another bowl, whisk flour and baking soda; gradually beat into creamed mixture. Stir in nuts and baking chips.

2. Drop by heaping teaspoonfuls 2 in. apart onto ungreased baking sheets. Bake 10-12 minutes or until golden brown. Cool on pans 1 minute. Remove to wire racks to cool completely.

FREEZE OPTION *Freeze cookies, layered between waxed paper, in freezer containers. To use, thaw before serving or, if desired, reheat on a baking sheet in a preheated 350° oven 3-4 minutes.*

WHITE CHOCOLATE MACADAMIA COOKIES

General Recipe Index

This handy index lists every recipe by food category, major ingredient and cooking method, so you can easily locate the recipes that suit your needs.

✓Recipe includes Nutrition Facts

IIIIIIIIIIIIIIIIIIIIIIIIIIIIIIIIIIIIIIIIIIIIIIIIIIIIIIIIIIIIIIIIIIIIIIIIIIIIIIIIIIIIII

BERRY GRANOLA PANCAKES
PAGE 79

BALSAMIC CHICKEN WITH
BROCCOLI COUSCOUS
PAGE 32

CHOCOLATE-DIPPED STRAWBERRY
MERINGUE ROSES
PAGE 53

PINEAPPLE-STRAWBERRY
CRANBERRY RELISH
PAGE 273

TOMATO-ONION GREEN BEANS
PAGE 229

SHRIMP KABOBS WITH
SPICY-SWEET SAUCE
PAGE 207

GNOCCHI ALFREDO
PAGE 30

PESTO PASTA & POTATOES
PAGE 244

RHUBARB COMPOTE WITH
YOGURT & ALMONDS
PAGE 110

SPICY TILAPIA RICE BOWL
PAGE 20

SAUCY BBQ CHICKEN THIGHS
PAGE 180

SAUSAGE PIZZA PASTA
PAGE 77

Alphabetical Recipe Index

This index lists every recipe in alphabetical order so you can easily find all your favorites.

✓Recipe includes Nutrition Facts

CHICKEN CORDON BLEU CRESCENT RING PAGE 158

CRANBERRY-BRIE TARTLETS
PAGE 125

LOADED STUFFED POTATO PANCAKES
PAGE 238

M

N

O

P

Q

**SMOKED SALMON BAGEL SANDWICHES
PAGE 109**

TURKEY & NOODLE TOMATO SOUP
PAGE 132